JUSTICE SOCIETY of AMERICA

THY KINGDOM COME PART THREE

DAN DIDIO SENIOR VP-EXECUTIVE EDITOR MICHAEL SIGLAIN EDITOR-ORIGINAL SERIES HARVEY RICHARDS ASSISTANT EDITOR-ORIGINAL SERIES
ANTON KAWASAKI EDITOR-COLLECTED EDITION ROBBIN BROSTERMAN SENIOR ART DIRECTOR PAUL LEVITZ PRESIDENT & PUBLISHER
GEORG BREWER VP-DESIGN & DC DIRECT CREATIVE RICHARD BRUNING SENIOR VP-CREATIVE DIRECTOR
PATRICK CALDON EXECUTIVE VP-FINANCE & OPERATIONS CHRIS CARAMALIS VP-FINANCE JOHN CUNNINGHAM VP-MARKETING
TERRI CUNNINGHAM VP-MANAGING EDITOR ALISON GILL VP-MANUFACTURING AMY GENKINS SENIOR VP-BUSINESS & LEGAL AFFAIRS
DAVID HYDE VP-PUBLICITY HANK KANALZ VP-GENERAL MANAGER, WILDSTORM JIM LEE EDITORIAL DIRECTOR-WILDSTORM
GREGORY NOVECK SENIOR VP-CREATIVE AFFAIRS SUE POHJA VP-BOOK TRADE SALES STEVE ROTTERDAM SENIOR VP-SALES & MARKETING
CHERYL RUBIN SENIOR VP-BRAND MANAGEMENT ALYSSE SOLL VP-ADVERTISING & CUSTOM PUBLISHING
JEFF TROJAN VP-BUSINESS DEVELOPMENT, DC DIRECT BOB WAYNE VP-SALES

Cover by Alex Ross

JUSTICE SOCIETY OF AMERICA: THY KINGDOM COME PART THREE

Published by DC Comics. Cover and compilation Copyright © 2009 DC Comics. All Rights Reserved.

Originally published in single magazine form in JUSTICE SOCIETY OF AMERICA #19-22, JUSTICE SOCIETY OF AMERICA KINGDOM COME SPECIAL: SUPERMAN, JUSTICE SOCIETY OF AMERICA KINGDOM COME SPECIAL: MAGOG, and JUSTICE SOCIETY OF AMERICA KINGDOM COME SPECIAL: THE KINGDOM. Copyright © 2008, 2009 DC Comics. All Rights Reserved. All characters, their distinctive likenesses and related elements featured in this publication are trademarks of DC Comics. The stories, characters and incidents featured in this publication are entirely fictional. DC Comics does not read or accept unsolicited submissions of ideas, stories or artwork.

DC Comics, 1700 Broadway, New York, NY 10019 | A Warner Bros. Entertainment Company | Printed in USA. First Printing. ISBN: 978-1-4012-2166-9 SC ISBN: 978-1-4012-2167-6

JUSTICE SOCIETY of AMERICA

THY KINGDOM COME Part Three

JSA #19-22

STORY BY **GEOFF JOHNS & ALEX ROSS** WRITER **GEOFF JOHNS**
ART **DALE EAGLESHAM & NATHAN MASSENGILL**
JERRY ORDWAY & BOB WIACEK (EARTH-2 SEQUENCES) **ALEX ROSS** (PAINTED PAGES)

KINGDOM COME SPECIAL: SUPERMAN
WRITER & ILLUSTRATOR **ALEX ROSS**

KINGDOM COME SPECIAL: MAGOG
WRITER **PETER J. TOMASI** ART **FERNANDO PASARIN & MICK GRAY**
STARMAN ORIGIN BY **GEOFF JOHNS & SCOTT KOLINS**

KINGDOM COME SPECIAL: THE KINGDOM
WRITER **GEOFF JOHNS** PENCILLER **FERNANDO PASARIN**
INKERS **MICK GRAY JACK PURCELL NORM RAPMUND FERNANDO PASARIN**

COLORISTS **HI-FI** ALEX SINCLAIR
LETTERERS **ROB LEIGH** JOHN J. HILL

SUPERMAN CREATED BY JERRY SIEGEL & JOE SHUSTER

CAST OF CHARACTERS

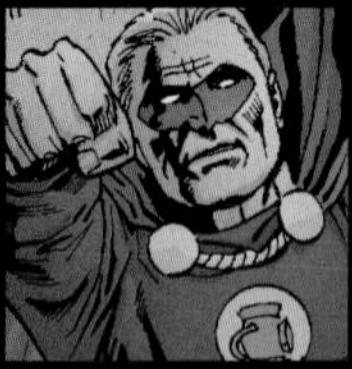

GREEN LANTERN Engineer Alan Scott found a lantern carved from a meteorite known as the Starheart. Fulfilling the lamp's prophecy to grant astonishing power, Scott tapped into the emerald energy and fought injustice as the Green Lantern. His ring can generate a variety of effects and energy constructs, sustained purely by his will.

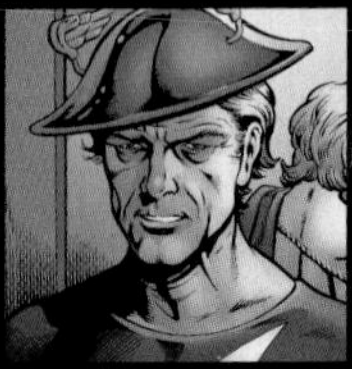

THE FLASH The first in a long line of super-speedsters, Jay Garrick is capable of running at velocities near the speed of light. A scientist, Garrick has also served as mentor to other speedsters, and to many heroes over several generations.

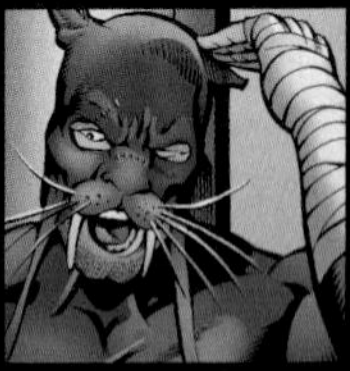

WILDCAT A former heavyweight boxing champ, Ted Grant, a.k.a. Wildcat, prowls the mean streets defending the helpless. One of the world's foremost hand-to-hand combatants, he has trained many of today's best fighters — including Black Canary, Catwoman, and the Batman himself.

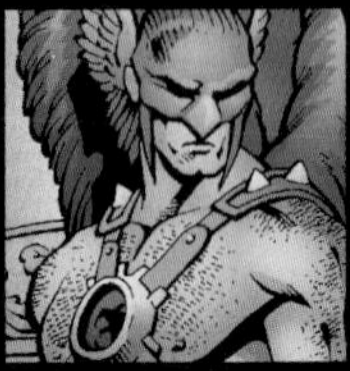

HAWKMAN Originally Prince Khufu of ancient Egypt, the hero who would become known as Hawkman discovered an alien spacecraft from the planet Thanagar, powered by a mysterious antigravity element called Nth metal. The unearthly energies of the metal transformed his soul, and he and his love Princess Chay-Ara were reincarnated over and over for centuries. Currently he is Carter Hall, archaeologist and adventurer.

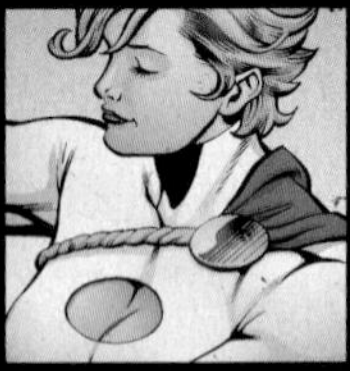

POWER GIRL Once confused about her origins, Karen Starr now knows she is the cousin of an alternate-Earth Superman — who gave his life in the Infinite Crisis. Her enhanced strength and powers of flight and invulnerability are matched only by her self-confidence in action, which sometimes borders on arrogance.

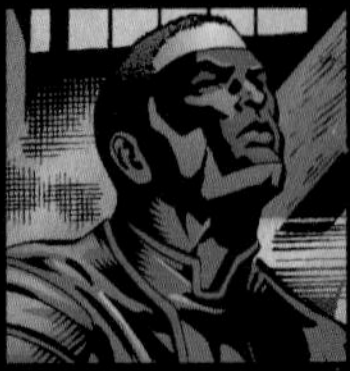

MR. TERRIFIC Haunted by the death of his wife, Olympic gold medal-winning decathlete Michael Holt was ready to take his own life. Instead, inspired by the Spectre's story of the original Mr. Terrific, he rededicated himself to ensuring fair play among the street youth using his wealth and technical skills to become the living embodiment of those ideals. He now divides his time between the JSA and the government agency known as Checkmate.

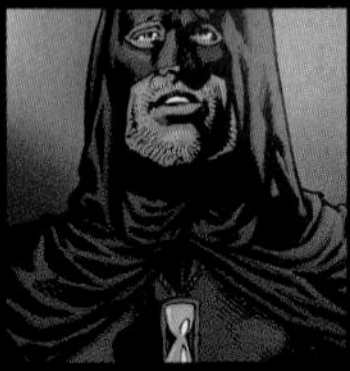

HOURMAN Rick Tyler struggled for a while before accepting his role as the son of the original Hourman. It hasn't been an easy road — he's endured addiction to the Miraclo drug that increases his strength and endurance, and nearly died from a strange disease. Now, after mastering the drug, he uses a special hourglass that enables him to see one hour into the future.

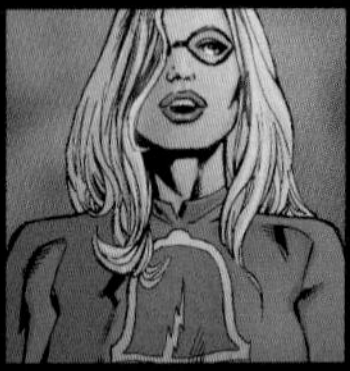

LIBERTY BELLE Jesse Chambers is the daughter of the Golden Age Johnny Quick and Liberty Belle. Originally adopting her father's speed formula, Jesse became the super-hero known as Jesse Quick. After a brief period without powers, Jesse has returned — now taking over her mother's role. As the new Liberty Belle, Jesse is an All-American Powerhouse.

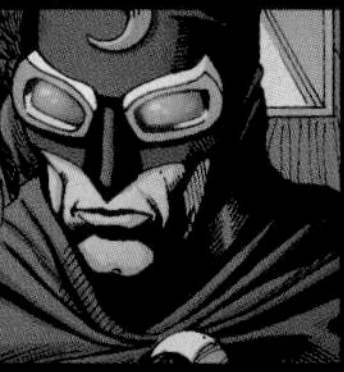

DR. MID-NITE A medical prodigy, Pieter Anton Cross refused to work within the limits of the system. Treating people on his own, he came into contact with a dangerous drug that altered his body chemistry, enabling him to see light in the infrared spectrum. Although he lost his normal sight in a murder attempt disguised as a car accident, his uncanny night vision allows him to protect the weak under the assumed identity of Dr. Mid-Nite.

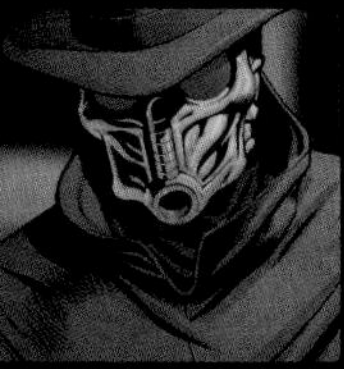

SANDMAN Sandy Hawkins was the ward of original Sandman Wesley Dodds, and he is the nephew of Dodds's lifelong partner, Dian Belmont. After a bizarre accident, Hawkins was able to transform himself into a pure silicon or sand form. Recently, he has been experiencing prophetic dreams. He also carries a gas mask, gas guns and other equipment.

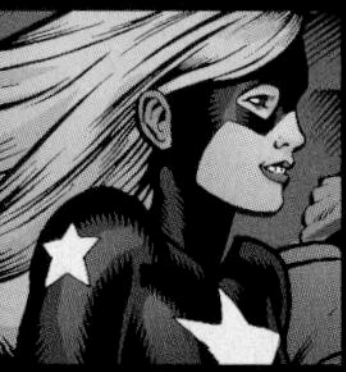

STARGIRL When Courtney Whitmore discovered the cosmic converter belt that had been worn by the JSA's original Star-Spangled Kid (her stepfather, Pat Dugan, was the Kid's sidekick Stripesy), she saw it as an opportunity to cut class and kick some butt. Now called Stargirl, she divides her time between her adventures with the JSA and bickering/teaming up with Pat — who sometimes monitors Courtney from his S.T.R.I.P.E. robot.

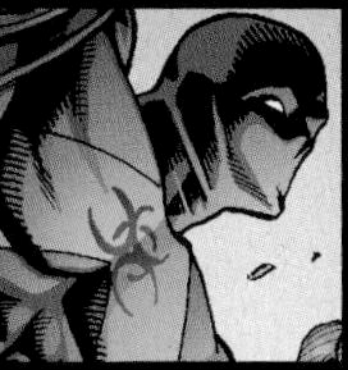

DAMAGE Grant Emerson has had a difficult life. Growing up, he was the victim of an abusive foster father. Then later, after discovering his explosive powers, he accidentally blew up half of downtown Atlanta. Last year, he was almost beaten to death by the super-speed villain known as Zoom. Grant has worn a full-face mask as Damage ever since.

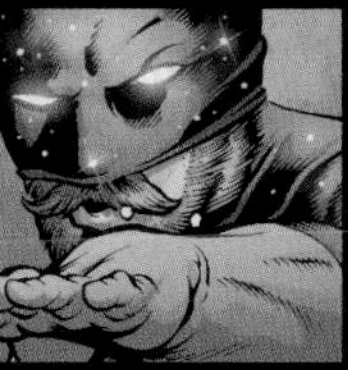

STARMAN A mysterious new Starman recently appeared in Opal City, saving its citizens numerous times. He apparently suffers from some form of schizophrenia, and hears voices in his head. Voluntarily residing in the Sunshine Sanitarium, Starman will occasionally leave and use his gravity-altering powers to fight crime.

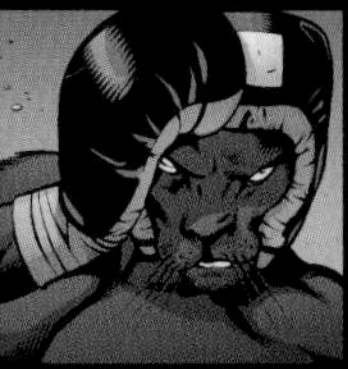

WILDCAT II Tommy Bronson is the newly discovered son of original Wildcat Ted Grant. But it's not quite "like father, like son" here. For one thing, Tom doesn't want to be a fighter like his dad. And second, this new Wildcat has the ability to turn into a feral creature, with enhanced agility and animalistic senses...

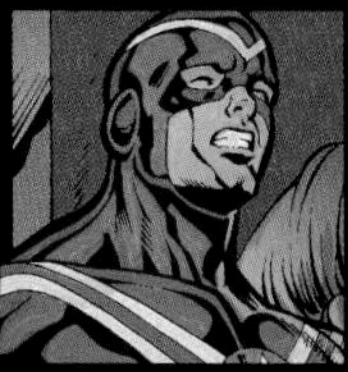

CITIZEN STEEL The grandson of the original Steel, Nathan Heywood is a former football hero who has suffered numerous tragedies. First, an injury and infection required his leg to be amputated. Then, a vicious attack by the Fourth Reich wiped out most of his family. But during the attack, a bizarre incident left him with metal-like skin and superhuman strength.

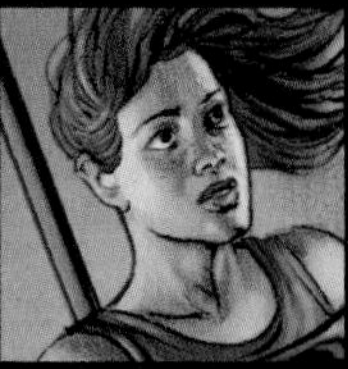

CYCLONE Maxine Hunkel is the granddaughter of the original Red Tornado, Abigail Mathilda "Ma" Hunkel (who is the current custodian of the Justice Society Museum). Maxine grew up idolizing her grandmother's allies in the JSA and still can't believe she's now part of the team. Maxine has the power of wind manipulation and can summon up cyclones and whirlwinds while gliding through the air.

PREVIOUSLY...

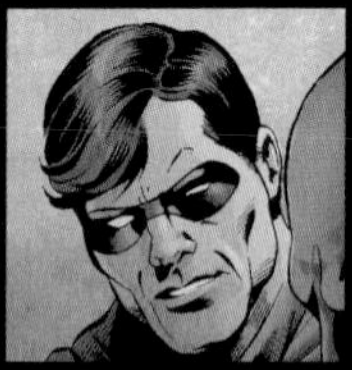

The Justice Society of America is back, bigger and better than ever. Formed by Green Lantern, the Flash, and Wildcat and led by new team leader Power Girl, the Society continues to welcome new members whose powers stem from the legacies of past heroes: Mr. America, a former FBI special agent and expert profiler of super-villains who inherited the mantle from his murdered partner. Lightning, the electrically powered daughter of Justice League member Black Lightning. Jakeem Thunder, a returning member of the Society who wields the power of the mystical genie Johnny Thunderbolt. Amazing-Man, grandson and heir to the powers of one of the greatest African-American super-heroes in history. Judomaster, an expert fighter who is literally unhittable in combat and seeks vengeance for her father, a slain Yakuza assassin. Lance Corporal David Reid, grandson of Justice Society founder President Franklin Delano Roosevelt and veteran of the wars in Afghanistan and Iraq, capable of concentrated energy blasts.

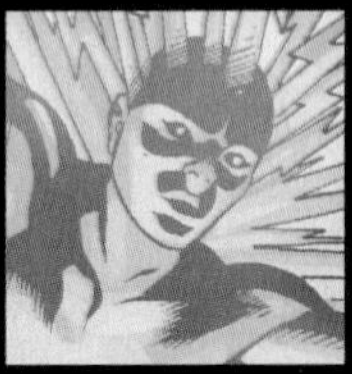

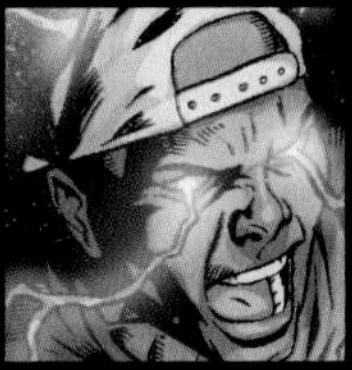

When the Society's powerful, seemingly schizophrenic new Starman accidentally opens a pathway to another universe, the team's most unexpected addition arrives: the "Kingdom Come" Superman! This aged Man of Steel has seen his Earth fall victim to heroes gone extreme, killing indiscriminately in the name of "justice" under the influence of a brazen anti-hero named Magog.

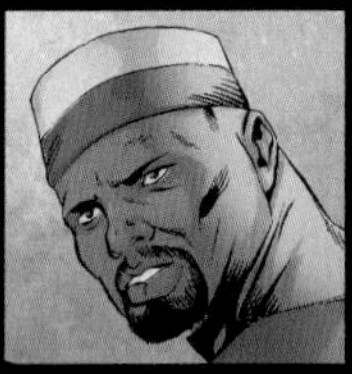

Torn from his world just as its remaining heroes fell victim to a nuclear strike, Superman has chosen to remain with the Justice Society, aiding in their mission in order to prevent this Earth from suffering the same fate — yet it may already be too late.

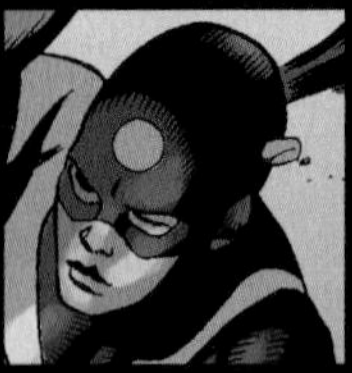

A powerful god calling himself Gog has arrived in Africa, promising to make the world better, and immediately makes drastic changes to several members of the JSA: suddenly Dr. Mid-Nite has the ability to see; Starman is cured of his schizophrenia; Sandman's insomnia is gone and he goes to sleep for 24 hours; and Lance Corporal David Reid is transformed into...Magog — possibly setting into motion events that the "Kingdom Come" Superman wants to prevent.

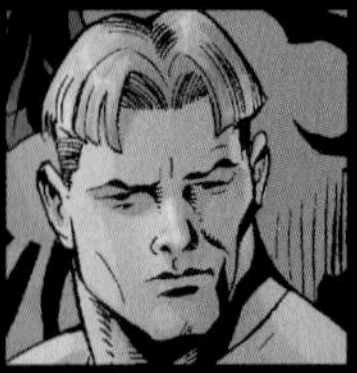

Meanwhile, Power Girl is sent "home" to Earth-2...only to discover the world Gog sends her to is *still* not quite hers. And the heroes of *that* world — Justice Society Infinity — want answers. As they hunt her down, Power Girl locates that Earth's Michael Holt — who in this reality became a professor of physics instead of Mr. Terrific — to help her find her way back home again...

JUSTICE SOCIETY OF AMERICA #19 cover A by Alex Ross

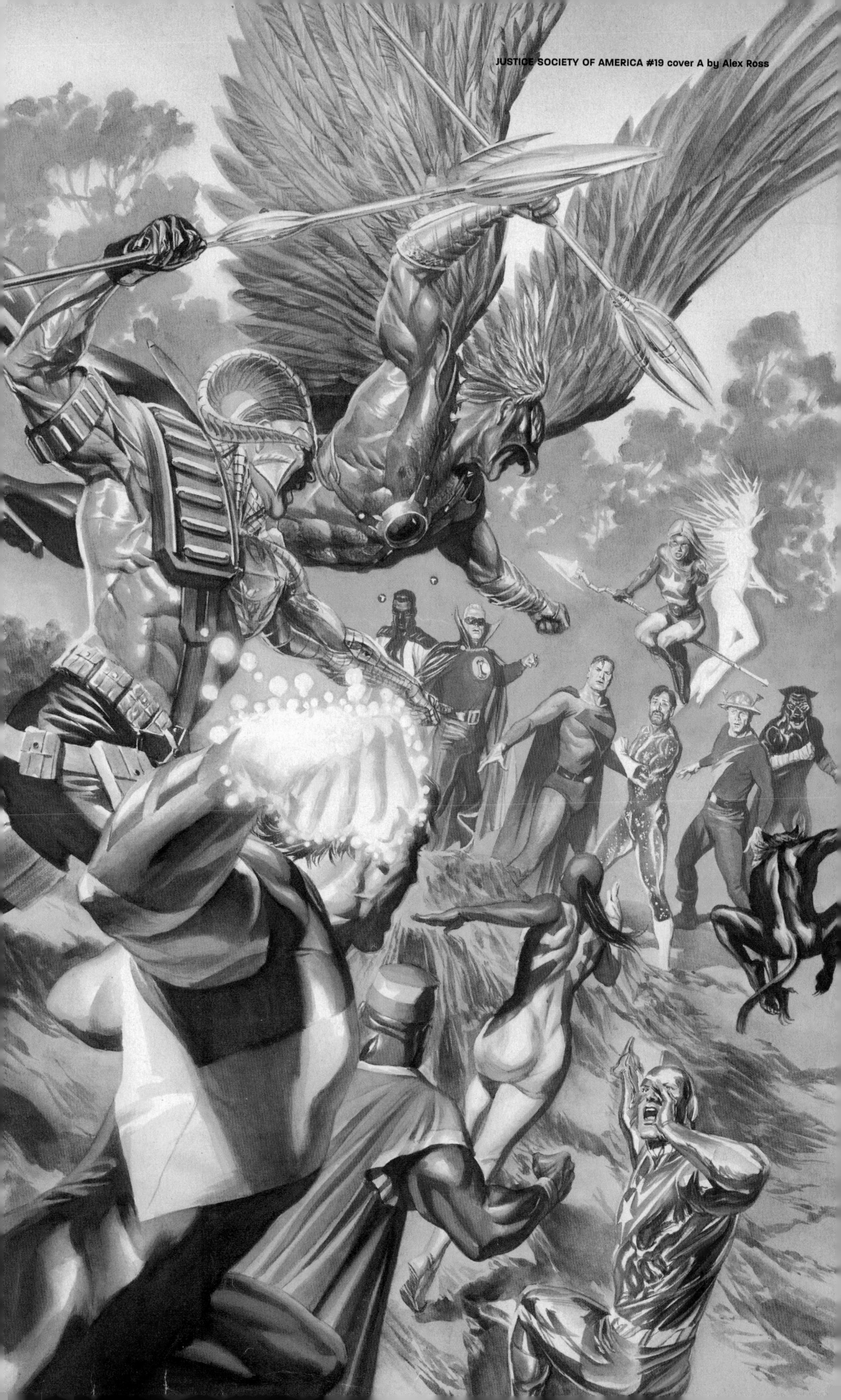

JUSTICE SOCIETY OF AMERICA #19 cover B
by Dale Eaglesham & Nathan Massengill
Interior art by Eaglesham & Massengill,
with Earth-2 sequence by Jerry Ordway

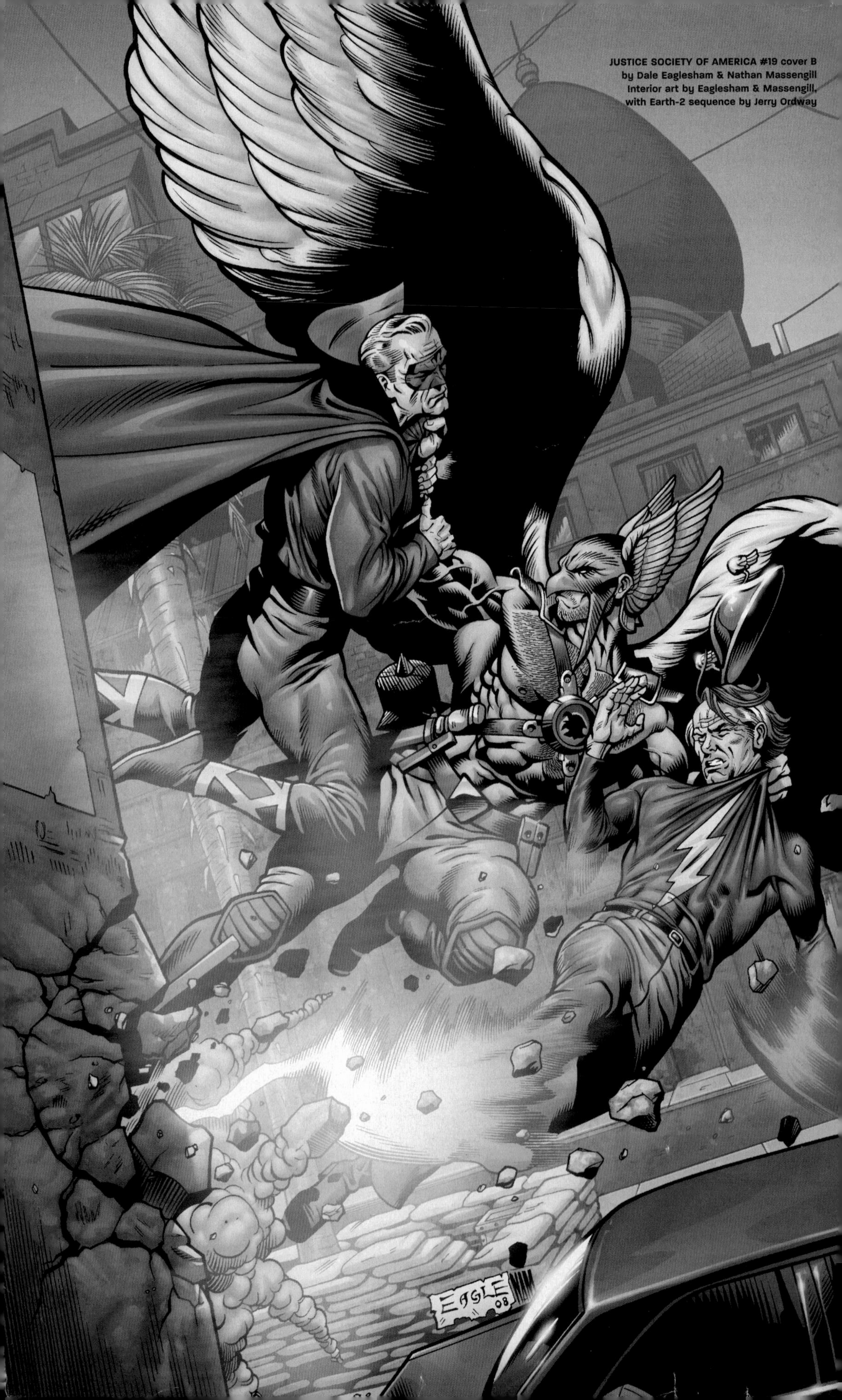

EAGLE 08

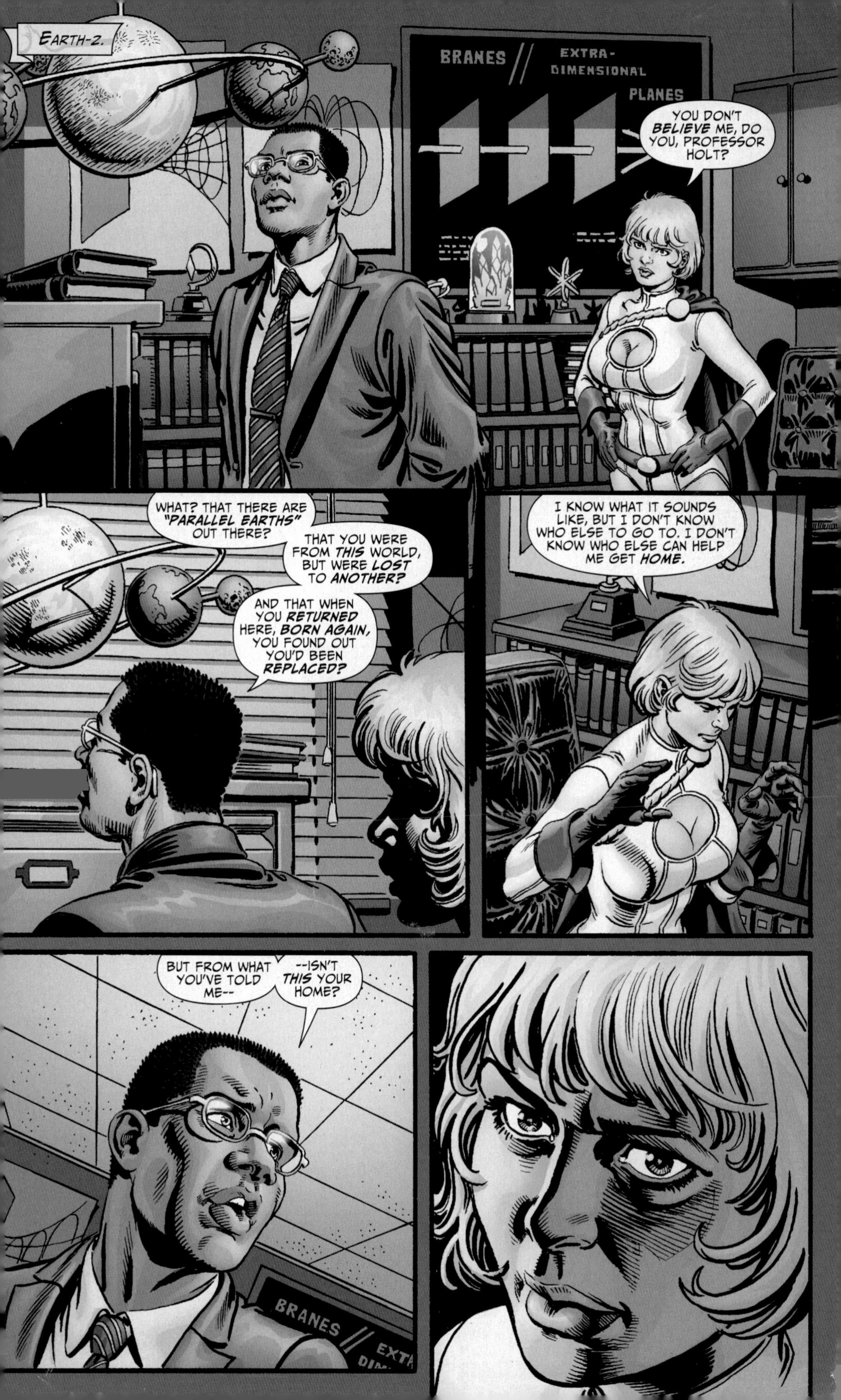
EARTH-2.
BRANES // EXTRA-DIMENSIONAL PLANES
YOU DON'T BELIEVE ME, DO YOU, PROFESSOR HOLT?
WHAT? THAT THERE ARE "PARALLEL EARTHS" OUT THERE?
THAT YOU WERE FROM THIS WORLD, BUT WERE LOST TO ANOTHER?
AND THAT WHEN YOU RETURNED HERE, BORN AGAIN, YOU FOUND OUT YOU'D BEEN REPLACED?
I KNOW WHAT IT SOUNDS LIKE, BUT I DON'T KNOW WHO ELSE TO GO TO. I DON'T KNOW WHO ELSE CAN HELP ME GET HOME.
BUT FROM WHAT YOU'VE TOLD ME--
--ISN'T THIS YOUR HOME?
BRANES

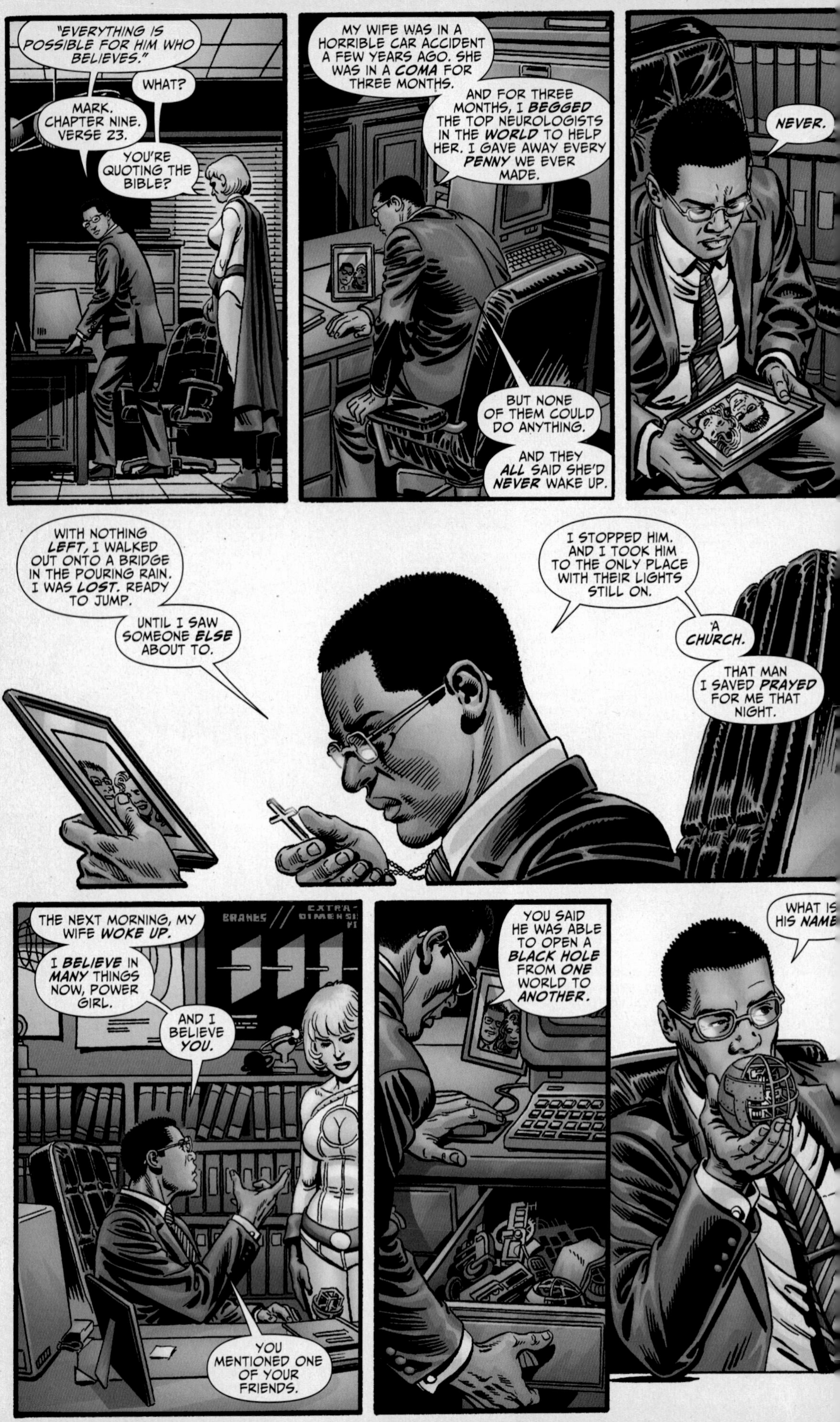
"EVERYTHING IS POSSIBLE FOR HIM WHO BELIEVES."
WHAT?
MARK. CHAPTER NINE. VERSE 23.
YOU'RE QUOTING THE BIBLE?
MY WIFE WAS IN A HORRIBLE CAR ACCIDENT A FEW YEARS AGO. SHE WAS IN A COMA FOR THREE MONTHS.
AND FOR THREE MONTHS, I BEGGED THE TOP NEUROLOGISTS IN THE WORLD TO HELP HER. I GAVE AWAY EVERY PENNY WE EVER MADE.
BUT NONE OF THEM COULD DO ANYTHING.
AND THEY ALL SAID SHE'D NEVER WAKE UP.
NEVER.
WITH NOTHING LEFT, I WALKED OUT ONTO A BRIDGE IN THE POURING RAIN. I WAS LOST. READY TO JUMP.
UNTIL I SAW SOMEONE ELSE ABOUT TO.
I STOPPED HIM. AND I TOOK HIM TO THE ONLY PLACE WITH THEIR LIGHTS STILL ON.
A CHURCH.
THAT MAN I SAVED PRAYED FOR ME THAT NIGHT.
THE NEXT MORNING, MY WIFE WOKE UP.
I BELIEVE IN MANY THINGS NOW, POWER GIRL.
AND I BELIEVE YOU.
YOU MENTIONED ONE OF YOUR FRIENDS.
YOU SAID HE WAS ABLE TO OPEN A BLACK HOLE FROM ONE WORLD TO ANOTHER.
WHAT IS HIS NAME

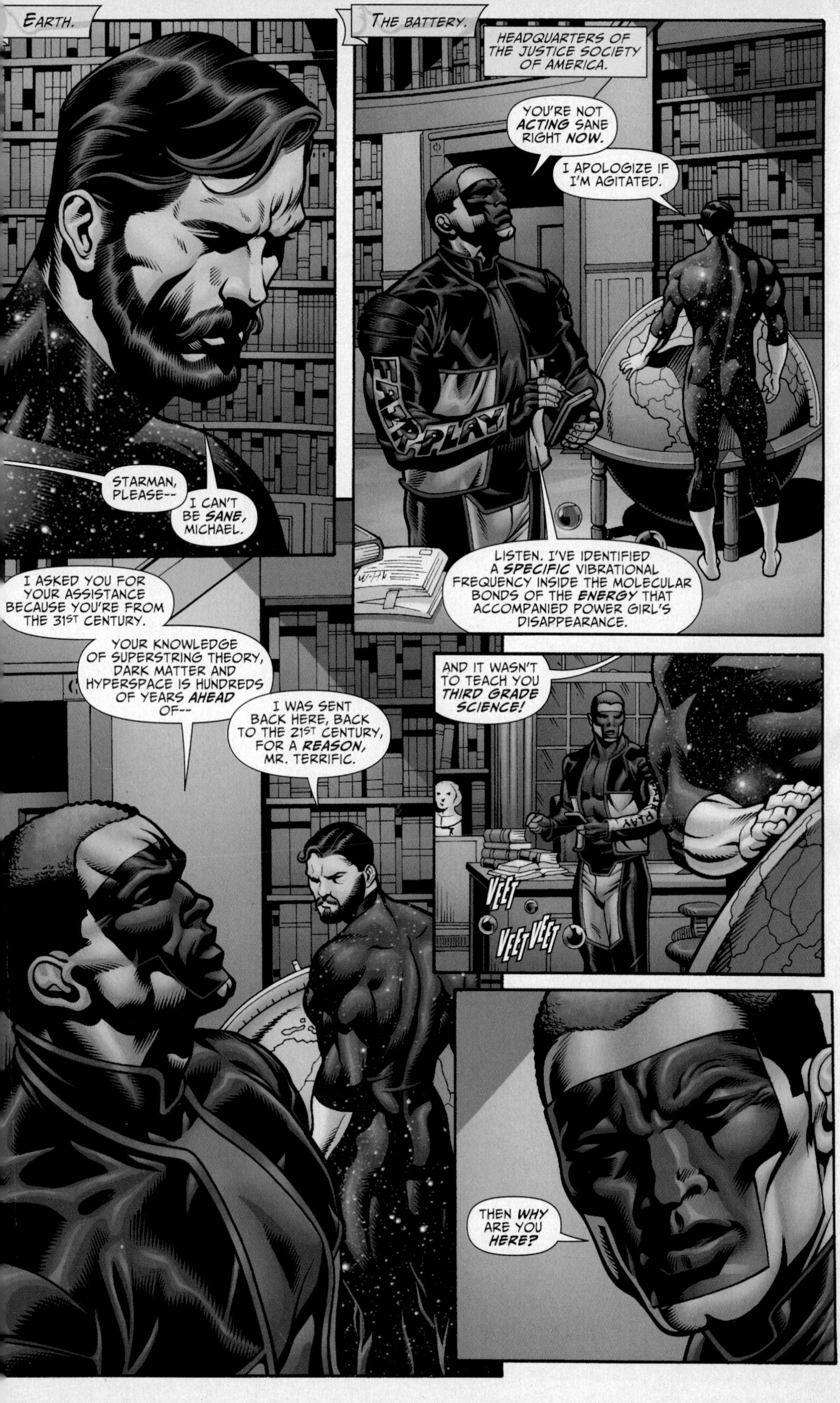
EARTH.
STARMAN, PLEASE--
I CAN'T BE SANE, MICHAEL.
THE BATTERY.
HEADQUARTERS OF THE JUSTICE SOCIETY OF AMERICA.
YOU'RE NOT ACTING SANE RIGHT NOW.
I APOLOGIZE IF I'M AGITATED.
FAIR PLAY
LISTEN. I'VE IDENTIFIED A SPECIFIC VIBRATIONAL FREQUENCY INSIDE THE MOLECULAR BONDS OF THE ENERGY THAT ACCOMPANIED POWER GIRL'S DISAPPEARANCE.
I ASKED YOU FOR YOUR ASSISTANCE BECAUSE YOU'RE FROM THE 31ST CENTURY.
YOUR KNOWLEDGE OF SUPERSTRING THEORY, DARK MATTER AND HYPERSPACE IS HUNDREDS OF YEARS AHEAD OF--
I WAS SENT BACK HERE, BACK TO THE 21ST CENTURY, FOR A REASON, MR. TERRIFIC.
AND IT WASN'T TO TEACH YOU THIRD GRADE SCIENCE!
VEET
VEET VEET
THEN WHY ARE YOU HERE?

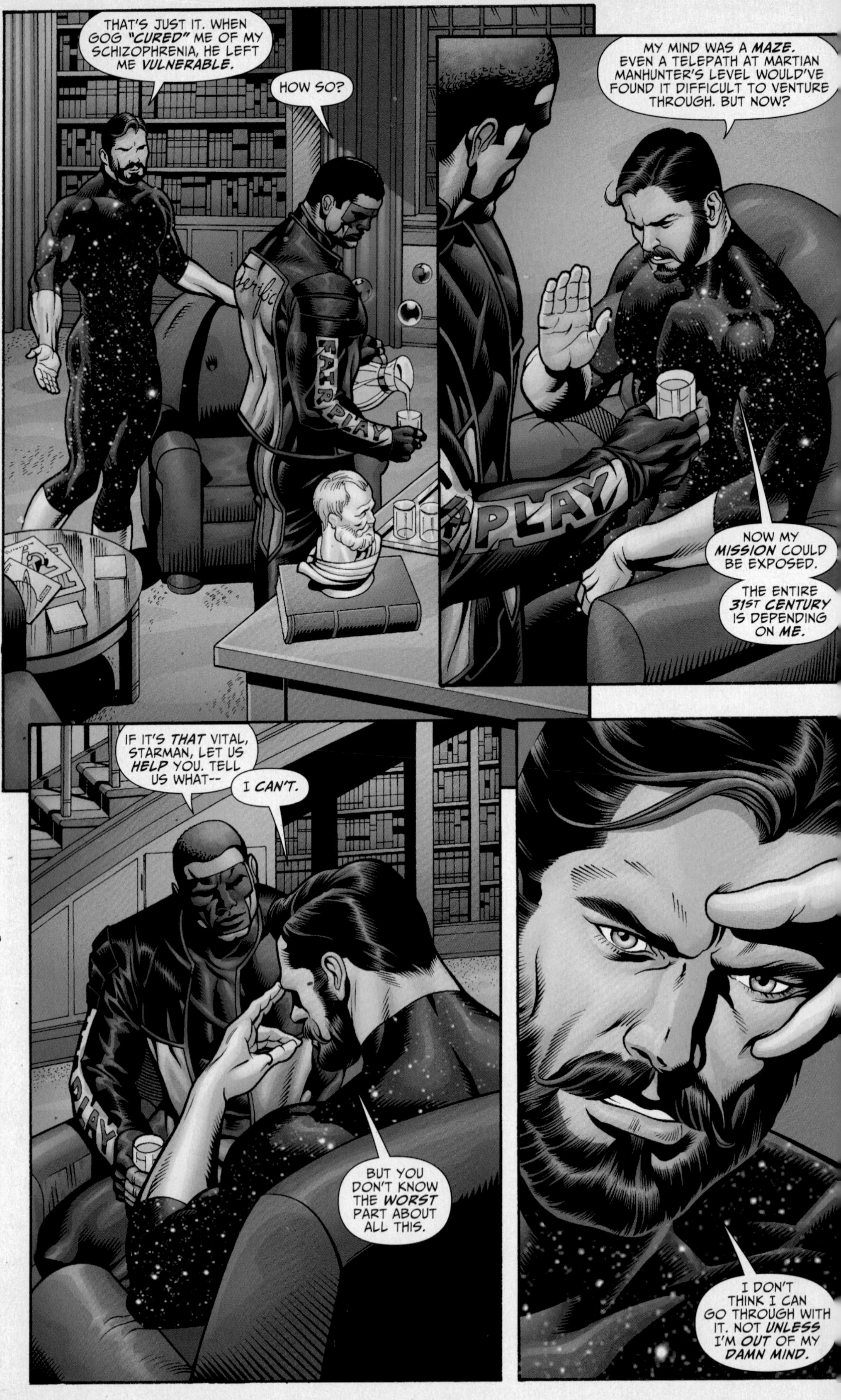
THAT'S JUST IT. WHEN GOG "CURED" ME OF MY SCHIZOPHRENIA, HE LEFT ME VULNERABLE.
HOW SO?
MY MIND WAS A MAZE. EVEN A TELEPATH AT MARTIAN MANHUNTER'S LEVEL WOULD'VE FOUND IT DIFFICULT TO VENTURE THROUGH. BUT NOW?
NOW MY MISSION COULD BE EXPOSED.
THE ENTIRE 31ST CENTURY IS DEPENDING ON ME.
IF IT'S THAT VITAL, STARMAN, LET US HELP YOU. TELL US WHAT--
I CAN'T.
BUT YOU DON'T KNOW THE WORST PART ABOUT ALL THIS.
I DON'T THINK I CAN GO THROUGH WITH IT. NOT UNLESS I'M OUT OF MY DAMN MIND.

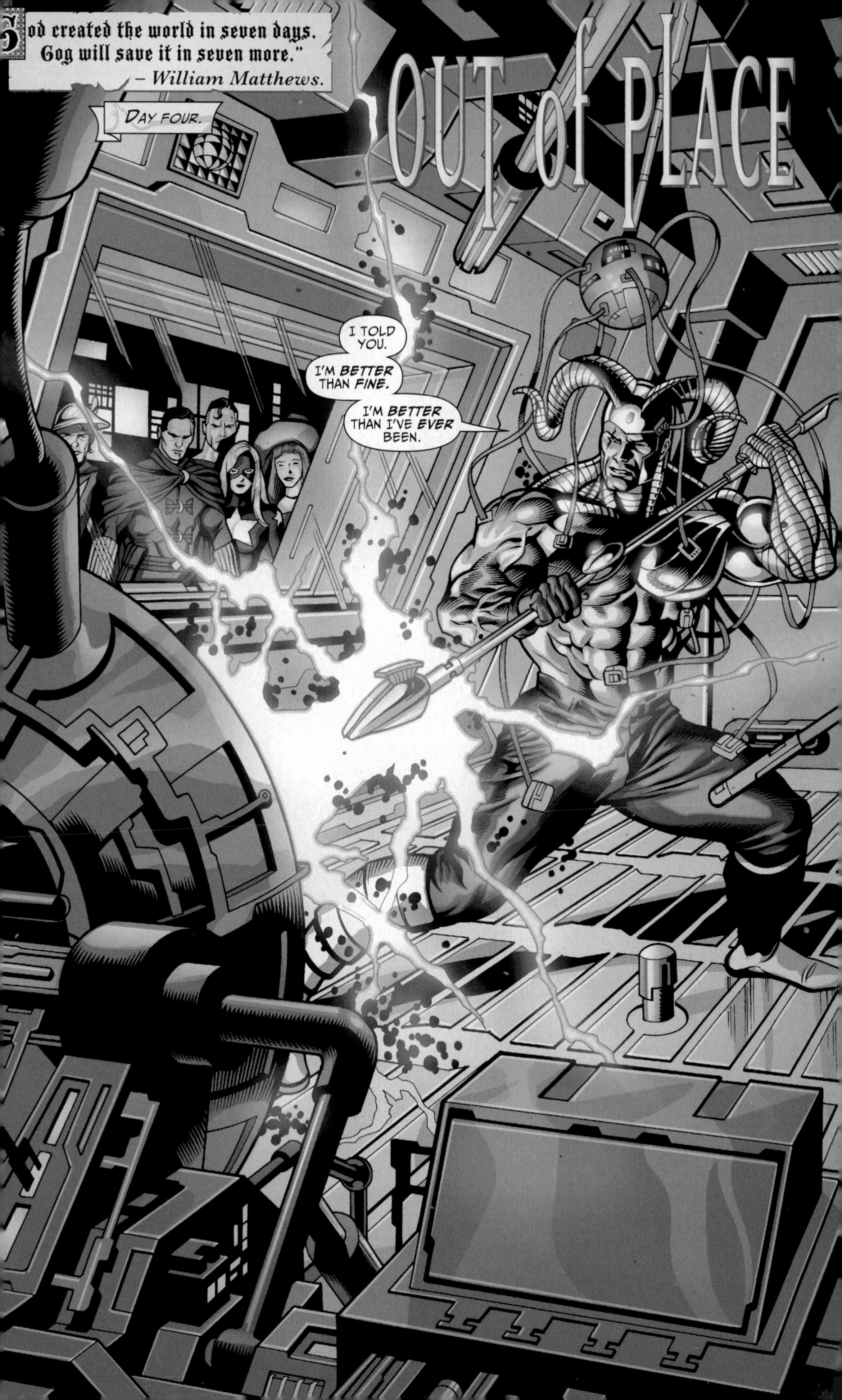
"God created the world in seven days. Gog will save it in seven more."
– William Matthews.
DAY FOUR.
OUT of PLACE
I TOLD YOU.
I'M BETTER THAN FINE.
I'M BETTER THAN I'VE EVER BEEN.

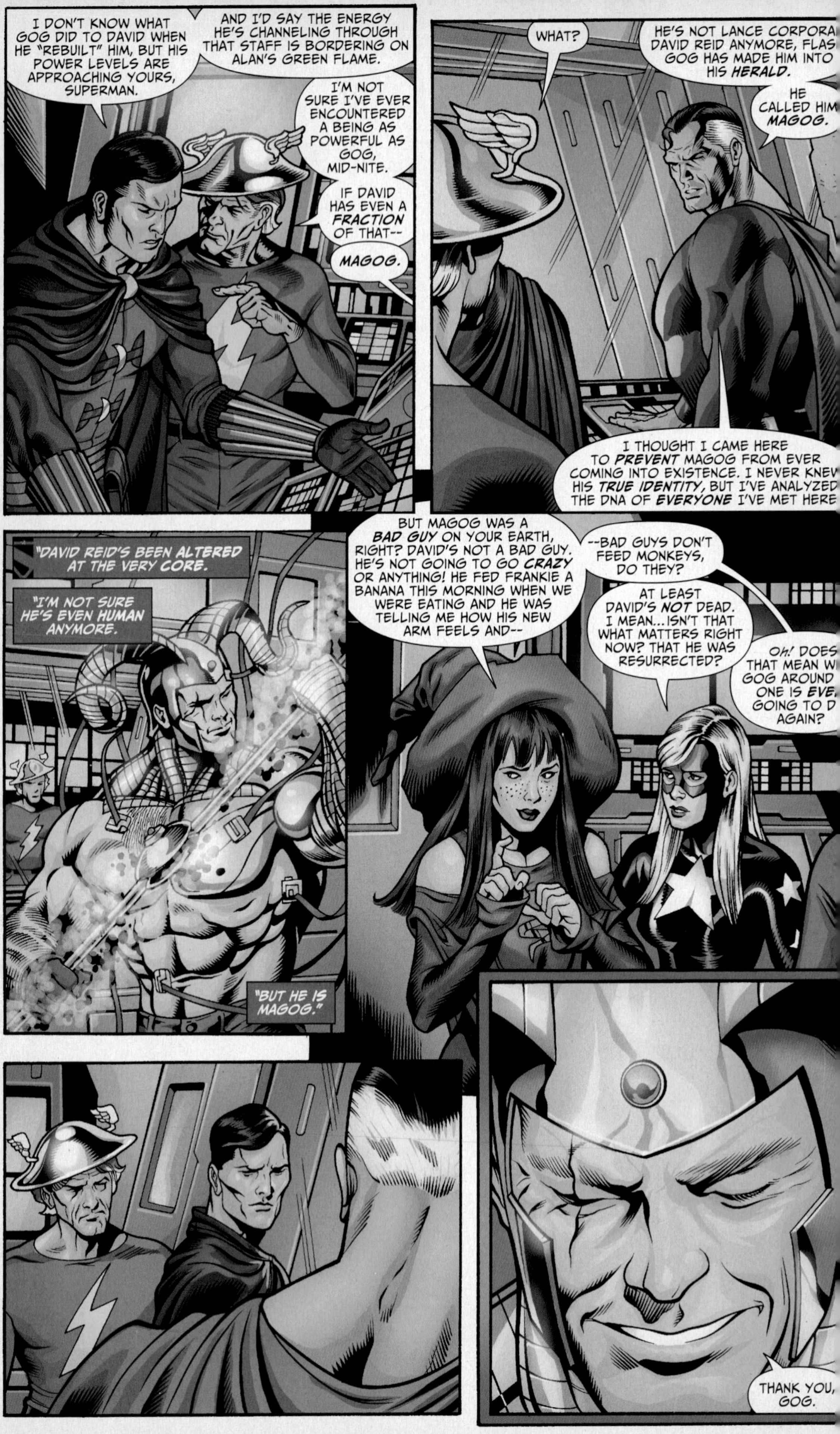
I DON'T KNOW WHAT GOG DID TO DAVID WHEN HE "REBUILT" HIM, BUT HIS POWER LEVELS ARE APPROACHING YOURS, SUPERMAN.
AND I'D SAY THE ENERGY HE'S CHANNELING THROUGH THAT STAFF IS BORDERING ON ALAN'S GREEN FLAME.
I'M NOT SURE I'VE EVER ENCOUNTERED A BEING AS POWERFUL AS GOG, MID-NITE.
IF DAVID HAS EVEN A FRACTION OF THAT--
MAGOG.
WHAT?
HE'S NOT LANCE CORPORA DAVID REID ANYMORE, FLAS GOG HAS MADE HIM INTO HIS HERALD.
HE CALLED HIM MAGOG.
I THOUGHT I CAME HERE TO PREVENT MAGOG FROM EVER COMING INTO EXISTENCE. I NEVER KNEW HIS TRUE IDENTITY, BUT I'VE ANALYZED THE DNA OF EVERYONE I'VE MET HERE
"DAVID REID'S BEEN ALTERED AT THE VERY CORE.
"I'M NOT SURE HE'S EVEN HUMAN ANYMORE.
"BUT HE IS MAGOG."
BUT MAGOG WAS A BAD GUY ON YOUR EARTH, RIGHT? DAVID'S NOT A BAD GUY. HE'S NOT GOING TO GO CRAZY OR ANYTHING! HE FED FRANKIE A BANANA THIS MORNING WHEN WE WERE EATING AND HE WAS TELLING ME HOW HIS NEW ARM FEELS AND--
--BAD GUYS DON'T FEED MONKEYS, DO THEY?
AT LEAST DAVID'S NOT DEAD. I MEAN...ISN'T THAT WHAT MATTERS RIGHT NOW? THAT HE WAS RESURRECTED?
OH! DOES THAT MEAN W GOG AROUND ONE IS EVE GOING TO D AGAIN?
THANK YOU, GOG.

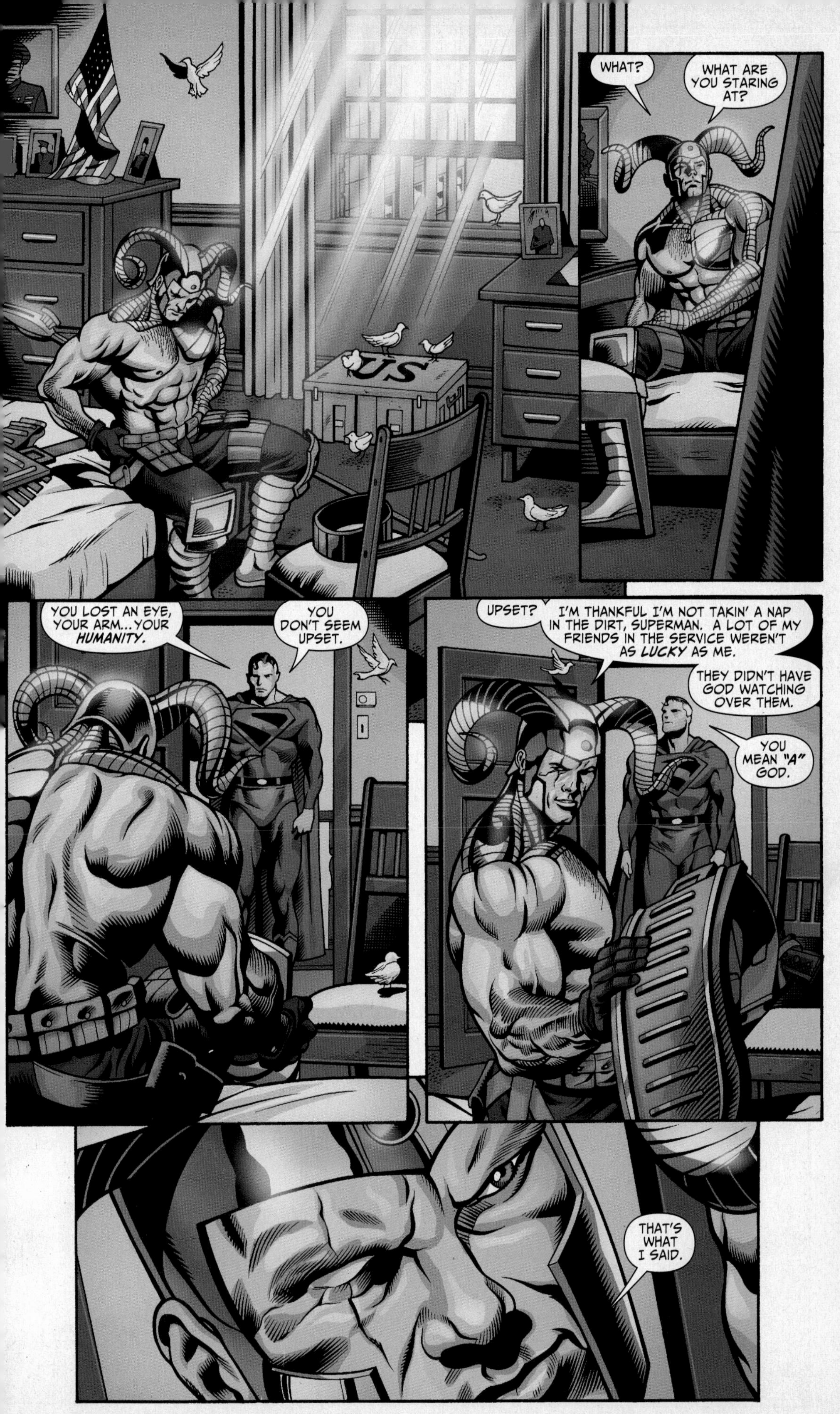
WHAT?
WHAT ARE YOU STARING AT?
YOU LOST AN EYE, YOUR ARM...YOUR HUMANITY.
YOU DON'T SEEM UPSET.
UPSET?
I'M THANKFUL I'M NOT TAKIN' A NAP IN THE DIRT, SUPERMAN. A LOT OF MY FRIENDS IN THE SERVICE WEREN'T AS LUCKY AS ME.
THEY DIDN'T HAVE GOD WATCHING OVER THEM.
YOU MEAN "A" GOD.
THAT'S WHAT I SAID.

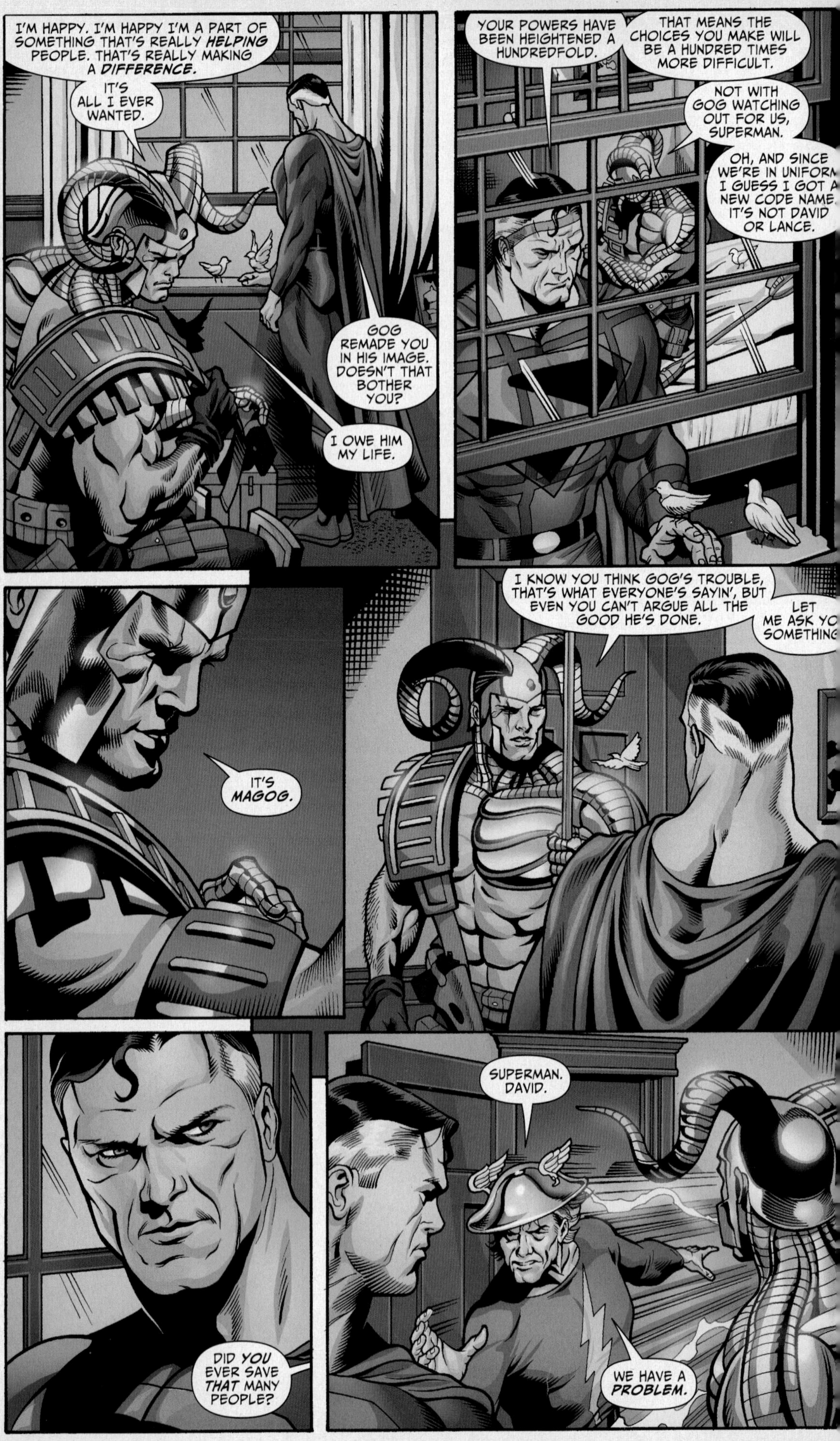

I'M HAPPY. I'M HAPPY I'M A PART OF SOMETHING THAT'S REALLY *HELPING* PEOPLE. THAT'S REALLY MAKING A *DIFFERENCE.*
IT'S ALL I EVER WANTED.
GOG REMADE YOU IN HIS IMAGE. DOESN'T THAT BOTHER YOU?
I OWE HIM MY LIFE.
YOUR POWERS HAVE BEEN HEIGHTENED A HUNDREDFOLD.
THAT MEANS THE CHOICES YOU MAKE WILL BE A HUNDRED TIMES MORE DIFFICULT.
NOT WITH GOG WATCHING OUT FOR US, SUPERMAN.
OH, AND SINCE WE'RE IN UNIFORM I GUESS I GOT A NEW CODE NAME. IT'S NOT DAVID OR LANCE.
IT'S *MAGOG.*
I KNOW YOU THINK GOG'S TROUBLE, THAT'S WHAT EVERYONE'S SAYIN', BUT EVEN YOU CAN'T ARGUE ALL THE GOOD HE'S DONE.
LET ME ASK YO SOMETHING
DID *YOU* EVER SAVE *THAT* MANY PEOPLE?
SUPERMAN. DAVID.
WE HAVE A *PROBLEM.*

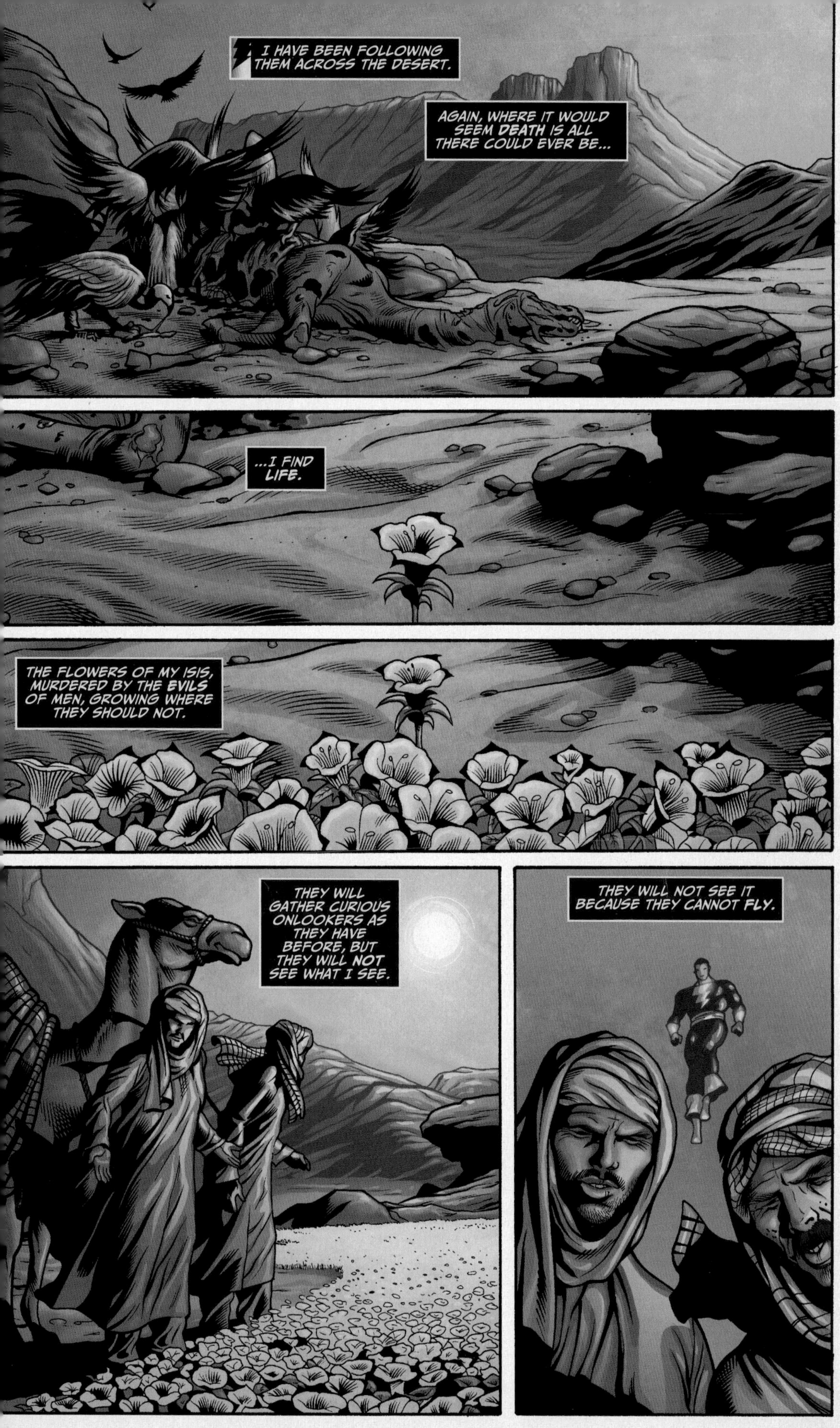

I HAVE BEEN FOLLOWING THEM ACROSS THE DESERT.
AGAIN, WHERE IT WOULD SEEM DEATH IS ALL THERE COULD EVER BE...
...I FIND LIFE.
THE FLOWERS OF MY ISIS, MURDERED BY THE EVILS OF MEN, GROWING WHERE THEY SHOULD NOT.
THEY WILL GATHER CURIOUS ONLOOKERS AS THEY HAVE BEFORE, BUT THEY WILL NOT SEE WHAT I SEE.
THEY WILL NOT SEE IT BECAUSE THEY CANNOT FLY.

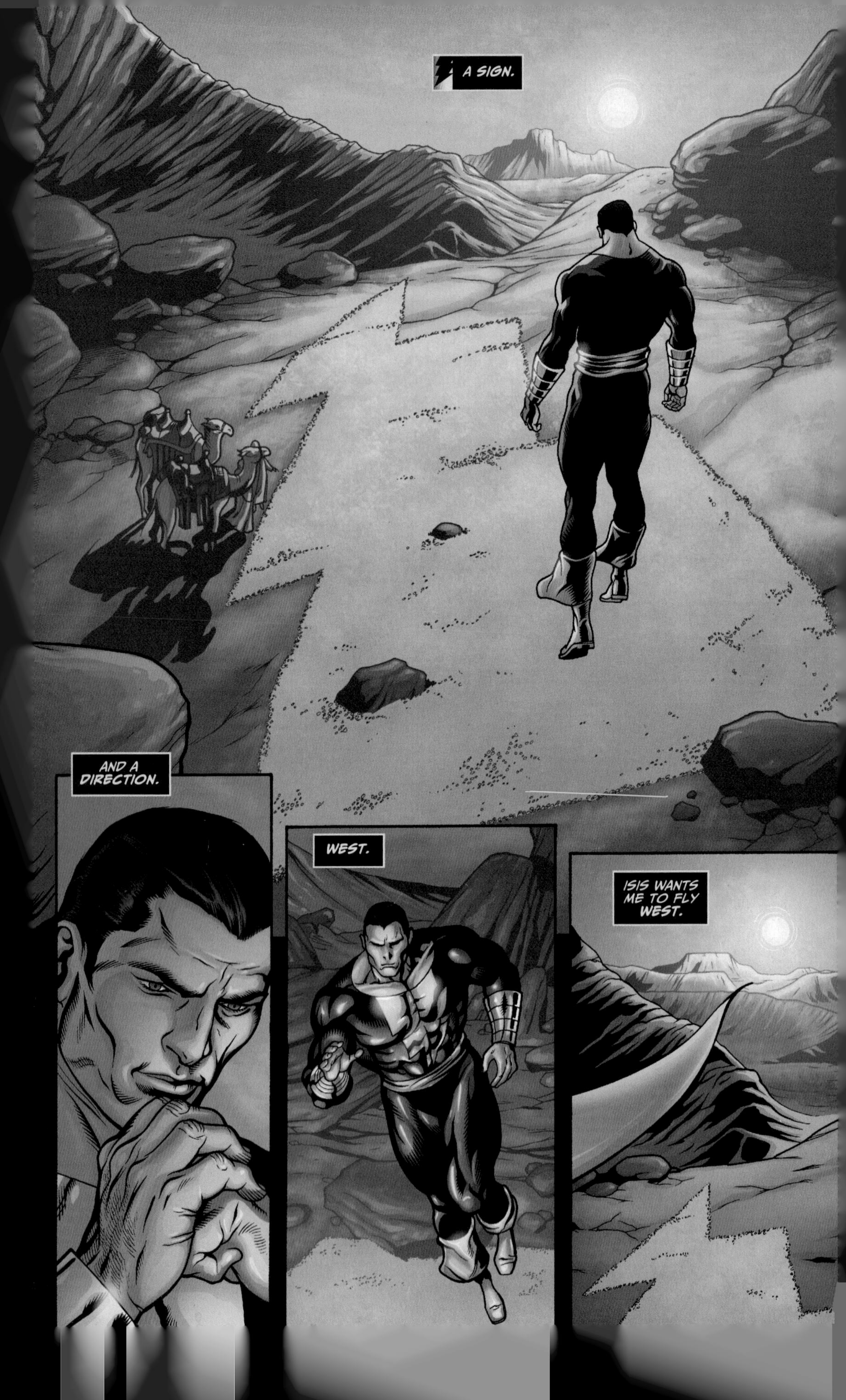
A SIGN.
AND A DIRECTION.
WEST.
ISIS WANTS ME TO FLY WEST.

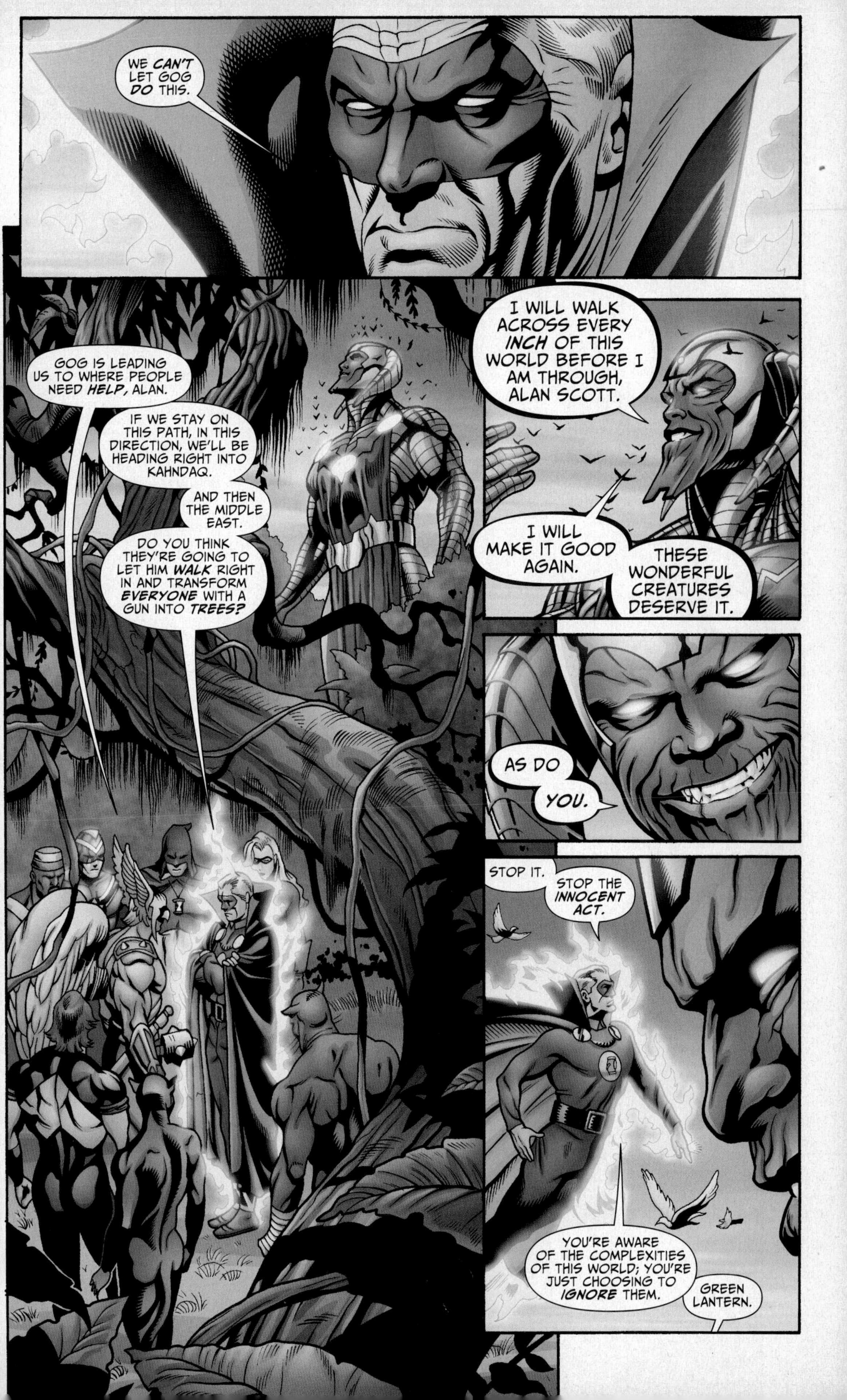
WE CAN'T LET GOG DO THIS.
GOG IS LEADING US TO WHERE PEOPLE NEED HELP, ALAN.
IF WE STAY ON THIS PATH, IN THIS DIRECTION, WE'LL BE HEADING RIGHT INTO KAHNDAQ.
AND THEN THE MIDDLE EAST.
DO YOU THINK THEY'RE GOING TO LET HIM WALK RIGHT IN AND TRANSFORM EVERYONE WITH A GUN INTO TREES?
I WILL WALK ACROSS EVERY INCH OF THIS WORLD BEFORE I AM THROUGH, ALAN SCOTT.
I WILL MAKE IT GOOD AGAIN.
THESE WONDERFUL CREATURES DESERVE IT.
AS DO
YOU.
STOP IT.
STOP THE INNOCENT ACT.
YOU'RE AWARE OF THE COMPLEXITIES OF THIS WORLD; YOU'RE JUST CHOOSING TO IGNORE THEM.
GREEN LANTERN.

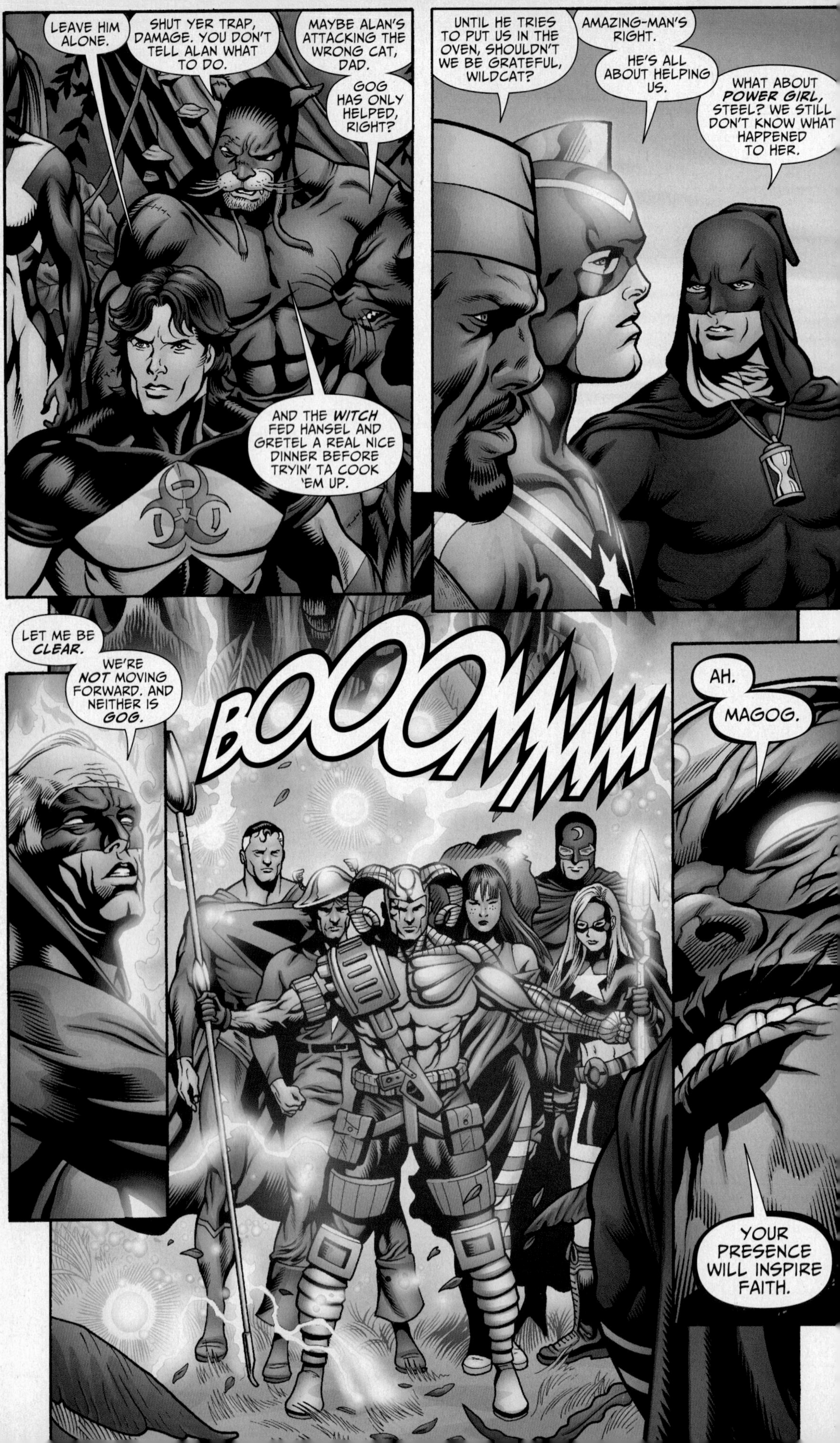
LEAVE HIM ALONE.
SHUT YER TRAP, DAMAGE. YOU DON'T TELL ALAN WHAT TO DO.
MAYBE ALAN'S ATTACKING THE WRONG CAT, DAD.
GOG HAS ONLY HELPED, RIGHT?
AND THE WITCH FED HANSEL AND GRETEL A REAL NICE DINNER BEFORE TRYIN' TA COOK 'EM UP.
UNTIL HE TRIES TO PUT US IN THE OVEN, SHOULDN'T WE BE GRATEFUL, WILDCAT?
AMAZING-MAN'S RIGHT.
HE'S ALL ABOUT HELPING US.
WHAT ABOUT POWER GIRL, STEEL? WE STILL DON'T KNOW WHAT HAPPENED TO HER.
LET ME BE CLEAR.
WE'RE NOT MOVING FORWARD. AND NEITHER IS GOG.
BOOOMMM
AH.
MAGOG.
YOUR PRESENCE WILL INSPIRE FAITH.

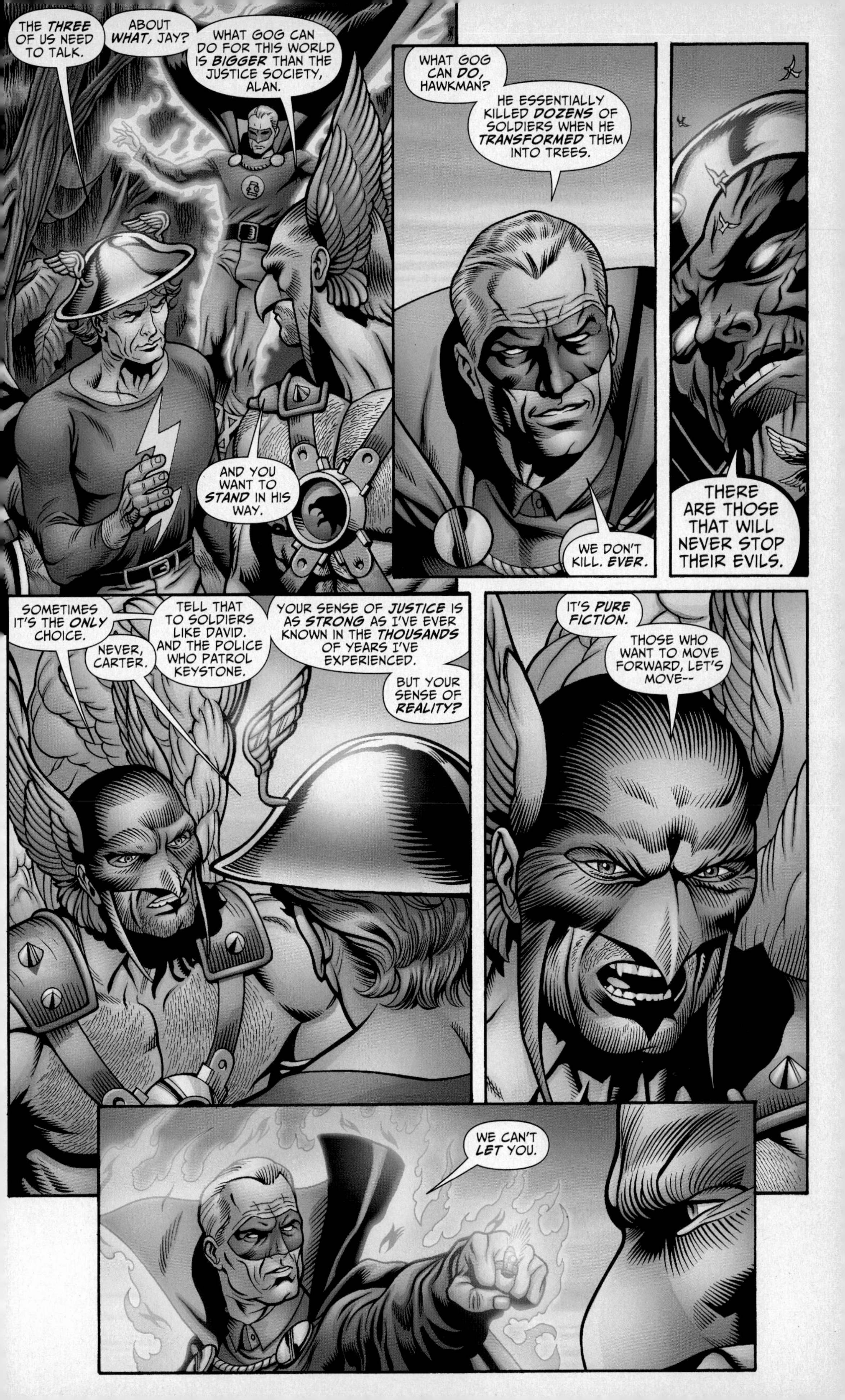
THE THREE OF US NEED TO TALK.
ABOUT WHAT, JAY?
WHAT GOG CAN DO FOR THIS WORLD IS BIGGER THAN THE JUSTICE SOCIETY, ALAN.
AND YOU WANT TO STAND IN HIS WAY.
WHAT GOG CAN DO, HAWKMAN?
HE ESSENTIALLY KILLED DOZENS OF SOLDIERS WHEN HE TRANSFORMED THEM INTO TREES.
WE DON'T KILL. EVER.
THERE ARE THOSE THAT WILL NEVER STOP THEIR EVILS.
SOMETIMES IT'S THE ONLY CHOICE.
NEVER, CARTER.
TELL THAT TO SOLDIERS LIKE DAVID. AND THE POLICE WHO PATROL KEYSTONE.
YOUR SENSE OF JUSTICE IS AS STRONG AS I'VE EVER KNOWN IN THE THOUSANDS OF YEARS I'VE EXPERIENCED.
BUT YOUR SENSE OF REALITY?
IT'S PURE FICTION.
THOSE WHO WANT TO MOVE FORWARD, LET'S MOVE--
WE CAN'T LET YOU.

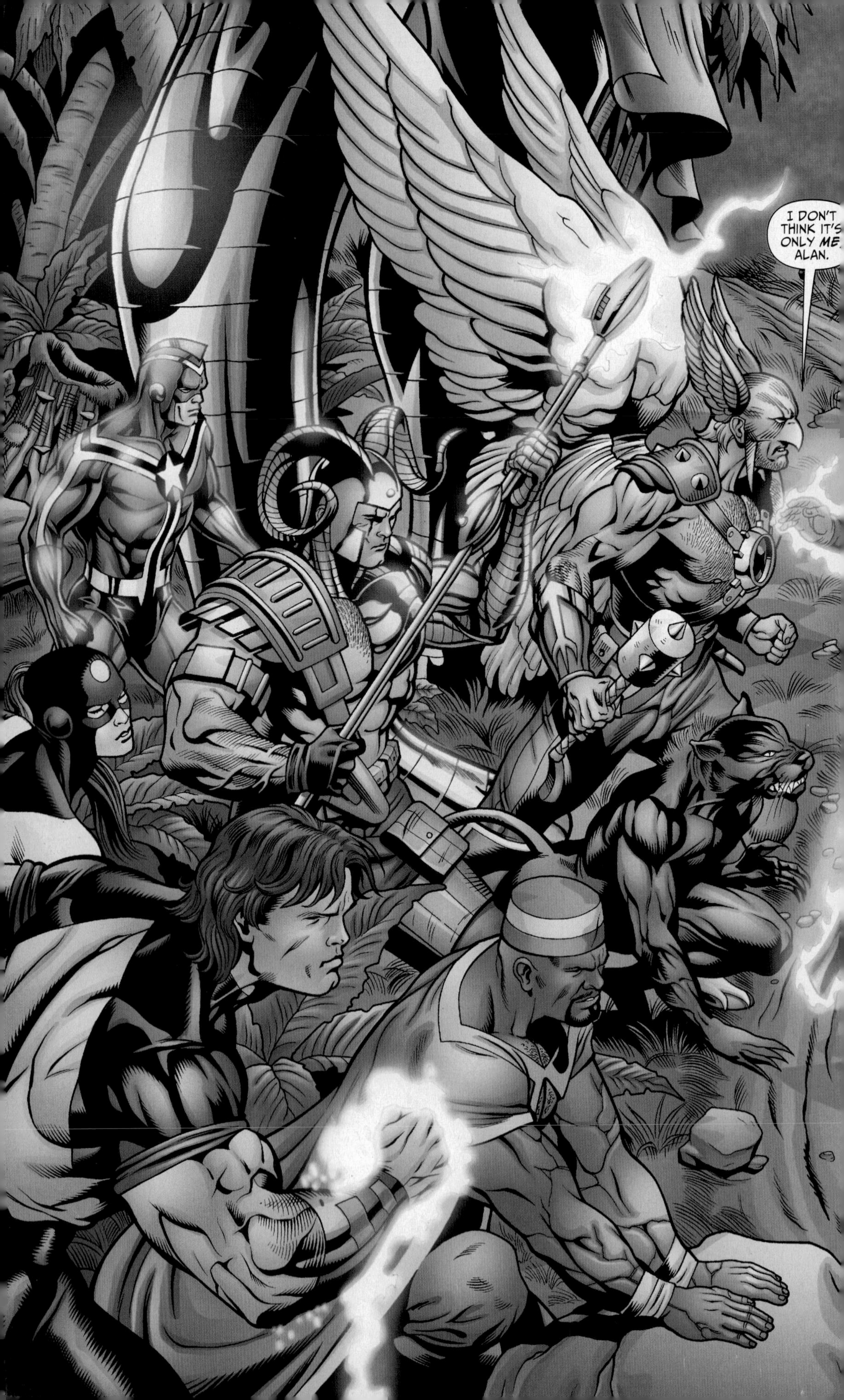
I DON'T THINK IT'S ONLY *ME*, ALAN.

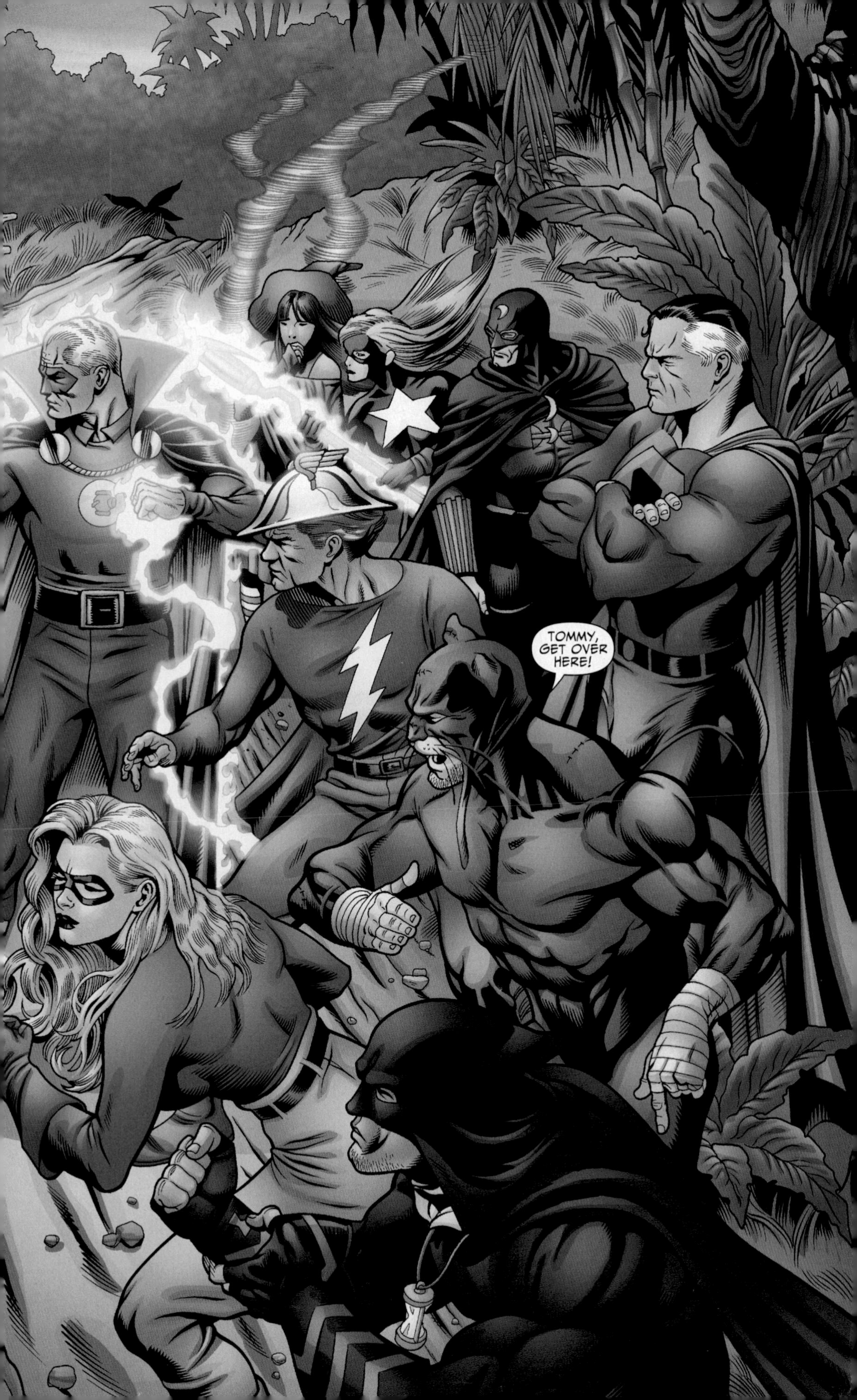
TOMMY, GET OVER HERE!

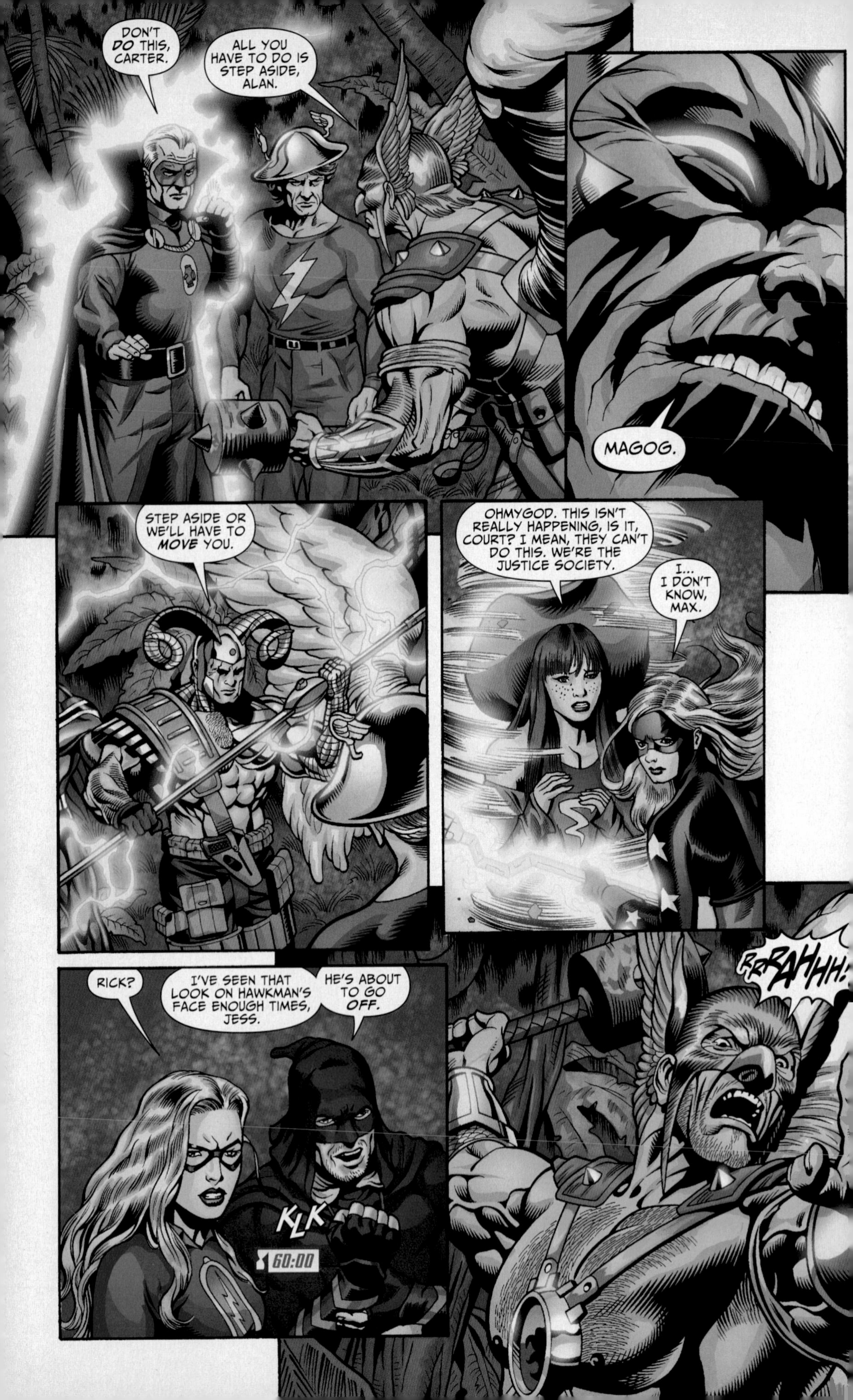
DON'T DO THIS, CARTER.
ALL YOU HAVE TO DO IS STEP ASIDE, ALAN.
MAGOG.
STEP ASIDE OR WE'LL HAVE TO MOVE YOU.
OHMYGOD. THIS ISN'T REALLY HAPPENING, IS IT, COURT? I MEAN, THEY CAN'T DO THIS. WE'RE THE JUSTICE SOCIETY.
I... I DON'T KNOW, MAX.
RICK?
I'VE SEEN THAT LOOK ON HAWKMAN'S FACE ENOUGH TIMES, JESS.
HE'S ABOUT TO GO OFF.
KLK
60:00
RRRAHHH!

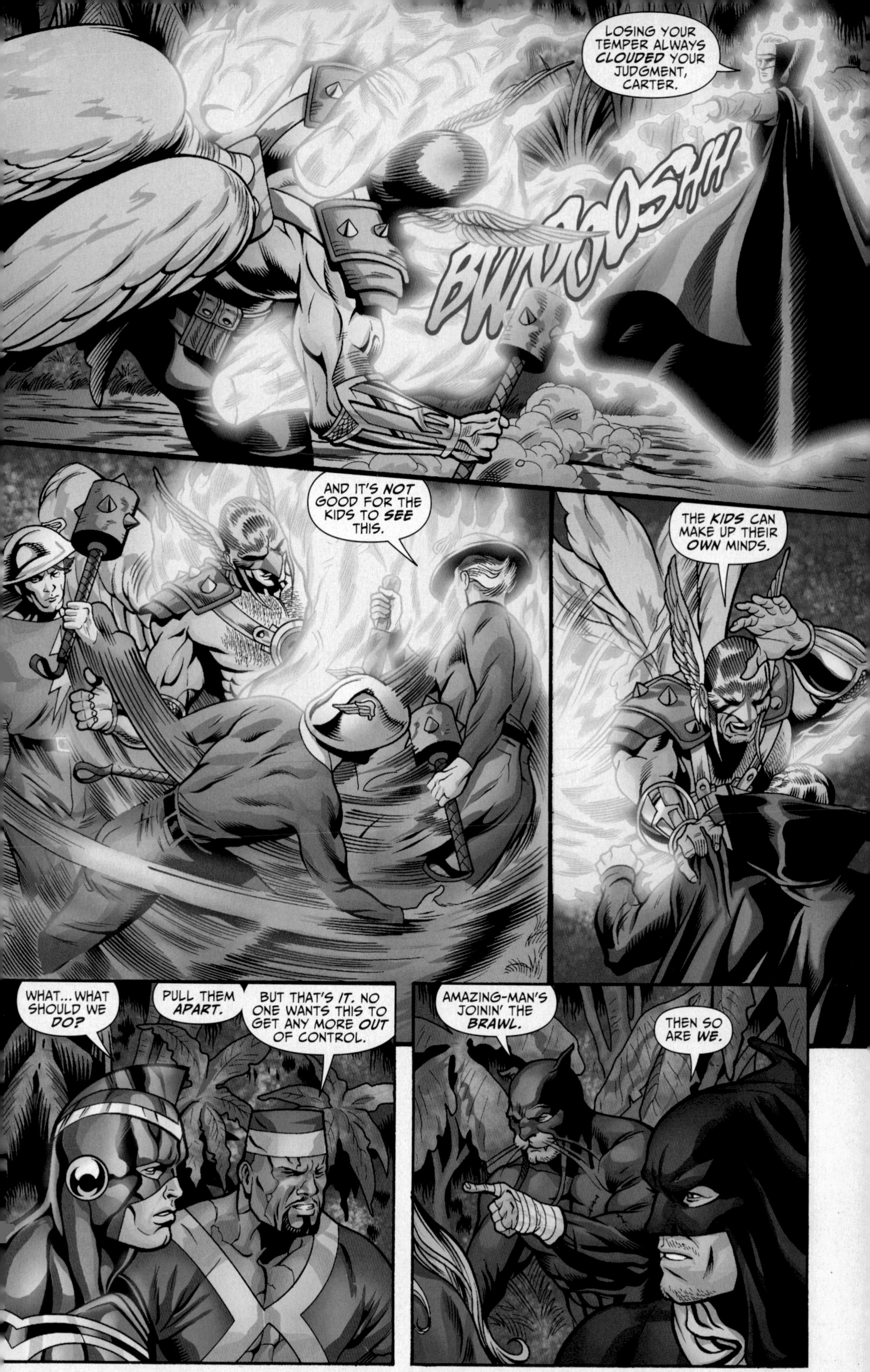
LOSING YOUR TEMPER ALWAYS CLOUDED YOUR JUDGMENT, CARTER.
BWOOOOSHH
AND IT'S NOT GOOD FOR THE KIDS TO SEE THIS.
THE KIDS CAN MAKE UP THEIR OWN MINDS.
WHAT...WHAT SHOULD WE DO?
PULL THEM APART.
BUT THAT'S IT. NO ONE WANTS THIS TO GET ANY MORE OUT OF CONTROL.
AMAZING-MAN'S JOININ' THE BRAWL.
THEN SO ARE WE.

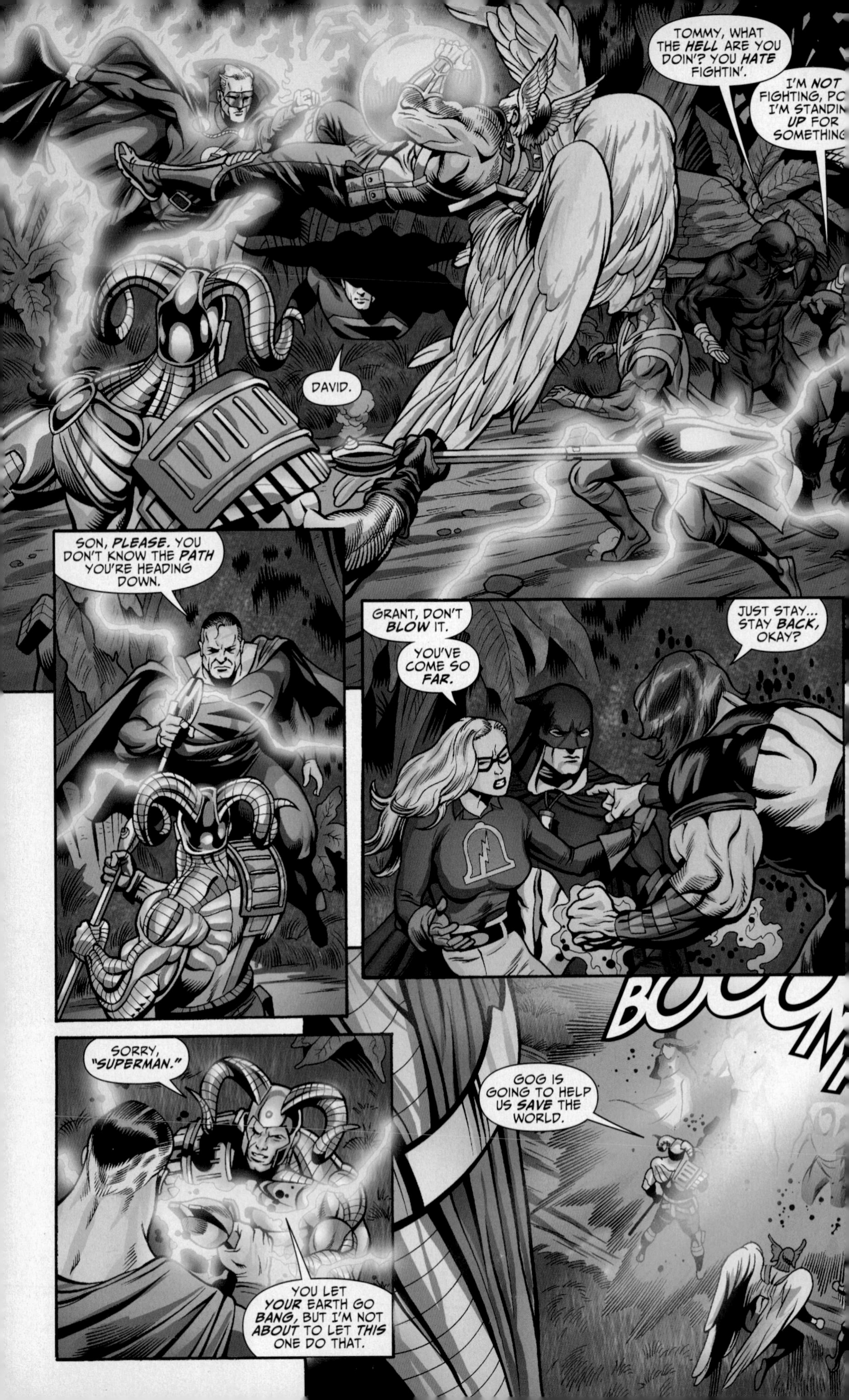
TOMMY, WHAT THE HELL ARE YOU DOIN'? YOU HATE FIGHTIN'.
I'M NOT FIGHTING, PO I'M STANDIN UP FOR SOMETHING
DAVID.
SON, PLEASE. YOU DON'T KNOW THE PATH YOU'RE HEADING DOWN.
GRANT, DON'T BLOW IT.
YOU'VE COME SO FAR.
JUST STAY... STAY BACK, OKAY?
SORRY, "SUPERMAN."
YOU LET YOUR EARTH GO BANG, BUT I'M NOT ABOUT TO LET THIS ONE DO THAT.
GOG IS GOING TO HELP US SAVE THE WORLD.
BOOOM

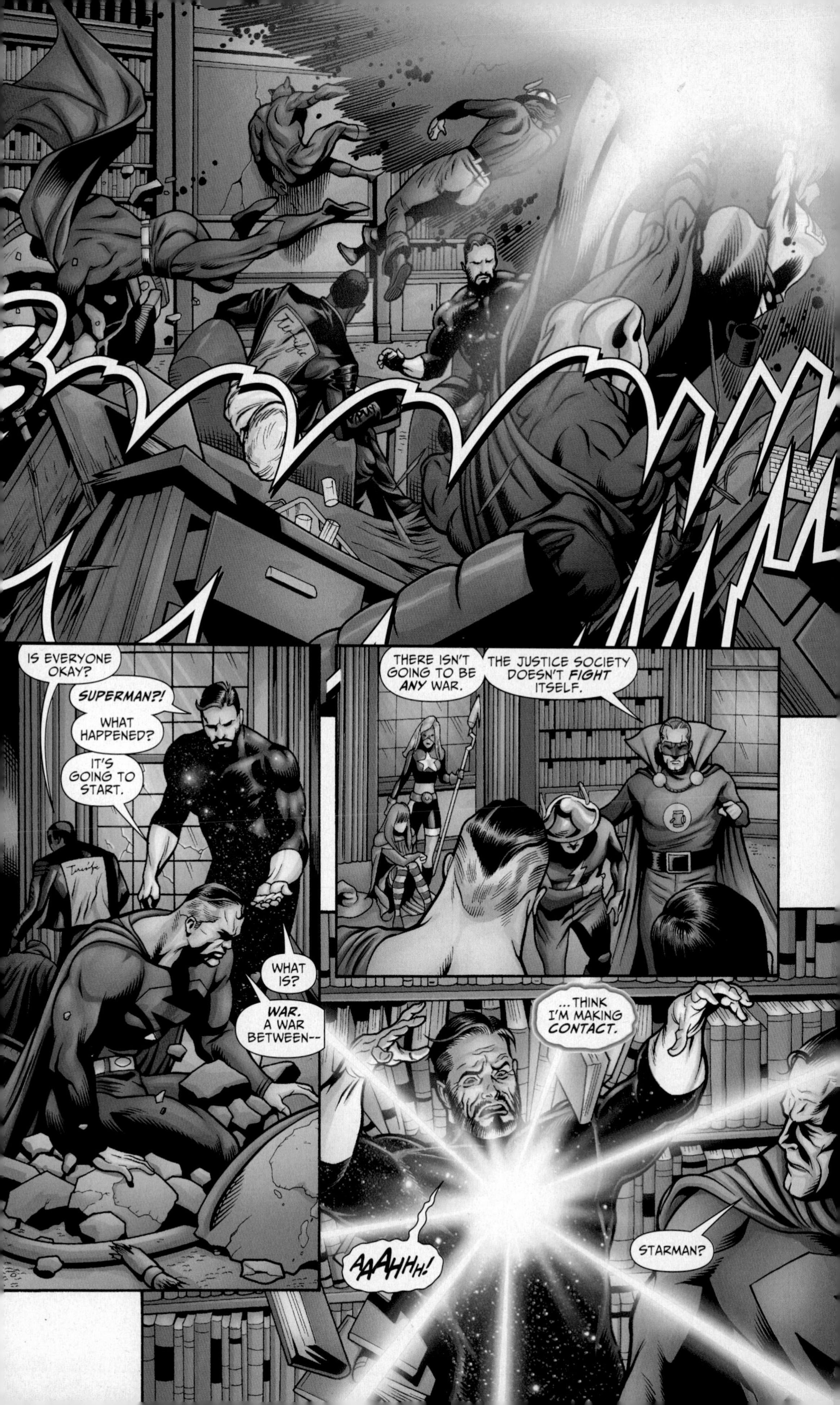
IS EVERYONE OKAY?
SUPERMAN?!
WHAT HAPPENED?
IT'S GOING TO START.
WHAT IS?
WAR. A WAR BETWEEN--
THERE ISN'T GOING TO BE ANY WAR.
THE JUSTICE SOCIETY DOESN'T FIGHT ITSELF.
...THINK I'M MAKING CONTACT.
AAAHHH!
STARMAN?

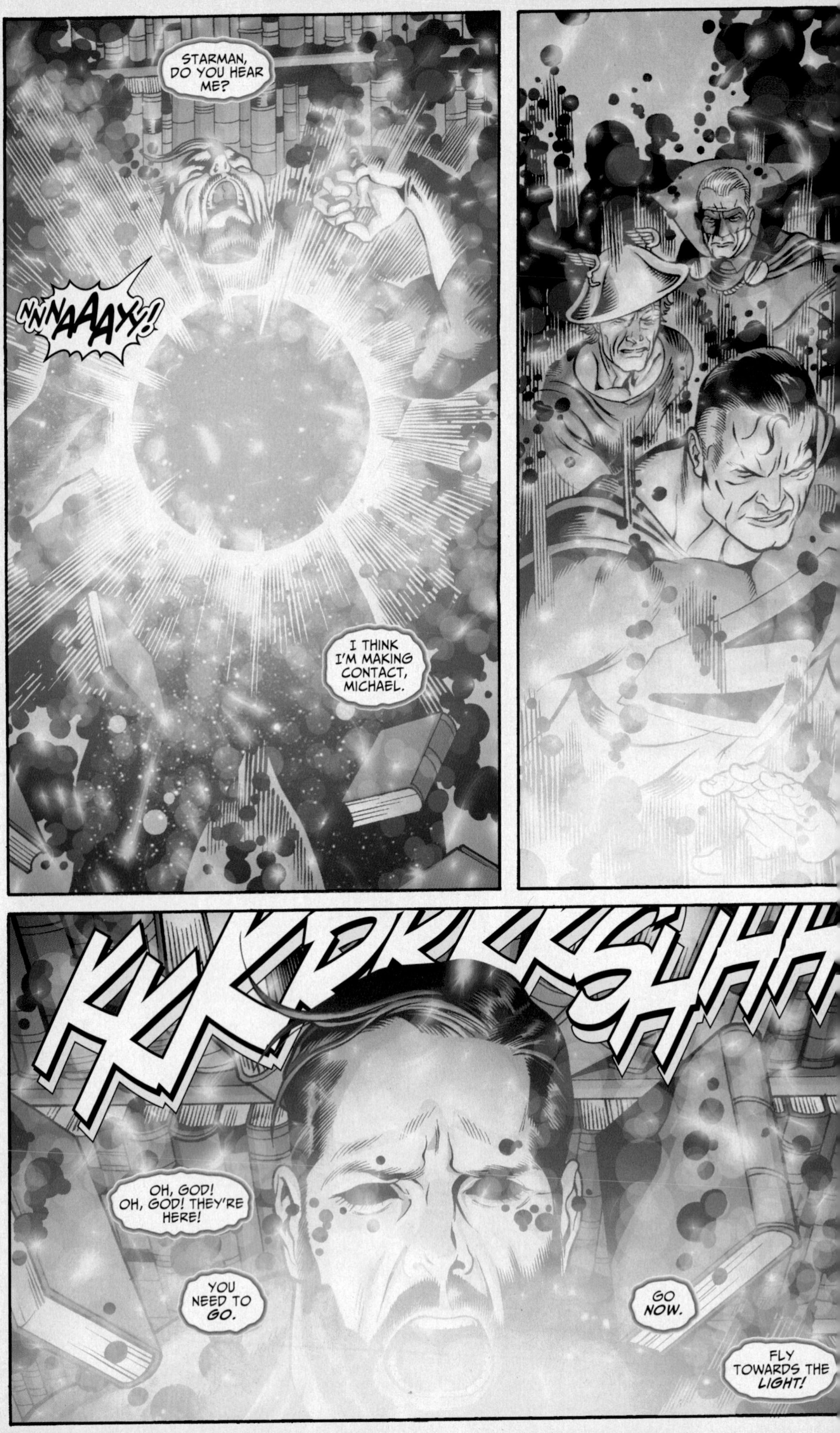
STARMAN, DO YOU HEAR ME?
NNNAAAYY!
I THINK I'M MAKING CONTACT, MICHAEL.
KKKDRRKSHHH
OH, GOD! OH, GOD! THEY'RE HERE!
YOU NEED TO GO.
GO NOW.
FLY TOWARDS THE LIGHT!

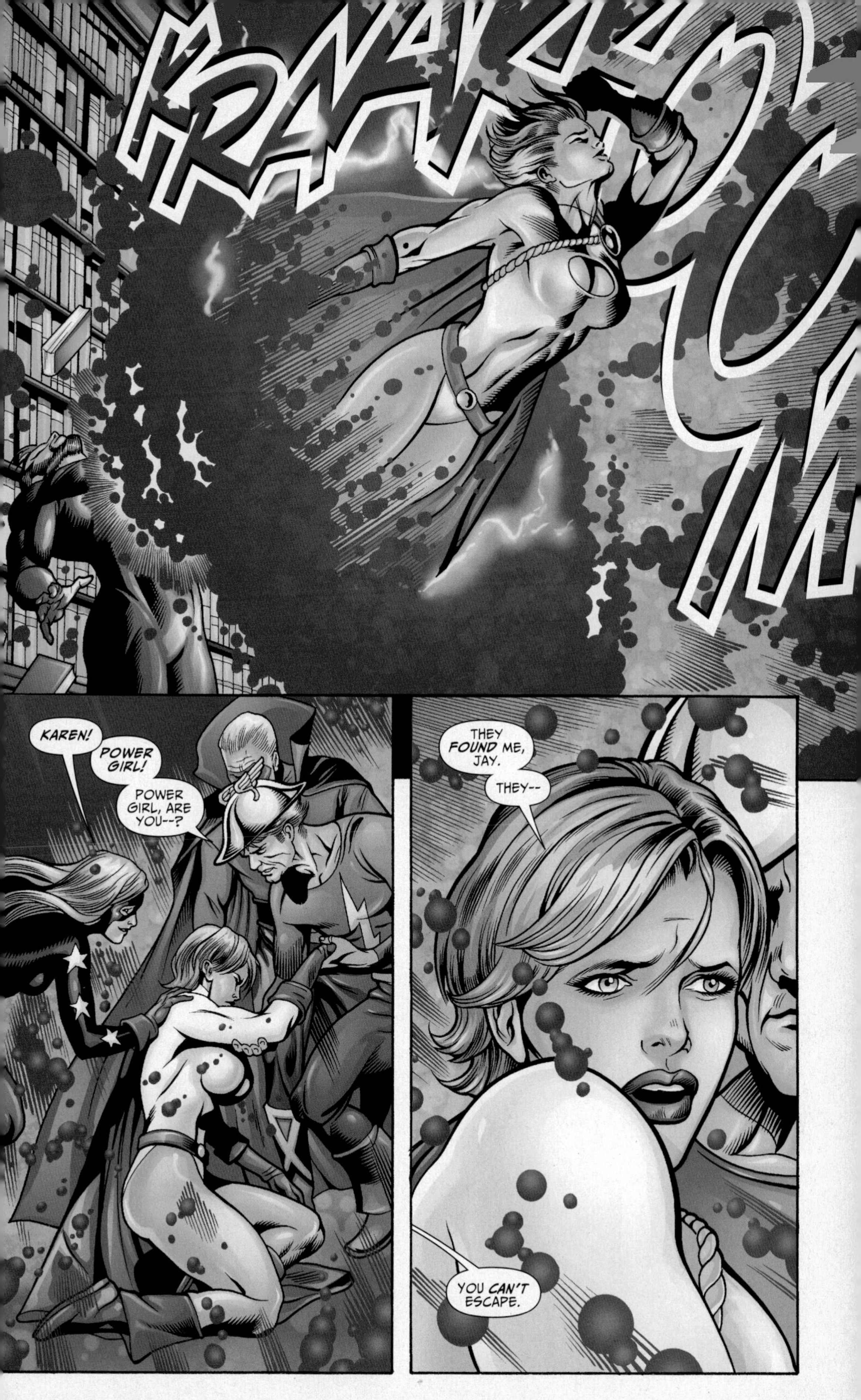
KARAKOOM
KAREN!
POWER GIRL!
POWER GIRL, ARE YOU--?
THEY FOUND ME, JAY.
THEY--
YOU CAN'T ESCAPE.

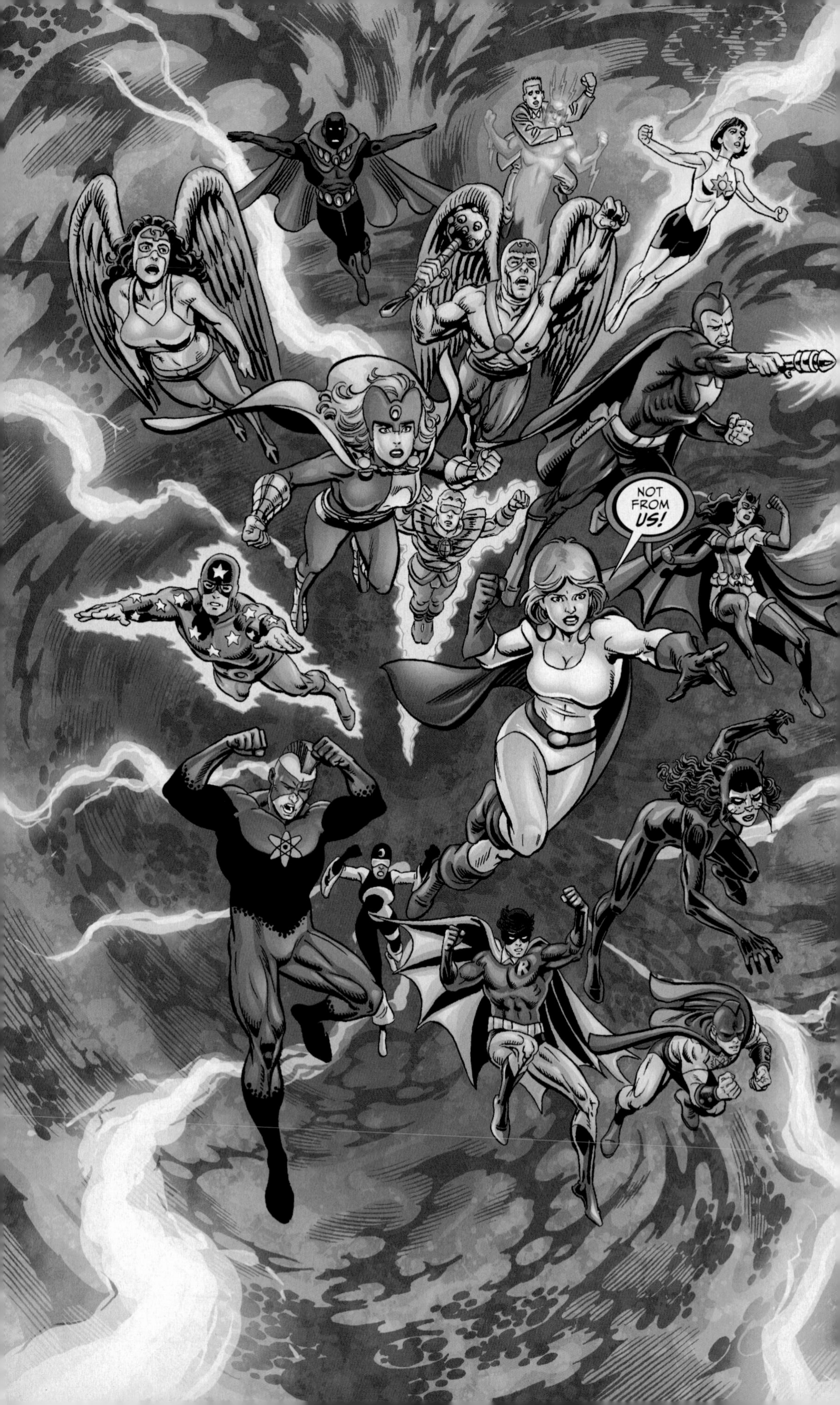
NOT FROM US!

JUSTICE SOCIETY OF AMERICA #20 cover A by Alex Ross

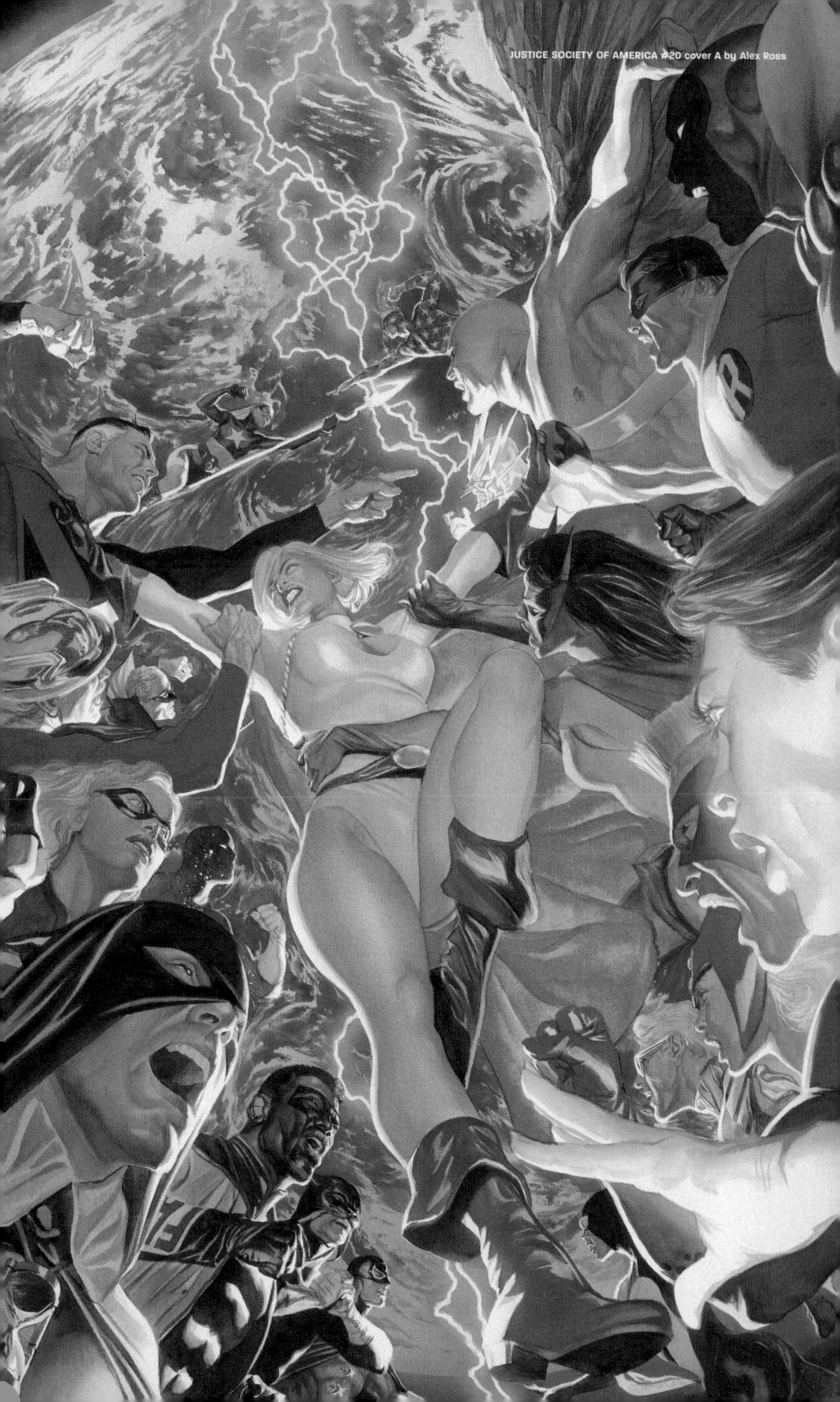

JUSTICE SOCIETY OF AMERICA #20 cover B by Dale Eaglesham & Mark McKenna

Interior art by Eaglesham & Massengill, with Earth-2 sequence by Jerry Ordway & Bob Wiacek

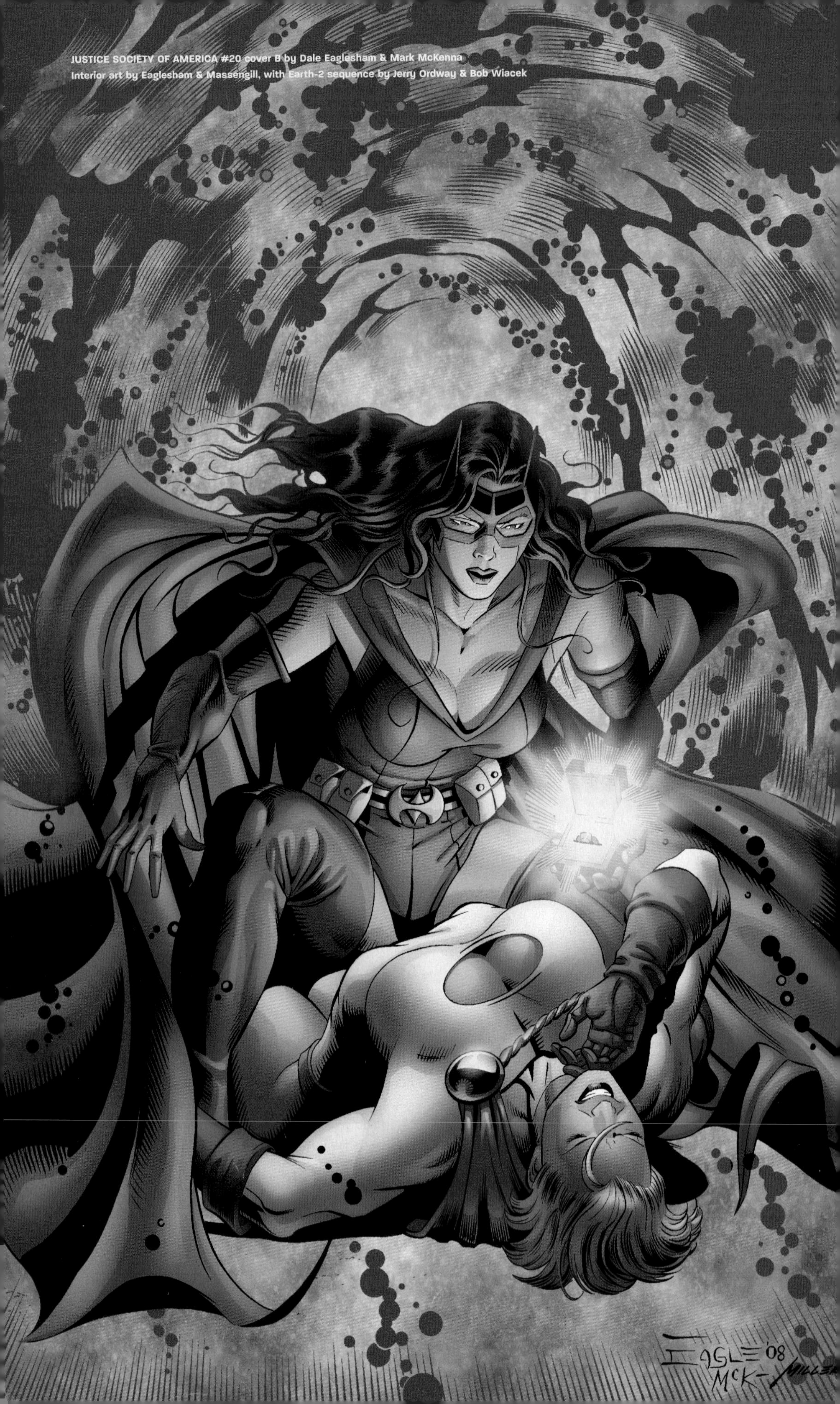

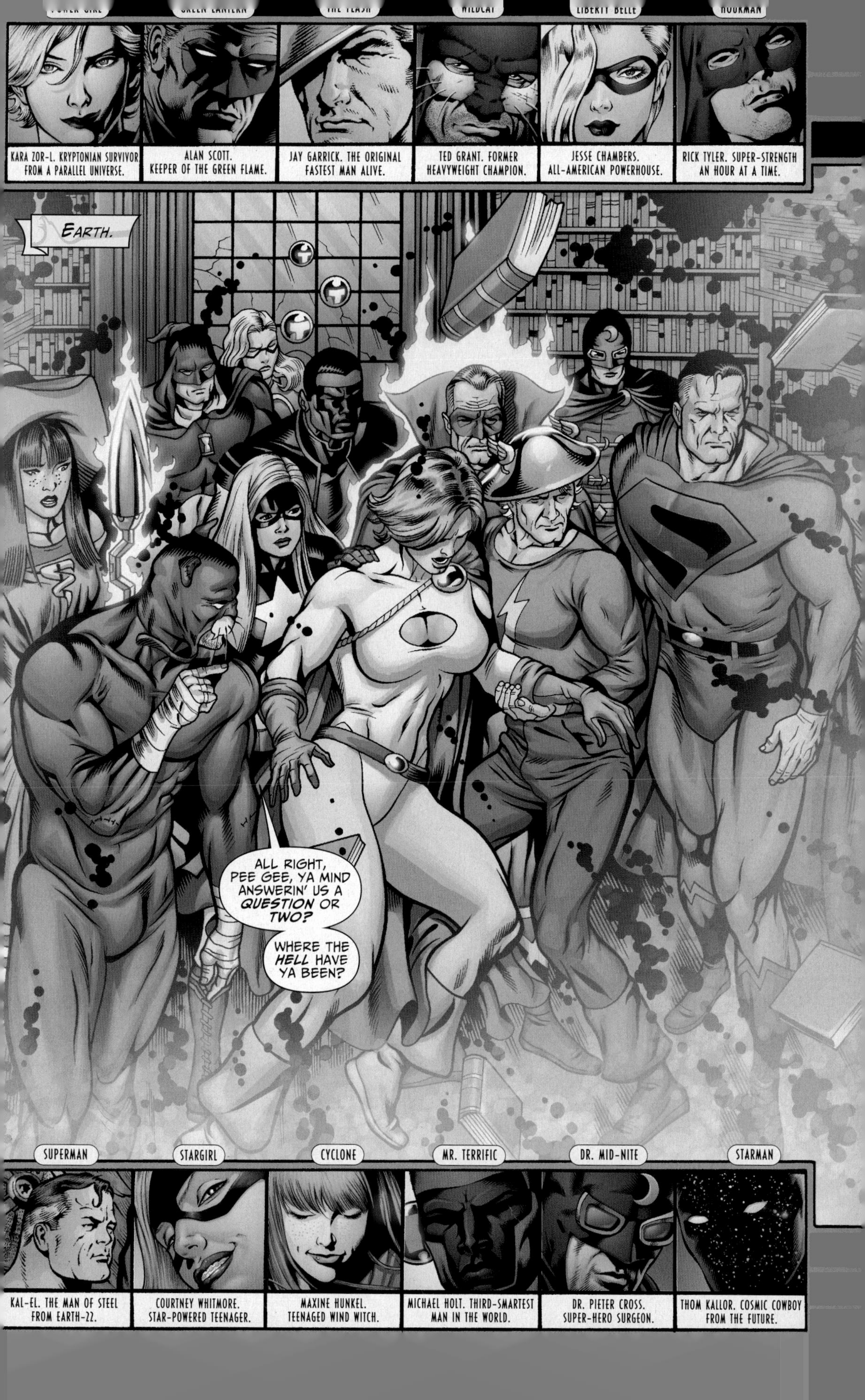
KARA ZOR-L. KRYPTONIAN SURVIVOR FROM A PARALLEL UNIVERSE.
ALAN SCOTT. KEEPER OF THE GREEN FLAME.
JAY GARRICK. THE ORIGINAL FASTEST MAN ALIVE.
TED GRANT. FORMER HEAVYWEIGHT CHAMPION.
JESSE CHAMBERS. ALL-AMERICAN POWERHOUSE.
RICK TYLER. SUPER-STRENGTH AN HOUR AT A TIME.
EARTH.
ALL RIGHT, PEE GEE, YA MIND ANSWERIN' US A *QUESTION* OR *TWO?*
WHERE THE *HELL* HAVE YA BEEN?
SUPERMAN
KAL-EL. THE MAN OF STEEL FROM EARTH-22.
STARGIRL
COURTNEY WHITMORE. STAR-POWERED TEENAGER.
CYCLONE
MAXINE HUNKEL. TEENAGED WIND WITCH.
MR. TERRIFIC
MICHAEL HOLT. THIRD-SMARTEST MAN IN THE WORLD.
DR. MID-NITE
DR. PIETER CROSS. SUPER-HERO SURGEON.
STARMAN
THOM KALLOR. COSMIC COWBOY FROM THE FUTURE.

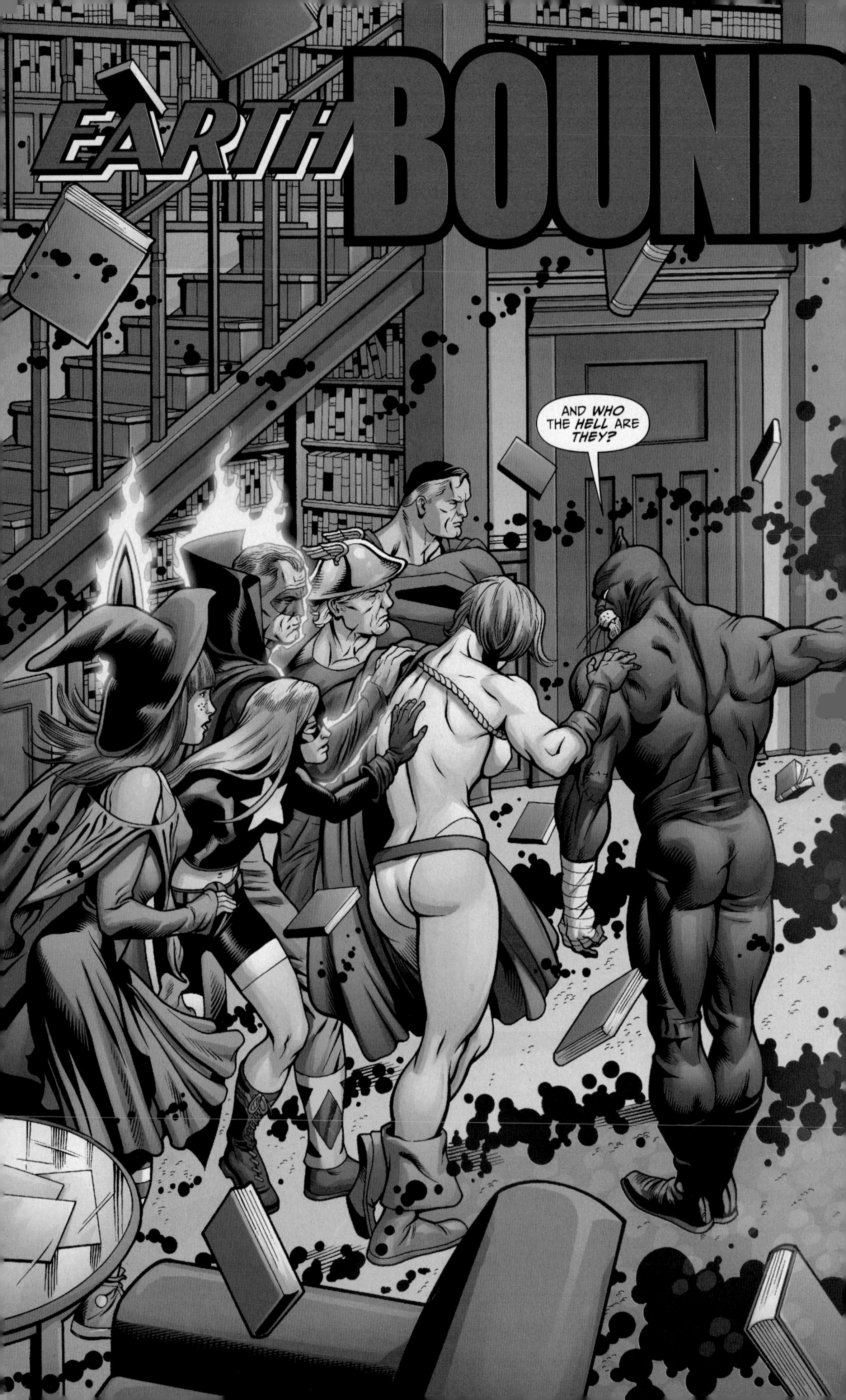
EARTH BOUND
AND WHO THE HELL ARE THEY?

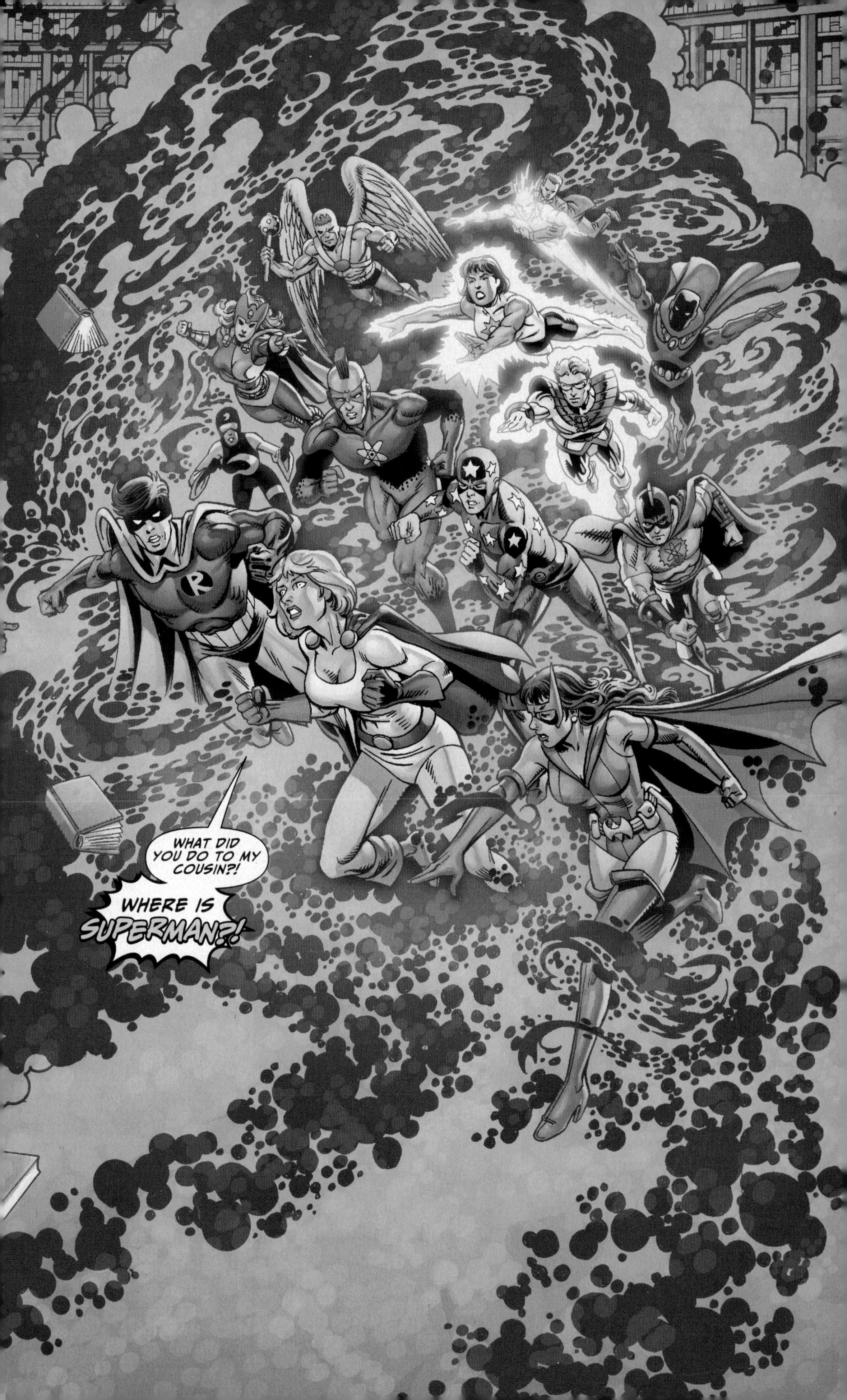
WHAT DID YOU DO TO MY COUSIN?!
WHERE IS SUPERMAN?!

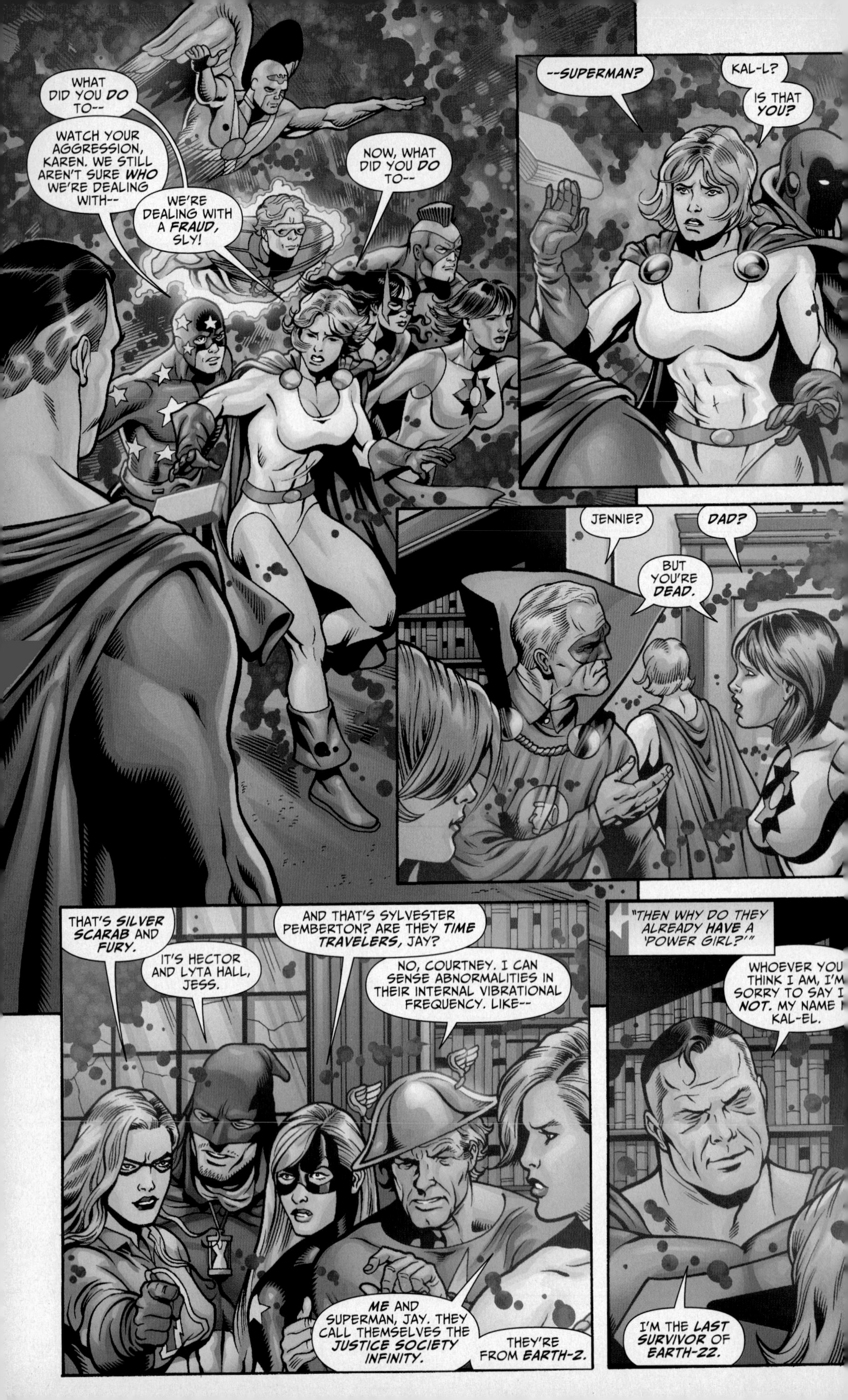
WHAT DID YOU DO TO--
WATCH YOUR AGGRESSION, KAREN. WE STILL AREN'T SURE WHO WE'RE DEALING WITH--
WE'RE DEALING WITH A FRAUD, SLY!
NOW, WHAT DID YOU DO TO--
--SUPERMAN?
KAL-L?
IS THAT YOU?
JENNIE?
DAD?
BUT YOU'RE DEAD.
THAT'S SILVER SCARAB AND FURY.
IT'S HECTOR AND LYTA HALL, JESS.
AND THAT'S SYLVESTER PEMBERTON? ARE THEY TIME TRAVELERS, JAY?
NO, COURTNEY. I CAN SENSE ABNORMALITIES IN THEIR INTERNAL VIBRATIONAL FREQUENCY. LIKE--
ME AND SUPERMAN, JAY. THEY CALL THEMSELVES THE JUSTICE SOCIETY INFINITY.
THEY'RE FROM EARTH-2.
"THEN WHY DO THEY ALREADY HAVE A 'POWER GIRL?'"
I'M THE LAST SURVIVOR OF EARTH-22.

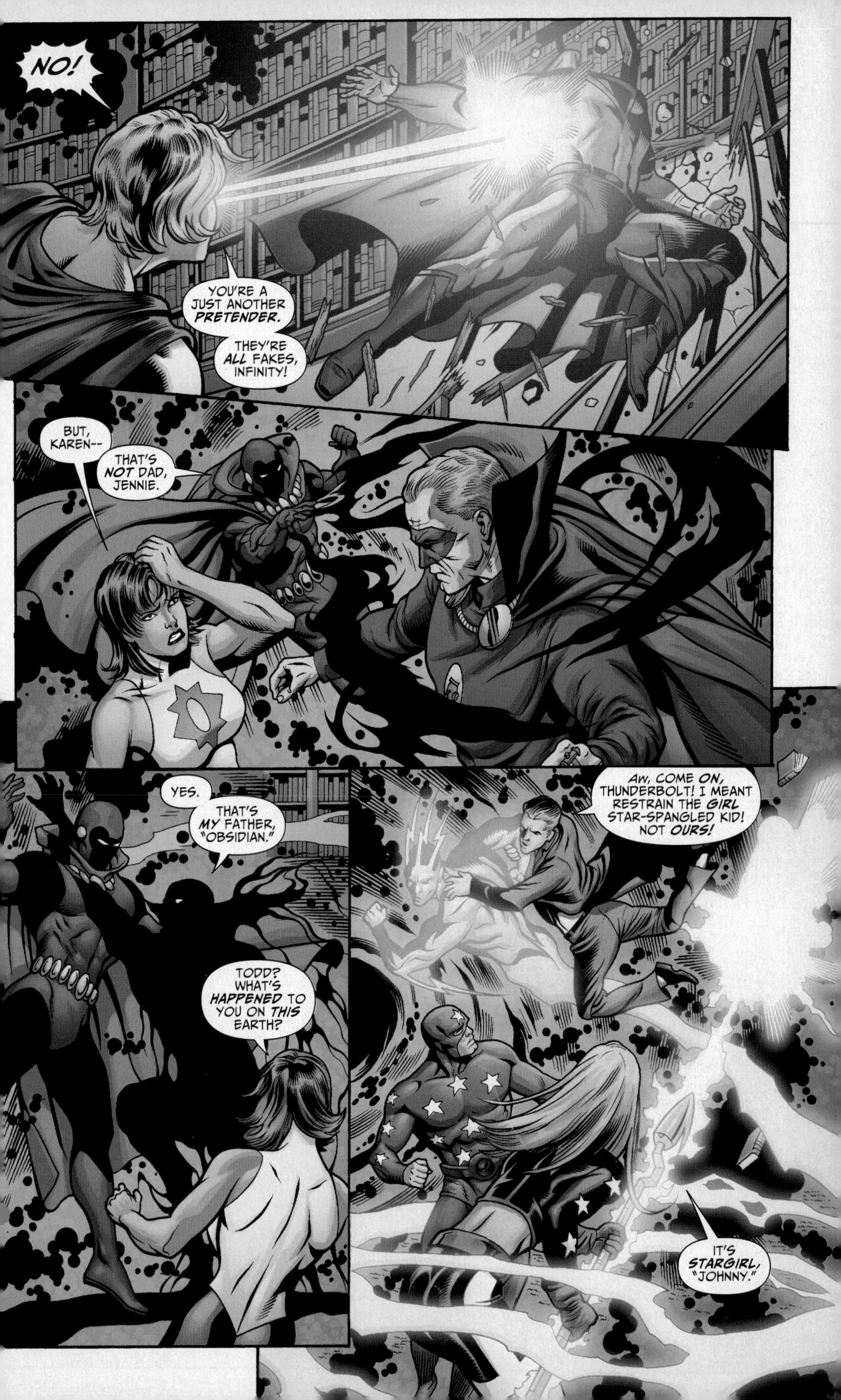
NO!
YOU'RE A JUST ANOTHER PRETENDER.
THEY'RE ALL FAKES, INFINITY!
BUT, KAREN--
THAT'S NOT DAD, JENNIE.
YES.
THAT'S MY FATHER, "OBSIDIAN."
TODD? WHAT'S HAPPENED TO YOU ON THIS EARTH?
AW, COME ON, THUNDERBOLT! I MEANT RESTRAIN THE GIRL STAR-SPANGLED KID! NOT OURS!
IT'S STARGIRL, "JOHNNY."

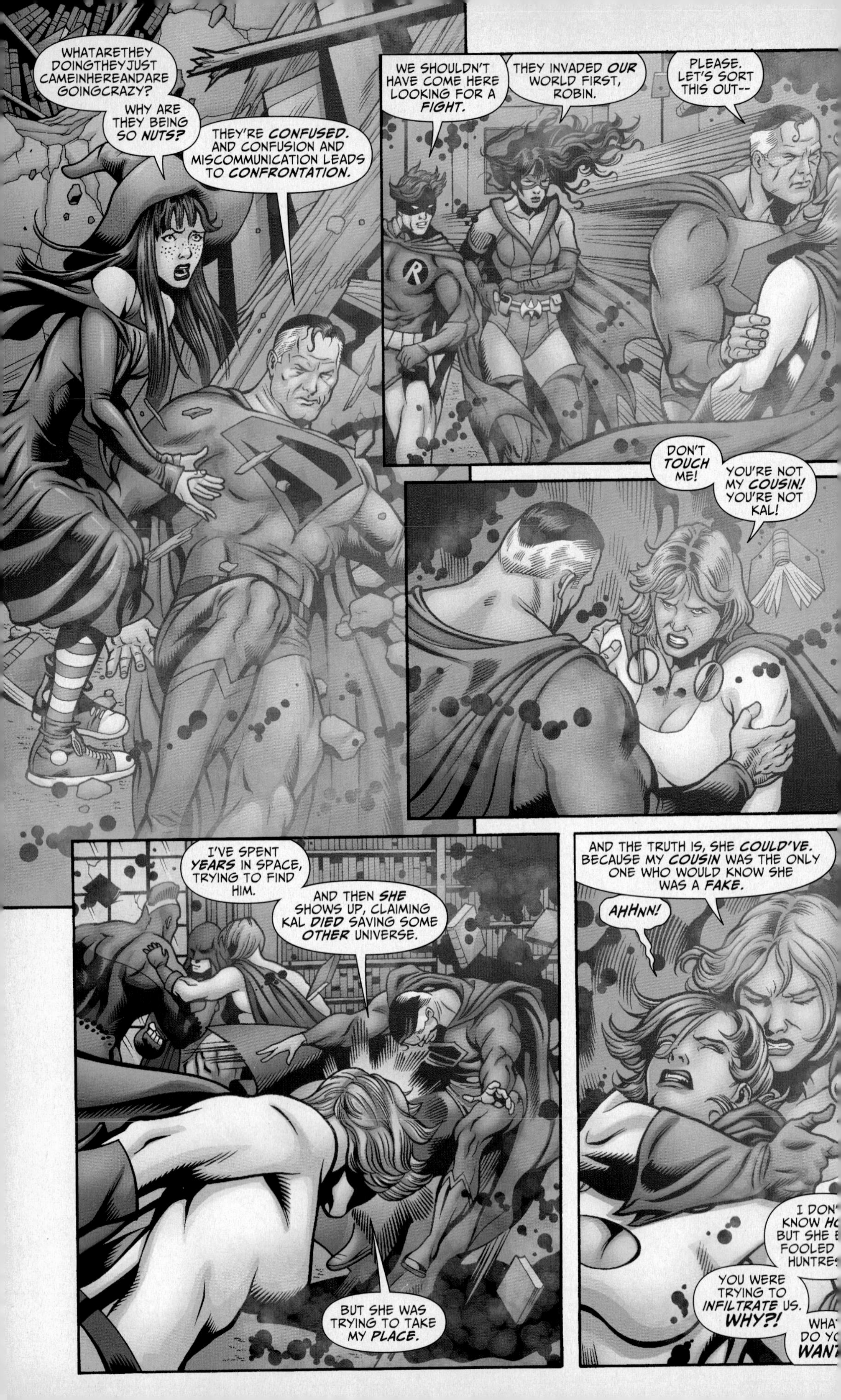
WHATARETHEY DOINGTHEYJUST CAMEINHEREANDARE GOINGCRAZY?
WHY ARE THEY BEING SO NUTS?
THEY'RE CONFUSED. AND CONFUSION AND MISCOMMUNICATION LEADS TO CONFRONTATION.
WE SHOULDN'T HAVE COME HERE LOOKING FOR A FIGHT.
THEY INVADED OUR WORLD FIRST, ROBIN.
PLEASE. LET'S SORT THIS OUT--
DON'T TOUCH ME!
YOU'RE NOT MY COUSIN! YOU'RE NOT KAL!
I'VE SPENT YEARS IN SPACE, TRYING TO FIND HIM.
AND THEN SHE SHOWS UP, CLAIMING KAL DIED SAVING SOME OTHER UNIVERSE.
BUT SHE WAS TRYING TO TAKE MY PLACE.
AND THE TRUTH IS, SHE COULD'VE. BECAUSE MY COUSIN WAS THE ONLY ONE WHO WOULD KNOW SHE WAS A FAKE.
AHHNN!
YOU WERE TRYING TO INFILTRATE US. WHY?!

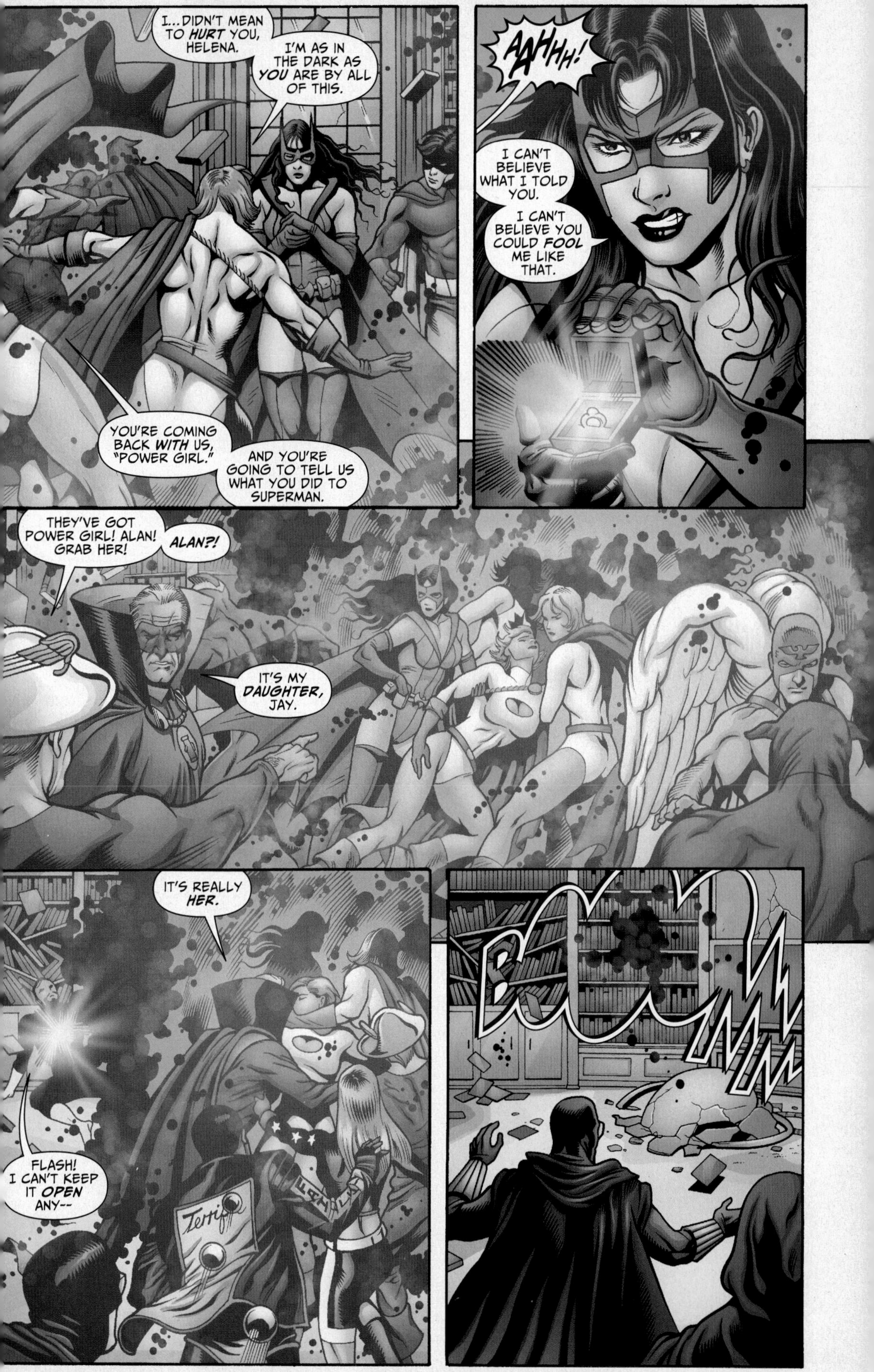

I...DIDN'T MEAN TO HURT YOU, HELENA.
I'M AS IN THE DARK AS YOU ARE BY ALL OF THIS.
YOU'RE COMING BACK WITH US, "POWER GIRL."
AND YOU'RE GOING TO TELL US WHAT YOU DID TO SUPERMAN.
AAHHH!
I CAN'T BELIEVE WHAT I TOLD YOU.
I CAN'T BELIEVE YOU COULD FOOL ME LIKE THAT.
THEY'VE GOT POWER GIRL! ALAN! GRAB HER!
ALAN?!
IT'S MY DAUGHTER, JAY.
IT'S REALLY HER.
FLASH! I CAN'T KEEP IT OPEN ANY--
BAMMM

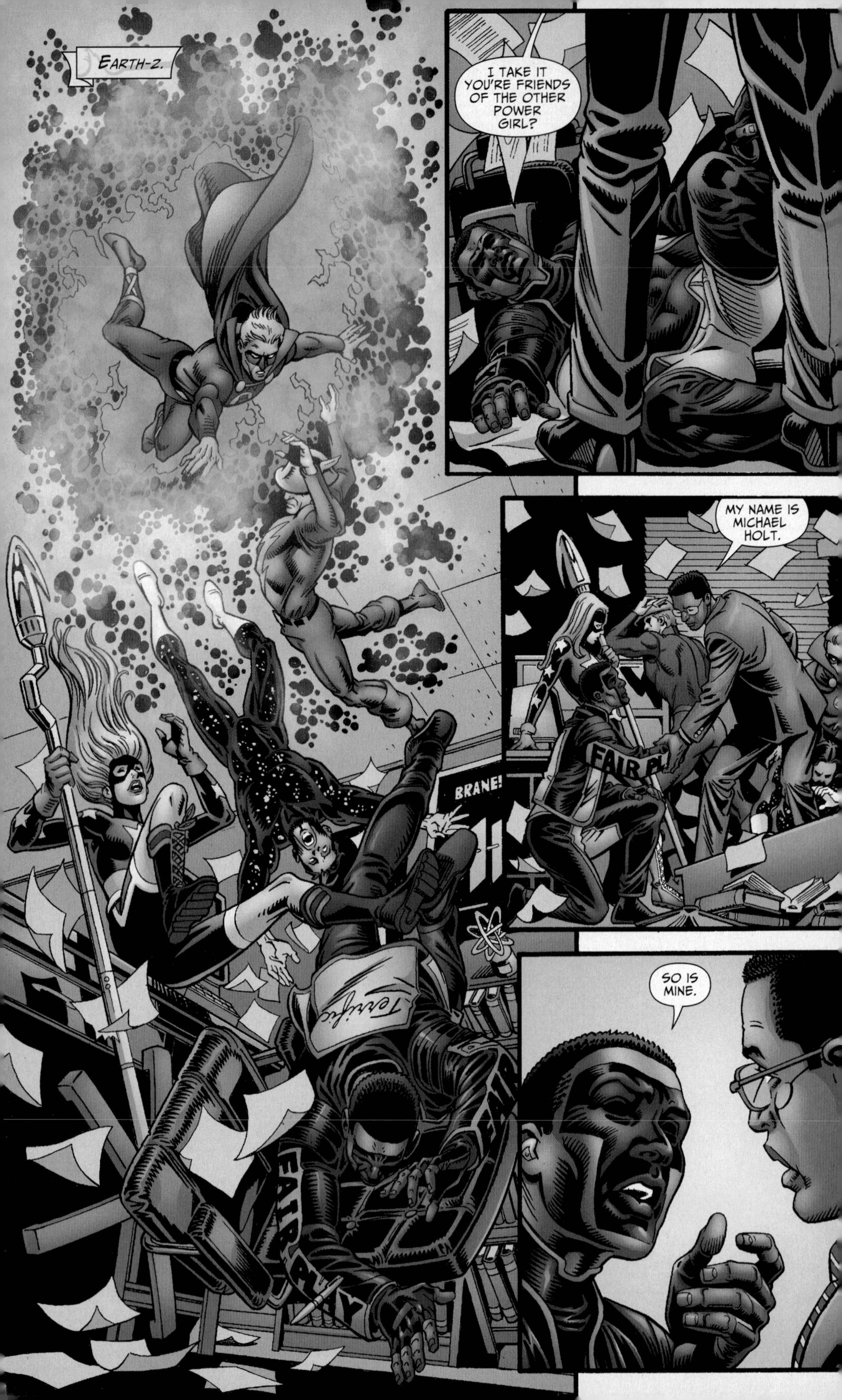
EARTH-2.
I TAKE IT YOU'RE FRIENDS OF THE OTHER POWER GIRL?
BRANE!
MY NAME IS MICHAEL HOLT.
SO IS MINE.

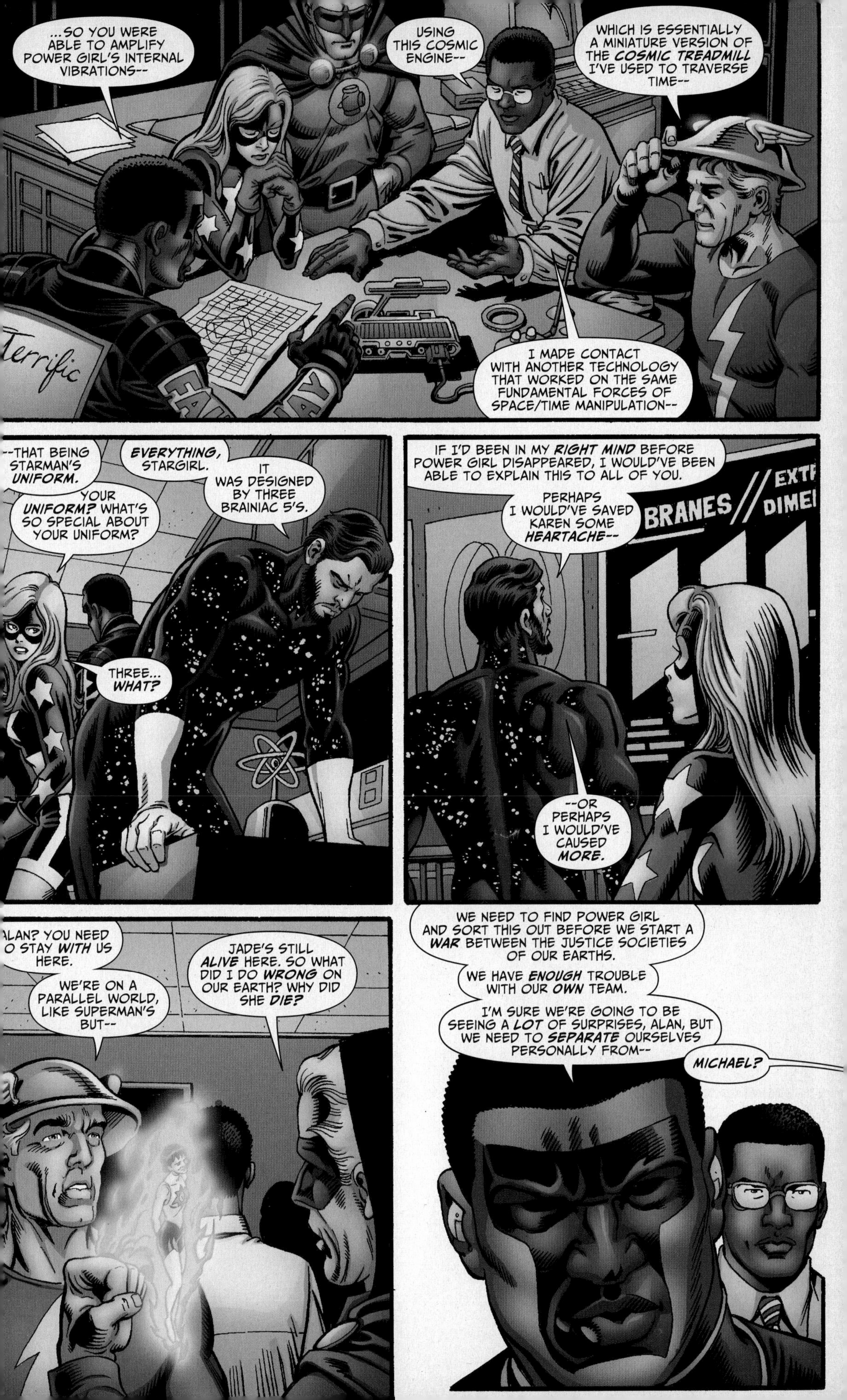
...SO YOU WERE ABLE TO AMPLIFY POWER GIRL'S INTERNAL VIBRATIONS--
USING THIS COSMIC ENGINE--
WHICH IS ESSENTIALLY A MINIATURE VERSION OF THE COSMIC TREADMILL I'VE USED TO TRAVERSE TIME--
I MADE CONTACT WITH ANOTHER TECHNOLOGY THAT WORKED ON THE SAME FUNDAMENTAL FORCES OF SPACE/TIME MANIPULATION--
Terrific
--THAT BEING STARMAN'S UNIFORM.
YOUR UNIFORM? WHAT'S SO SPECIAL ABOUT YOUR UNIFORM?
EVERYTHING, STARGIRL.
IT WAS DESIGNED BY THREE BRAINIAC 5'S.
THREE... WHAT?
IF I'D BEEN IN MY RIGHT MIND BEFORE POWER GIRL DISAPPEARED, I WOULD'VE BEEN ABLE TO EXPLAIN THIS TO ALL OF YOU.
PERHAPS I WOULD'VE SAVED KAREN SOME HEARTACHE--
BRANES
--OR PERHAPS I WOULD'VE CAUSED MORE.
ALAN? YOU NEED TO STAY WITH US HERE.
WE'RE ON A PARALLEL WORLD, LIKE SUPERMAN'S BUT--
JADE'S STILL ALIVE HERE. SO WHAT DID I DO WRONG ON OUR EARTH? WHY DID SHE DIE?
WE NEED TO FIND POWER GIRL AND SORT THIS OUT BEFORE WE START A WAR BETWEEN THE JUSTICE SOCIETIES OF OUR EARTHS.
WE HAVE ENOUGH TROUBLE WITH OUR OWN TEAM.
I'M SURE WE'RE GOING TO BE SEEING A LOT OF SURPRISES, ALAN, BUT WE NEED TO SEPARATE OURSELVES PERSONALLY FROM--
MICHAEL?

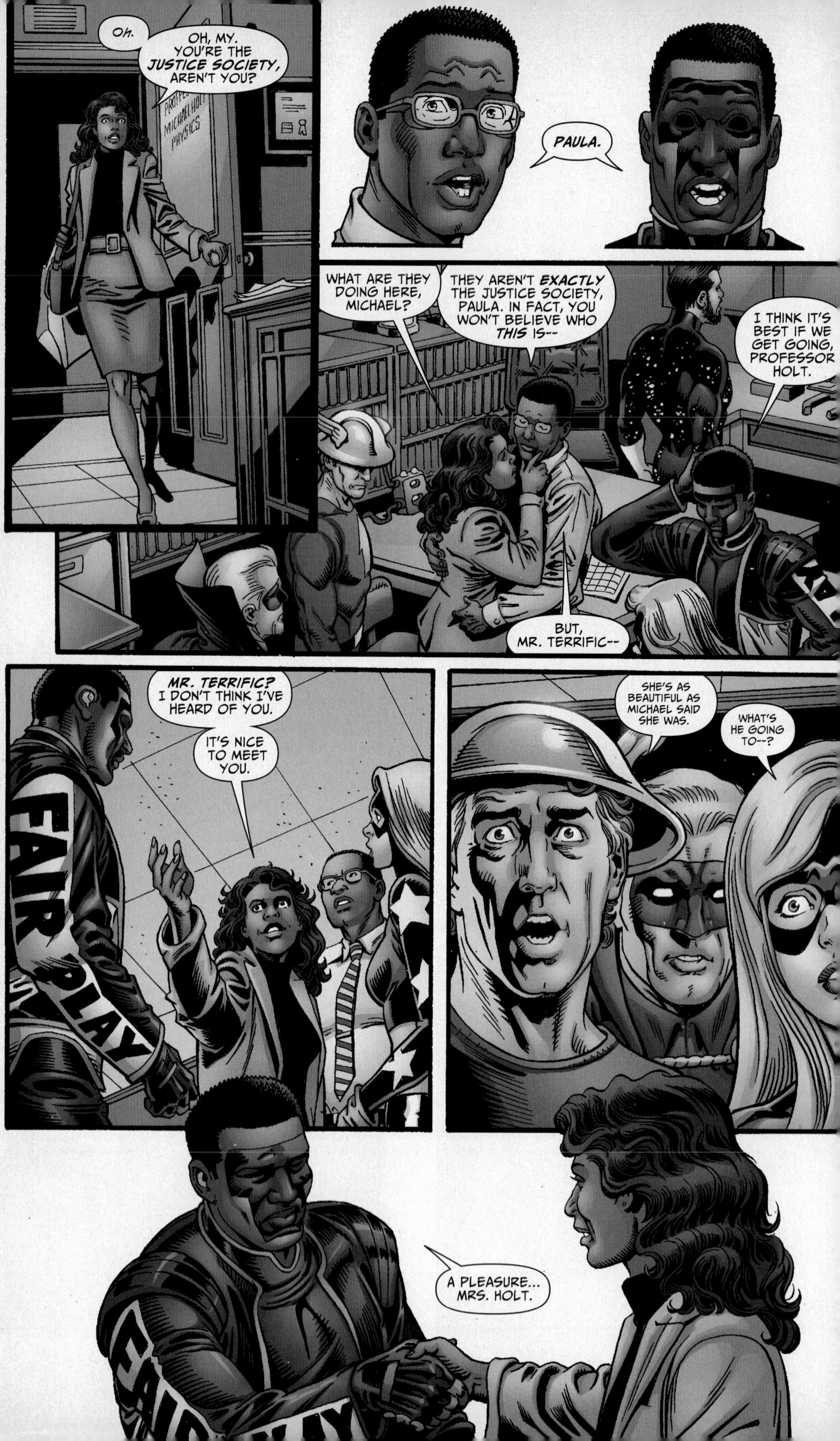
Oh.
OH, MY. YOU'RE THE JUSTICE SOCIETY, AREN'T YOU?
PROFESSOR MICHAEL HOLT PHYSICS
PAULA.
WHAT ARE THEY DOING HERE, MICHAEL?
THEY AREN'T EXACTLY THE JUSTICE SOCIETY, PAULA. IN FACT, YOU WON'T BELIEVE WHO THIS IS--
I THINK IT'S BEST IF WE GET GOING, PROFESSOR HOLT.
BUT, MR. TERRIFIC--
MR. TERRIFIC? I DON'T THINK I'VE HEARD OF YOU.
IT'S NICE TO MEET YOU.
FAIR PLAY
SHE'S AS BEAUTIFUL AS MICHAEL SAID SHE WAS.
WHAT'S HE GOING TO--?
A PLEASURE... MRS. HOLT.

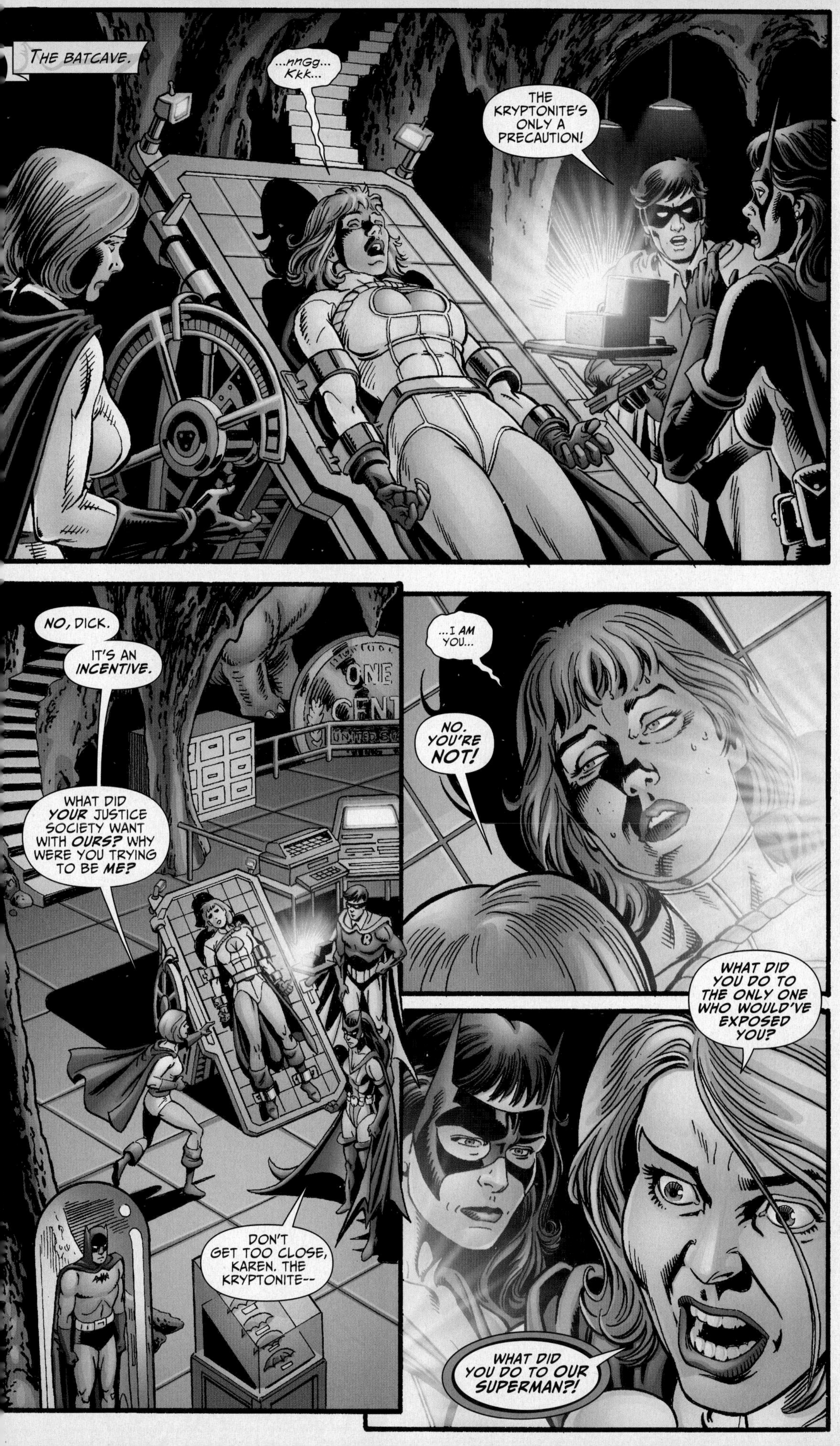

THE BATCAVE.
...nnGg... Kkk...
THE KRYPTONITE'S ONLY A PRECAUTION!
NO, DICK.
IT'S AN INCENTIVE.
WHAT DID YOUR JUSTICE SOCIETY WANT WITH OURS? WHY WERE YOU TRYING TO BE ME?
DON'T GET TOO CLOSE, KAREN. THE KRYPTONITE--
...I AM YOU...
NO. YOU'RE NOT!
WHAT DID YOU DO TO THE ONLY ONE WHO WOULD'VE EXPOSED YOU?
WHAT DID YOU DO TO OUR SUPERMAN?!

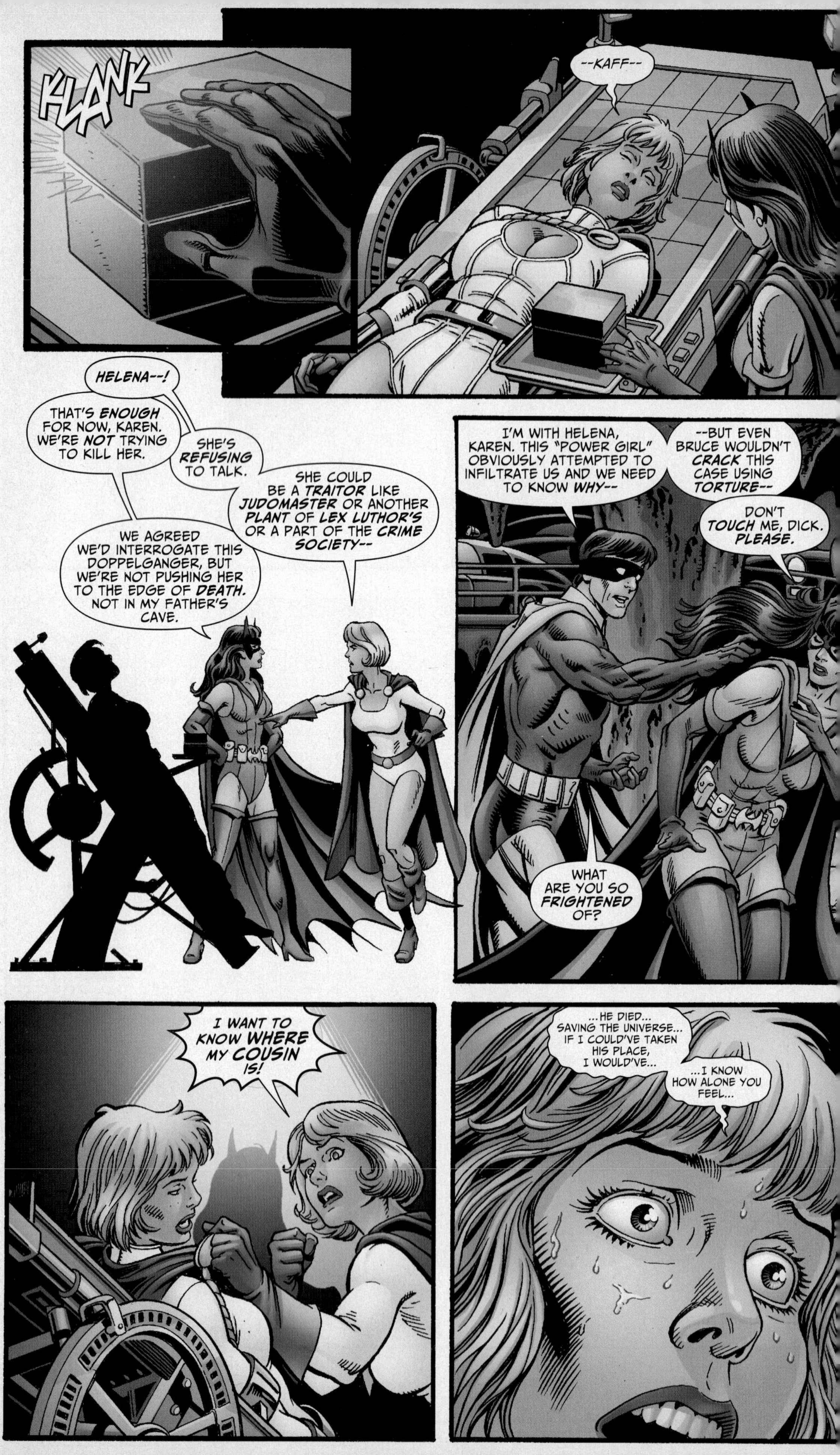
KLANK
--KAFF--
HELENA--!
THAT'S ENOUGH FOR NOW, KAREN. WE'RE NOT TRYING TO KILL HER.
SHE'S REFUSING TO TALK.
SHE COULD BE A TRAITOR LIKE JUDOMASTER OR ANOTHER PLANT OF LEX LUTHOR'S OR A PART OF THE CRIME SOCIETY--
WE AGREED WE'D INTERROGATE THIS DOPPELGANGER, BUT WE'RE NOT PUSHING HER TO THE EDGE OF DEATH. NOT IN MY FATHER'S CAVE.
I'M WITH HELENA, KAREN. THIS "POWER GIRL" OBVIOUSLY ATTEMPTED TO INFILTRATE US AND WE NEED TO KNOW WHY--
--BUT EVEN BRUCE WOULDN'T CRACK THIS CASE USING TORTURE--
DON'T TOUCH ME, DICK. PLEASE.
WHAT ARE YOU SO FRIGHTENED OF?
I WANT TO KNOW WHERE MY COUSIN IS!
...HE DIED... SAVING THE UNIVERSE... IF I COULD'VE TAKEN HIS PLACE, I WOULD'VE...
...I KNOW HOW ALONE YOU FEEL...

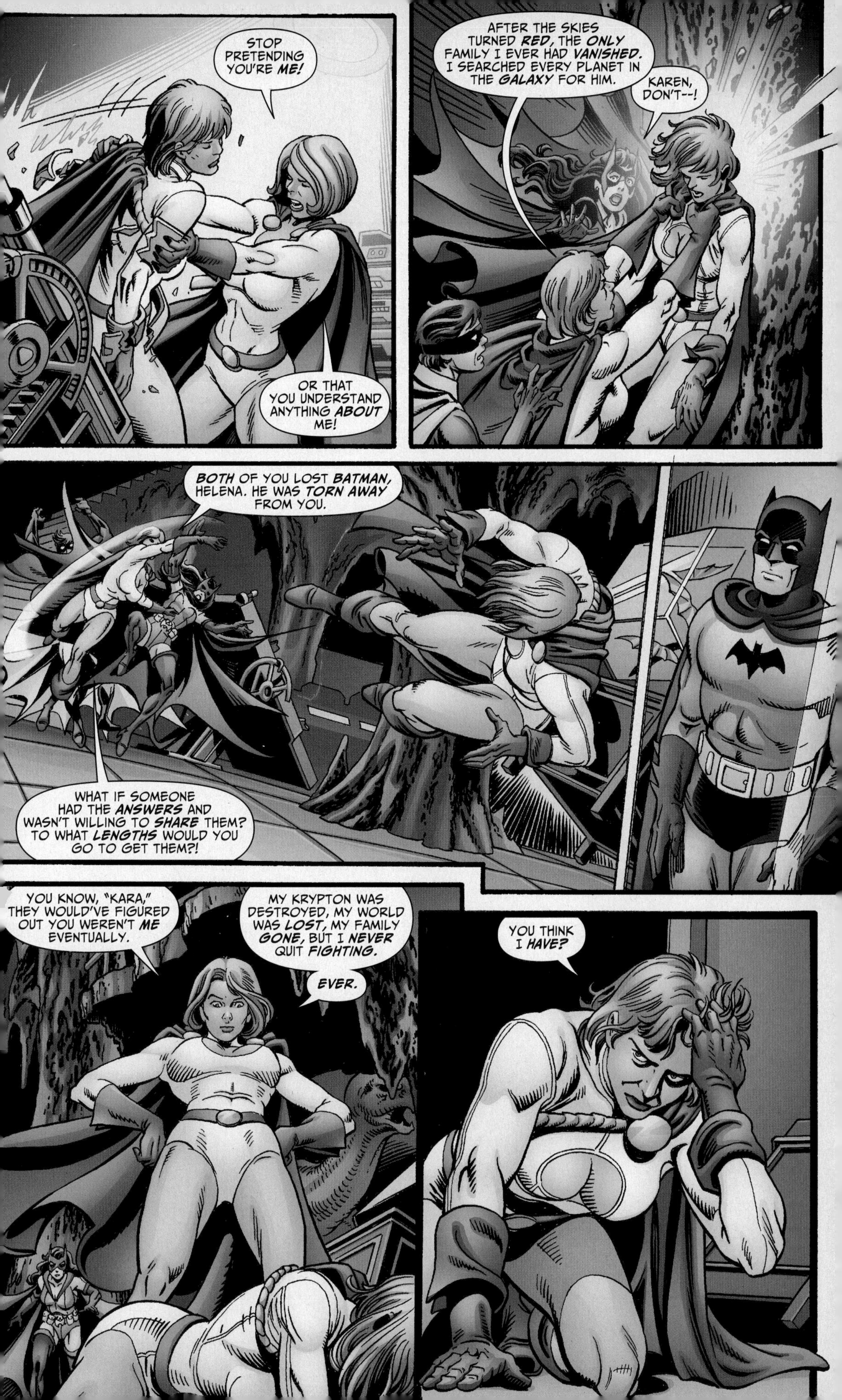

STOP PRETENDING YOU'RE ME!
OR THAT YOU UNDERSTAND ANYTHING ABOUT ME!
AFTER THE SKIES TURNED RED, THE ONLY FAMILY I EVER HAD VANISHED. I SEARCHED EVERY PLANET IN THE GALAXY FOR HIM.
KAREN, DON'T--!
BOTH OF YOU LOST BATMAN, HELENA. HE WAS TORN AWAY FROM YOU.
WHAT IF SOMEONE HAD THE ANSWERS AND WASN'T WILLING TO SHARE THEM? TO WHAT LENGTHS WOULD YOU GO TO GET THEM?!
YOU KNOW, "KARA," THEY WOULD'VE FIGURED OUT YOU WEREN'T ME EVENTUALLY.
MY KRYPTON WAS DESTROYED, MY WORLD WAS LOST, MY FAMILY GONE, BUT I NEVER QUIT FIGHTING.
EVER.
YOU THINK I HAVE?

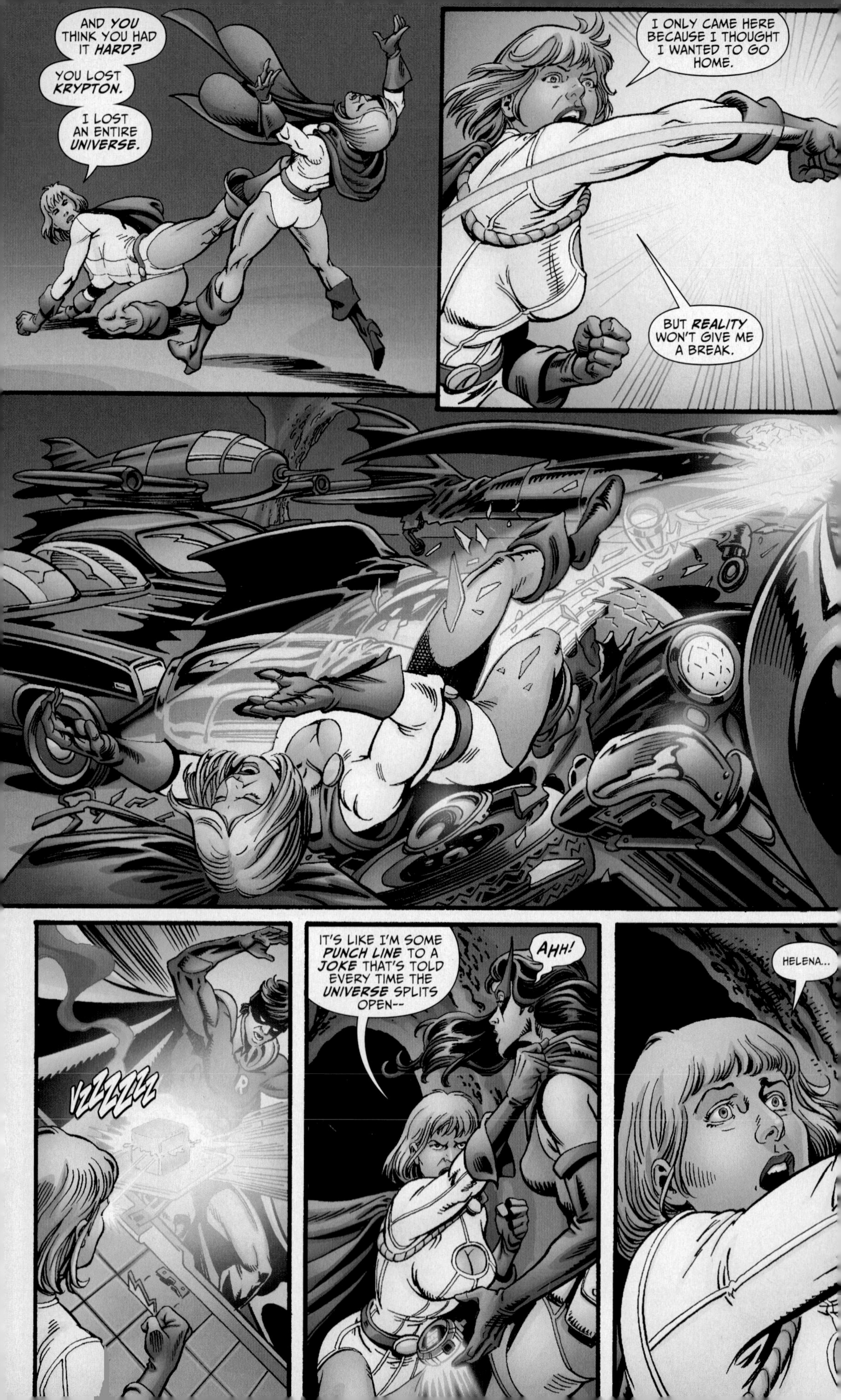
AND YOU THINK YOU HAD IT HARD?
YOU LOST KRYPTON.
I LOST AN ENTIRE UNIVERSE.
I ONLY CAME HERE BECAUSE I THOUGHT I WANTED TO GO HOME.
BUT REALITY WON'T GIVE ME A BREAK.
VZZZZZZ
IT'S LIKE I'M SOME PUNCH LINE TO A JOKE THAT'S TOLD EVERY TIME THE UNIVERSE SPLITS OPEN--
AHH!
HELENA...

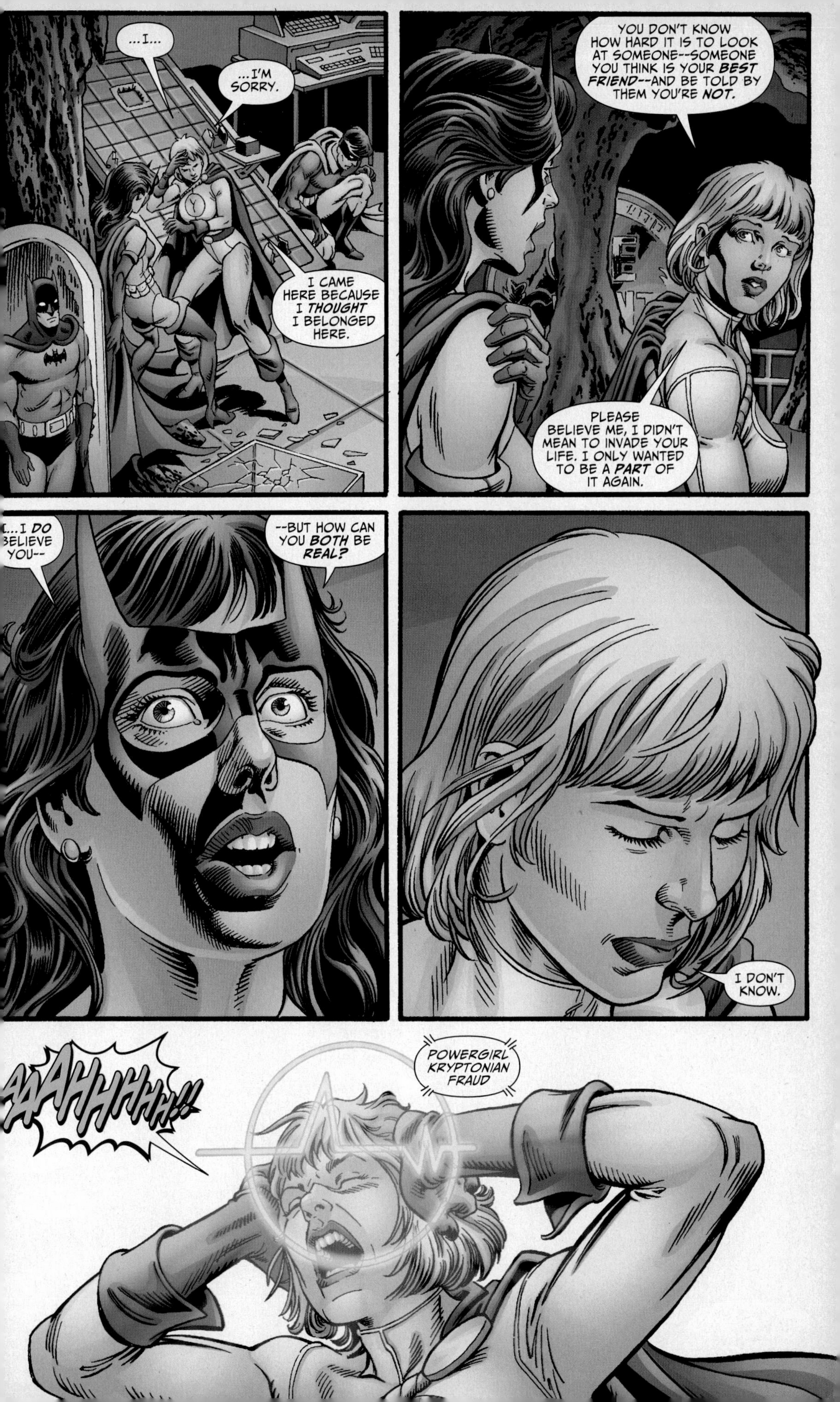

...I...
...I'M SORRY.
I CAME HERE BECAUSE I THOUGHT I BELONGED HERE.
YOU DON'T KNOW HOW HARD IT IS TO LOOK AT SOMEONE--SOMEONE YOU THINK IS YOUR BEST FRIEND--AND BE TOLD BY THEM YOU'RE NOT.
PLEASE BELIEVE ME, I DIDN'T MEAN TO INVADE YOUR LIFE. I ONLY WANTED TO BE A PART OF IT AGAIN.
...I DO BELIEVE YOU--
--BUT HOW CAN YOU BOTH BE REAL?
I DON'T KNOW.
AAAHHHHHH!!
POWERGIRL KRYPTONIAN FRAUD

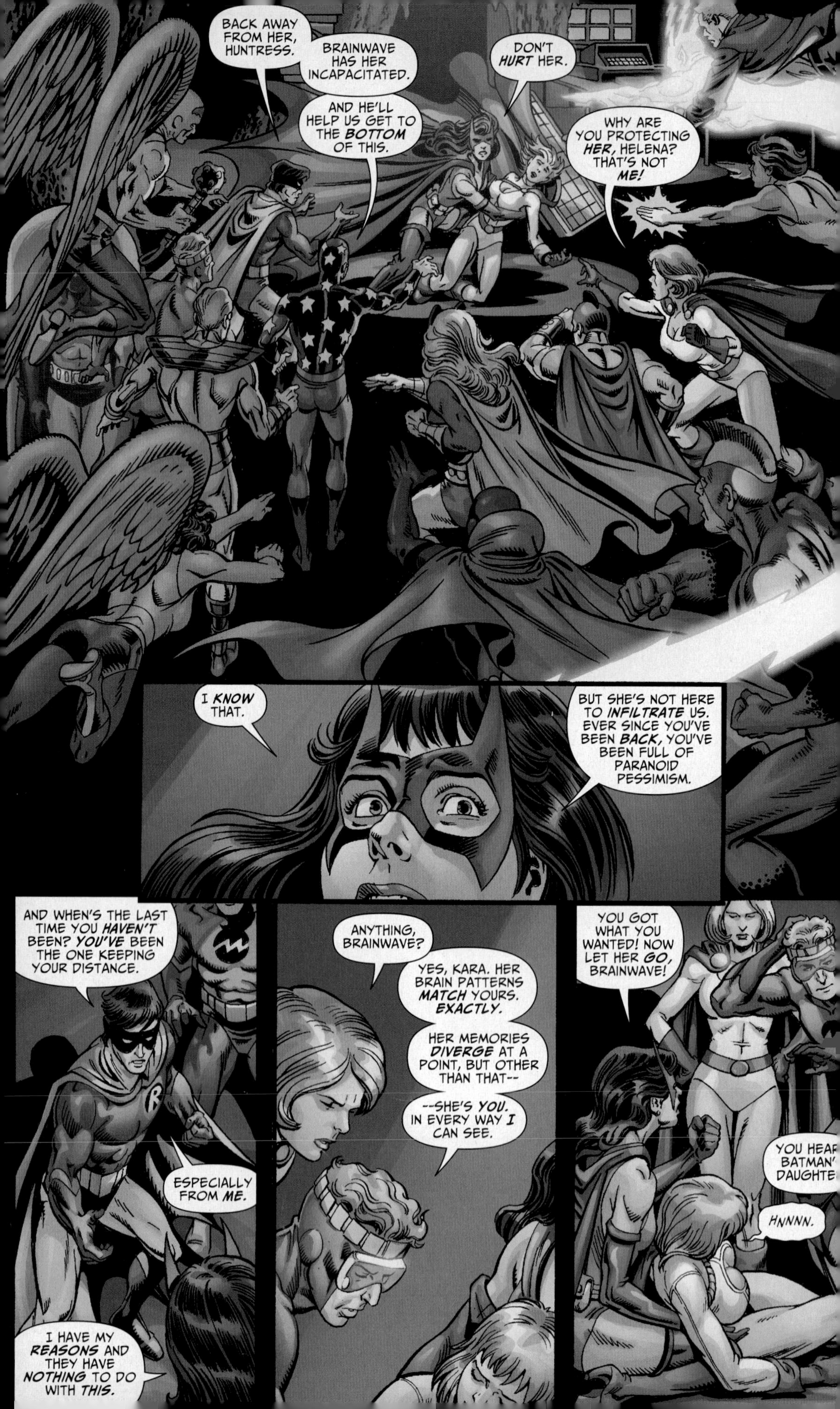

BACK AWAY FROM HER, HUNTRESS.
BRAINWAVE HAS HER INCAPACITATED.
AND HE'LL HELP US GET TO THE BOTTOM OF THIS.
DON'T HURT HER.
WHY ARE YOU PROTECTING HER, HELENA? THAT'S NOT ME!
I KNOW THAT.
BUT SHE'S NOT HERE TO INFILTRATE US. EVER SINCE YOU'VE BEEN BACK, YOU'VE BEEN FULL OF PARANOID PESSIMISM.
AND WHEN'S THE LAST TIME YOU HAVEN'T BEEN? YOU'VE BEEN THE ONE KEEPING YOUR DISTANCE.
ESPECIALLY FROM ME.
I HAVE MY REASONS AND THEY HAVE NOTHING TO DO WITH THIS.
ANYTHING, BRAINWAVE?
YES, KARA. HER BRAIN PATTERNS MATCH YOURS. EXACTLY.
HER MEMORIES DIVERGE AT A POINT, BUT OTHER THAN THAT--
--SHE'S YOU. IN EVERY WAY I CAN SEE.
YOU GOT WHAT YOU WANTED! NOW LET HER GO, BRAINWAVE!
HNNNN.

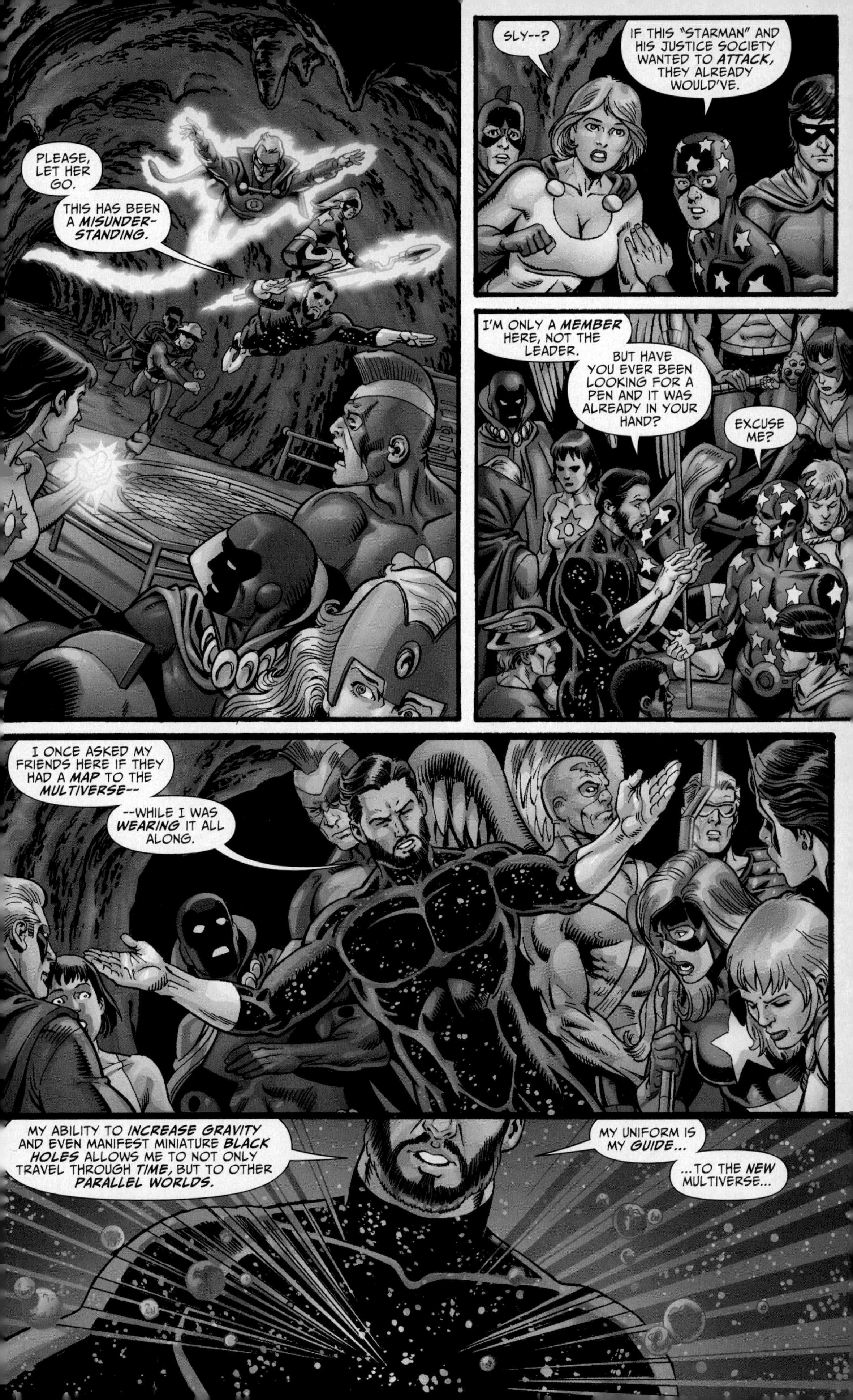

PLEASE, LET HER GO.
THIS HAS BEEN A MISUNDER-STANDING.
SLY--?
IF THIS "STARMAN" AND HIS JUSTICE SOCIETY WANTED TO ATTACK, THEY ALREADY WOULD'VE.
I'M ONLY A MEMBER HERE, NOT THE LEADER.
BUT HAVE YOU EVER BEEN LOOKING FOR A PEN AND IT WAS ALREADY IN YOUR HAND?
EXCUSE ME?
I ONCE ASKED MY FRIENDS HERE IF THEY HAD A MAP TO THE MULTIVERSE--
--WHILE I WAS WEARING IT ALL ALONG.
MY ABILITY TO INCREASE GRAVITY AND EVEN MANIFEST MINIATURE BLACK HOLES ALLOWS ME TO NOT ONLY TRAVEL THROUGH TIME, BUT TO OTHER PARALLEL WORLDS.
MY UNIFORM IS MY GUIDE...
...TO THE NEW MULTIVERSE...

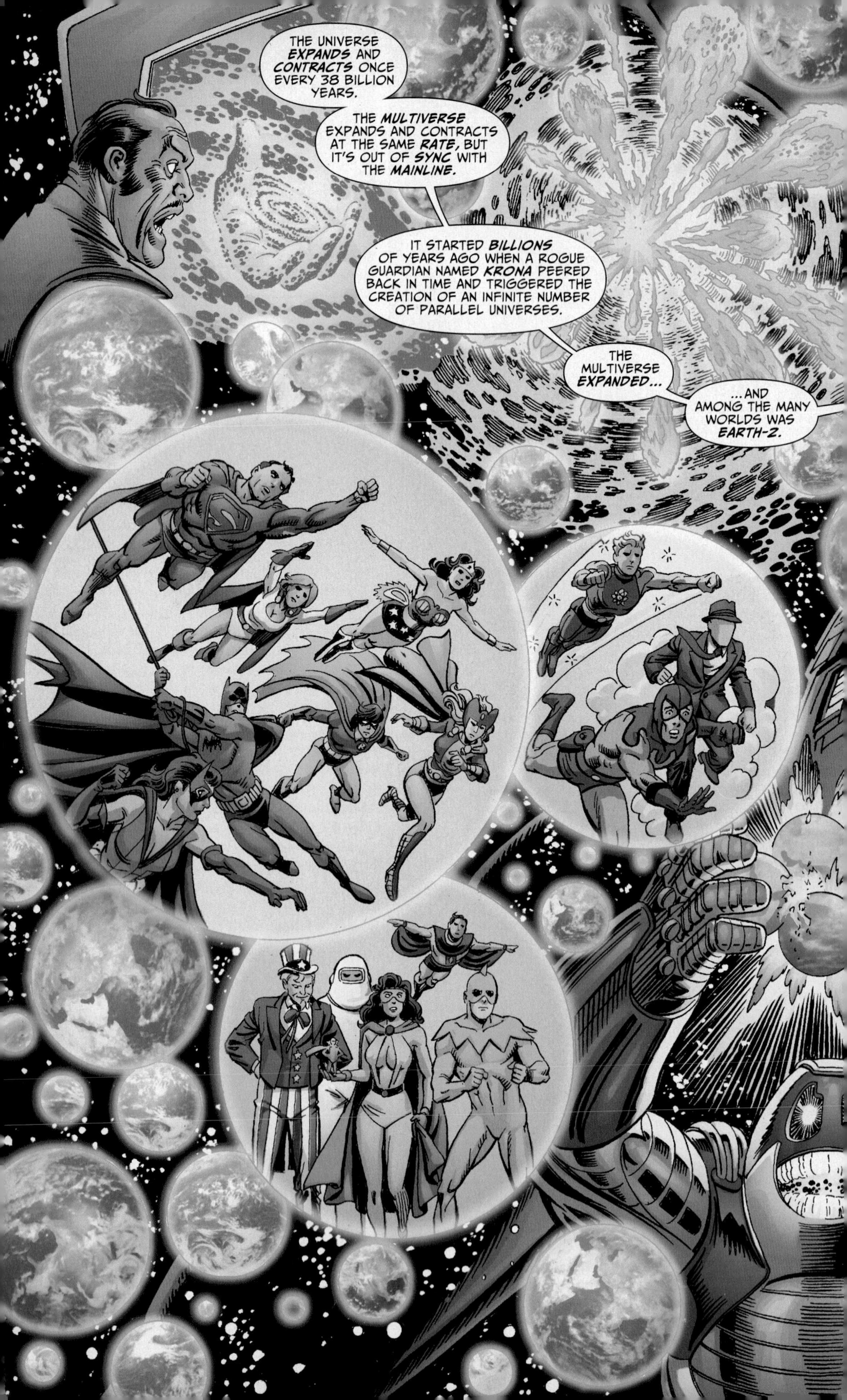
THE UNIVERSE EXPANDS AND CONTRACTS ONCE EVERY 38 BILLION YEARS.
THE MULTIVERSE EXPANDS AND CONTRACTS AT THE SAME RATE, BUT IT'S OUT OF SYNC WITH THE MAINLINE.
IT STARTED BILLIONS OF YEARS AGO WHEN A ROGUE GUARDIAN NAMED KRONA PEERED BACK IN TIME AND TRIGGERED THE CREATION OF AN INFINITE NUMBER OF PARALLEL UNIVERSES.
THE MULTIVERSE EXPANDED...
...AND AMONG THE MANY WORLDS WAS EARTH-2.

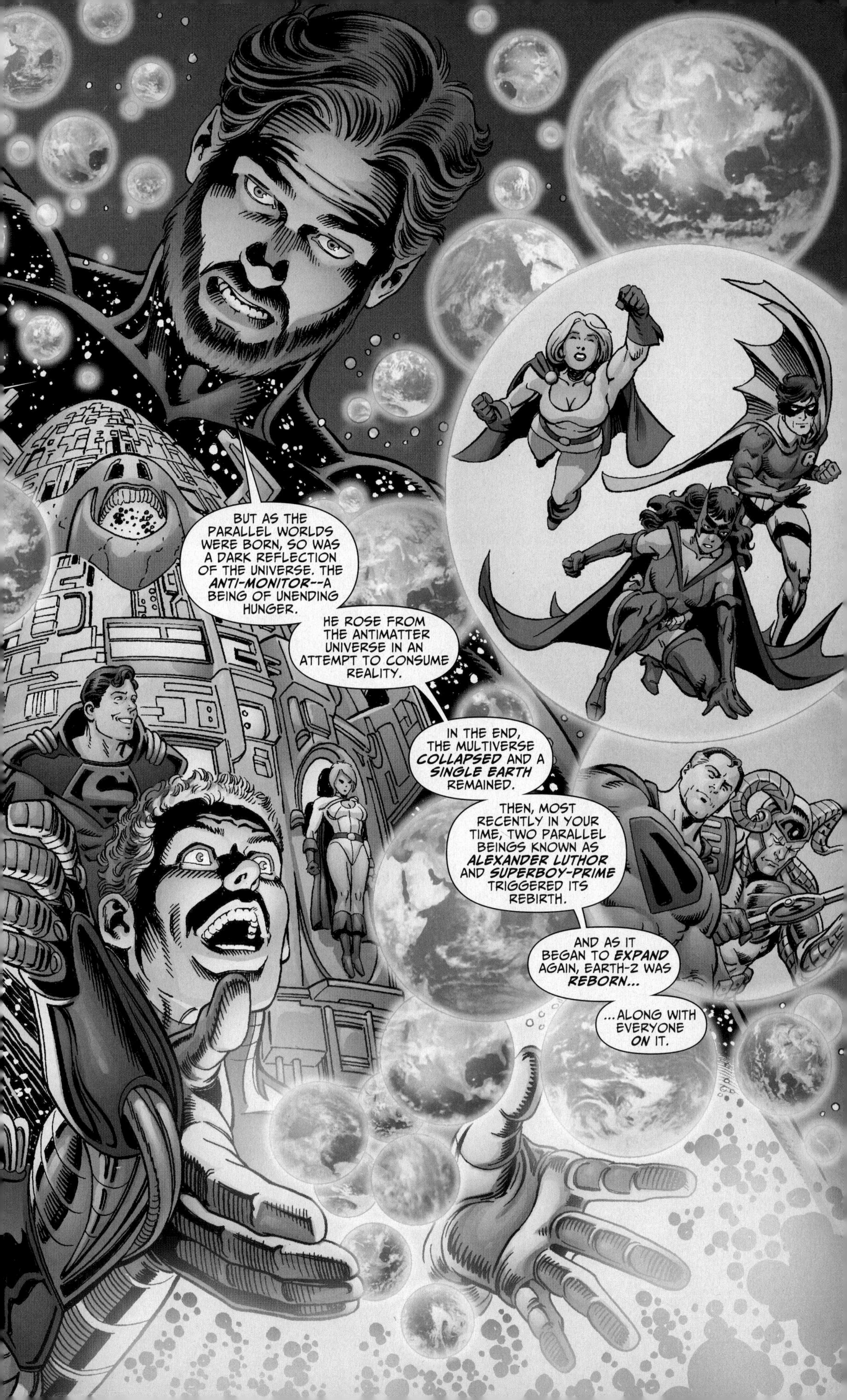

BUT AS THE PARALLEL WORLDS WERE BORN, SO WAS A DARK REFLECTION OF THE UNIVERSE. THE ANTI-MONITOR--A BEING OF UNENDING HUNGER.
HE ROSE FROM THE ANTIMATTER UNIVERSE IN AN ATTEMPT TO CONSUME REALITY.
IN THE END, THE MULTIVERSE COLLAPSED AND A SINGLE EARTH REMAINED.
THEN, MOST RECENTLY IN YOUR TIME, TWO PARALLEL BEINGS KNOWN AS ALEXANDER LUTHOR AND SUPERBOY-PRIME TRIGGERED ITS REBIRTH.
AND AS IT BEGAN TO EXPAND AGAIN, EARTH-2 WAS REBORN...
...ALONG WITH EVERYONE ON IT.

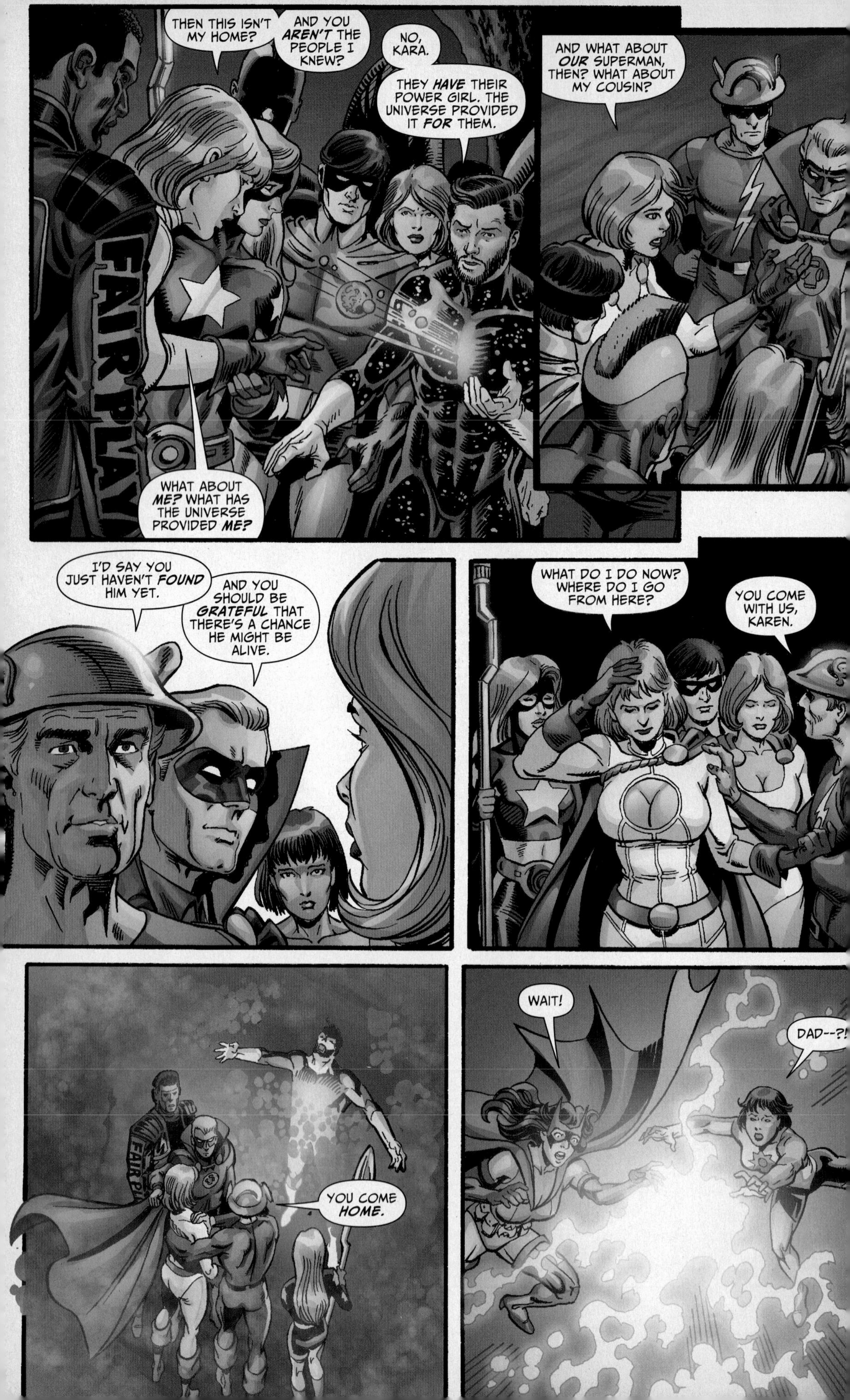

THEN THIS ISN'T MY HOME?
AND YOU *AREN'T* THE PEOPLE I KNEW?
NO, KARA.
THEY *HAVE* THEIR POWER GIRL. THE UNIVERSE PROVIDED IT *FOR* THEM.
FAIR PLAY
WHAT ABOUT *ME?* WHAT HAS THE UNIVERSE PROVIDED *ME?*
AND WHAT ABOUT *OUR* SUPERMAN, THEN? WHAT ABOUT MY COUSIN?
I'D SAY YOU JUST HAVEN'T *FOUND* HIM YET.
AND YOU SHOULD BE *GRATEFUL* THAT THERE'S A CHANCE HE MIGHT BE ALIVE.
WHAT DO I DO NOW? WHERE DO I GO FROM HERE?
YOU COME WITH US, KAREN.
FAIR PL
YOU COME *HOME.*
WAIT!
DAD--?!

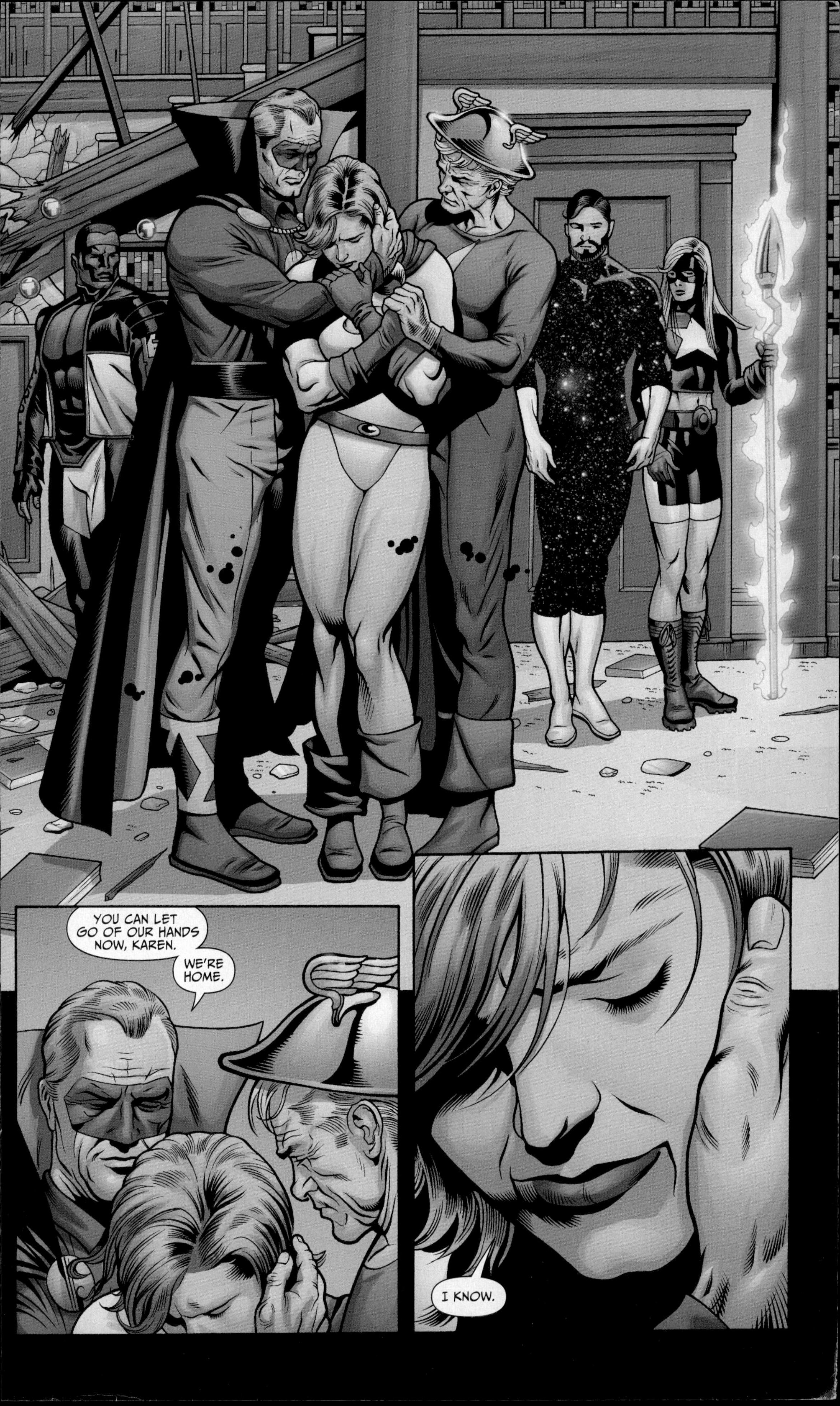
YOU CAN LET GO OF OUR HANDS NOW, KAREN.
WE'RE HOME.
I KNOW.

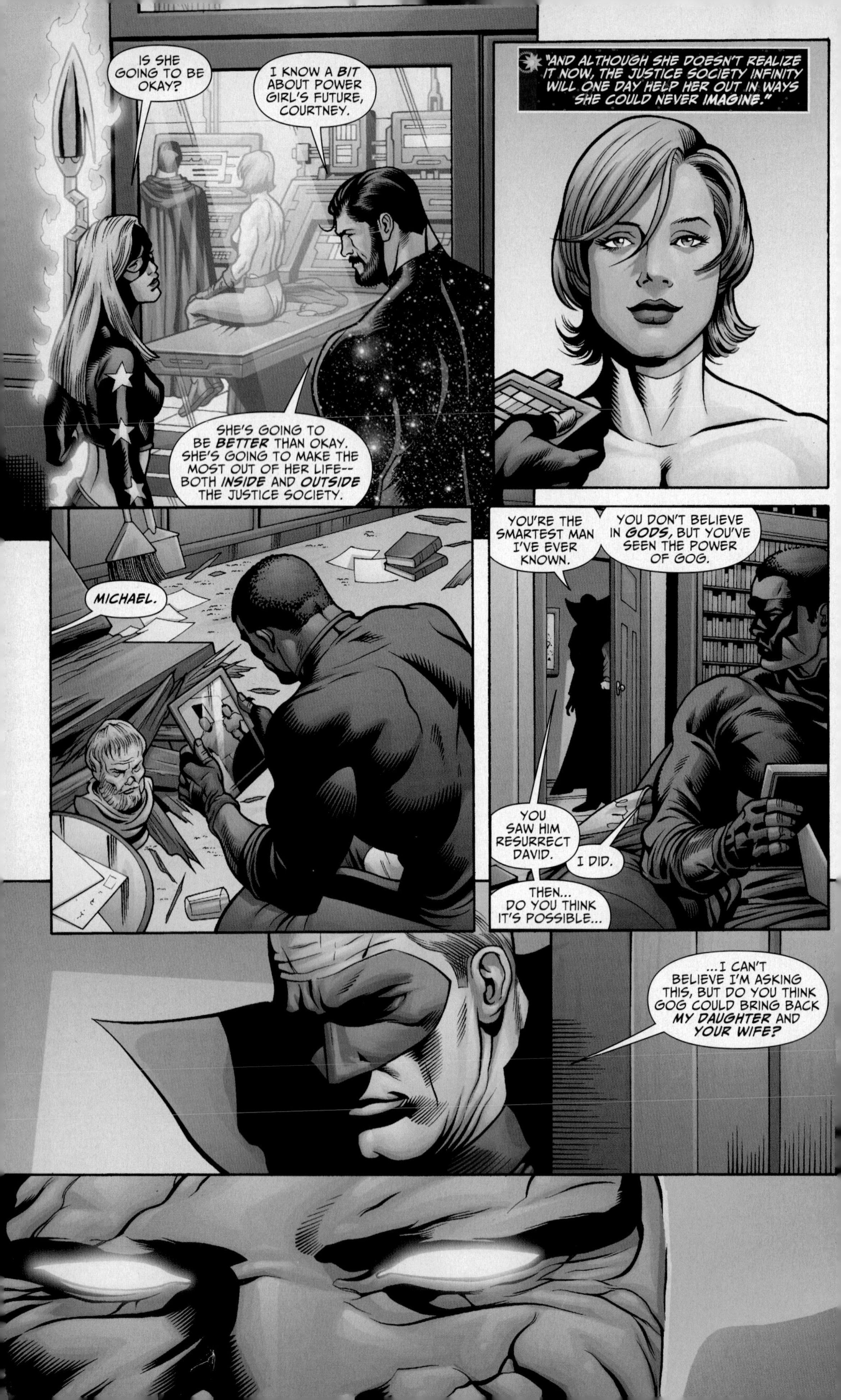
IS SHE GOING TO BE OKAY?
I KNOW A BIT ABOUT POWER GIRL'S FUTURE, COURTNEY.
SHE'S GOING TO BE BETTER THAN OKAY. SHE'S GOING TO MAKE THE MOST OUT OF HER LIFE-- BOTH INSIDE AND OUTSIDE THE JUSTICE SOCIETY.
"AND ALTHOUGH SHE DOESN'T REALIZE IT NOW, THE JUSTICE SOCIETY INFINITY WILL ONE DAY HELP HER OUT IN WAYS SHE COULD NEVER IMAGINE."
MICHAEL.
YOU'RE THE SMARTEST MAN I'VE EVER KNOWN.
YOU DON'T BELIEVE IN GODS, BUT YOU'VE SEEN THE POWER OF GOG.
YOU SAW HIM RESURRECT DAVID.
I DID.
THEN... DO YOU THINK IT'S POSSIBLE...
...I CAN'T BELIEVE I'M ASKING THIS, BUT DO YOU THINK GOG COULD BRING BACK MY DAUGHTER AND YOUR WIFE?

JUSTICE SOCIETY OF AMERICA KINGDOM COME SPECIAL: SUPERMAN #1 cover A by Alex Ross

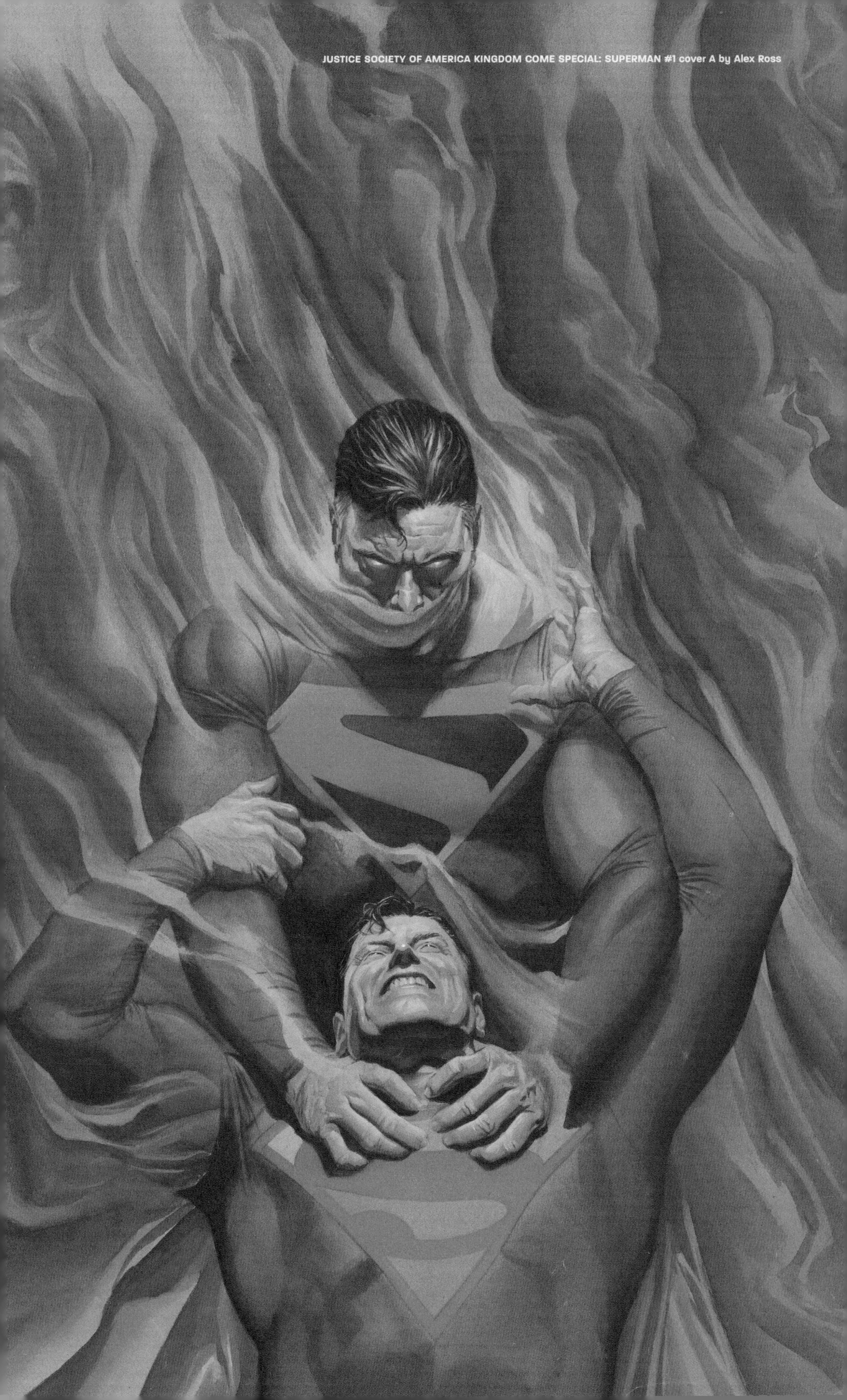

JUSTICE SOCIETY OF AMERICA KINGDOM COME SPECIAL: SUPERMAN #1 cover B by Dale Eaglesham with Brian Miller
Interior art by Alex Ross with Alex Sinclair

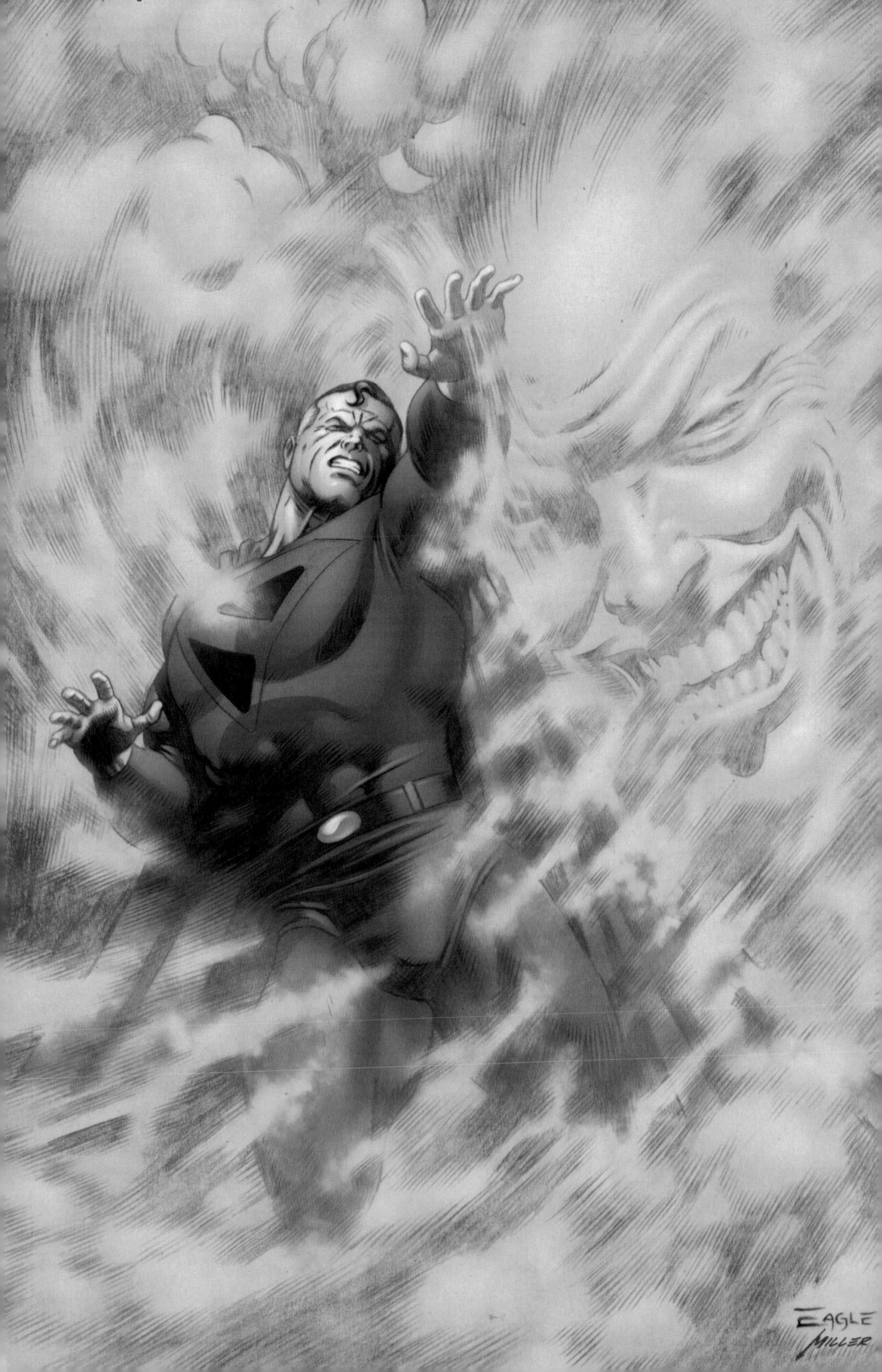
EAGLE
MILLER

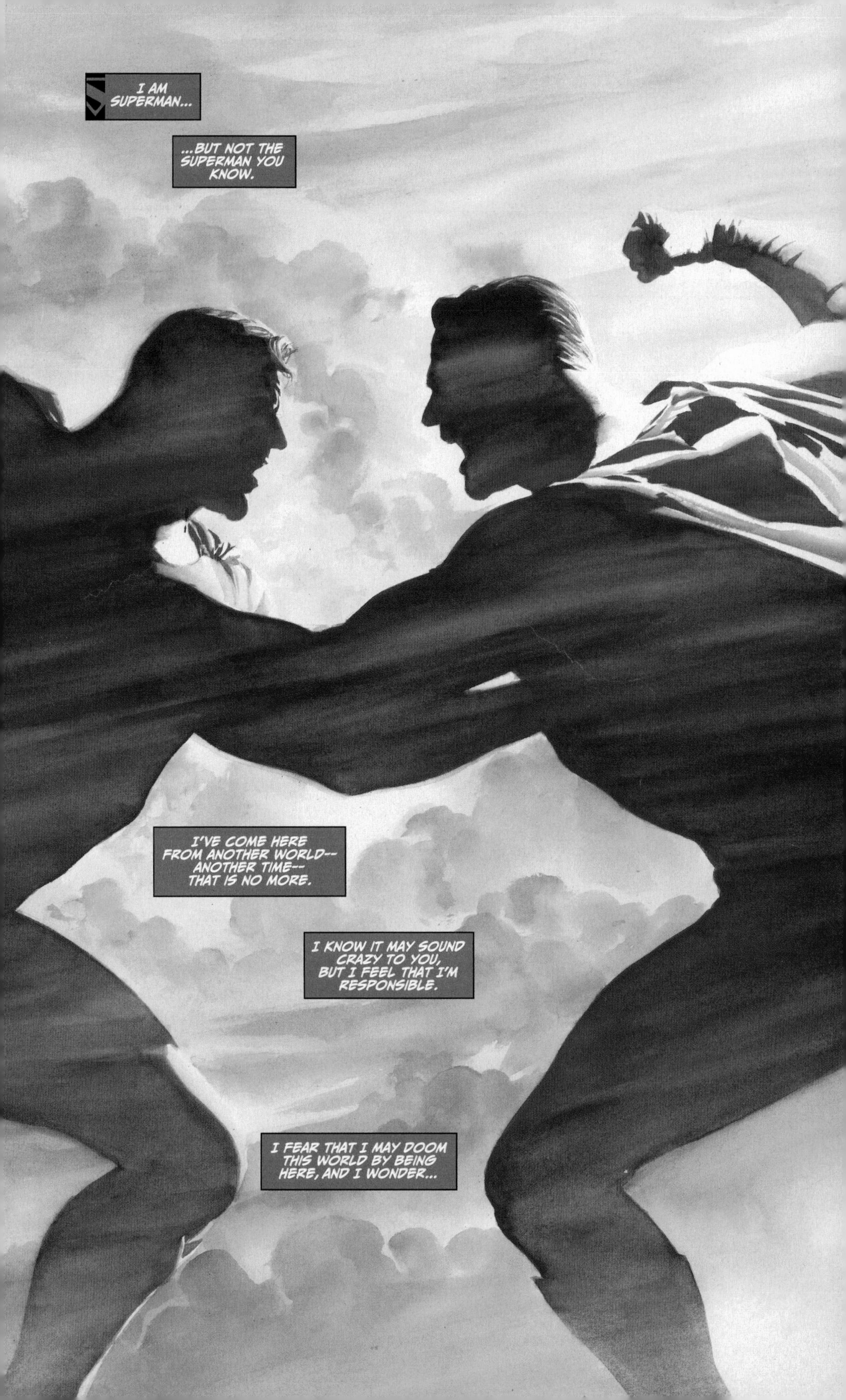
I AM SUPERMAN...
...BUT NOT THE SUPERMAN YOU KNOW.
I'VE COME HERE FROM ANOTHER WORLD-- ANOTHER TIME-- THAT IS NO MORE.
I KNOW IT MAY SOUND CRAZY TO YOU, BUT I FEEL THAT I'M RESPONSIBLE.
I FEAR THAT I MAY DOOM THIS WORLD BY BEING HERE, AND I WONDER...

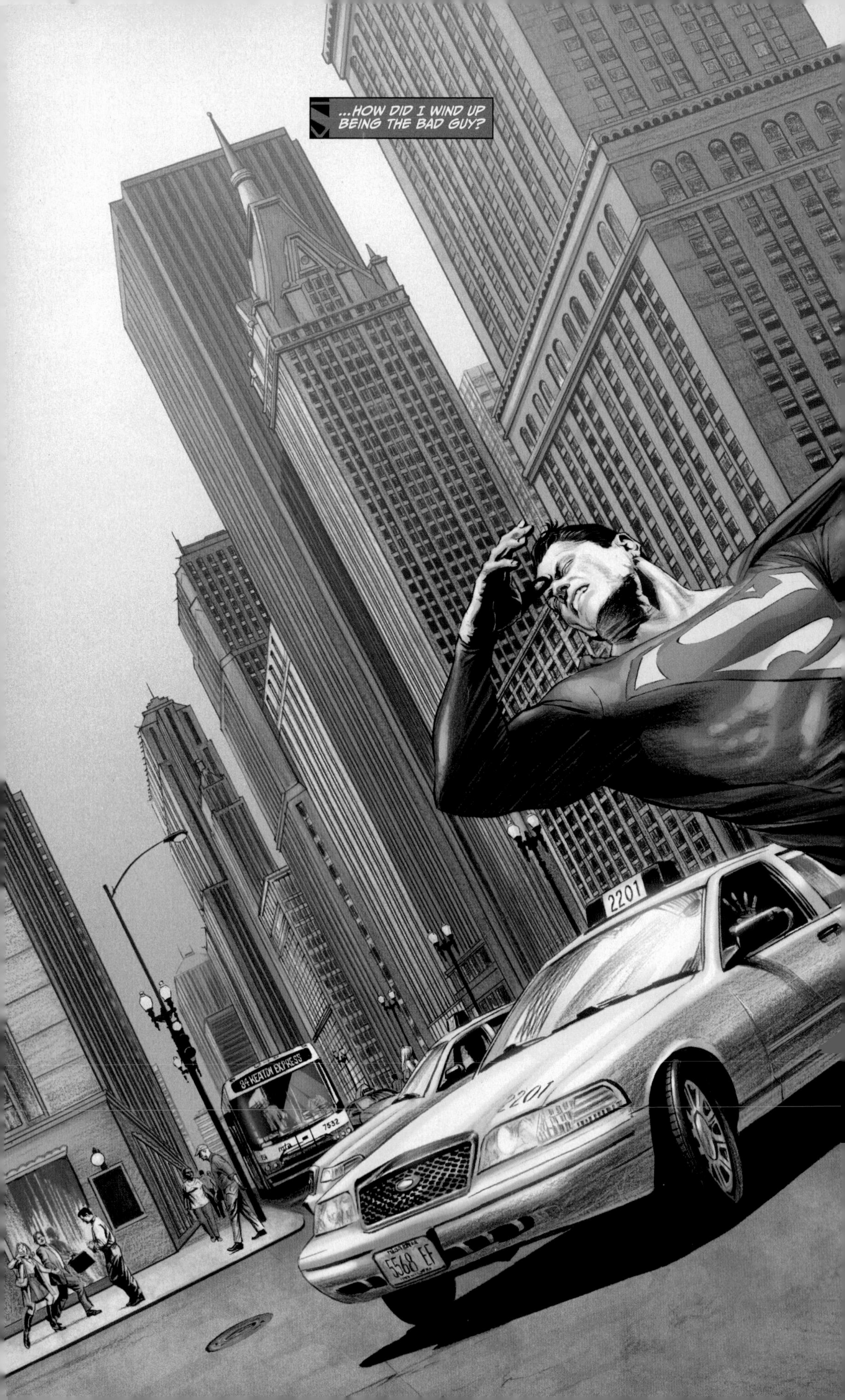
...HOW DID I WIND UP BEING THE BAD GUY?
84 KEATON EXPRESS
7532
2201
2201
5568 EF

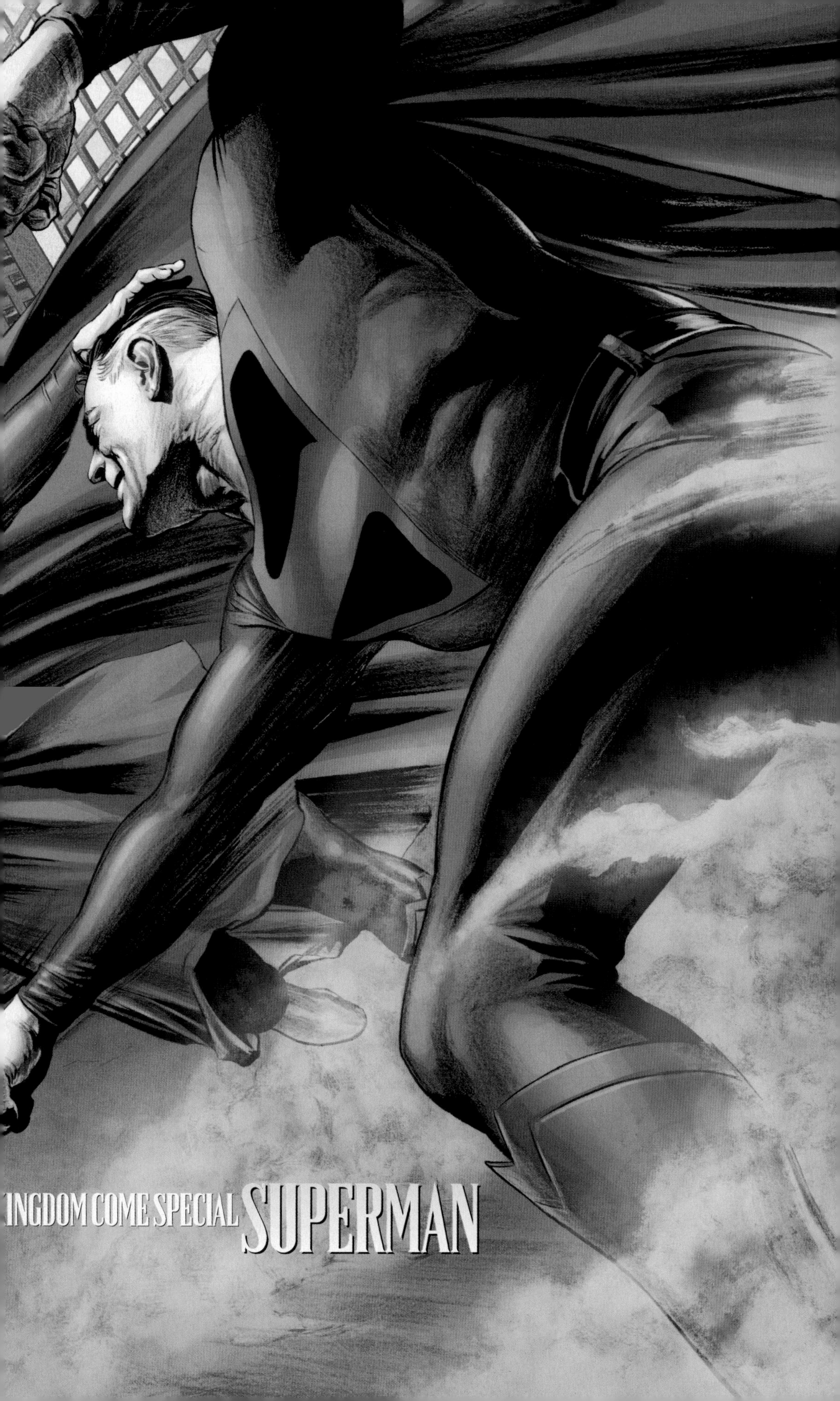
INGDOM COME SPECIAL
SUPERMAN

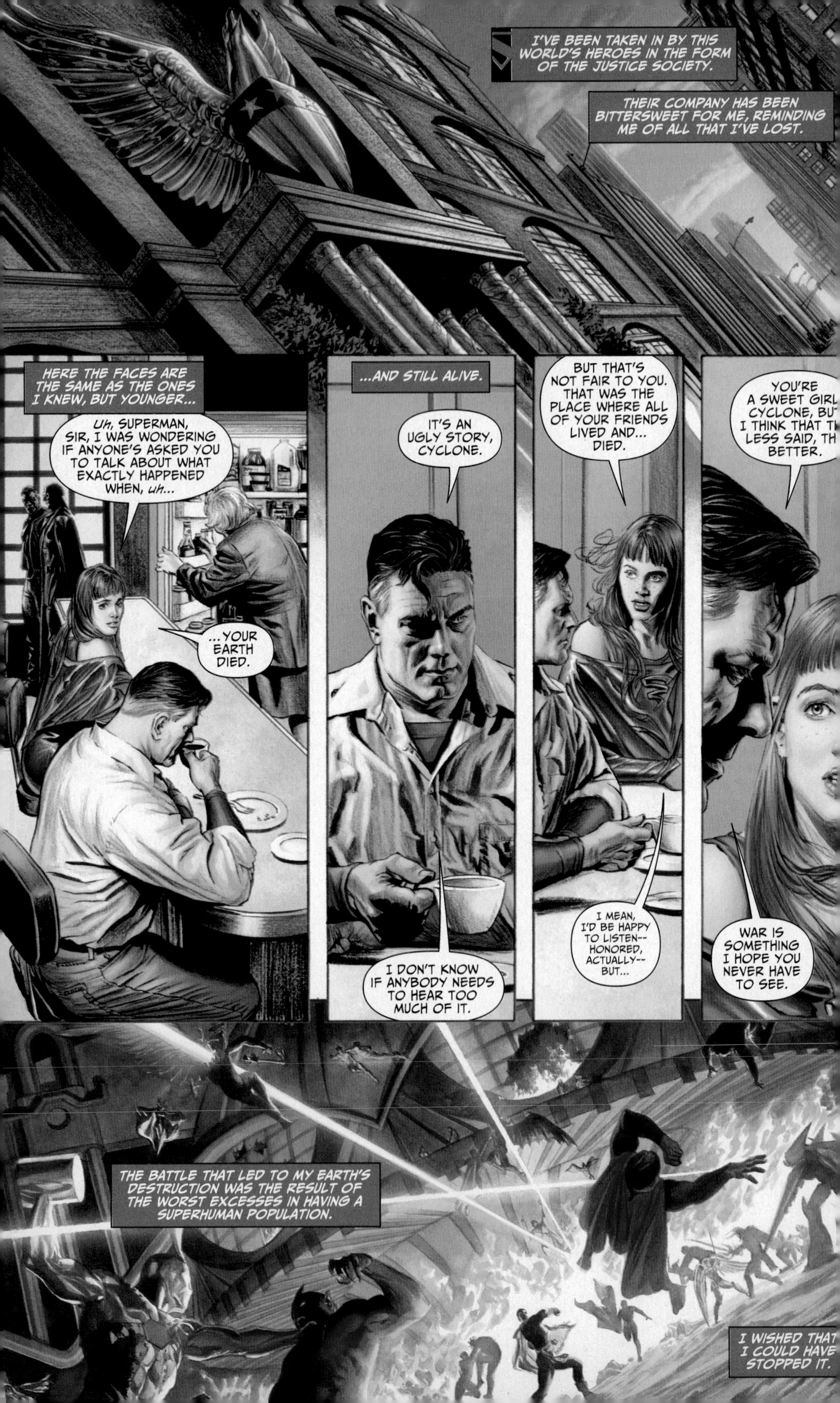
I'VE BEEN TAKEN IN BY THIS WORLD'S HEROES IN THE FORM OF THE JUSTICE SOCIETY.
THEIR COMPANY HAS BEEN BITTERSWEET FOR ME, REMINDING ME OF ALL THAT I'VE LOST.
HERE THE FACES ARE THE SAME AS THE ONES I KNEW, BUT YOUNGER...
Uh, SUPERMAN, SIR, I WAS WONDERING IF ANYONE'S ASKED YOU TO TALK ABOUT WHAT EXACTLY HAPPENED WHEN, *uh*...
...YOUR EARTH DIED.
...AND STILL ALIVE.
IT'S AN UGLY STORY, CYCLONE.
I DON'T KNOW IF ANYBODY NEEDS TO HEAR TOO MUCH OF IT.
BUT THAT'S NOT FAIR TO YOU. THAT WAS THE PLACE WHERE ALL OF YOUR FRIENDS LIVED AND... DIED.
I MEAN, I'D BE HAPPY TO LISTEN--HONORED, ACTUALLY--BUT...
YOU'RE A SWEET GIRL CYCLONE, BU I THINK THAT T LESS SAID, TH BETTER.
WAR IS SOMETHING I HOPE YOU NEVER HAVE TO SEE.
THE BATTLE THAT LED TO MY EARTH'S DESTRUCTION WAS THE RESULT OF THE WORST EXCESSES IN HAVING A SUPERHUMAN POPULATION.
I WISHED THAT I COULD HAVE STOPPED IT.

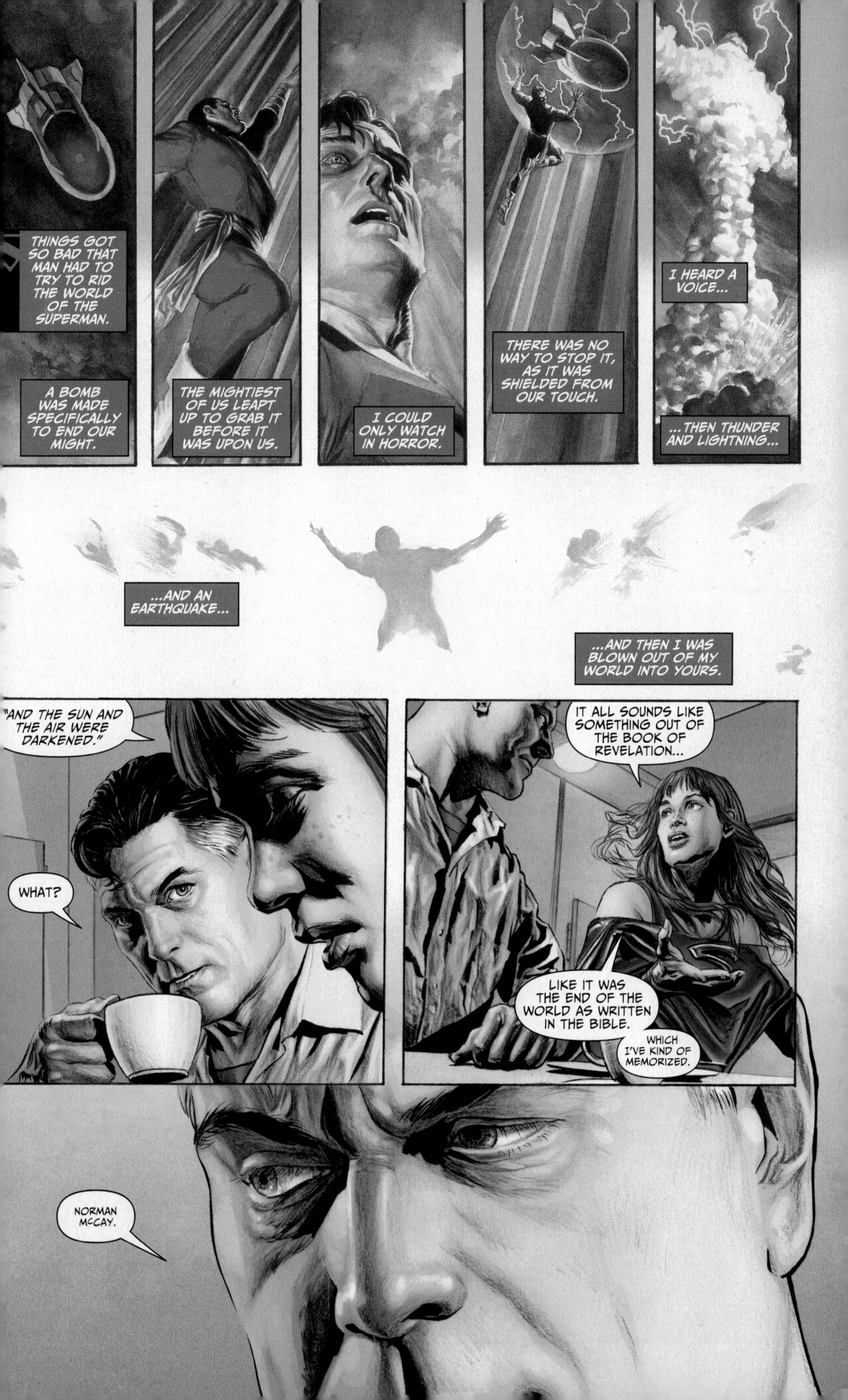
THINGS GOT SO BAD THAT MAN HAD TO TRY TO RID THE WORLD OF THE SUPERMAN.
A BOMB WAS MADE SPECIFICALLY TO END OUR MIGHT.
THE MIGHTIEST OF US LEAPT UP TO GRAB IT BEFORE IT WAS UPON US.
I COULD ONLY WATCH IN HORROR.
THERE WAS NO WAY TO STOP IT, AS IT WAS SHIELDED FROM OUR TOUCH.
I HEARD A VOICE...
...THEN THUNDER AND LIGHTNING...
...AND AN EARTHQUAKE...
...AND THEN I WAS BLOWN OUT OF MY WORLD INTO YOURS.
"AND THE SUN AND THE AIR WERE DARKENED."
WHAT?
IT ALL SOUNDS LIKE SOMETHING OUT OF THE BOOK OF REVELATION...
LIKE IT WAS THE END OF THE WORLD AS WRITTEN IN THE BIBLE.
WHICH I'VE KIND OF MEMORIZED.
NORMAN McCAY.

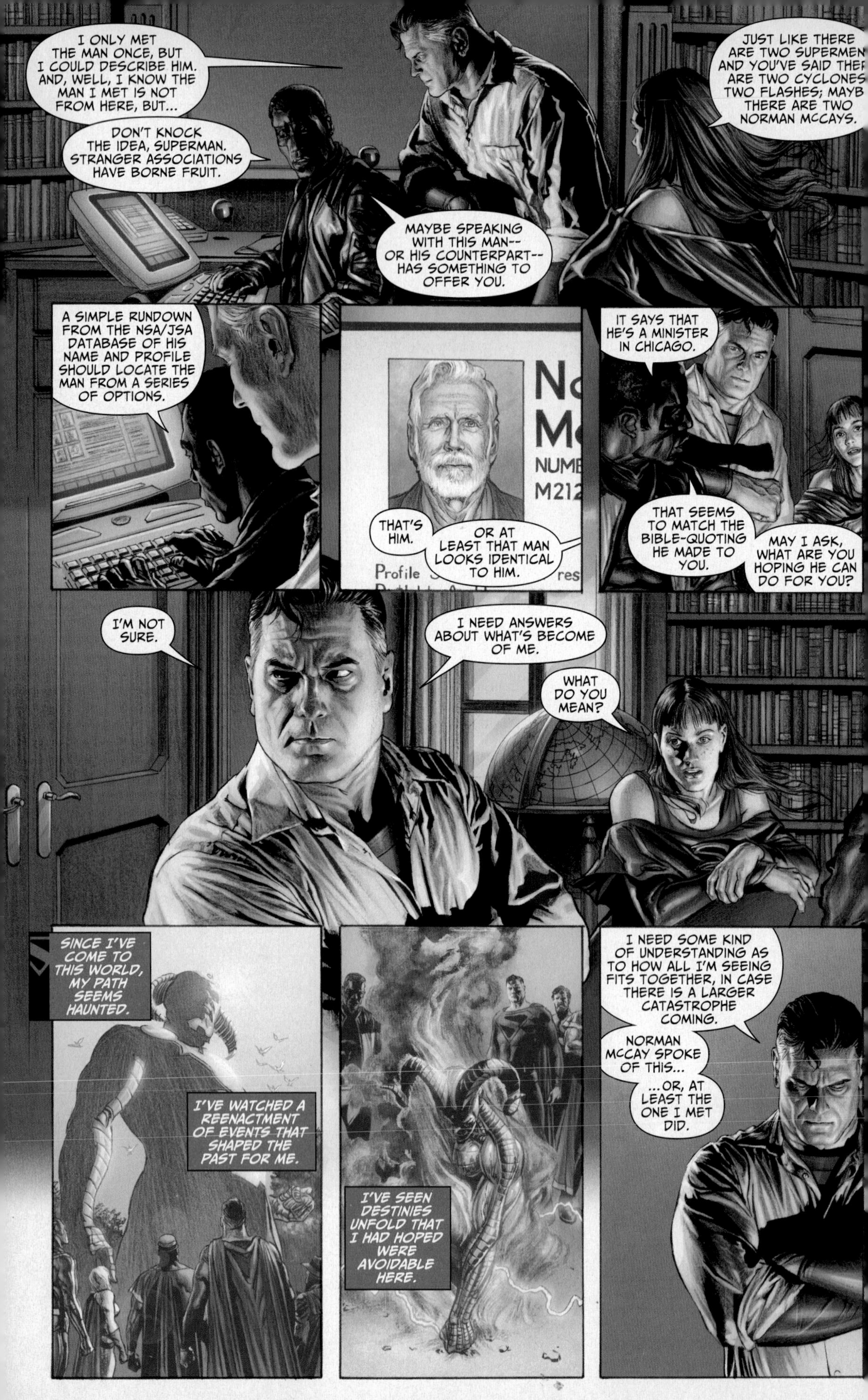
I ONLY MET THE MAN ONCE, BUT I COULD DESCRIBE HIM. AND, WELL, I KNOW THE MAN I MET IS NOT FROM HERE, BUT...
DON'T KNOCK THE IDEA, SUPERMAN. STRANGER ASSOCIATIONS HAVE BORNE FRUIT.
JUST LIKE THERE ARE TWO SUPERMEN AND YOU'VE SAID THER ARE TWO CYCLONES TWO FLASHES; MAYB THERE ARE TWO NORMAN McCAYS.
MAYBE SPEAKING WITH THIS MAN-- OR HIS COUNTERPART-- HAS SOMETHING TO OFFER YOU.
A SIMPLE RUNDOWN FROM THE NSA/JSA DATABASE OF HIS NAME AND PROFILE SHOULD LOCATE THE MAN FROM A SERIES OF OPTIONS.
No
Mc
NUMB
M212
THAT'S HIM.
OR AT LEAST THAT MAN LOOKS IDENTICAL TO HIM.
IT SAYS THAT HE'S A MINISTER IN CHICAGO.
THAT SEEMS TO MATCH THE BIBLE-QUOTING HE MADE TO YOU.
MAY I ASK, WHAT ARE YOU HOPING HE CAN DO FOR YOU?
I'M NOT SURE.
I NEED ANSWERS ABOUT WHAT'S BECOME OF ME.
WHAT DO YOU MEAN?
SINCE I'VE COME TO THIS WORLD, MY PATH SEEMS HAUNTED.
I'VE WATCHED A REENACTMENT OF EVENTS THAT SHAPED THE PAST FOR ME.
I'VE SEEN DESTINIES UNFOLD THAT I HAD HOPED WERE AVOIDABLE HERE.
I NEED SOME KIND OF UNDERSTANDING AS TO HOW ALL I'M SEEING FITS TOGETHER, IN CASE THERE IS A LARGER CATASTROPHE COMING.
NORMAN McCAY SPOKE OF THIS...
...OR, AT LEAST THE ONE I MET DID.

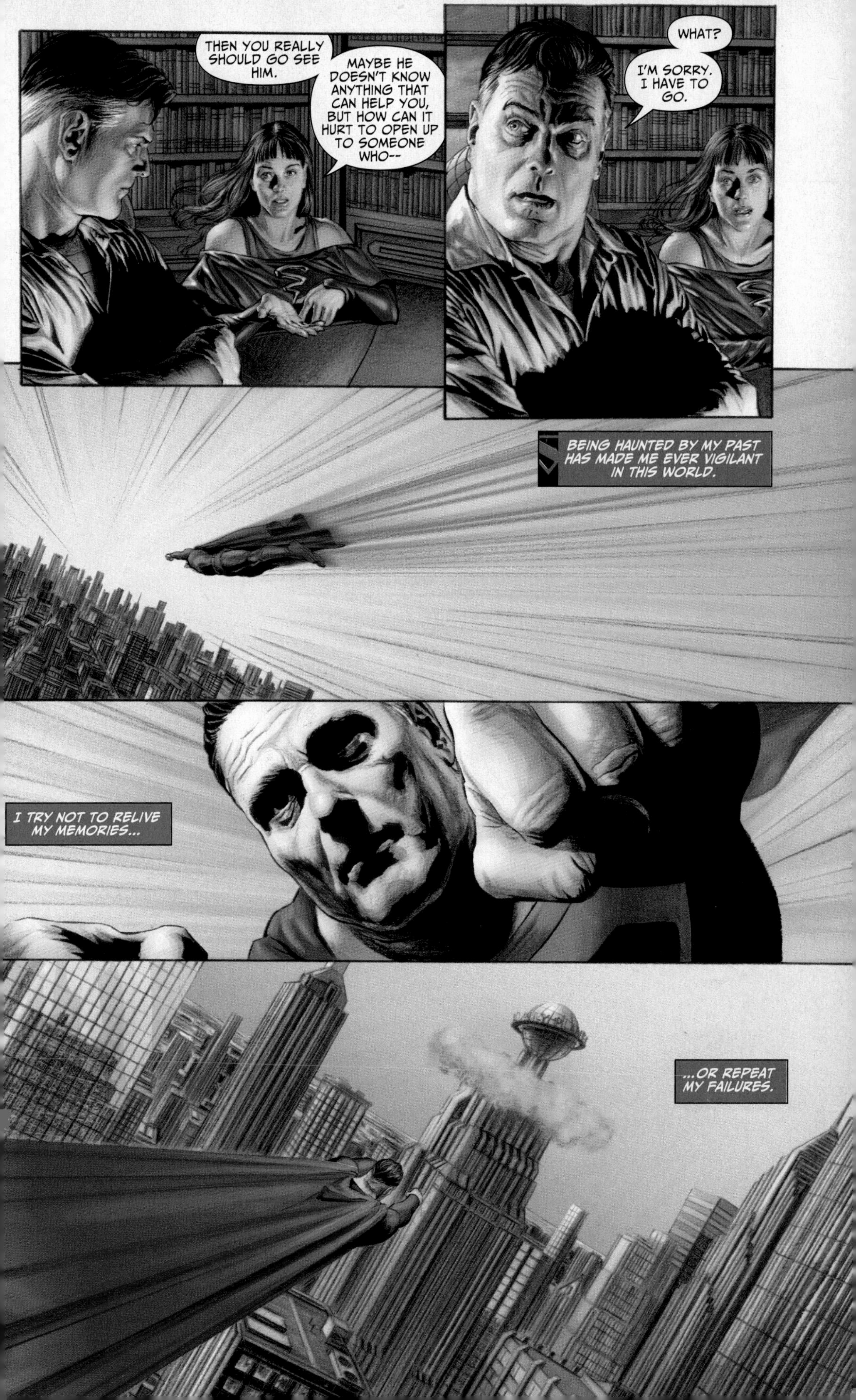
THEN YOU REALLY SHOULD GO SEE HIM.
MAYBE HE DOESN'T KNOW ANYTHING THAT CAN HELP YOU, BUT HOW CAN IT HURT TO OPEN UP TO SOMEONE WHO--
WHAT?
I'M SORRY. I HAVE TO GO.
BEING HAUNTED BY MY PAST HAS MADE ME EVER VIGILANT IN THIS WORLD.
I TRY NOT TO RELIVE MY MEMORIES...
...OR REPEAT MY FAILURES.

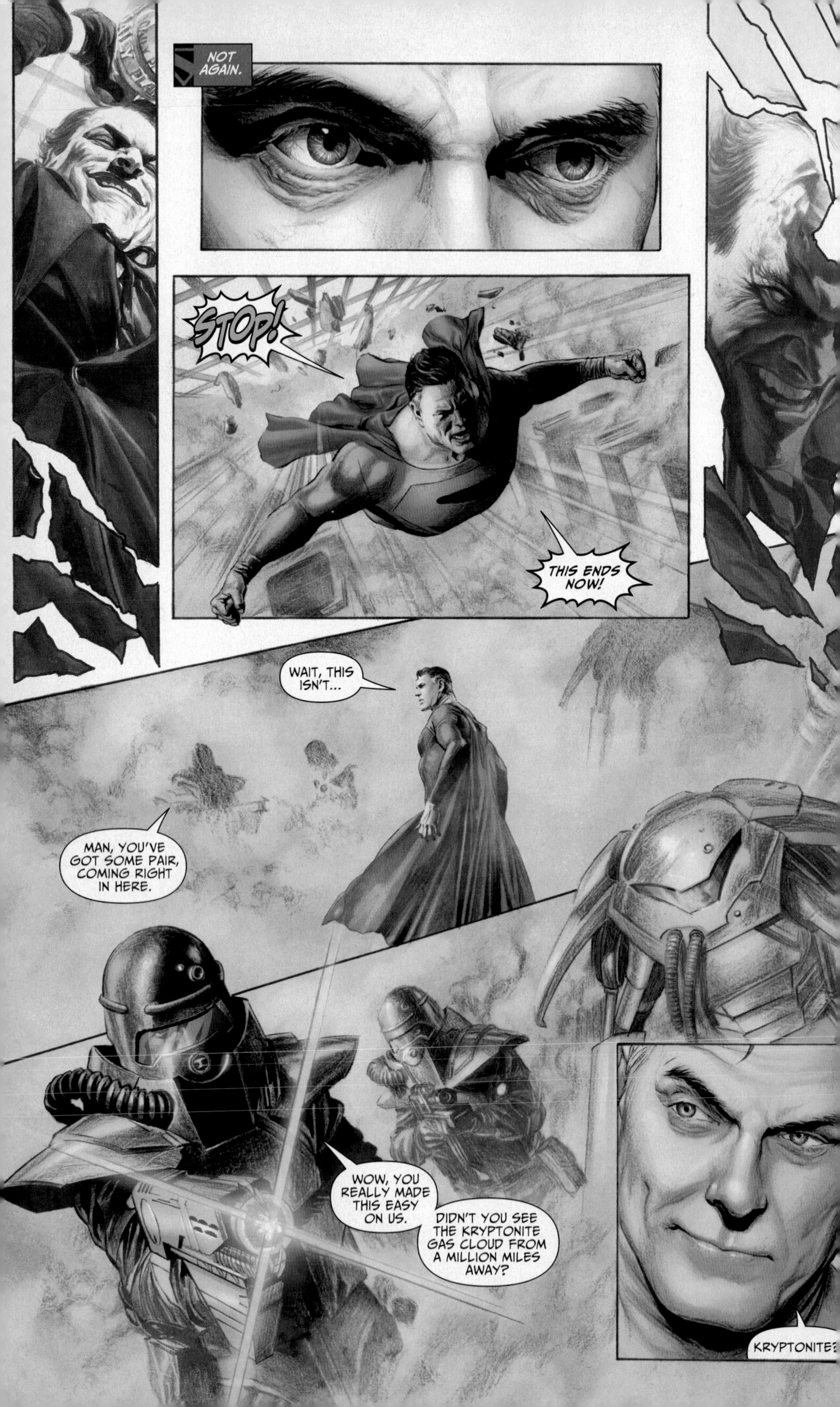

NOT AGAIN.
STOP!
THIS ENDS NOW!
WAIT, THIS ISN'T...
MAN, YOU'VE GOT SOME PAIR, COMING RIGHT IN HERE.
WOW, YOU REALLY MADE THIS EASY ON US.
DIDN'T YOU SEE THE KRYPTONITE GAS CLOUD FROM A MILLION MILES AWAY?
KRYPTONITE?

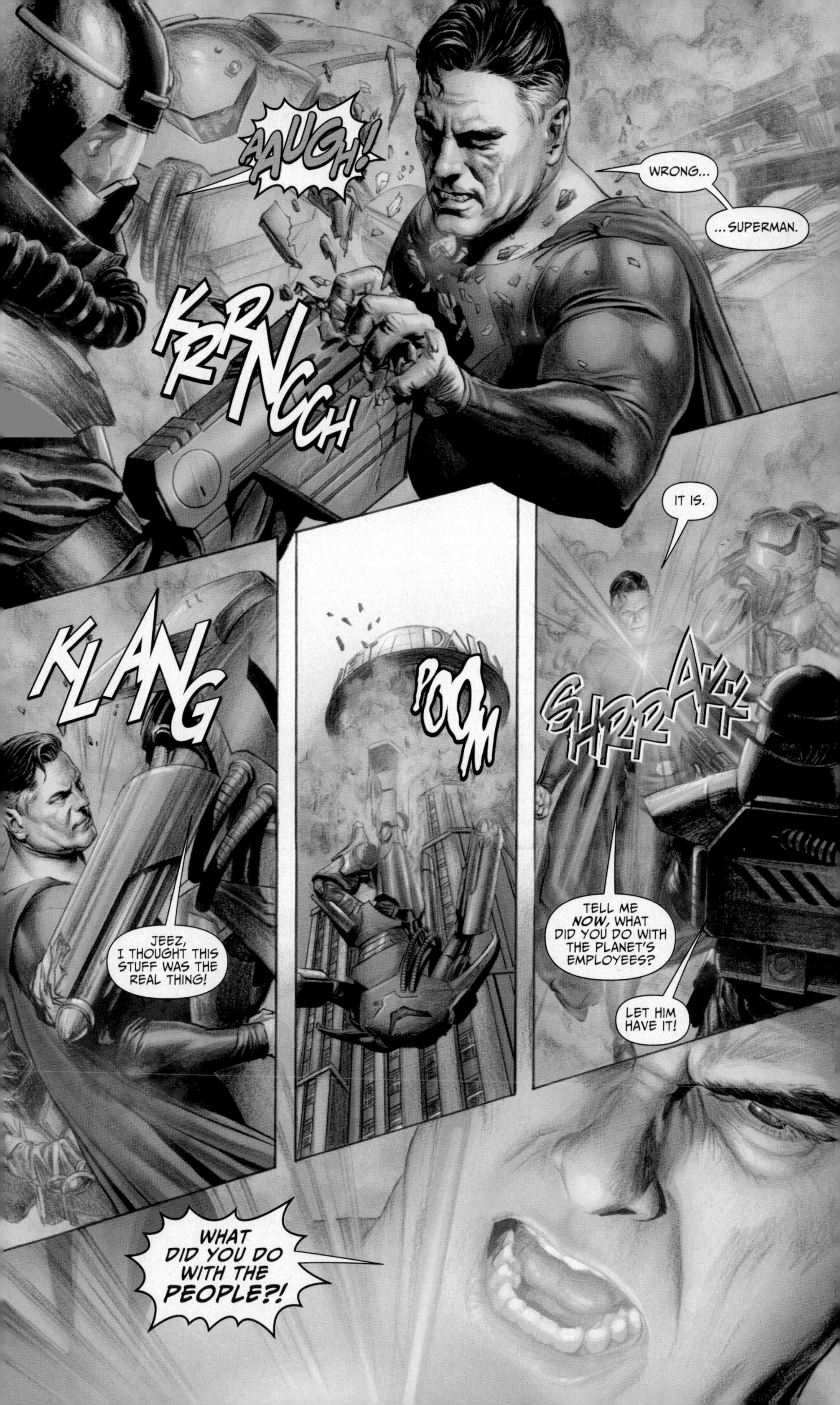
AAUGH!
WRONG...
...SUPERMAN.
KRRRNCCH
IT IS.
KLANG
POOM
SHRRAKK
JEEZ, I THOUGHT THIS STUFF WAS THE REAL THING!
TELL ME NOW, WHAT DID YOU DO WITH THE PLANET'S EMPLOYEES?
LET HIM HAVE IT!
WHAT DID YOU DO WITH THE PEOPLE?!

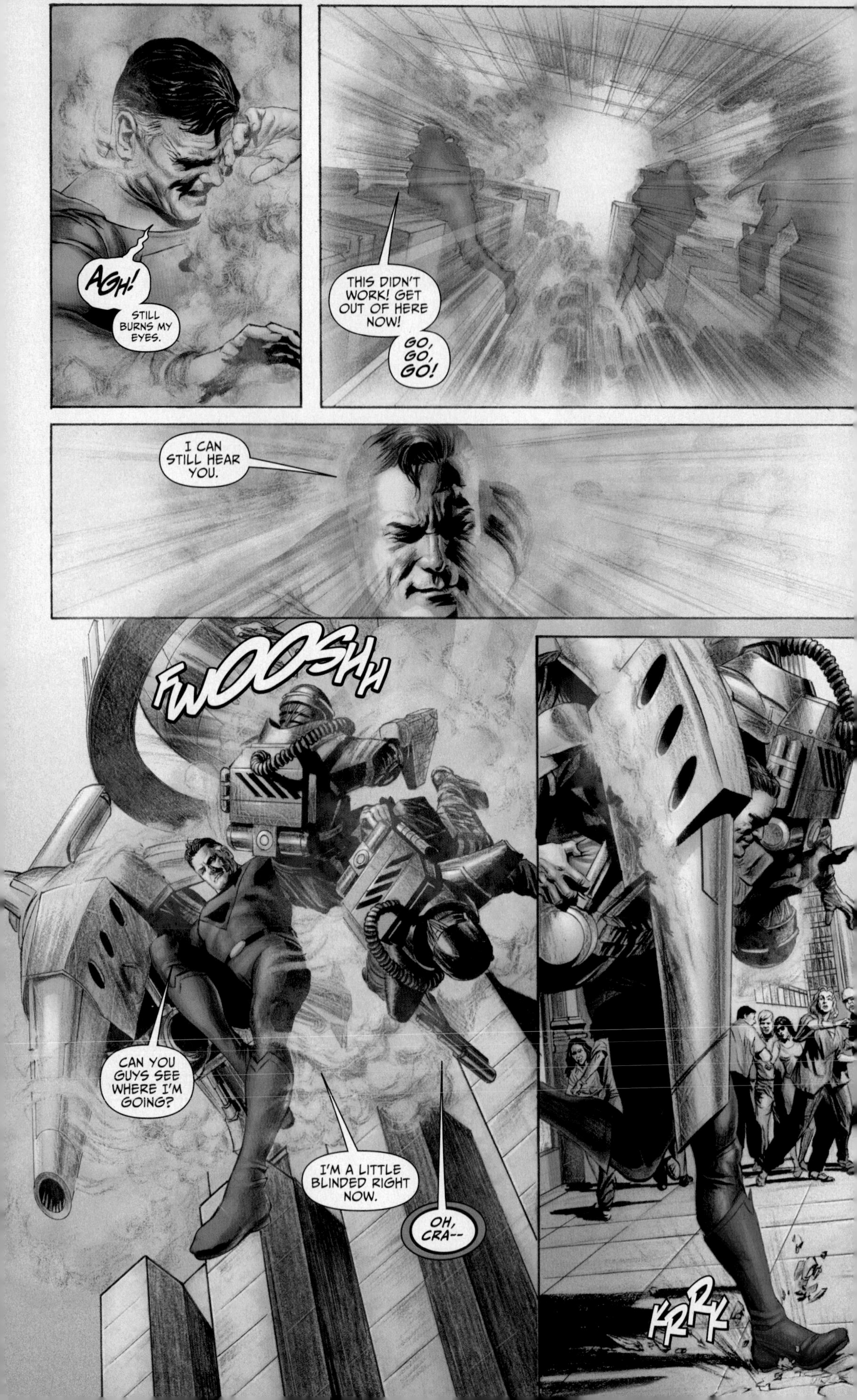
AGH!
STILL BURNS MY EYES.
THIS DIDN'T WORK! GET OUT OF HERE NOW!
GO, GO, GO!
I CAN STILL HEAR YOU.
FWOOSHH
CAN YOU GUYS SEE WHERE I'M GOING?
I'M A LITTLE BLINDED RIGHT NOW.
OH, CRA--
KRRK

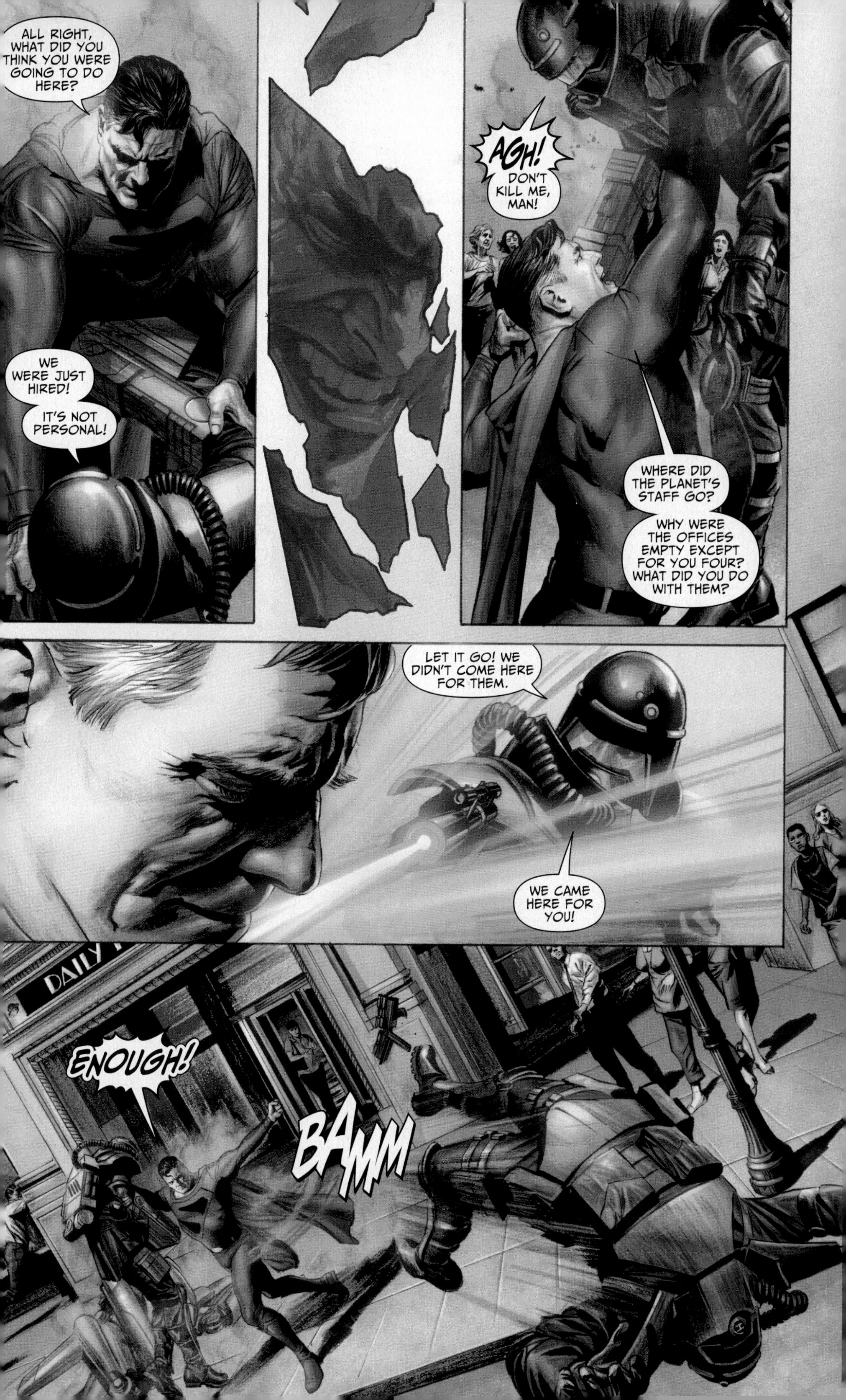
ALL RIGHT, WHAT DID YOU THINK YOU WERE GOING TO DO HERE?
WE WERE JUST HIRED!
IT'S NOT PERSONAL!
AGH!
DON'T KILL ME, MAN!
WHERE DID THE PLANET'S STAFF GO?
WHY WERE THE OFFICES EMPTY EXCEPT FOR YOU FOUR? WHAT DID YOU DO WITH THEM?
LET IT GO! WE DIDN'T COME HERE FOR THEM.
WE CAME HERE FOR YOU!
DAILY
ENOUGH!
BAMM

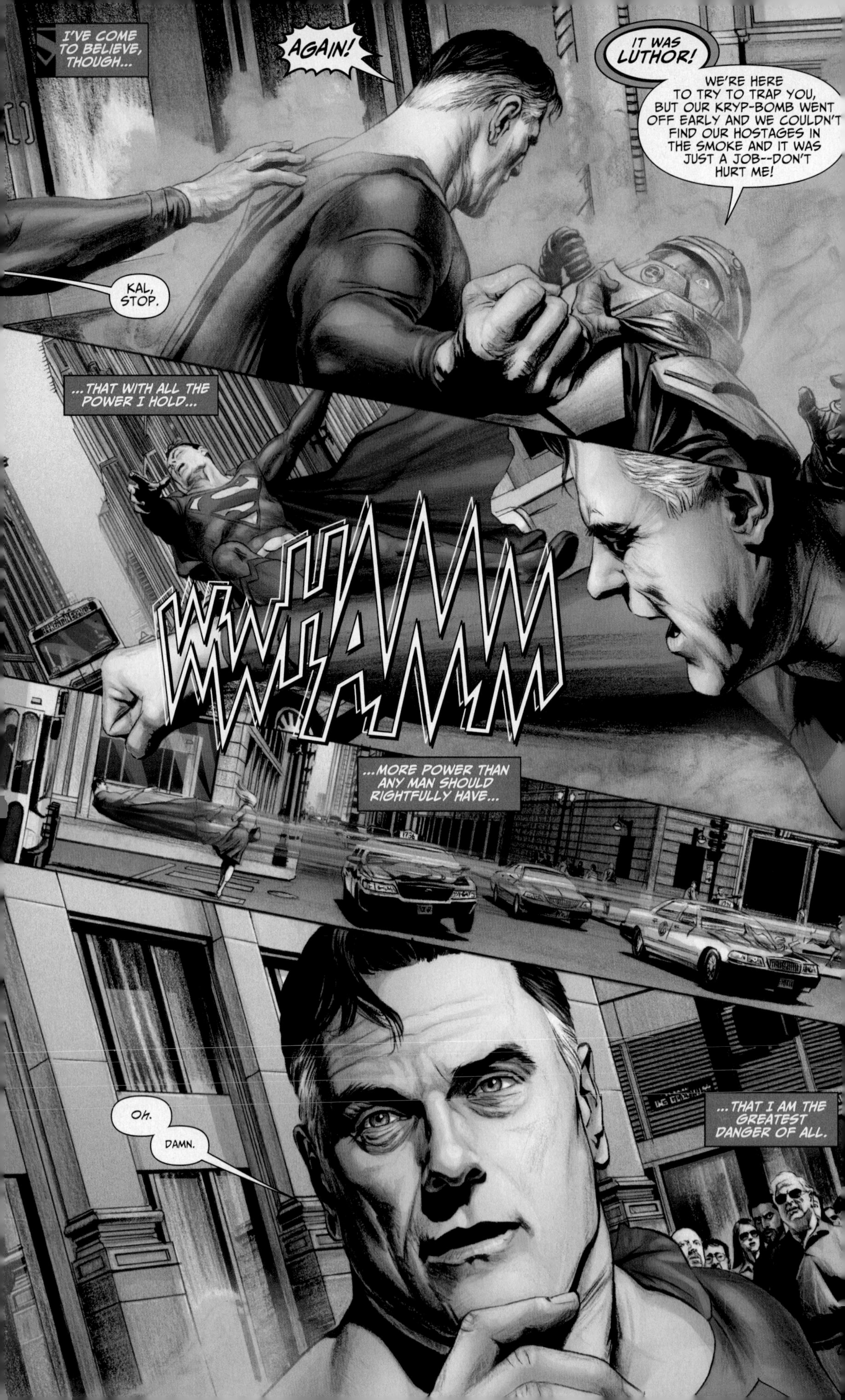
I'VE COME TO BELIEVE, THOUGH...
AGAIN!
IT WAS LUTHOR!
WE'RE HERE TO TRY TO TRAP YOU, BUT OUR KRYP-BOMB WENT OFF EARLY AND WE COULDN'T FIND OUR HOSTAGES IN THE SMOKE AND IT WAS JUST A JOB--DON'T HURT ME!
KAL, STOP.
...THAT WITH ALL THE POWER I HOLD...
WHAMM
...MORE POWER THAN ANY MAN SHOULD RIGHTFULLY HAVE...
Oh.
DAMN.
...THAT I AM THE GREATEST DANGER OF ALL.

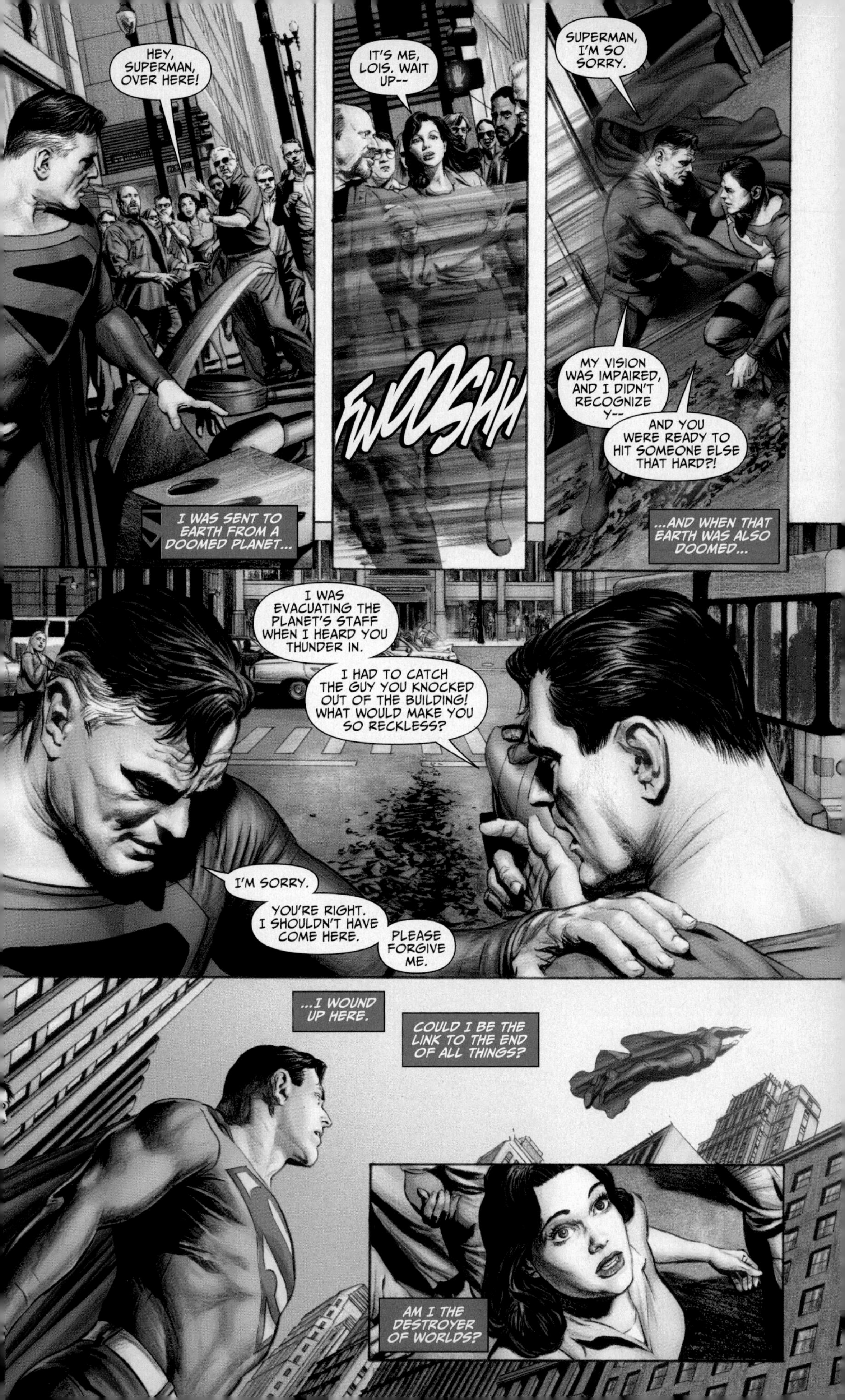
HEY, SUPERMAN, OVER HERE!
I WAS SENT TO EARTH FROM A DOOMED PLANET...
IT'S ME, LOIS. WAIT UP--
FWOOSHH
SUPERMAN, I'M SO SORRY.
MY VISION WAS IMPAIRED, AND I DIDN'T RECOGNIZE Y--
AND YOU WERE READY TO HIT SOMEONE ELSE THAT HARD?!
...AND WHEN THAT EARTH WAS ALSO DOOMED...
I WAS EVACUATING THE PLANET'S STAFF WHEN I HEARD YOU THUNDER IN.
I HAD TO CATCH THE GUY YOU KNOCKED OUT OF THE BUILDING! WHAT WOULD MAKE YOU SO RECKLESS?
I'M SORRY.
YOU'RE RIGHT. I SHOULDN'T HAVE COME HERE.
PLEASE FORGIVE ME.
...I WOUND UP HERE.
COULD I BE THE LINK TO THE END OF ALL THINGS?
AM I THE DESTROYER OF WORLDS?

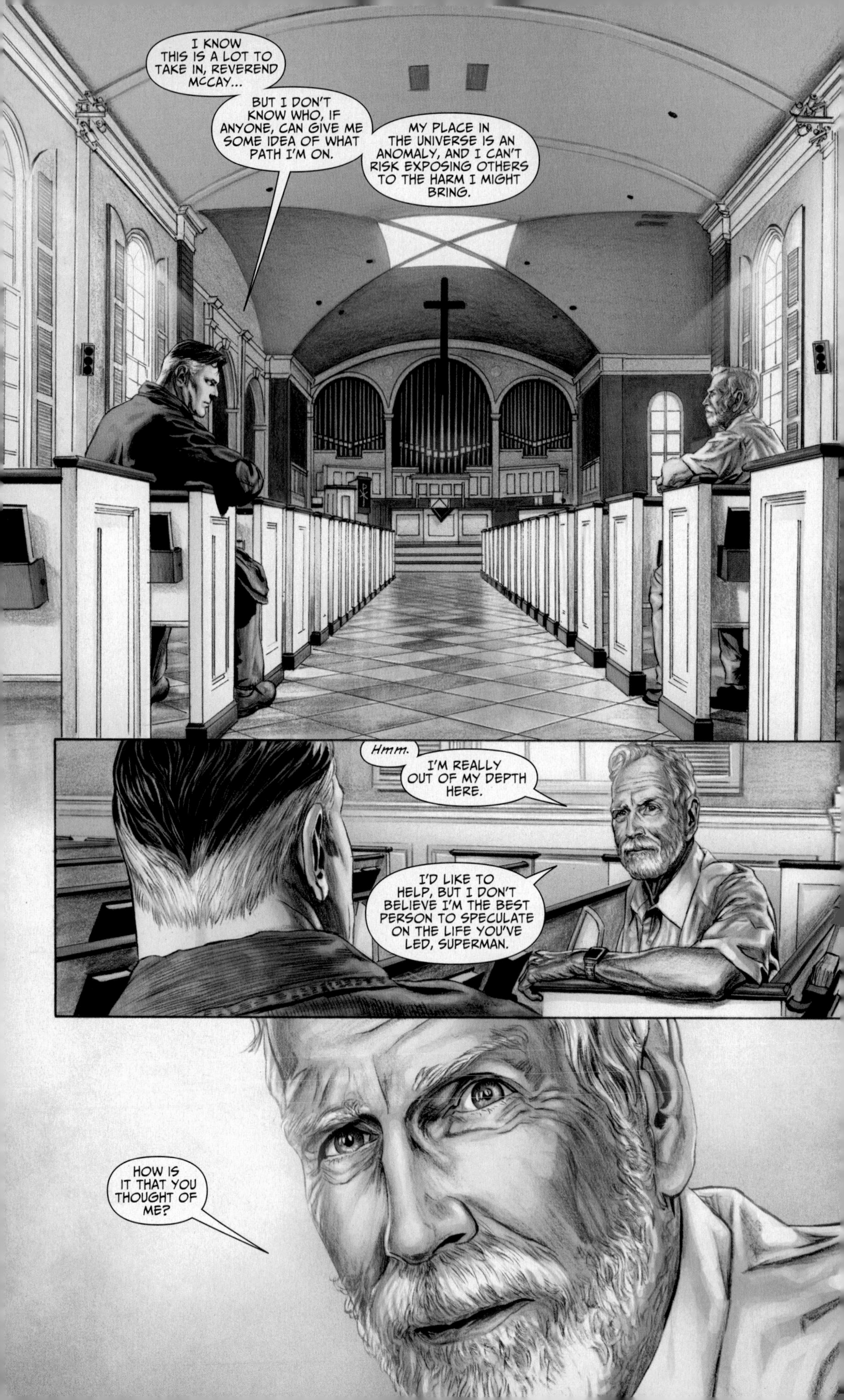
I KNOW THIS IS A LOT TO TAKE IN, REVEREND McCAY...
BUT I DON'T KNOW WHO, IF ANYONE, CAN GIVE ME SOME IDEA OF WHAT PATH I'M ON.
MY PLACE IN THE UNIVERSE IS AN ANOMALY, AND I CAN'T RISK EXPOSING OTHERS TO THE HARM I MIGHT BRING.
Hmm.
I'M REALLY OUT OF MY DEPTH HERE.
I'D LIKE TO HELP, BUT I DON'T BELIEVE I'M THE BEST PERSON TO SPECULATE ON THE LIFE YOU'VE LED, SUPERMAN.
HOW IS IT THAT YOU THOUGHT OF ME?

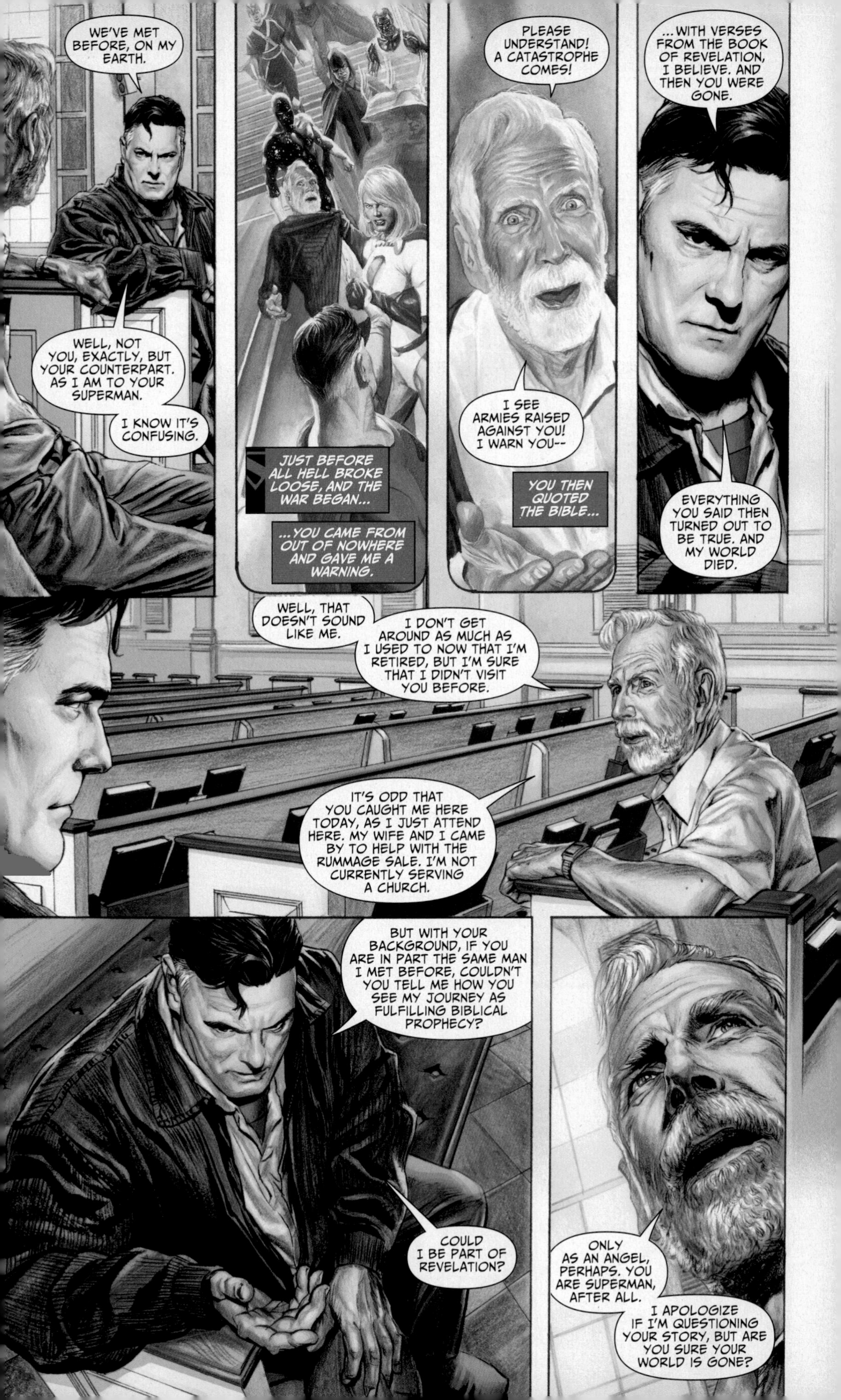
WE'VE MET BEFORE, ON MY EARTH.
WELL, NOT YOU, EXACTLY, BUT YOUR COUNTERPART. AS I AM TO YOUR SUPERMAN.
I KNOW IT'S CONFUSING.
JUST BEFORE ALL HELL BROKE LOOSE, AND THE WAR BEGAN...
...YOU CAME FROM OUT OF NOWHERE AND GAVE ME A WARNING.
PLEASE UNDERSTAND! A CATASTROPHE COMES!
I SEE ARMIES RAISED AGAINST YOU! I WARN YOU--
YOU THEN QUOTED THE BIBLE...
...WITH VERSES FROM THE BOOK OF REVELATION, I BELIEVE. AND THEN YOU WERE GONE.
EVERYTHING YOU SAID THEN TURNED OUT TO BE TRUE. AND MY WORLD DIED.
WELL, THAT DOESN'T SOUND LIKE ME.
I DON'T GET AROUND AS MUCH AS I USED TO NOW THAT I'M RETIRED, BUT I'M SURE THAT I DIDN'T VISIT YOU BEFORE.
IT'S ODD THAT YOU CAUGHT ME HERE TODAY, AS I JUST ATTEND HERE. MY WIFE AND I CAME BY TO HELP WITH THE RUMMAGE SALE. I'M NOT CURRENTLY SERVING A CHURCH.
BUT WITH YOUR BACKGROUND, IF YOU ARE IN PART THE SAME MAN I MET BEFORE, COULDN'T YOU TELL ME HOW YOU SEE MY JOURNEY AS FULFILLING BIBLICAL PROPHECY?
COULD I BE PART OF REVELATION?
ONLY AS AN ANGEL, PERHAPS. YOU ARE SUPERMAN, AFTER ALL.
I APOLOGIZE IF I'M QUESTIONING YOUR STORY, BUT ARE YOU SURE YOUR WORLD IS GONE?

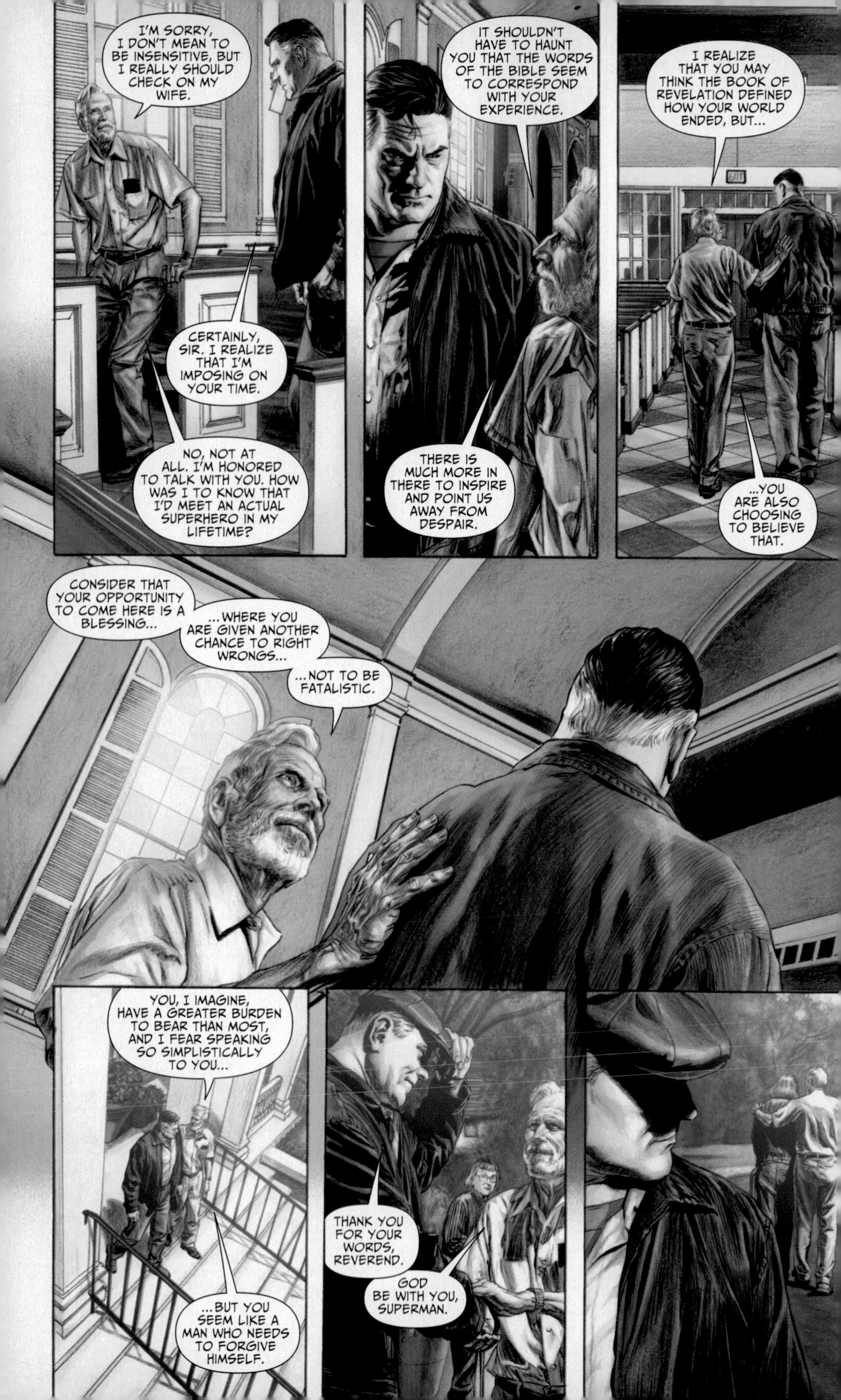
I'M SORRY, I DON'T MEAN TO BE INSENSITIVE, BUT I REALLY SHOULD CHECK ON MY WIFE.
CERTAINLY, SIR. I REALIZE THAT I'M IMPOSING ON YOUR TIME.
NO, NOT AT ALL. I'M HONORED TO TALK WITH YOU. HOW WAS I TO KNOW THAT I'D MEET AN ACTUAL SUPERHERO IN MY LIFETIME?
IT SHOULDN'T HAVE TO HAUNT YOU THAT THE WORDS OF THE BIBLE SEEM TO CORRESPOND WITH YOUR EXPERIENCE.
THERE IS MUCH MORE IN THERE TO INSPIRE AND POINT US AWAY FROM DESPAIR.
I REALIZE THAT YOU MAY THINK THE BOOK OF REVELATION DEFINED HOW YOUR WORLD ENDED, BUT...
EXIT
...YOU ARE ALSO CHOOSING TO BELIEVE THAT.
CONSIDER THAT YOUR OPPORTUNITY TO COME HERE IS A BLESSING...
...WHERE YOU ARE GIVEN ANOTHER CHANCE TO RIGHT WRONGS...
...NOT TO BE FATALISTIC.
YOU, I IMAGINE, HAVE A GREATER BURDEN TO BEAR THAN MOST, AND I FEAR SPEAKING SO SIMPLISTICALLY TO YOU...
...BUT YOU SEEM LIKE A MAN WHO NEEDS TO FORGIVE HIMSELF.
THANK YOU FOR YOUR WORDS, REVEREND.
GOD BE WITH YOU, SUPERMAN.

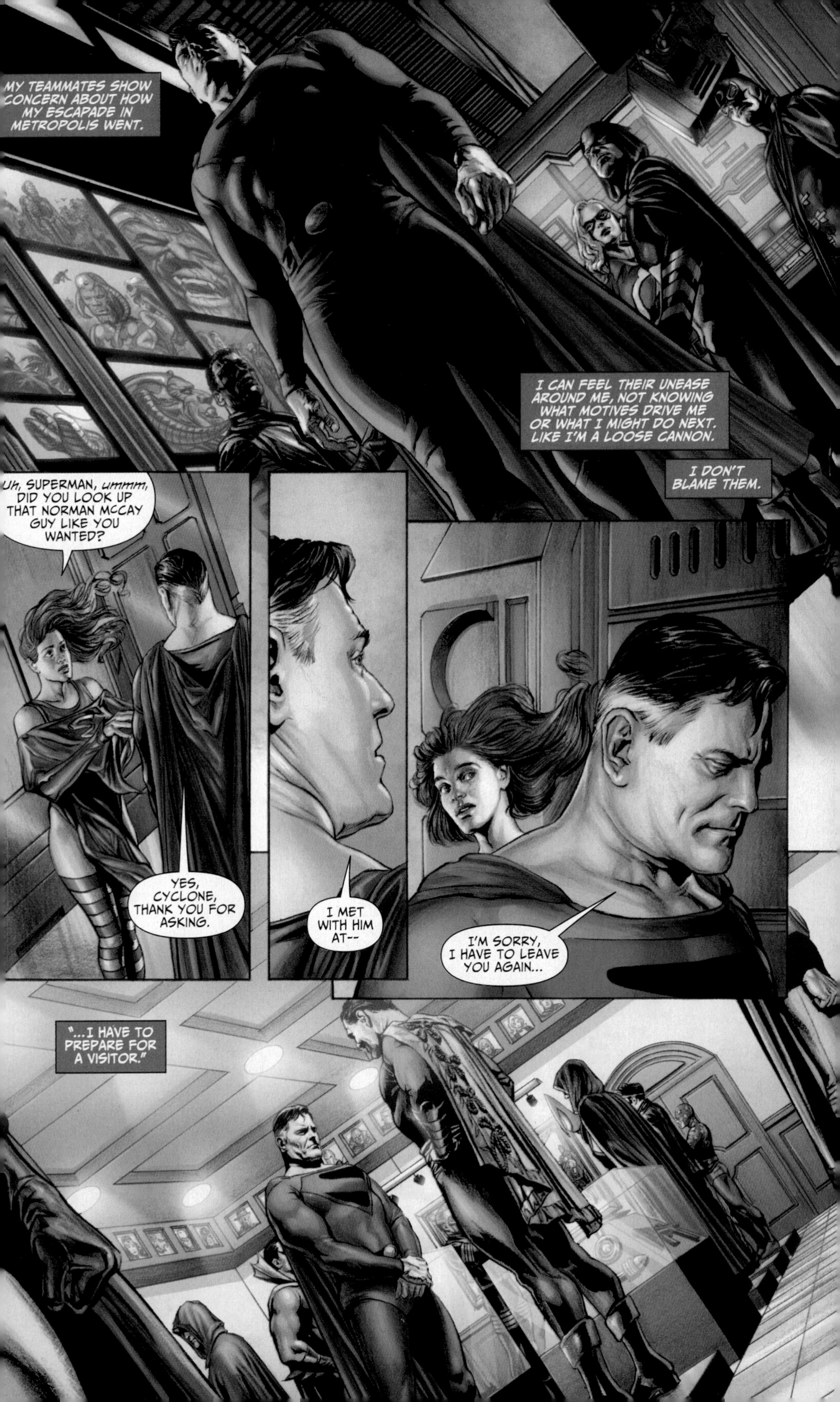
MY TEAMMATES SHOW CONCERN ABOUT HOW MY ESCAPADE IN METROPOLIS WENT.
I CAN FEEL THEIR UNEASE AROUND ME, NOT KNOWING WHAT MOTIVES DRIVE ME OR WHAT I MIGHT DO NEXT. LIKE I'M A LOOSE CANNON.
I DON'T BLAME THEM.
Uh, SUPERMAN, ummm, DID YOU LOOK UP THAT NORMAN McCAY GUY LIKE YOU WANTED?
YES, CYCLONE, THANK YOU FOR ASKING.
I MET WITH HIM AT--
I'M SORRY, I HAVE TO LEAVE YOU AGAIN...
"...I HAVE TO PREPARE FOR A VISITOR."

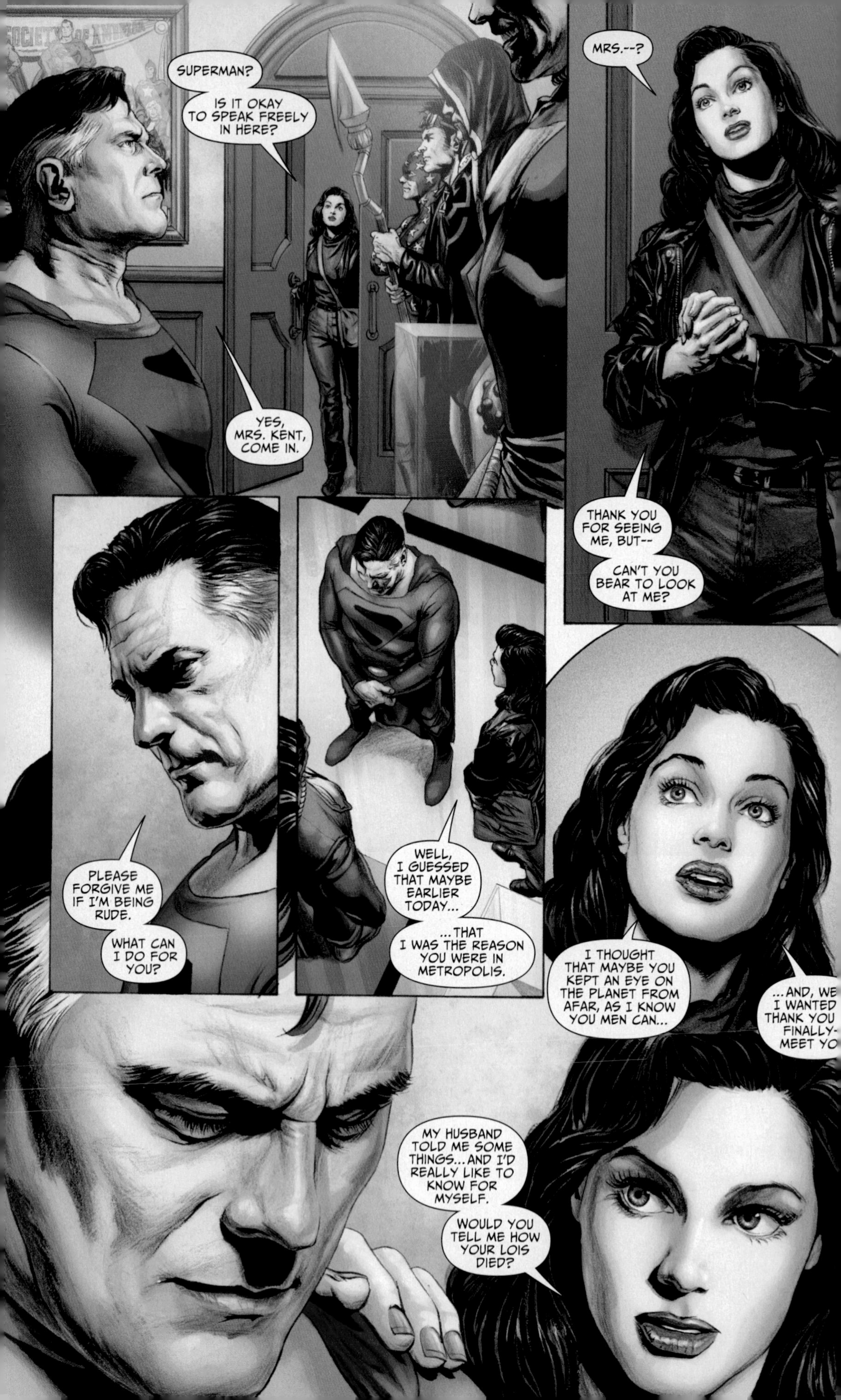
SUPERMAN?
IS IT OKAY TO SPEAK FREELY IN HERE?
YES, MRS. KENT, COME IN.
MRS.--?
THANK YOU FOR SEEING ME, BUT--
CAN'T YOU BEAR TO LOOK AT ME?
PLEASE FORGIVE ME IF I'M BEING RUDE.
WHAT CAN I DO FOR YOU?
WELL, I GUESSED THAT MAYBE EARLIER TODAY...
...THAT I WAS THE REASON YOU WERE IN METROPOLIS.
I THOUGHT THAT MAYBE YOU KEPT AN EYE ON THE PLANET FROM AFAR, AS I KNOW YOU MEN CAN...
...AND, WE I WANTED THANK YOU FINALLY- MEET YO
MY HUSBAND TOLD ME SOME THINGS...AND I'D REALLY LIKE TO KNOW FOR MYSELF.
WOULD YOU TELL ME HOW YOUR LOIS DIED?

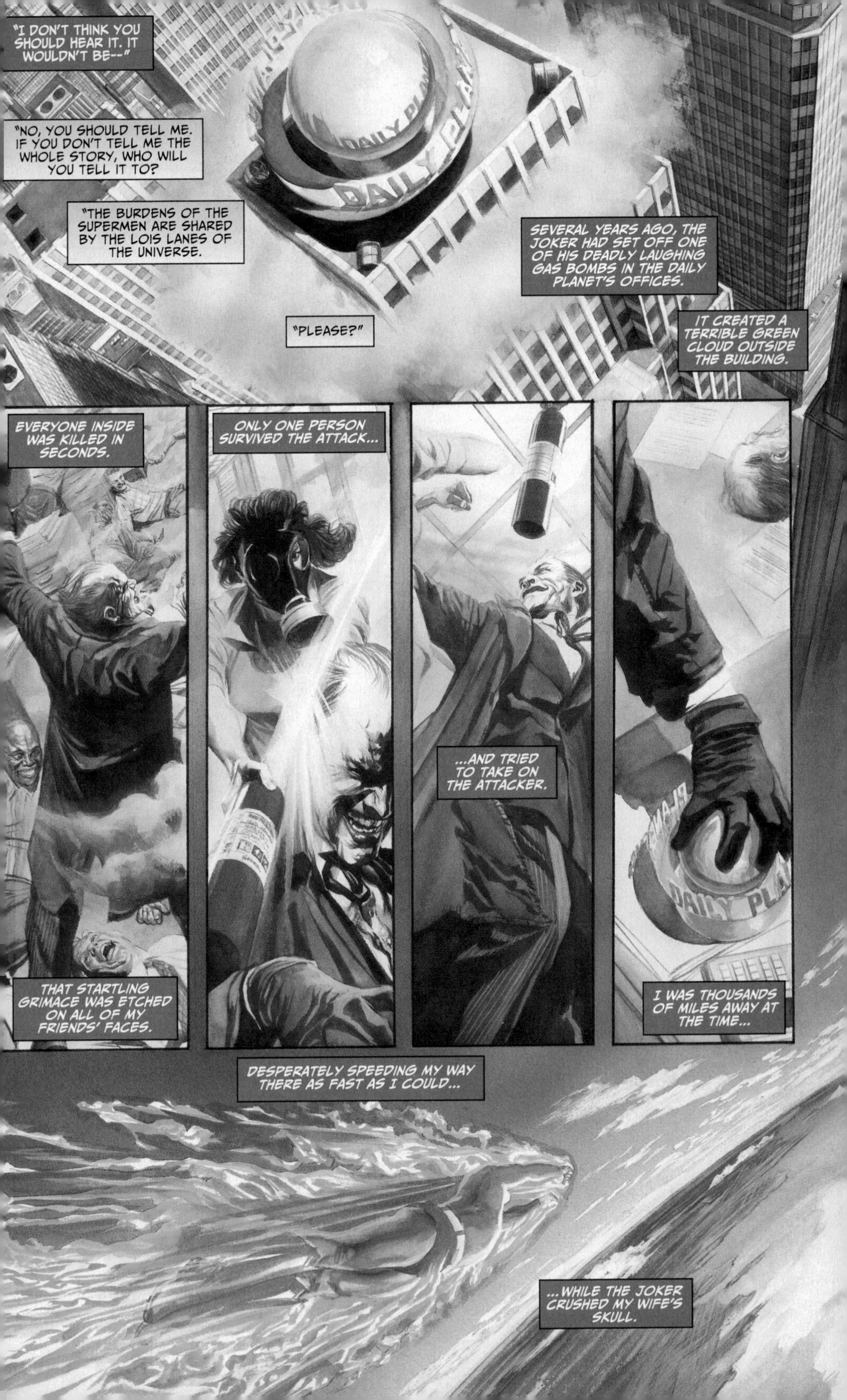

"I DON'T THINK YOU SHOULD HEAR IT. IT WOULDN'T BE--"
"NO, YOU SHOULD TELL ME. IF YOU DON'T TELL ME THE WHOLE STORY, WHO WILL YOU TELL IT TO?
"THE BURDENS OF THE SUPERMEN ARE SHARED BY THE LOIS LANES OF THE UNIVERSE.
"PLEASE?"
SEVERAL YEARS AGO, THE JOKER HAD SET OFF ONE OF HIS DEADLY LAUGHING GAS BOMBS IN THE DAILY PLANET'S OFFICES.
IT CREATED A TERRIBLE GREEN CLOUD OUTSIDE THE BUILDING.
EVERYONE INSIDE WAS KILLED IN SECONDS.
THAT STARTLING GRIMACE WAS ETCHED ON ALL OF MY FRIENDS' FACES.
ONLY ONE PERSON SURVIVED THE ATTACK...
...AND TRIED TO TAKE ON THE ATTACKER.
I WAS THOUSANDS OF MILES AWAY AT THE TIME...
DESPERATELY SPEEDING MY WAY THERE AS FAST AS I COULD...
...WHILE THE JOKER CRUSHED MY WIFE'S SKULL.

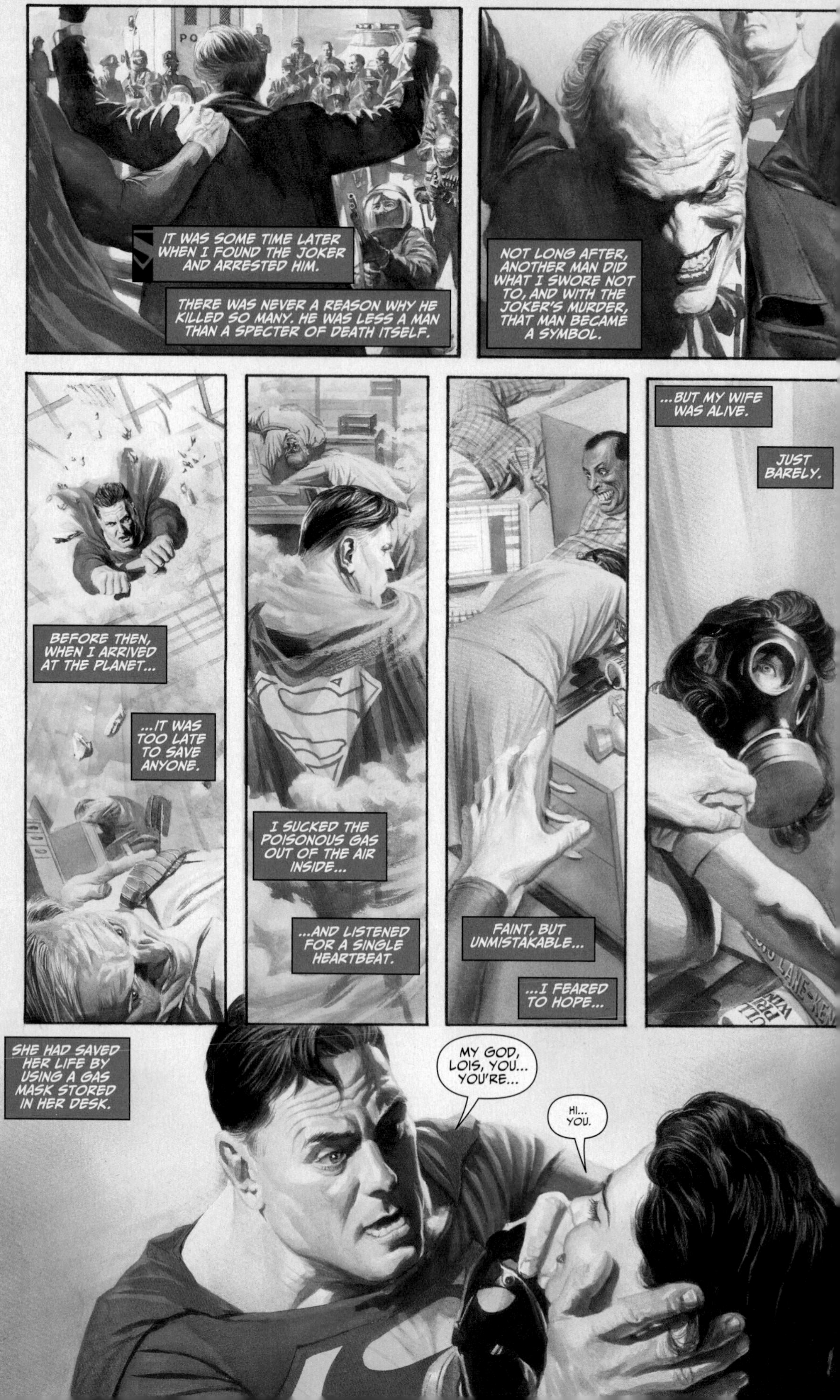
IT WAS SOME TIME LATER WHEN I FOUND THE JOKER AND ARRESTED HIM.
THERE WAS NEVER A REASON WHY HE KILLED SO MANY. HE WAS LESS A MAN THAN A SPECTER OF DEATH ITSELF.
NOT LONG AFTER, ANOTHER MAN DID WHAT I SWORE NOT TO, AND WITH THE JOKER'S MURDER, THAT MAN BECAME A SYMBOL.
BEFORE THEN, WHEN I ARRIVED AT THE PLANET...
...IT WAS TOO LATE TO SAVE ANYONE.
I SUCKED THE POISONOUS GAS OUT OF THE AIR INSIDE...
...AND LISTENED FOR A SINGLE HEARTBEAT.
FAINT, BUT UNMISTAKABLE...
...I FEARED TO HOPE...
...BUT MY WIFE WAS ALIVE.
JUST BARELY.
SHE HAD SAVED HER LIFE BY USING A GAS MASK STORED IN HER DESK.
MY GOD, LOIS, YOU... YOU'RE...
HI... YOU.

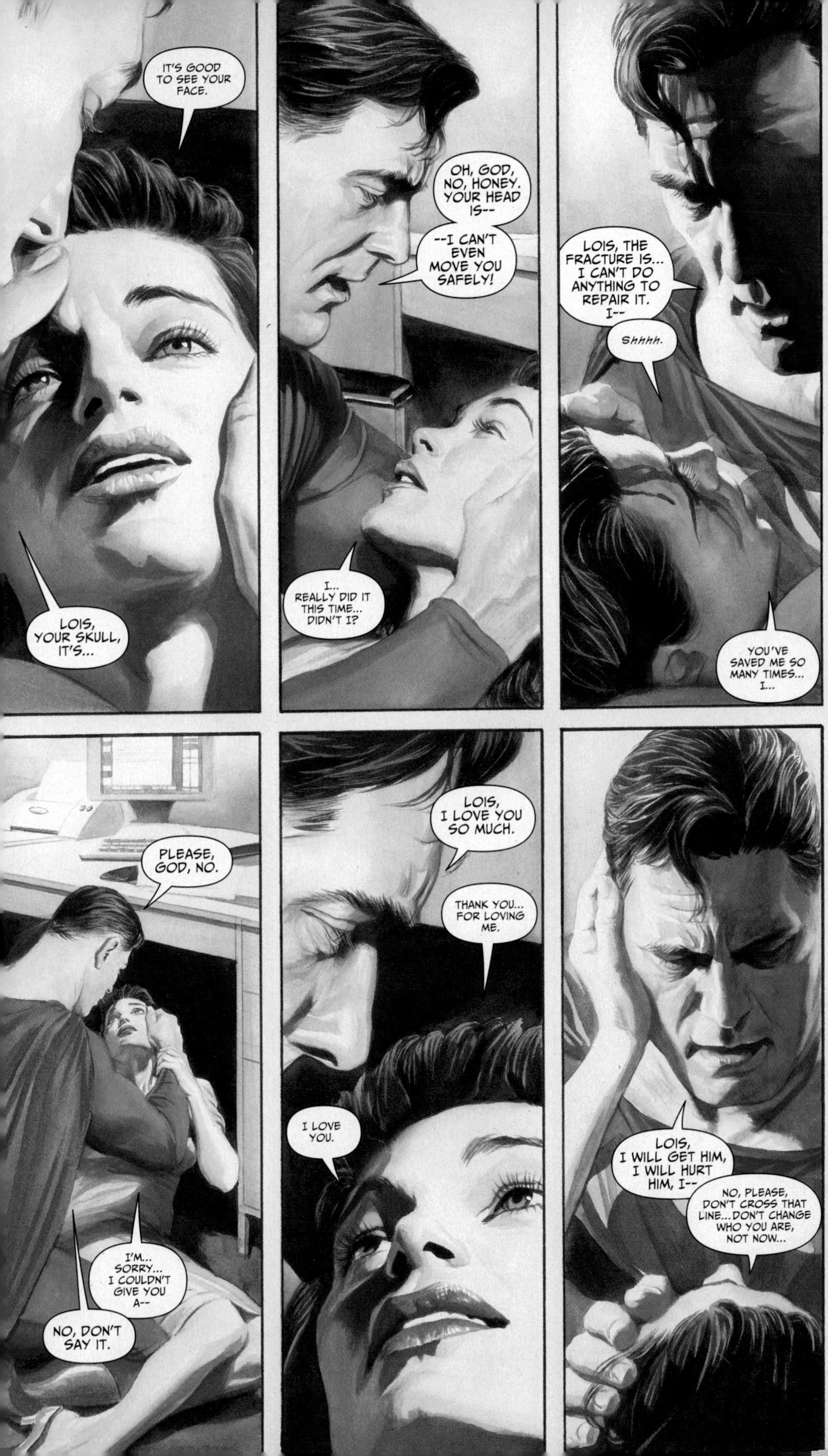
IT'S GOOD TO SEE YOUR FACE.
LOIS, YOUR SKULL, IT'S...
OH, GOD, NO, HONEY. YOUR HEAD IS--
--I CAN'T EVEN MOVE YOU SAFELY!
I... REALLY DID IT THIS TIME... DIDN'T I?
LOIS, THE FRACTURE IS... I CAN'T DO ANYTHING TO REPAIR IT. I--
Shhhh.
YOU'VE SAVED ME SO MANY TIMES... I...
PLEASE, GOD, NO.
I'M... SORRY... I COULDN'T GIVE YOU A--
NO, DON'T SAY IT.
LOIS, I LOVE YOU SO MUCH.
THANK YOU... FOR LOVING ME.
I LOVE YOU.
LOIS, I WILL GET HIM, I WILL HURT HIM, I--
NO, PLEASE, DON'T CROSS THAT LINE... DON'T CHANGE WHO YOU ARE, NOT NOW...

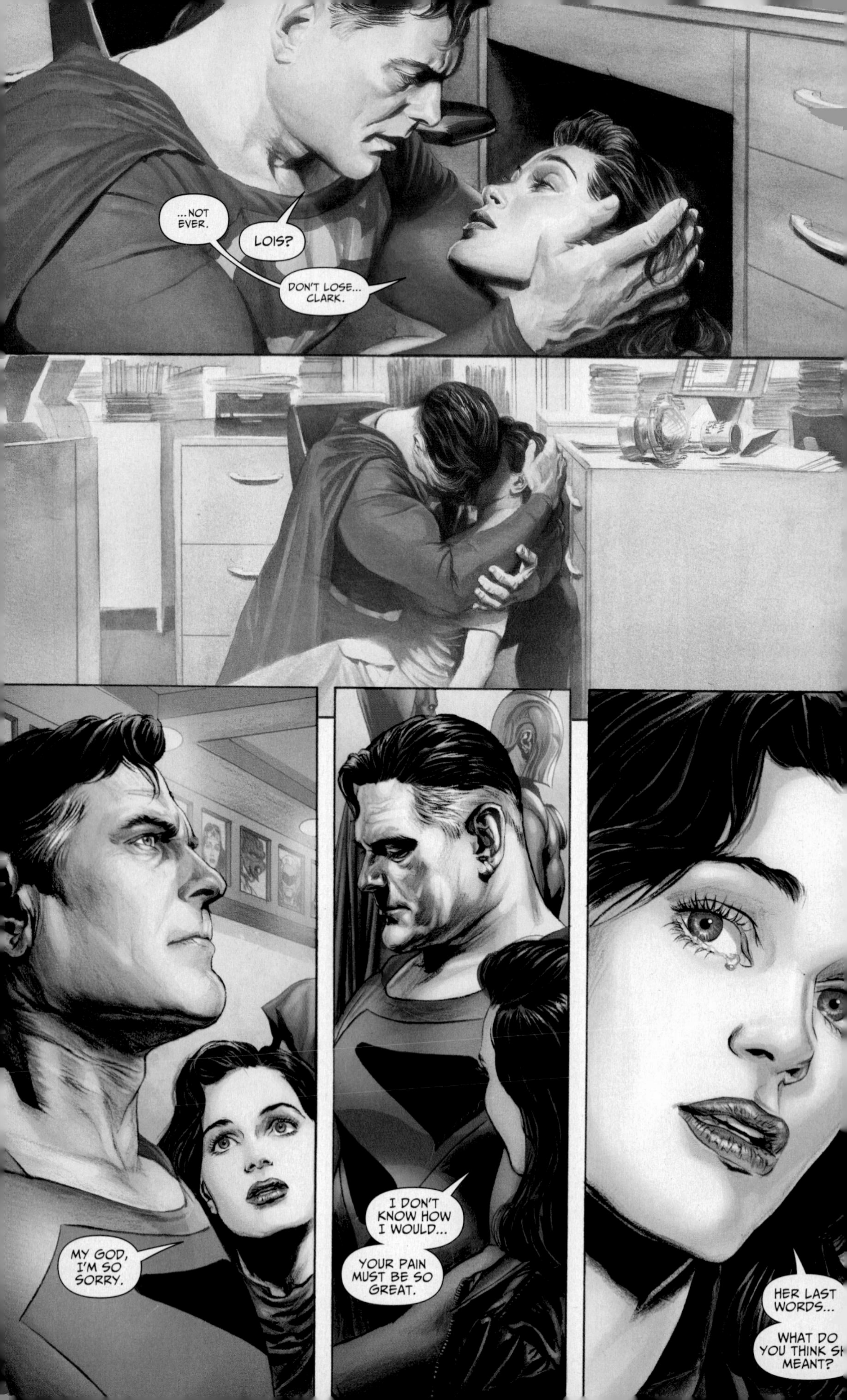
...NOT EVER.
LOIS?
DON'T LOSE... CLARK.
MY GOD, I'M SO SORRY.
I DON'T KNOW HOW I WOULD...
YOUR PAIN MUST BE SO GREAT.
HER LAST WORDS...
WHAT DO YOU THINK SH MEANT?

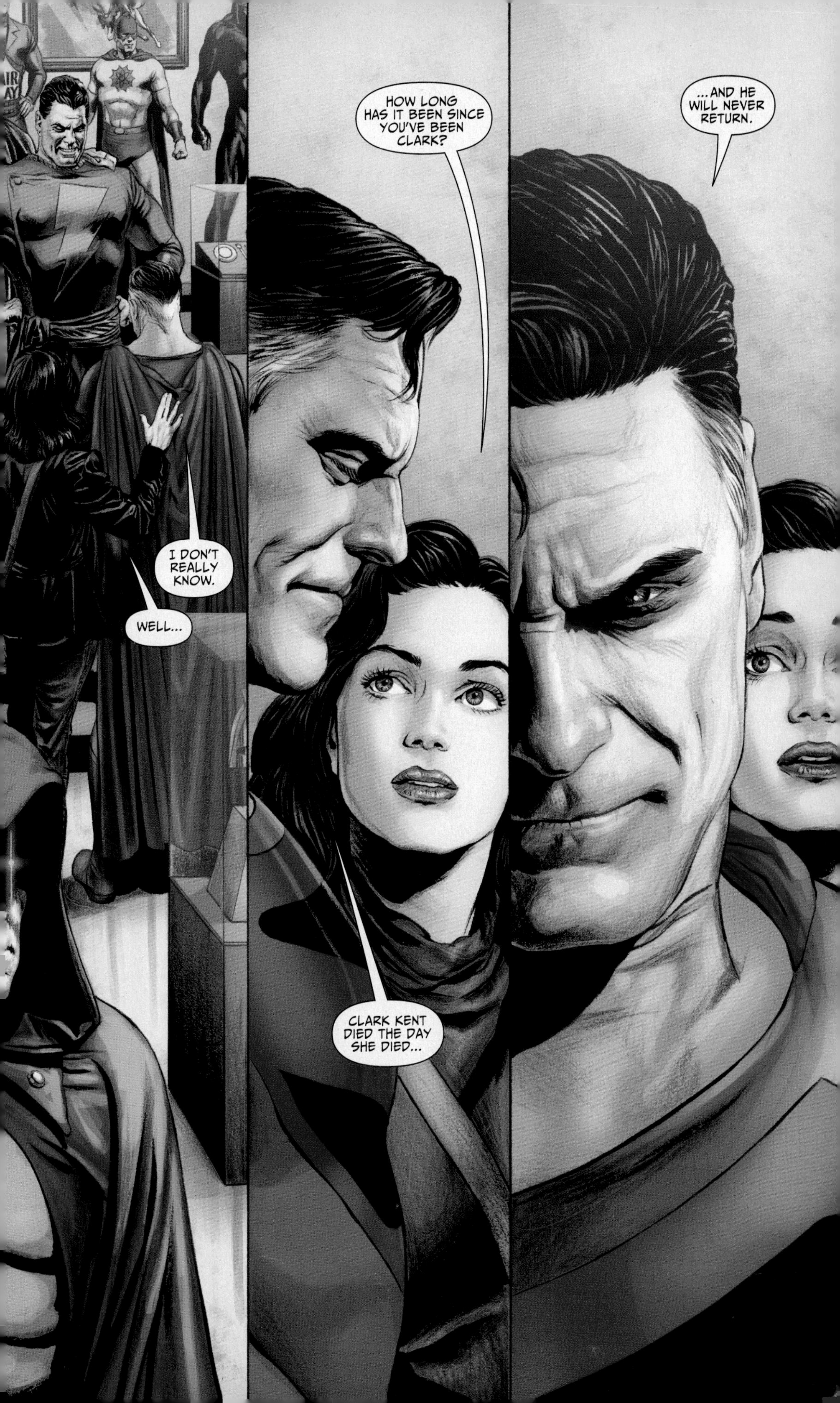
WELL...
I DON'T REALLY KNOW.
HOW LONG HAS IT BEEN SINCE YOU'VE BEEN CLARK?
CLARK KENT DIED THE DAY SHE DIED...
...AND HE WILL NEVER RETURN.

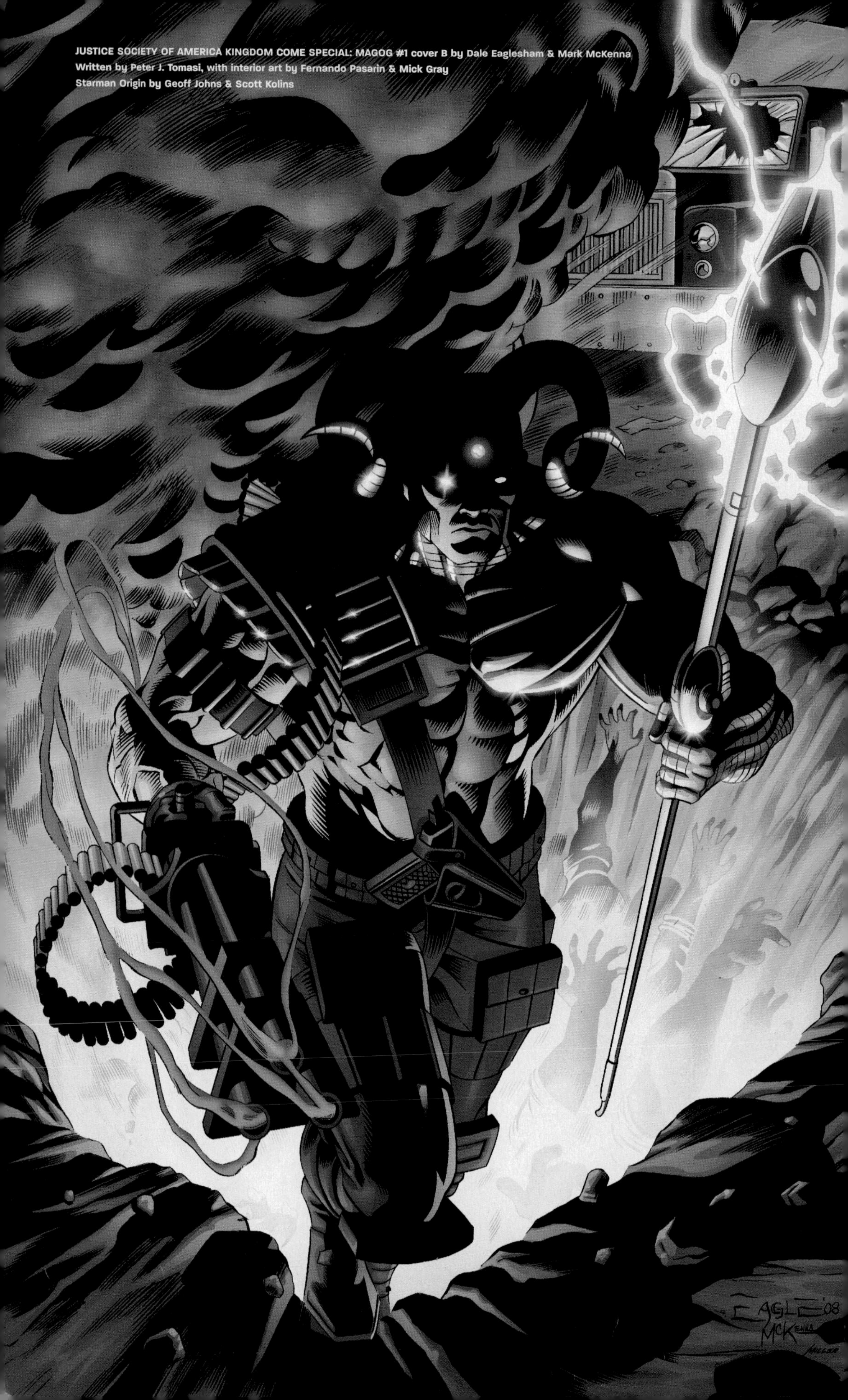
EAGLE '08
McKENNA

JUSTICE SOCIETY OF AMERICA KINGDOM COME SPECIAL: MAGOG #1 cover B by Dale Eaglesham & Mark McKenna
Written by Peter J. Tomasi, with interior art by Fernando Pasarin & Mick Gray
Starman Origin by Geoff Johns & Scott Kolins

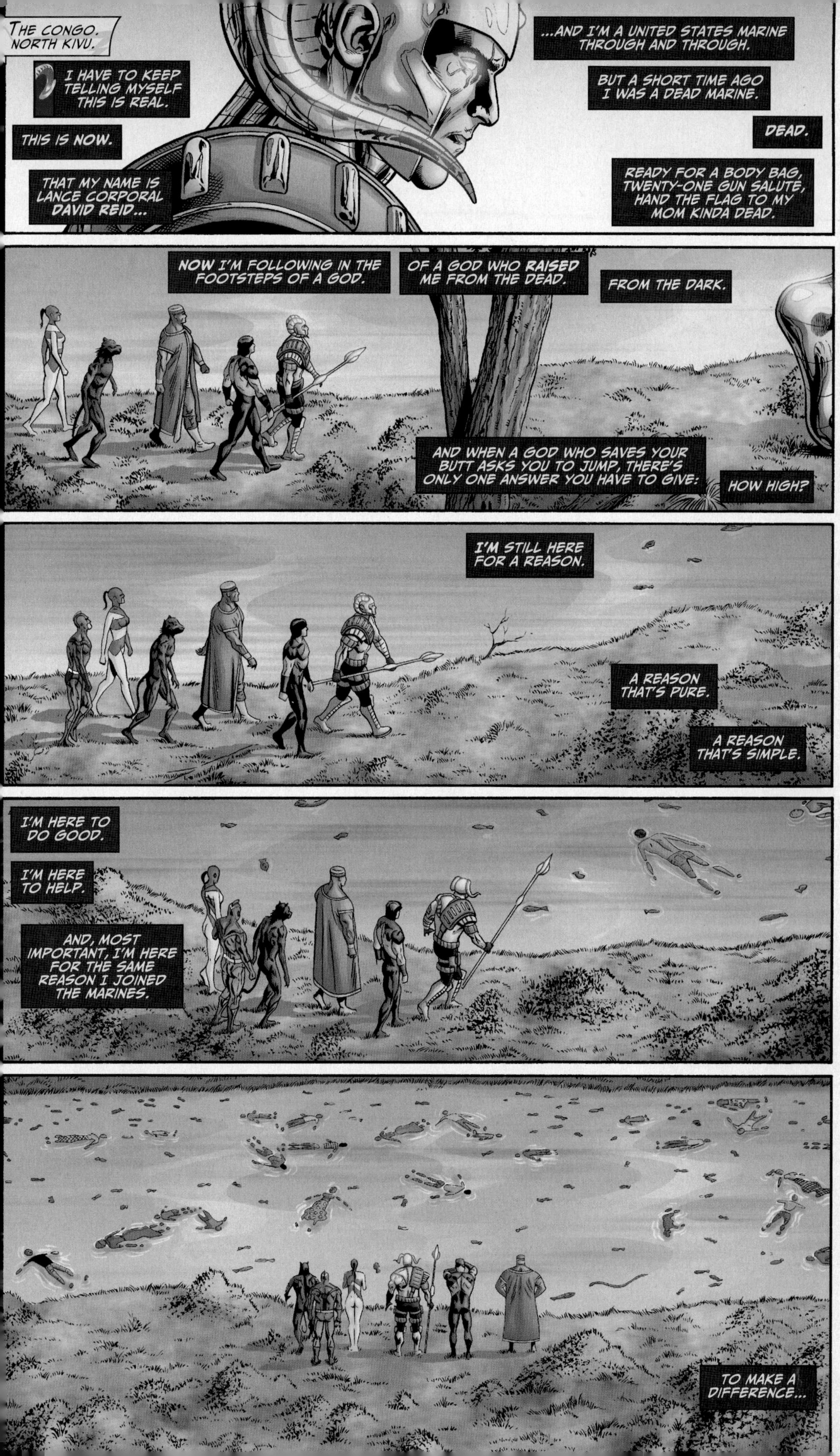
THE CONGO. NORTH KIVU.
I HAVE TO KEEP TELLING MYSELF THIS IS REAL.
THIS IS NOW.
THAT MY NAME IS LANCE CORPORAL DAVID REID...
...AND I'M A UNITED STATES MARINE THROUGH AND THROUGH.
BUT A SHORT TIME AGO I WAS A DEAD MARINE.
DEAD.
READY FOR A BODY BAG, TWENTY-ONE GUN SALUTE, HAND THE FLAG TO MY MOM KINDA DEAD.
NOW I'M FOLLOWING IN THE FOOTSTEPS OF A GOD.
OF A GOD WHO RAISED ME FROM THE DEAD.
FROM THE DARK.
AND WHEN A GOD WHO SAVES YOUR BUTT ASKS YOU TO JUMP, THERE'S ONLY ONE ANSWER YOU HAVE TO GIVE:
HOW HIGH?
I'M STILL HERE FOR A REASON.
A REASON THAT'S PURE.
A REASON THAT'S SIMPLE.
I'M HERE TO DO GOOD.
I'M HERE TO HELP.
AND, MOST IMPORTANT, I'M HERE FOR THE SAME REASON I JOINED THE MARINES.
TO MAKE A DIFFERENCE...

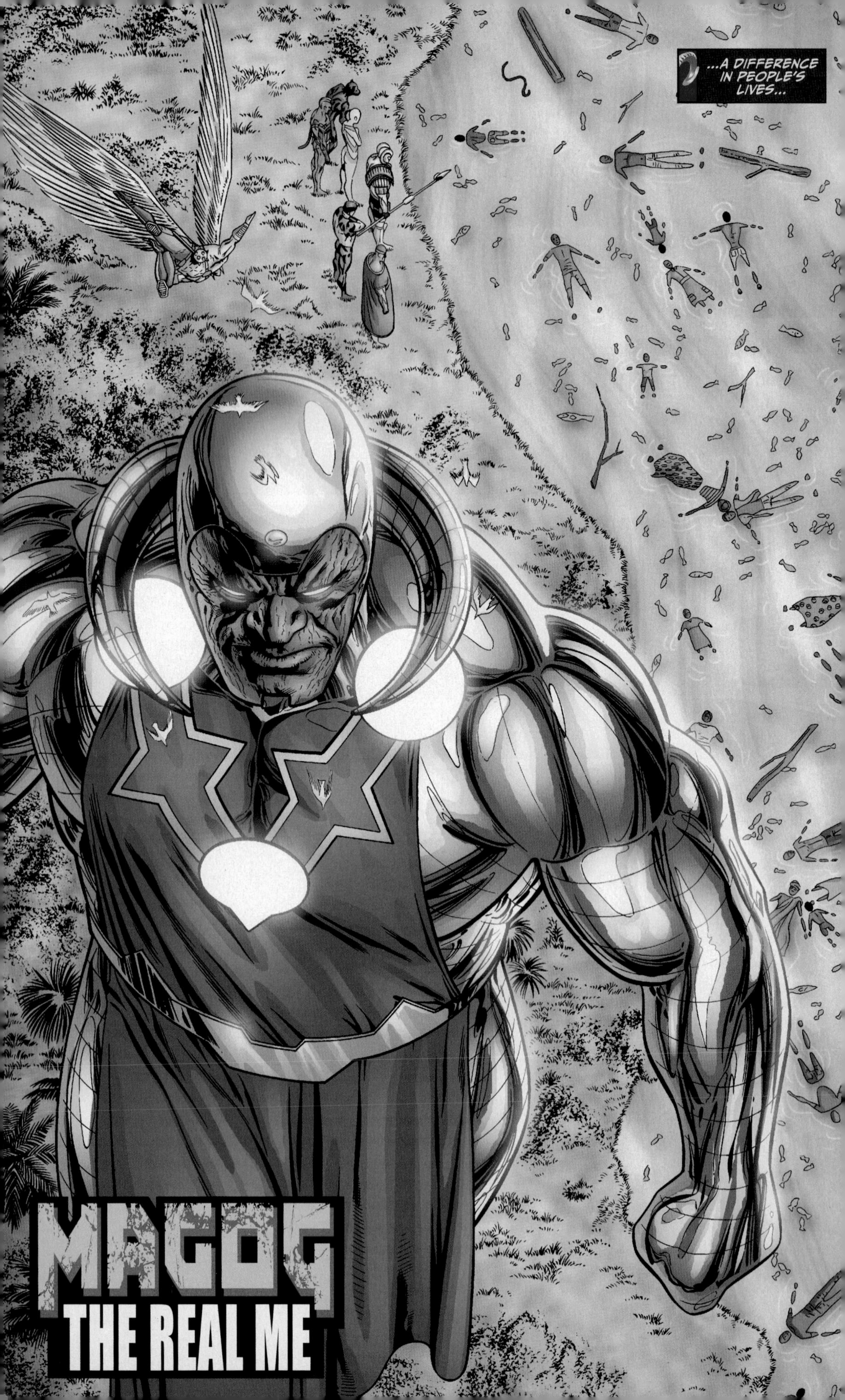
...A DIFFERENCE IN PEOPLE'S LIVES...
MAGOG
THE REAL ME

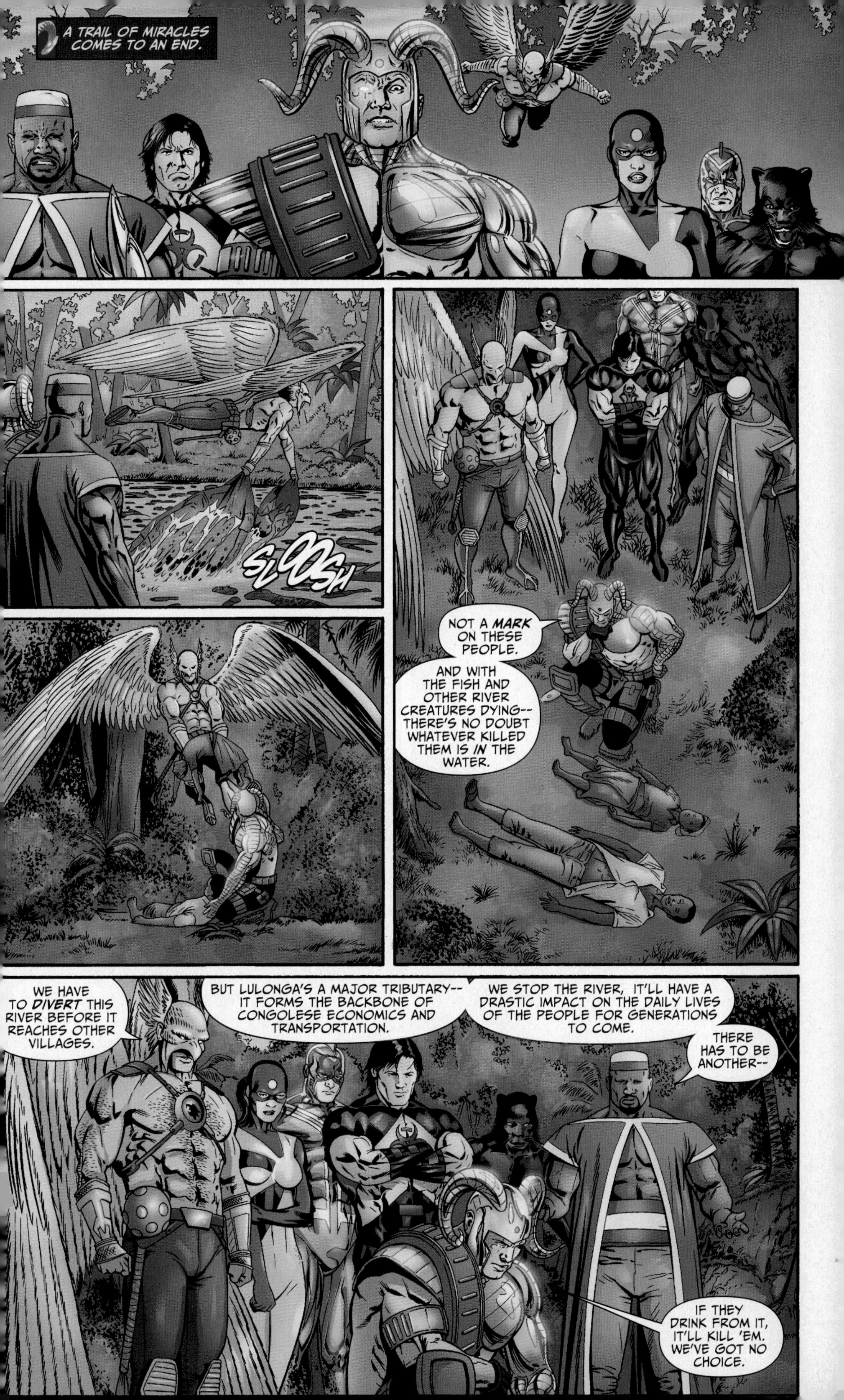
A TRAIL OF MIRACLES COMES TO AN END.
SLOOSH
NOT A MARK ON THESE PEOPLE.
AND WITH THE FISH AND OTHER RIVER CREATURES DYING-- THERE'S NO DOUBT WHATEVER KILLED THEM IS IN THE WATER.
WE HAVE TO DIVERT THIS RIVER BEFORE IT REACHES OTHER VILLAGES.
BUT LULONGA'S A MAJOR TRIBUTARY-- IT FORMS THE BACKBONE OF CONGOLESE ECONOMICS AND TRANSPORTATION.
WE STOP THE RIVER, IT'LL HAVE A DRASTIC IMPACT ON THE DAILY LIVES OF THE PEOPLE FOR GENERATIONS TO COME.
THERE HAS TO BE ANOTHER--
IF THEY DRINK FROM IT, IT'LL KILL 'EM. WE'VE GOT NO CHOICE.

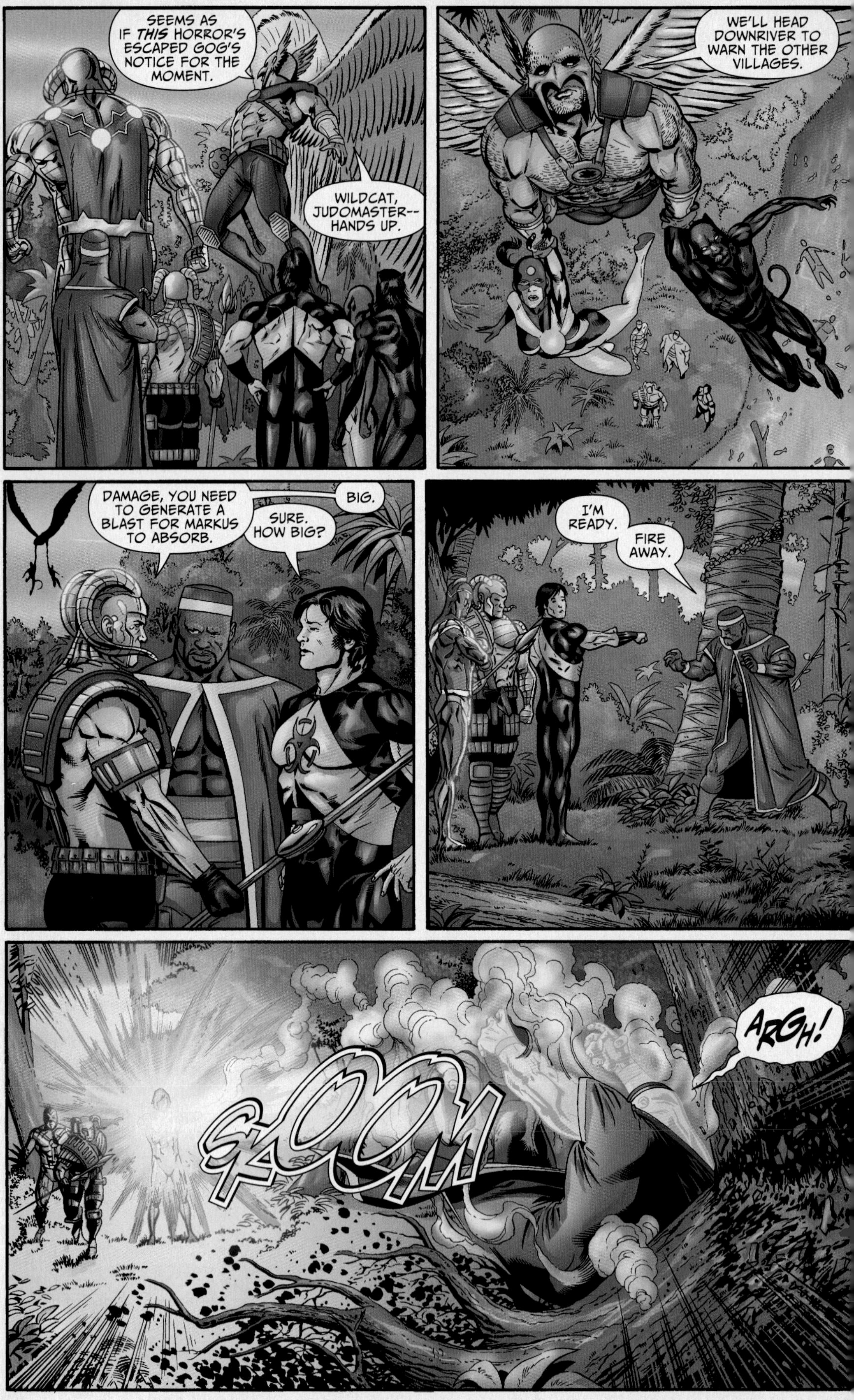
SEEMS AS IF *THIS* HORROR'S ESCAPED GOG'S NOTICE FOR THE MOMENT.
WILDCAT, JUDOMASTER-- HANDS UP.
WE'LL HEAD DOWNRIVER TO WARN THE OTHER VILLAGES.
DAMAGE, YOU NEED TO GENERATE A BLAST FOR MARKUS TO ABSORB.
SURE. HOW BIG?
BIG.
I'M READY.
FIRE AWAY.
ARGH!

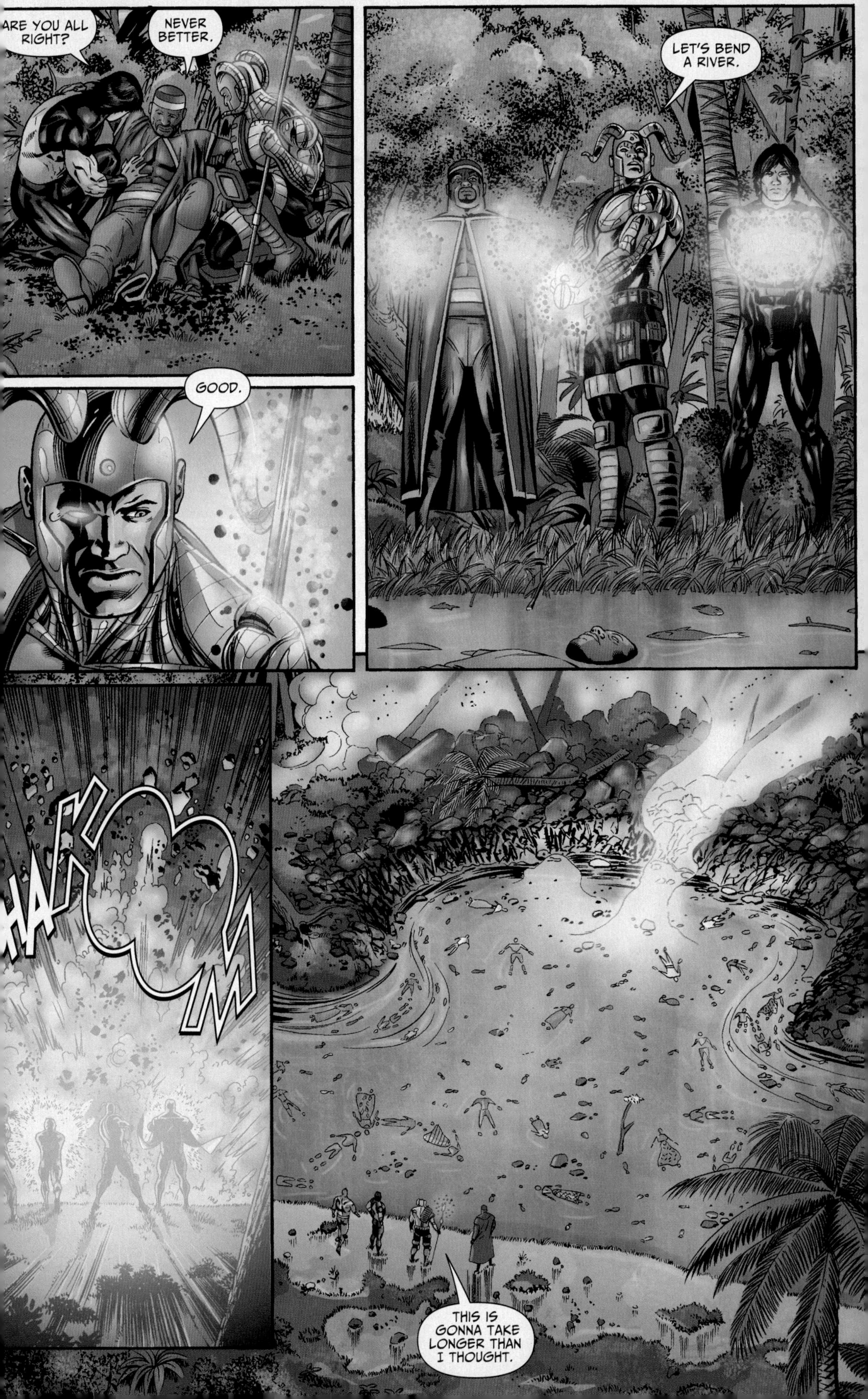
ARE YOU ALL RIGHT?
NEVER BETTER.
LET'S BEND A RIVER.
GOOD.
THAKOOM
THIS IS GONNA TAKE LONGER THAN I THOUGHT.

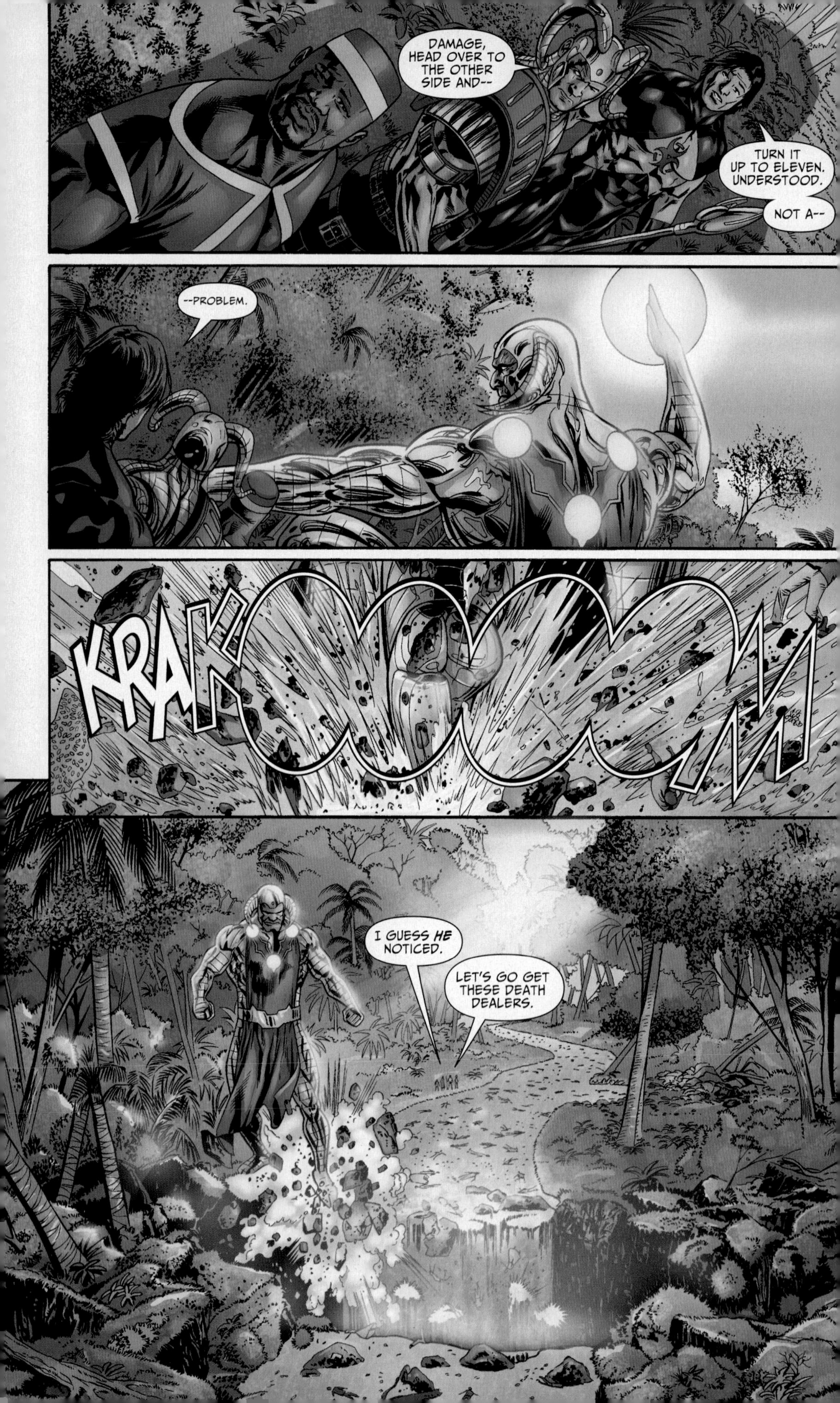
DAMAGE, HEAD OVER TO THE OTHER SIDE AND--
TURN IT UP TO ELEVEN. UNDERSTOOD.
NOT A--
--PROBLEM.
KRAKOOOOM
I GUESS *HE* NOTICED.
LET'S GO GET THESE DEATH DEALERS.

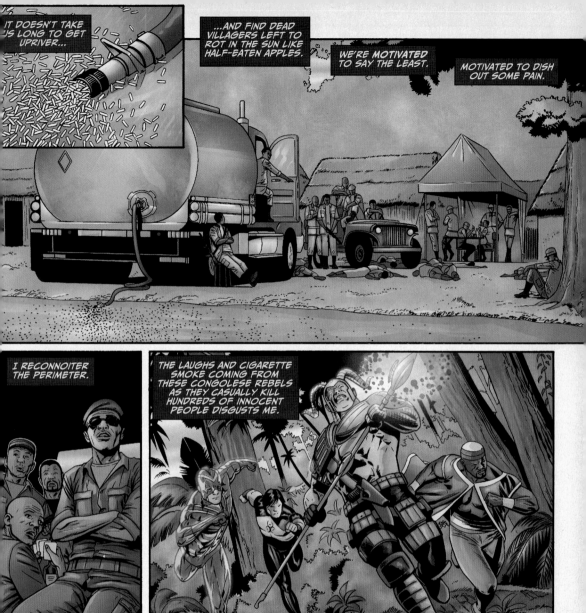

IT DOESN'T TAKE US LONG TO GET UPRIVER...

...AND FIND DEAD VILLAGERS LEFT TO ROT IN THE SUN LIKE HALF-EATEN APPLES.

WE'RE MOTIVATED TO SAY THE LEAST.

MOTIVATED TO DISH OUT SOME PAIN.

I RECONNOITER THE PERIMETER.

THE LAUGHS AND CIGARETTE SMOKE COMING FROM THESE CONGOLESE REBELS AS THEY CASUALLY KILL HUNDREDS OF INNOCENT PEOPLE DISGUSTS ME.

MUCH AS I HATE TO ADMIT IT, I'M LOOKING FORWARD TO HEARING THEM SCREAM.

BOOOOM

BRATTABRATTA

BRATTABRATTABRATTA

STEEL, TAKE OUT *THAT* TRUCK!

ALREADY ON IT!

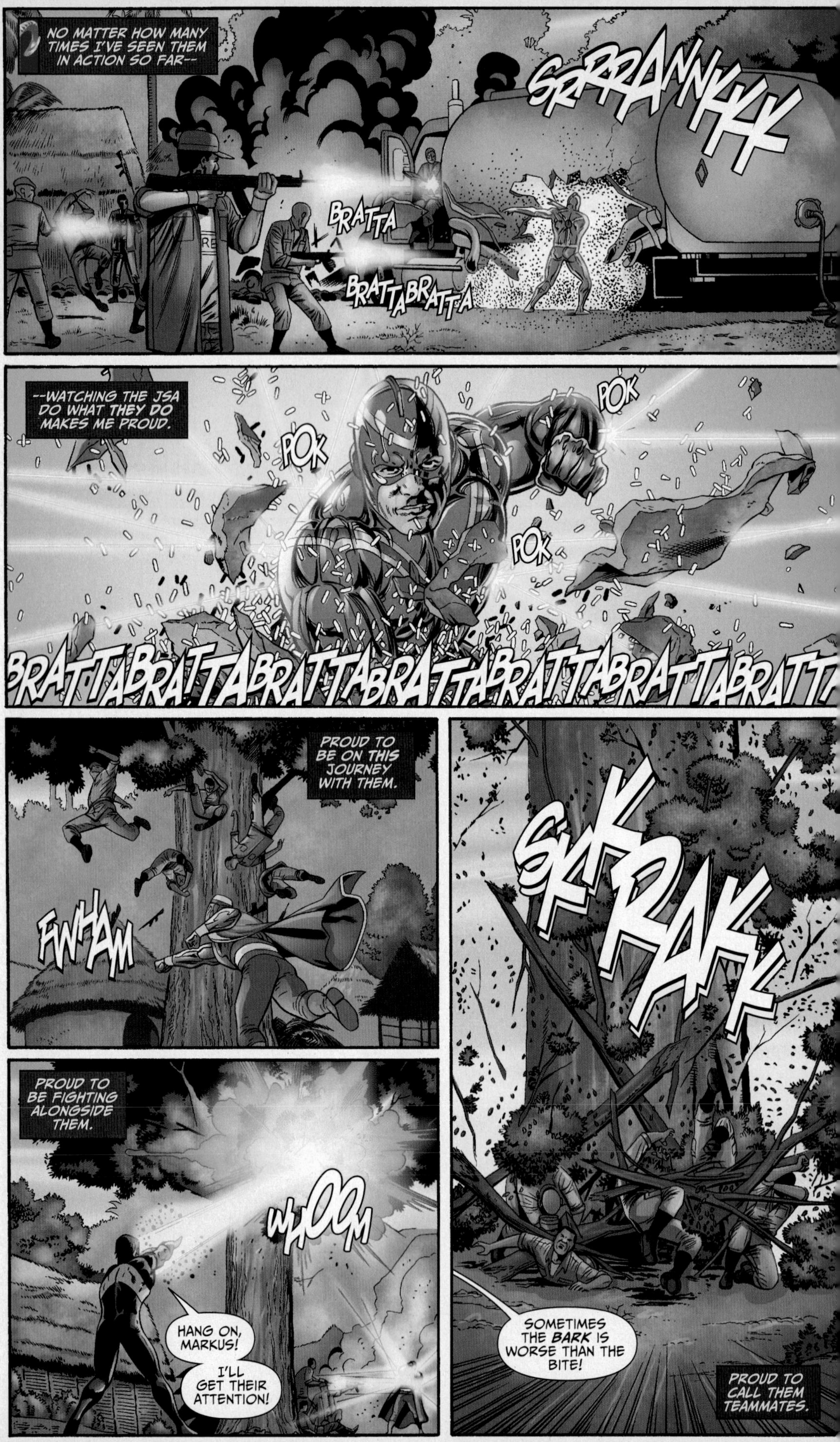
NO MATTER HOW MANY TIMES I'VE SEEN THEM IN ACTION SO FAR--
SRRRANNKKK
BRATTA
BRATTABRATTA
--WATCHING THE JSA DO WHAT THEY DO MAKES ME PROUD.
POK
POK
POK
BRATTABRATTABRATTABRATTABRATTABRATTABRATTA
PROUD TO BE ON THIS JOURNEY WITH THEM.
FWHAM
PROUD TO BE FIGHTING ALONGSIDE THEM.
WHOOM
HANG ON, MARKUS!
I'LL GET THEIR ATTENTION!
SKKRAKK
SOMETIMES THE BARK IS WORSE THAN THE BITE!
PROUD TO CALL THEM TEAMMATES.

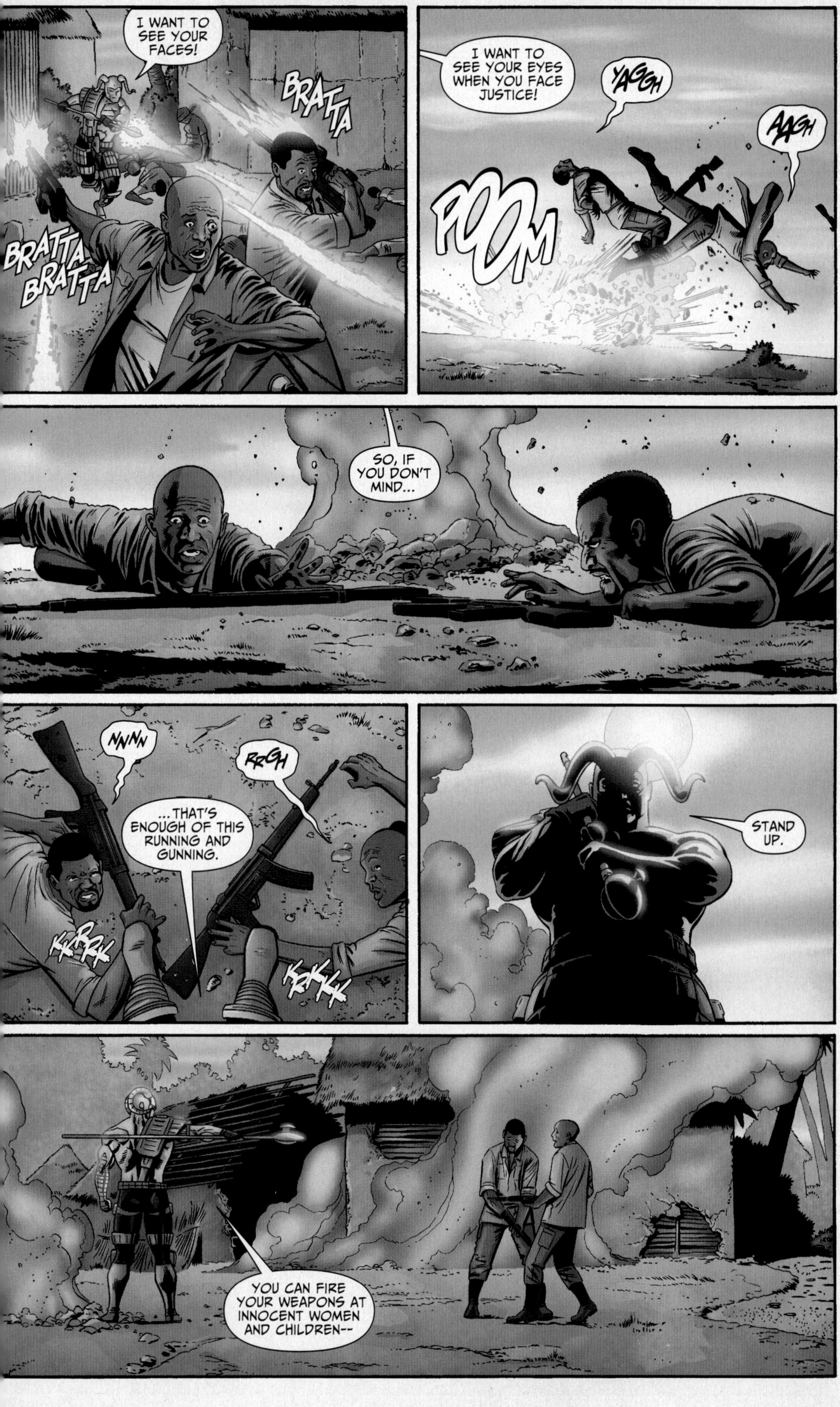
I WANT TO SEE YOUR FACES!
BRATTA
BRATTA BRATTA
I WANT TO SEE YOUR EYES WHEN YOU FACE JUSTICE!
YAGGH
AAGH
POOM
SO, IF YOU DON'T MIND...
NNNN
RRGH
...THAT'S ENOUGH OF THIS RUNNING AND GUNNING.
KKRRK
KRKKK
STAND UP.
YOU CAN FIRE YOUR WEAPONS AT INNOCENT WOMEN AND CHILDREN--

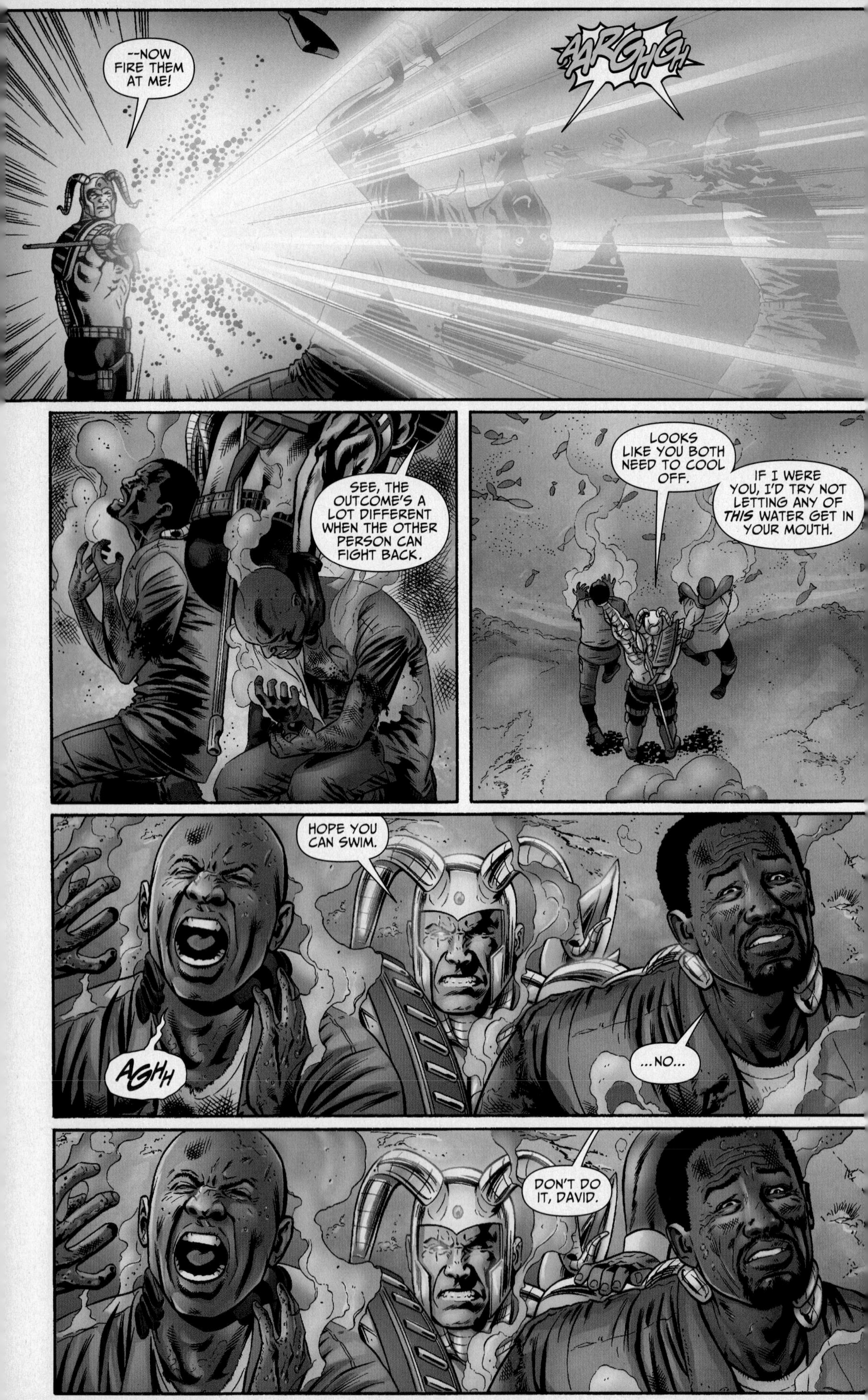
--NOW FIRE THEM AT ME!
AARGHGH
SEE, THE OUTCOME'S A LOT DIFFERENT WHEN THE OTHER PERSON CAN FIGHT BACK.
LOOKS LIKE YOU BOTH NEED TO COOL OFF.
IF I WERE YOU, I'D TRY NOT LETTING ANY OF THIS WATER GET IN YOUR MOUTH.
HOPE YOU CAN SWIM.
AGHH
...NO...
DON'T DO IT, DAVID.

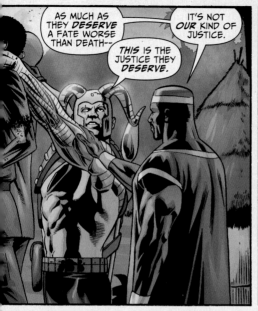

AS MUCH AS THEY *DESERVE* A FATE WORSE THAN DEATH--

IT'S NOT *OUR* KIND OF JUSTICE.

THIS IS THE JUSTICE THEY *DESERVE*.

THERE ARE MANY DIFFERENT FACETS OF JUSTICE.

HERE IS ANOTHER ONE.

AAIEE

NOOoo!

FAASSH

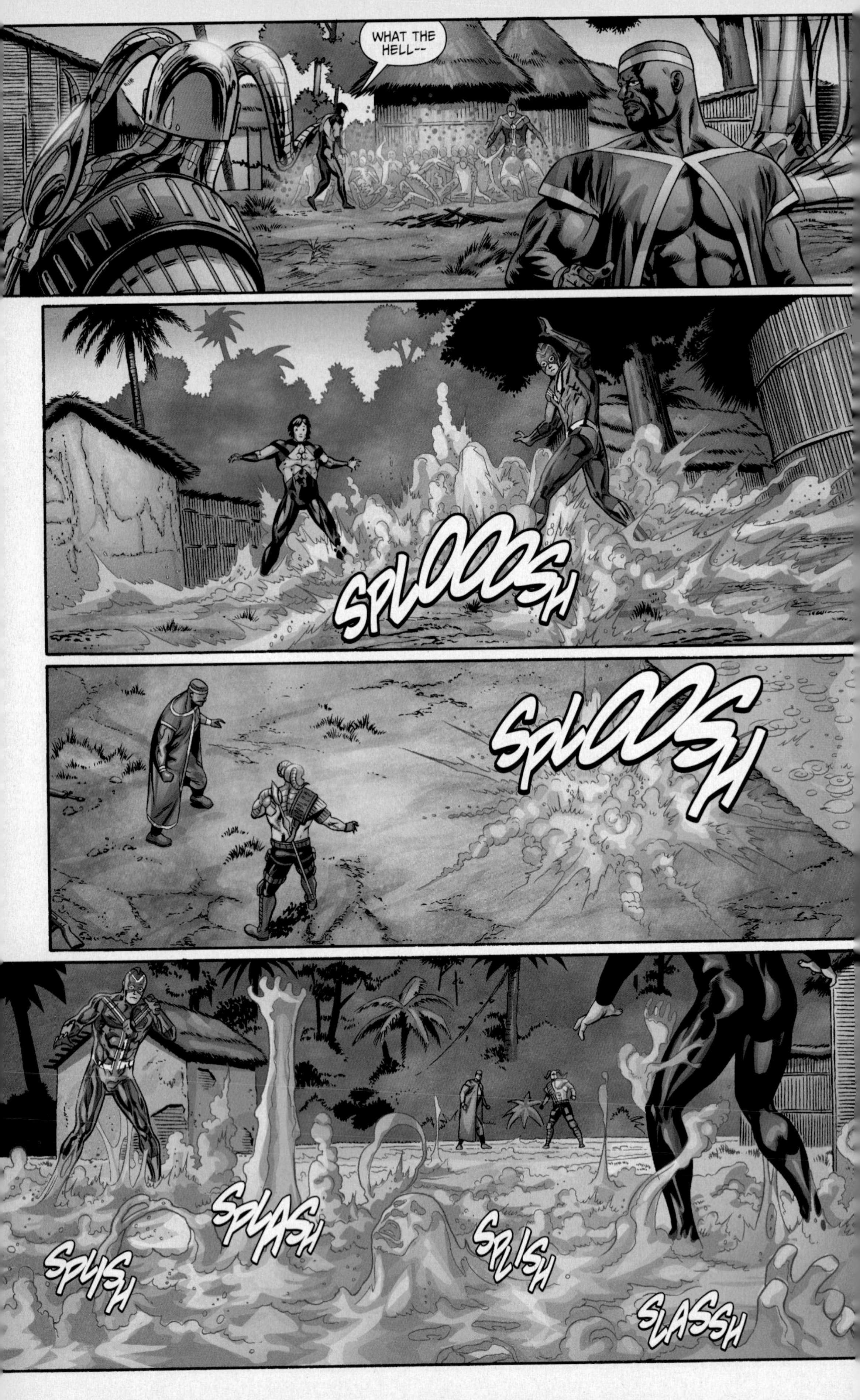
WHAT THE HELL--
SPLOOOSH
SPLOOSH
SPLISH
SPLASH
SPLISH
SLASSH

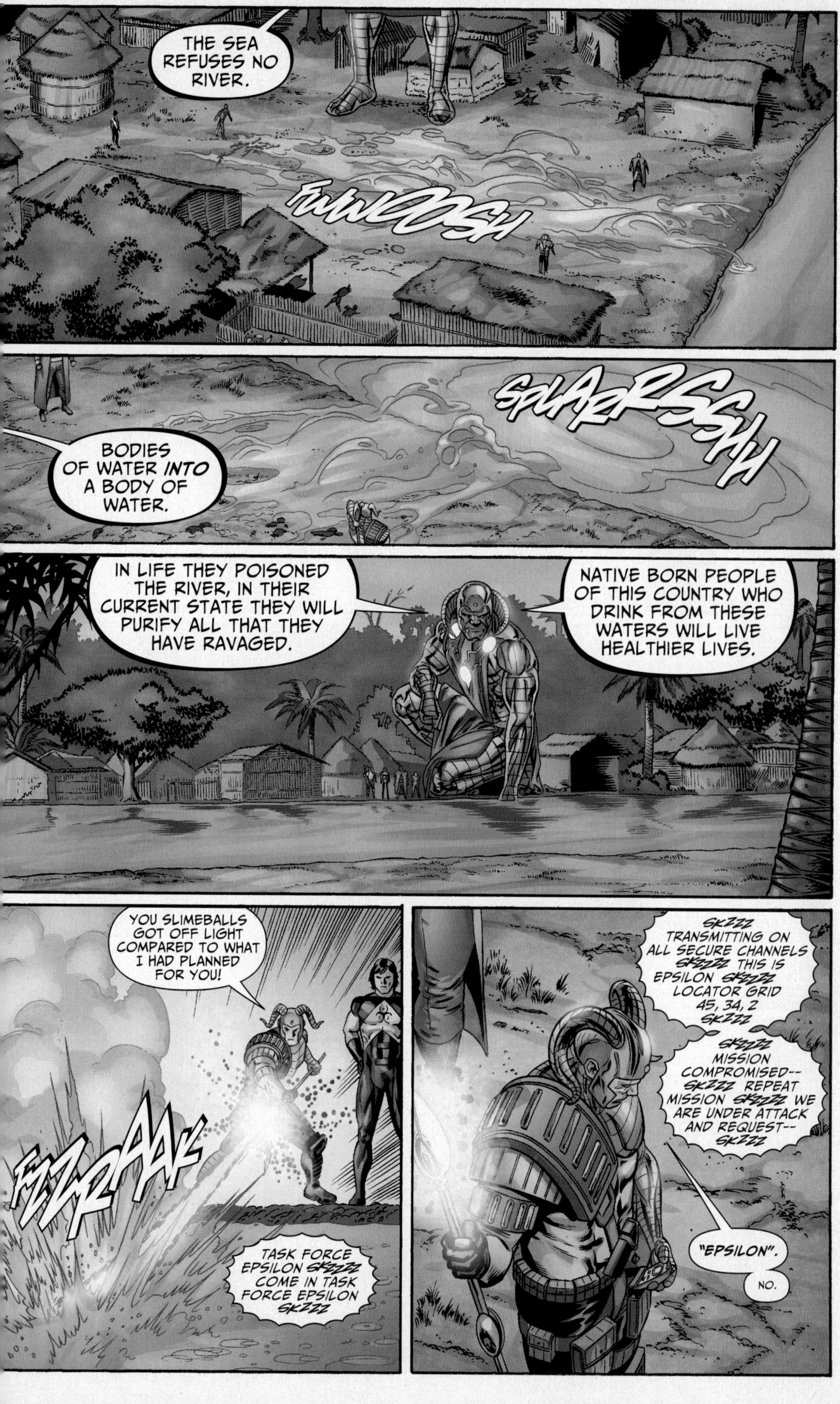
THE SEA REFUSES NO RIVER.
FWWOOSH
SPLARRSSHH
BODIES OF WATER *INTO* A BODY OF WATER.
IN LIFE THEY POISONED THE RIVER, IN THEIR CURRENT STATE THEY WILL PURIFY ALL THAT THEY HAVE RAVAGED.
NATIVE BORN PEOPLE OF THIS COUNTRY WHO DRINK FROM THESE WATERS WILL LIVE HEALTHIER LIVES.
YOU SLIMEBALLS GOT OFF LIGHT COMPARED TO WHAT I HAD PLANNED FOR YOU!
FZZRAAK
TASK FORCE EPSILON SKZZZZ COME IN TASK FORCE EPSILON SKZZZ
SKZZZ TRANSMITTING ON ALL SECURE CHANNELS SKZZZZ THIS IS EPSILON SKZZZZ LOCATOR GRID 45, 34, 2 SKZZZ
SKZZZZ MISSION COMPROMISED-- SKZZZ REPEAT MISSION SKZZZZ WE ARE UNDER ATTACK AND REQUEST-- SKZZZ
"EPSILON".
NO.

I HAVE TO GO. NOW.

WHAT? WHERE ARE YOU GOING?

THEY NEED MY HELP.

"THEY"?

MY OLD UNIT.

A MISSION'S GONE BAD. I HAVE TO GET TO THEM.

WITH GOG HEADING TO KAHNDAQ WE NEED TO STAY CLOSE--IT'S ALWAYS A HOTBED THERE, AND THAT WHOLE REGION IS STILL PRIMED FOR--

I UNDERSTAND WHAT YOU NEED TO DO.

BUT THESE ARE MY BROTHERS IN ARMS.

THEY'VE BEEN THERE TO SAVE ME.

I'M GONNA BE THERE TO SAVE THEM.

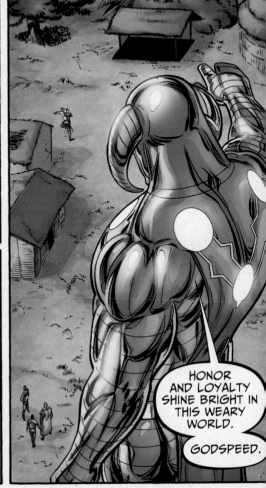

HONOR AND LOYALTY SHINE BRIGHT IN THIS WEARY WORLD.

GODSPEED.

I'M SORRY, BUT THEY TAKE TOP PRIORITY. I'LL SYNC UP WITH YOU SOON!

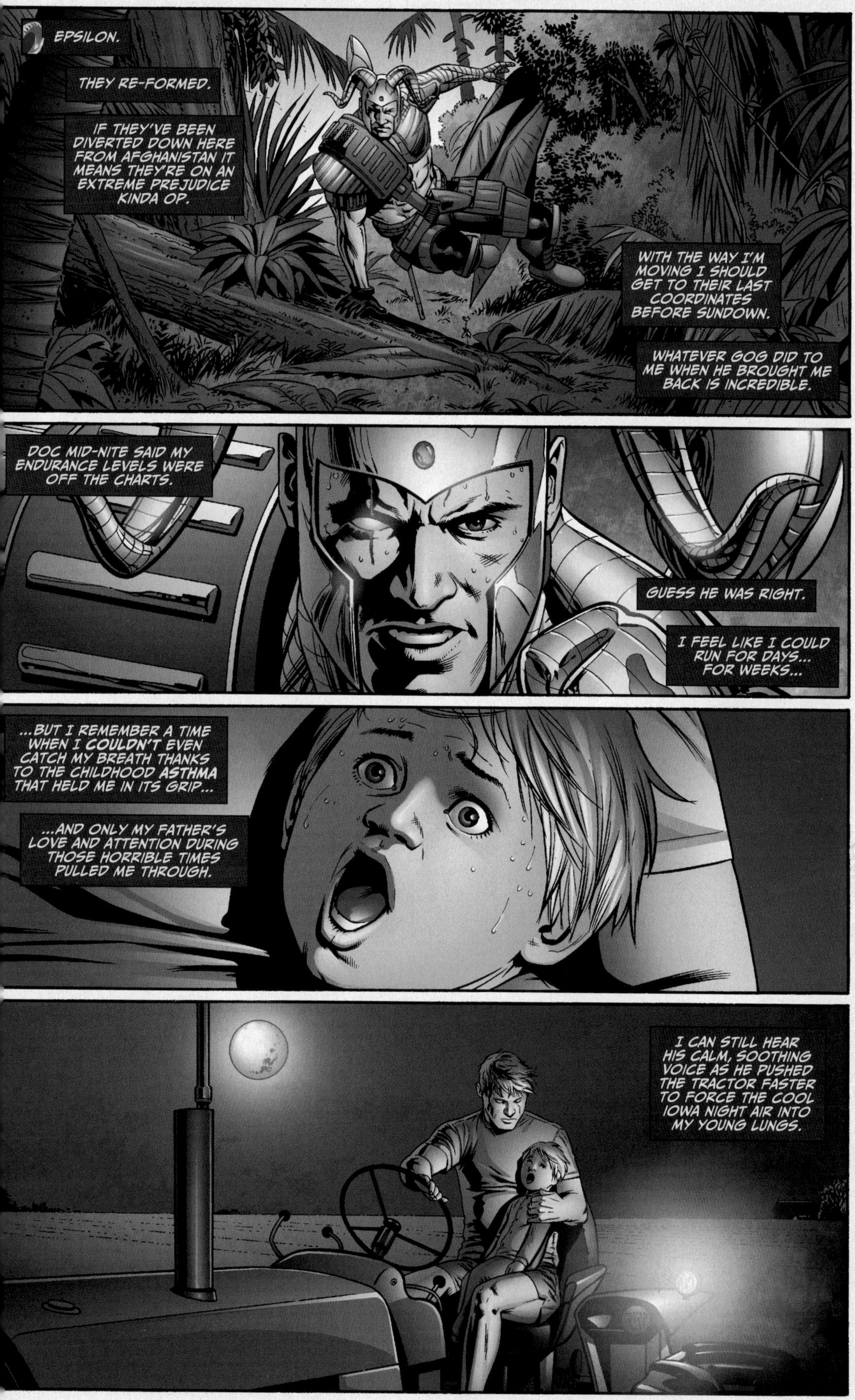
EPSILON.
THEY RE-FORMED.
IF THEY'VE BEEN DIVERTED DOWN HERE FROM AFGHANISTAN IT MEANS THEY'RE ON AN EXTREME PREJUDICE KINDA OP.
WITH THE WAY I'M MOVING I SHOULD GET TO THEIR LAST COORDINATES BEFORE SUNDOWN.
WHATEVER GOG DID TO ME WHEN HE BROUGHT ME BACK IS INCREDIBLE.
DOC MID-NITE SAID MY ENDURANCE LEVELS WERE OFF THE CHARTS.
GUESS HE WAS RIGHT.
I FEEL LIKE I COULD RUN FOR DAYS... FOR WEEKS...
...BUT I REMEMBER A TIME WHEN I COULDN'T EVEN CATCH MY BREATH THANKS TO THE CHILDHOOD ASTHMA THAT HELD ME IN ITS GRIP...
...AND ONLY MY FATHER'S LOVE AND ATTENTION DURING THOSE HORRIBLE TIMES PULLED ME THROUGH.
I CAN STILL HEAR HIS CALM, SOOTHING VOICE AS HE PUSHED THE TRACTOR FASTER TO FORCE THE COOL IOWA NIGHT AIR INTO MY YOUNG LUNGS.

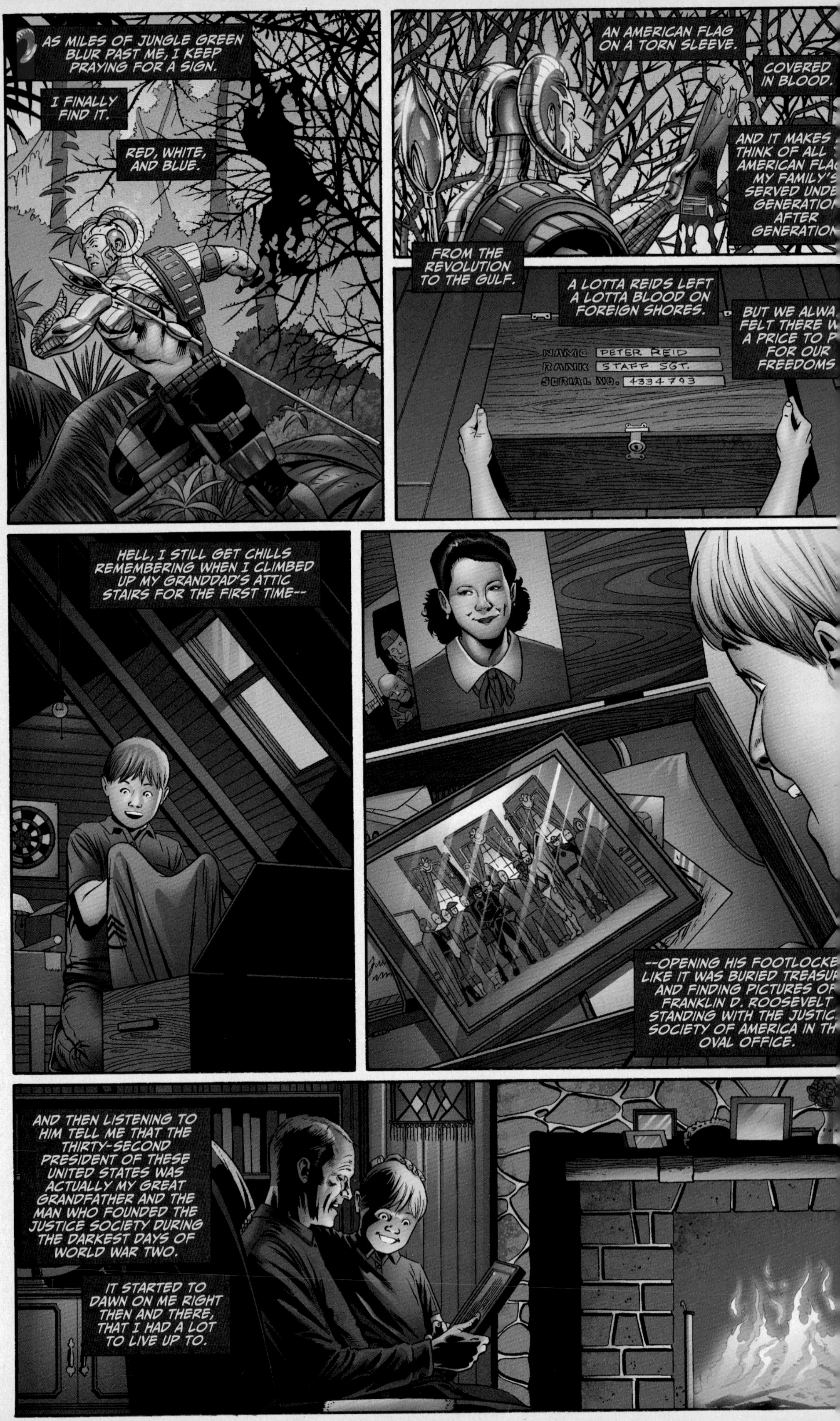
AS MILES OF JUNGLE GREEN BLUR PAST ME, I KEEP PRAYING FOR A SIGN.
I FINALLY FIND IT.
RED, WHITE, AND BLUE.
AN AMERICAN FLAG ON A TORN SLEEVE.
COVERED IN BLOOD.
AND IT MAKES THINK OF ALL AMERICAN FLA MY FAMILY'S SERVED UNDE GENERATIO AFTER GENERATIO
FROM THE REVOLUTION TO THE GULF.
A LOTTA REIDS LEFT A LOTTA BLOOD ON FOREIGN SHORES.
NAME PETER REID
RANK STAFF SGT.
SERIAL NO. 4334793
BUT WE ALWA FELT THERE W A PRICE TO P FOR OUR FREEDOMS
HELL, I STILL GET CHILLS REMEMBERING WHEN I CLIMBED UP MY GRANDDAD'S ATTIC STAIRS FOR THE FIRST TIME--
--OPENING HIS FOOTLOCKE LIKE IT WAS BURIED TREASU AND FINDING PICTURES OF FRANKLIN D. ROOSEVELT STANDING WITH THE JUSTIC SOCIETY OF AMERICA IN TH OVAL OFFICE.
AND THEN LISTENING TO HIM TELL ME THAT THE THIRTY-SECOND PRESIDENT OF THESE UNITED STATES WAS ACTUALLY MY GREAT GRANDFATHER AND THE MAN WHO FOUNDED THE JUSTICE SOCIETY DURING THE DARKEST DAYS OF WORLD WAR TWO.
IT STARTED TO DAWN ON ME RIGHT THEN AND THERE, THAT I HAD A LOT TO LIVE UP TO.

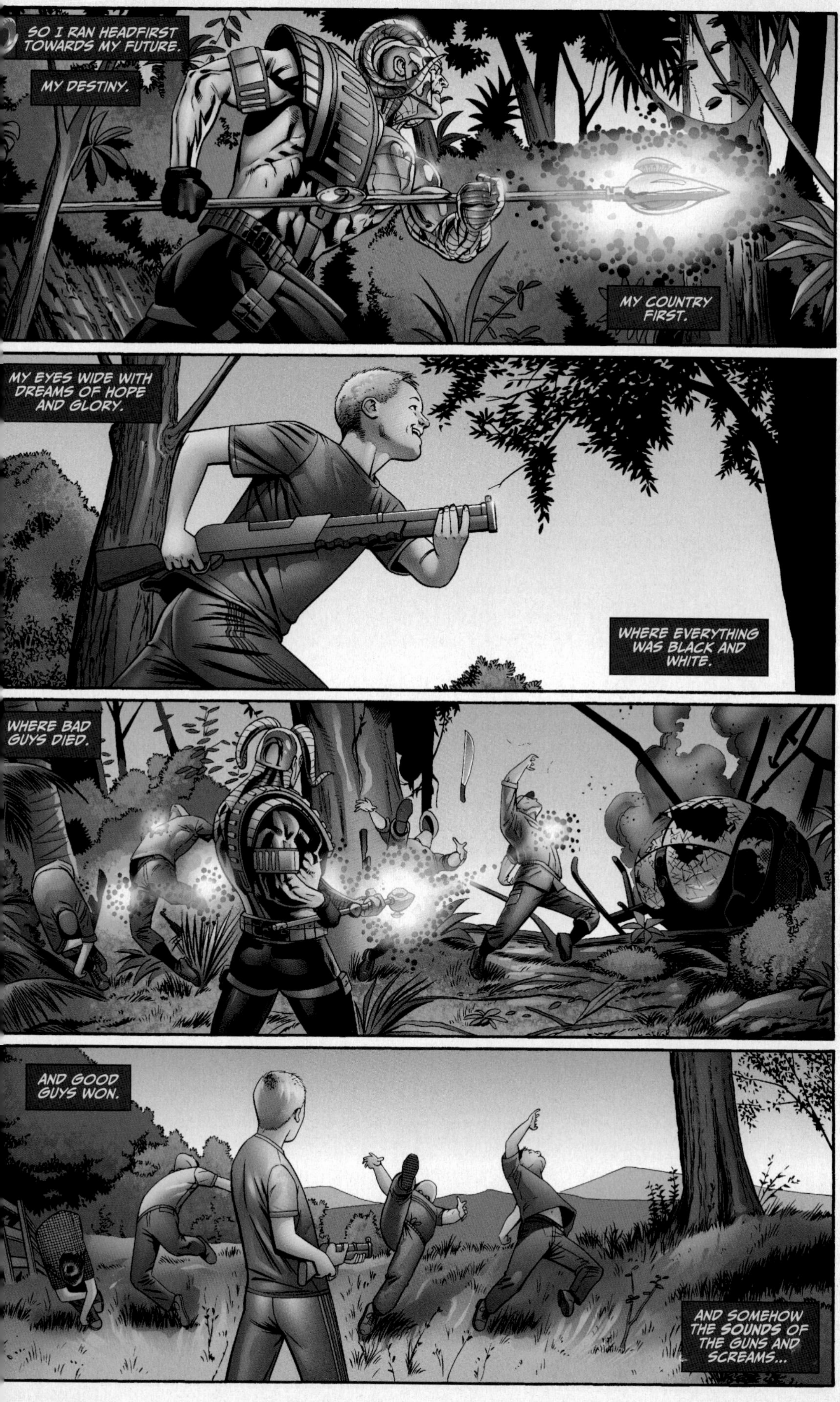
SO I RAN HEADFIRST TOWARDS MY FUTURE.
MY DESTINY.
MY COUNTRY FIRST.
MY EYES WIDE WITH DREAMS OF HOPE AND GLORY.
WHERE EVERYTHING WAS BLACK AND WHITE.
WHERE BAD GUYS DIED.
AND GOOD GUYS WON.
AND SOMEHOW THE SOUNDS OF THE GUNS AND SCREAMS...

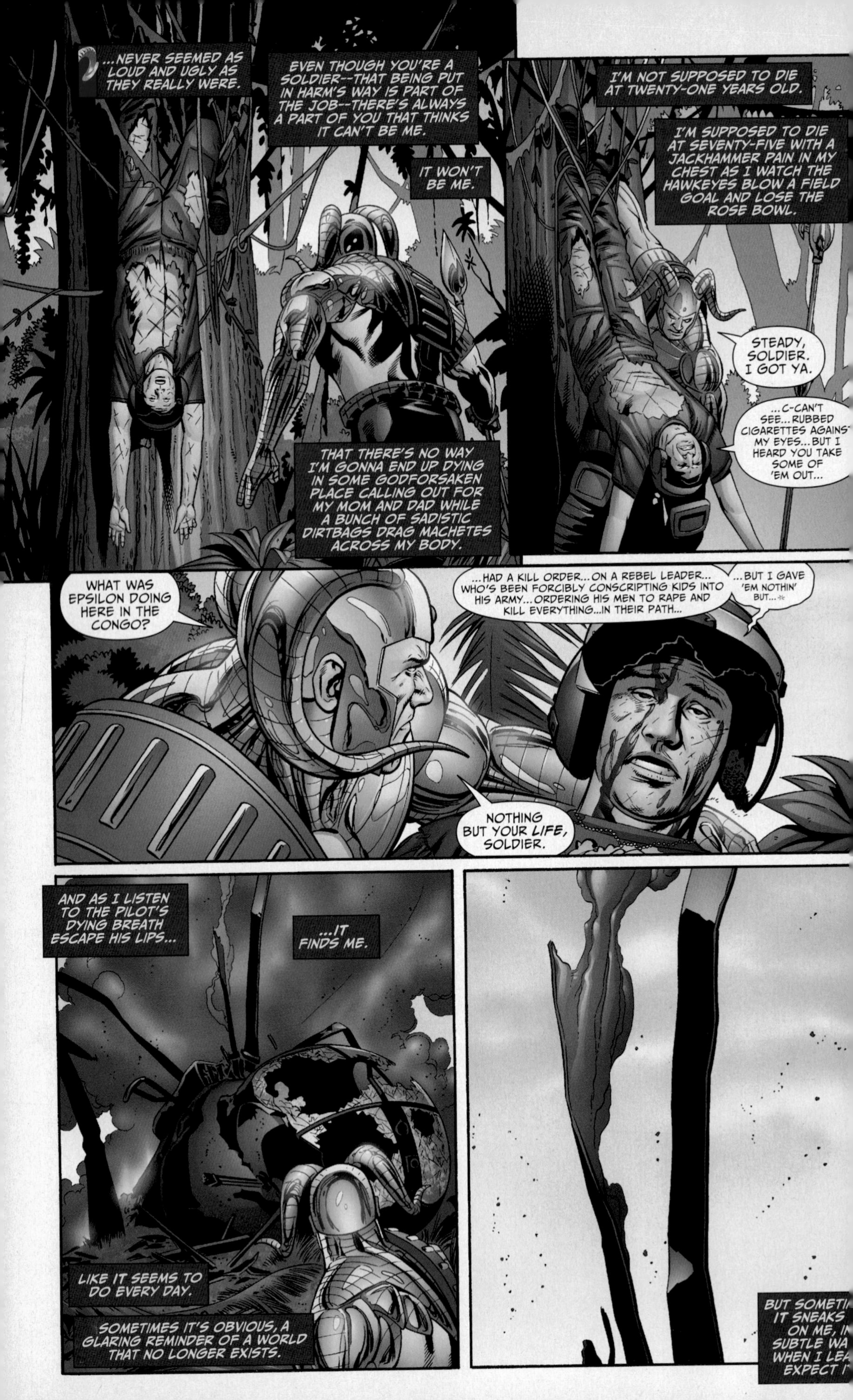
...NEVER SEEMED AS LOUD AND UGLY AS THEY REALLY WERE.
EVEN THOUGH YOU'RE A SOLDIER--THAT BEING PUT IN HARM'S WAY IS PART OF THE JOB--THERE'S ALWAYS A PART OF YOU THAT THINKS IT CAN'T BE ME.
IT WON'T BE ME.
THAT THERE'S NO WAY I'M GONNA END UP DYING IN SOME GODFORSAKEN PLACE CALLING OUT FOR MY MOM AND DAD WHILE A BUNCH OF SADISTIC DIRTBAGS DRAG MACHETES ACROSS MY BODY.
I'M NOT SUPPOSED TO DIE AT TWENTY-ONE YEARS OLD.
I'M SUPPOSED TO DIE AT SEVENTY-FIVE WITH A JACKHAMMER PAIN IN MY CHEST AS I WATCH THE HAWKEYES BLOW A FIELD GOAL AND LOSE THE ROSE BOWL.
STEADY, SOLDIER. I GOT YA.
...C-CAN'T SEE...RUBBED CIGARETTES AGAINST MY EYES...BUT I HEARD YOU TAKE SOME OF 'EM OUT...
WHAT WAS EPSILON DOING HERE IN THE CONGO?
...HAD A KILL ORDER...ON A REBEL LEADER... WHO'S BEEN FORCIBLY CONSCRIPTING KIDS INTO HIS ARMY...ORDERING HIS MEN TO RAPE AND KILL EVERYTHING...IN THEIR PATH...
...BUT I GAVE 'EM NOTHIN' BUT...
NOTHING BUT YOUR LIFE, SOLDIER.
AND AS I LISTEN TO THE PILOT'S DYING BREATH ESCAPE HIS LIPS...
...IT FINDS ME.
LIKE IT SEEMS TO DO EVERY DAY.
SOMETIMES IT'S OBVIOUS, A GLARING REMINDER OF A WORLD THAT NO LONGER EXISTS.

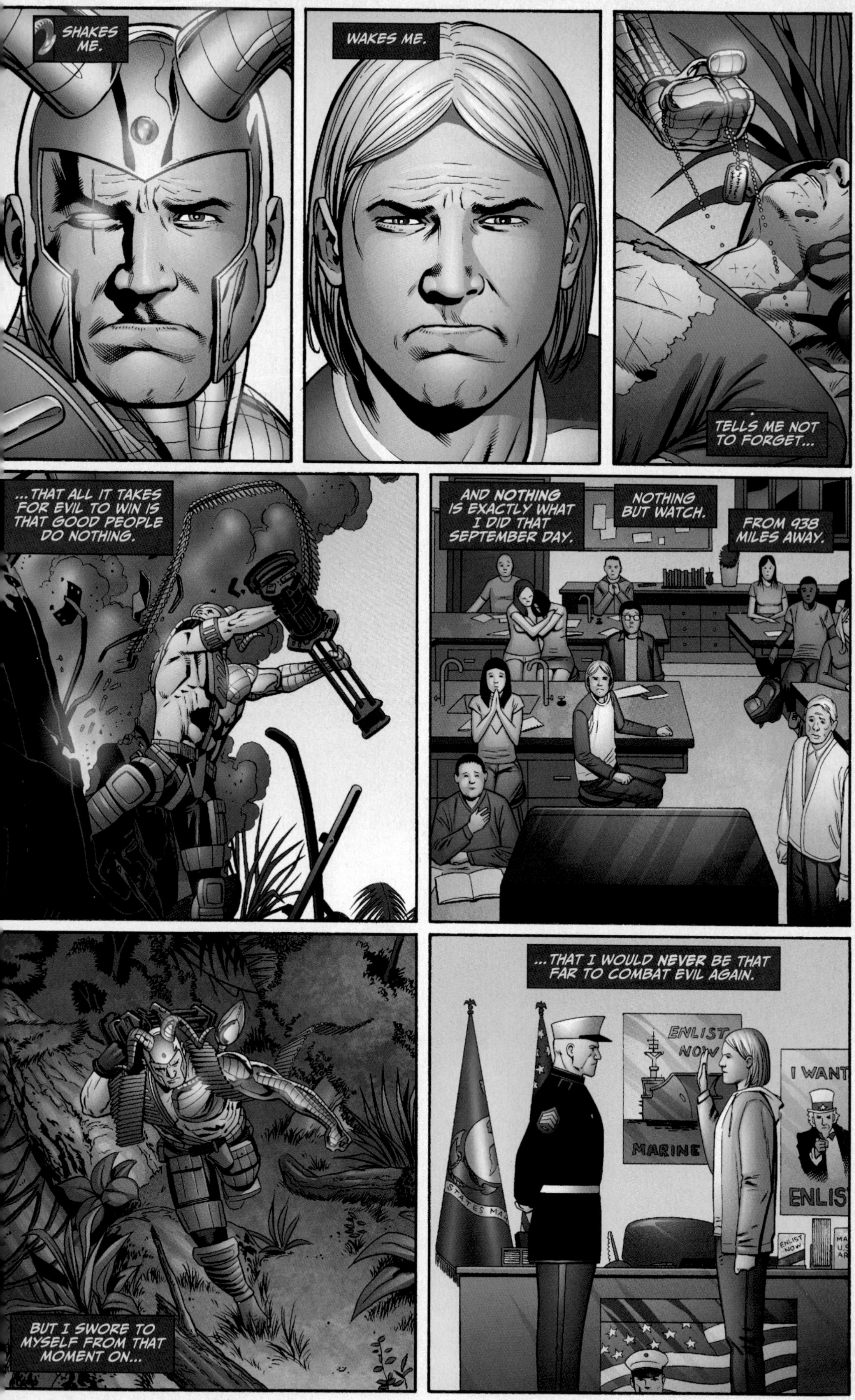
SHAKES ME.
WAKES ME.
TELLS ME NOT TO FORGET...
...THAT ALL IT TAKES FOR EVIL TO WIN IS THAT GOOD PEOPLE DO NOTHING.
AND NOTHING IS EXACTLY WHAT I DID THAT SEPTEMBER DAY.
NOTHING BUT WATCH.
FROM 938 MILES AWAY.
BUT I SWORE TO MYSELF FROM THAT MOMENT ON...
...THAT I WOULD NEVER BE THAT FAR TO COMBAT EVIL AGAIN.
ENLIST NOW
MARINE
I WANT
ENLIST
ENLIST NOW

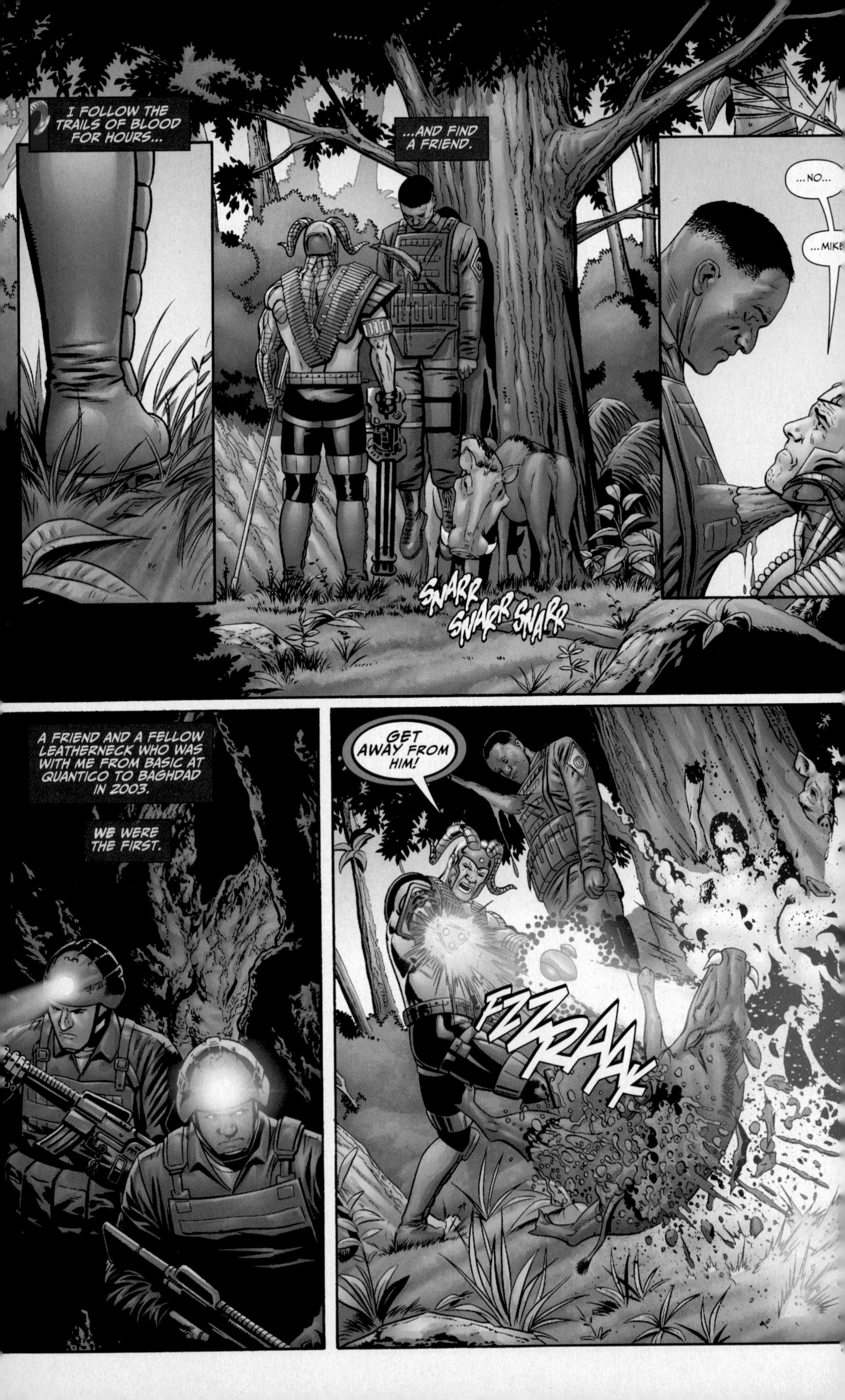
I FOLLOW THE TRAILS OF BLOOD FOR HOURS...
...AND FIND A FRIEND.
SNARR SNARR SNARR
...NO...
...MIKE
A FRIEND AND A FELLOW LEATHERNECK WHO WAS WITH ME FROM BASIC AT QUANTICO TO BAGHDAD IN 2003.
WE WERE THE FIRST.
GET AWAY FROM HIM!
FZZRAAK

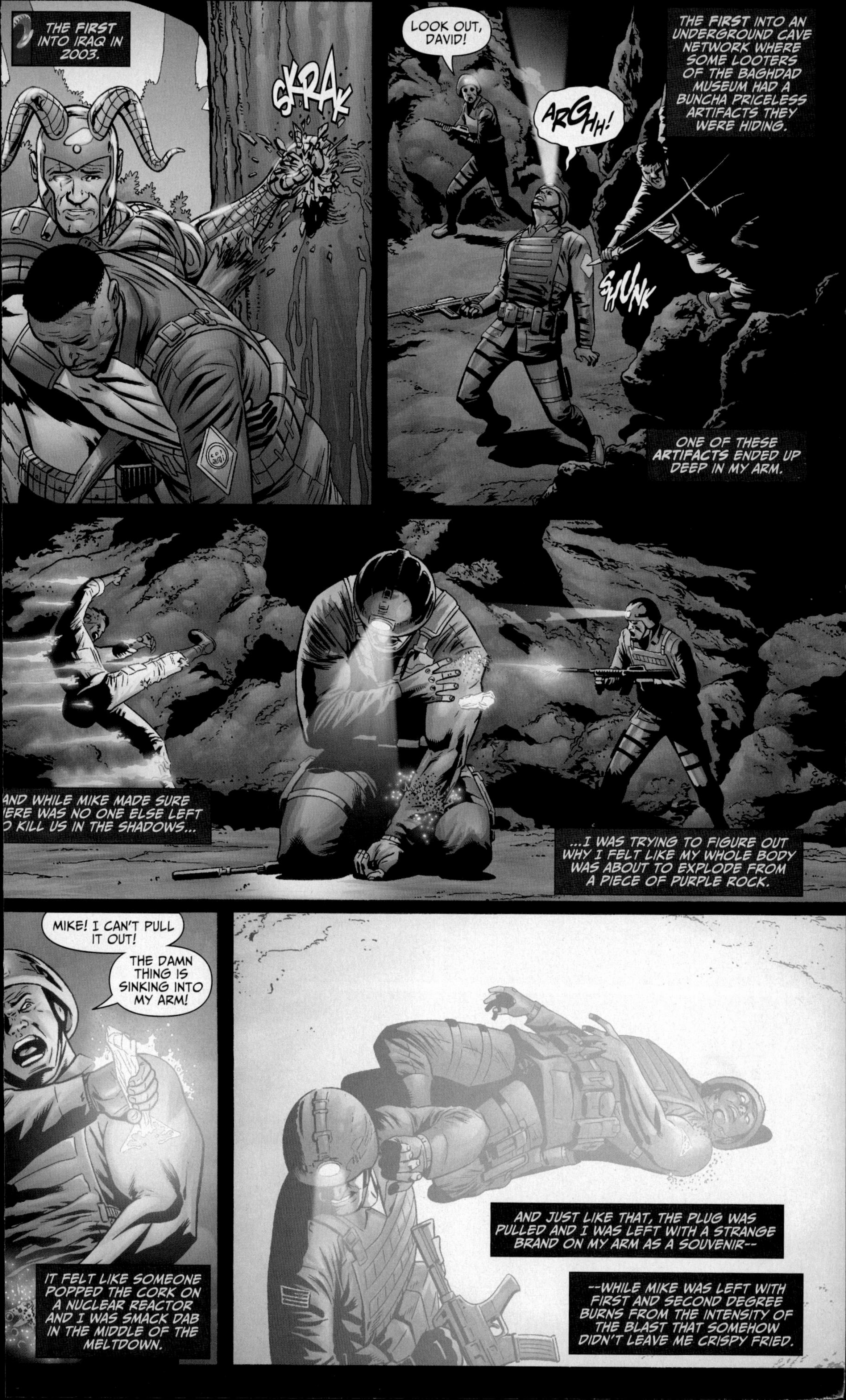

THE FIRST INTO IRAQ IN 2003.
SKRAK
LOOK OUT, DAVID!
THE FIRST INTO AN UNDERGROUND CAVE NETWORK WHERE SOME LOOTERS OF THE BAGHDAD MUSEUM HAD A BUNCHA PRICELESS ARTIFACTS THEY WERE HIDING.
ARGHH!
SHUNK
ONE OF THESE ARTIFACTS ENDED UP DEEP IN MY ARM.
AND WHILE MIKE MADE SURE THERE WAS NO ONE ELSE LEFT TO KILL US IN THE SHADOWS...
...I WAS TRYING TO FIGURE OUT WHY I FELT LIKE MY WHOLE BODY WAS ABOUT TO EXPLODE FROM A PIECE OF PURPLE ROCK.
MIKE! I CAN'T PULL IT OUT!
THE DAMN THING IS SINKING INTO MY ARM!
IT FELT LIKE SOMEONE POPPED THE CORK ON A NUCLEAR REACTOR AND I WAS SMACK DAB IN THE MIDDLE OF THE MELTDOWN.
AND JUST LIKE THAT, THE PLUG WAS PULLED AND I WAS LEFT WITH A STRANGE BRAND ON MY ARM AS A SOUVENIR--
--WHILE MIKE WAS LEFT WITH FIRST AND SECOND DEGREE BURNS FROM THE INTENSITY OF THE BLAST THAT SOMEHOW DIDN'T LEAVE ME CRISPY FRIED.

MIKE DONOVAN WAS A WARRIOR WHO WOULDN'T WANT ME WASTING TIME ON HIS LIFELESS BODY WHILE THERE STILL MAY BE AMERICAN LIVES TO SAVE.

I GIVE HIM HALF OF A VIKING FUNERAL, 'CAUSE THERE'S NO WAY IN HELL I'M LEAVING HIS BODY TO THE WILD ANIMALS.

I'LL REMEMBER HIM ALWAYS.

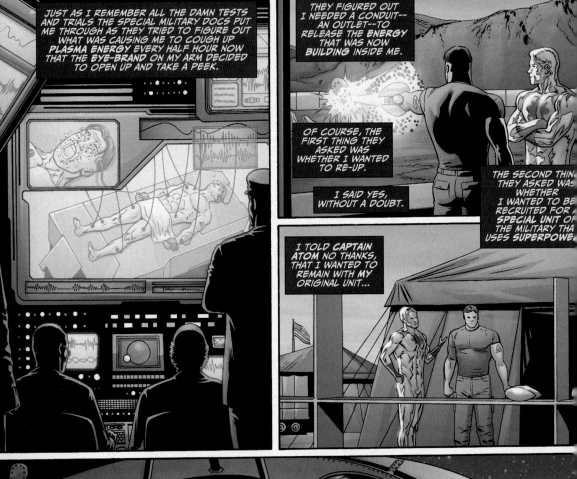

JUST AS I REMEMBER ALL THE DAMN TESTS AND TRIALS THE SPECIAL MILITARY DOCS PUT ME THROUGH AS THEY TRIED TO FIGURE OUT WHAT WAS CAUSING ME TO COUGH UP PLASMA ENERGY EVERY HALF HOUR NOW THAT THE EYE-BRAND ON MY ARM DECIDED TO OPEN UP AND TAKE A PEEK.

THEY FIGURED OUT I NEEDED A CONDUIT-- AN OUTLET--TO RELEASE THE ENERGY THAT WAS NOW BUILDING INSIDE ME.

OF COURSE, THE FIRST THING THEY ASKED WAS WHETHER I WANTED TO RE-UP.

I SAID YES, WITHOUT A DOUBT.

THE SECOND THING THEY ASKED WAS WHETHER I WANTED TO BE RECRUITED FOR A SPECIAL UNIT OF THE MILITARY THAT USES SUPERPOWE...

I TOLD CAPTAIN ATOM NO THANKS, THAT I WANTED TO REMAIN WITH MY ORIGINAL UNIT...

...WHICH HAD NOW FOLDED INTO AN ELITE BLACK OPS UNIT THAT WOULD ALWAYS BE IN THE THICK OF IT CALLED "EPSILON...

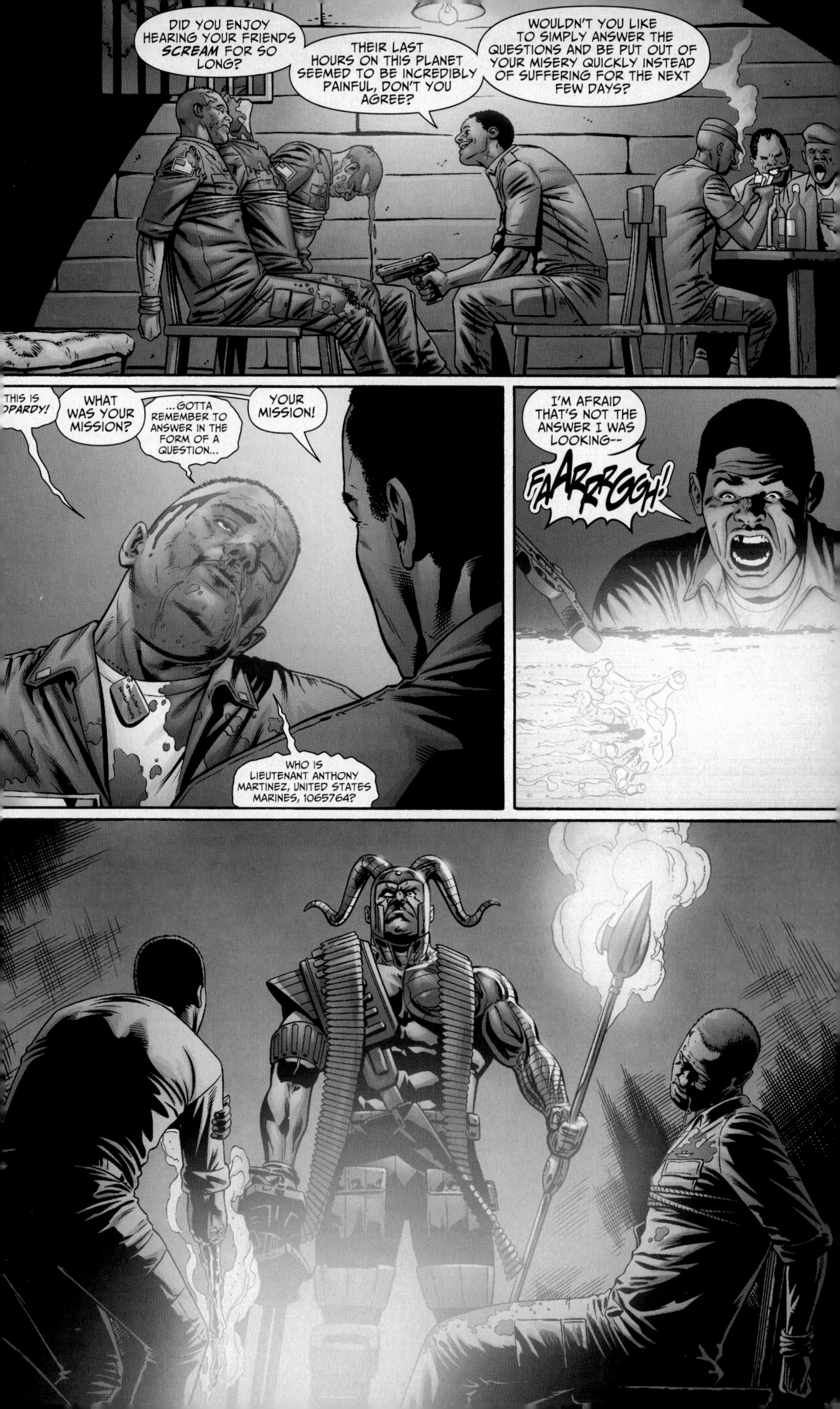

DID YOU ENJOY HEARING YOUR FRIENDS SCREAM FOR SO LONG?
THEIR LAST HOURS ON THIS PLANET SEEMED TO BE INCREDIBLY PAINFUL, DON'T YOU AGREE?
WOULDN'T YOU LIKE TO SIMPLY ANSWER THE QUESTIONS AND BE PUT OUT OF YOUR MISERY QUICKLY INSTEAD OF SUFFERING FOR THE NEXT FEW DAYS?
WHAT WAS YOUR MISSION?
...GOTTA REMEMBER TO ANSWER IN THE FORM OF A QUESTION...
YOUR MISSION!
WHO IS LIEUTENANT ANTHONY MARTINEZ, UNITED STATES MARINES, 1065764?
I'M AFRAID THAT'S NOT THE ANSWER I WAS LOOKING--
FAARRRGGH!

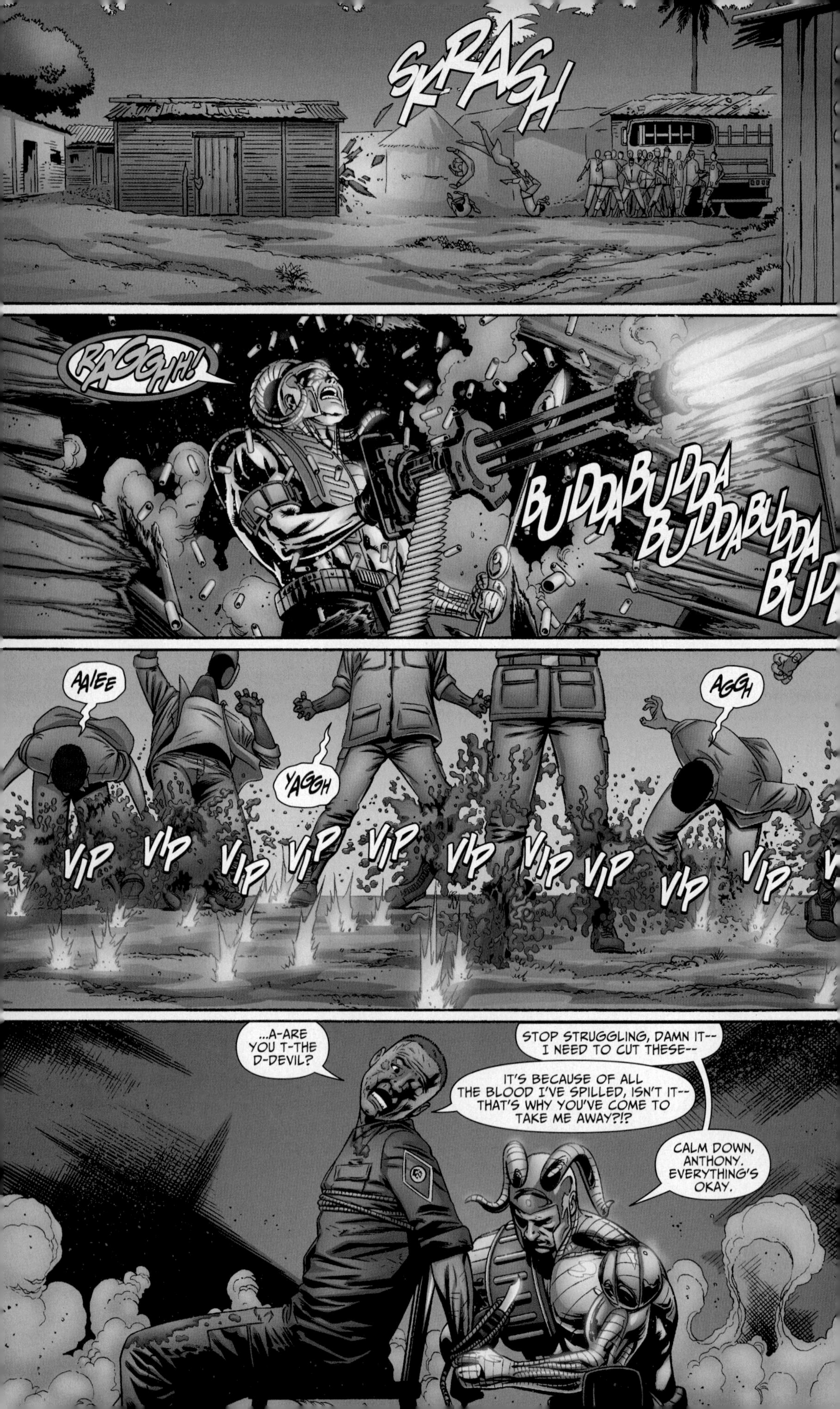
SKRASH
RAGGHH!
BUDDABUDDA BUDDABUDDA BUD
AAIEE
YAGGH
AGGH
VIP VIP VIP VIP VIP VIP VIP VIP VIP VIP
...A-ARE YOU T-THE D-DEVIL?
IT'S BECAUSE OF ALL THE BLOOD I'VE SPILLED, ISN'T IT-- THAT'S WHY YOU'VE COME TO TAKE ME AWAY?!?
STOP STRUGGLING, DAMN IT-- I NEED TO CUT THESE--
CALM DOWN, ANTHONY. EVERYTHING'S OKAY.

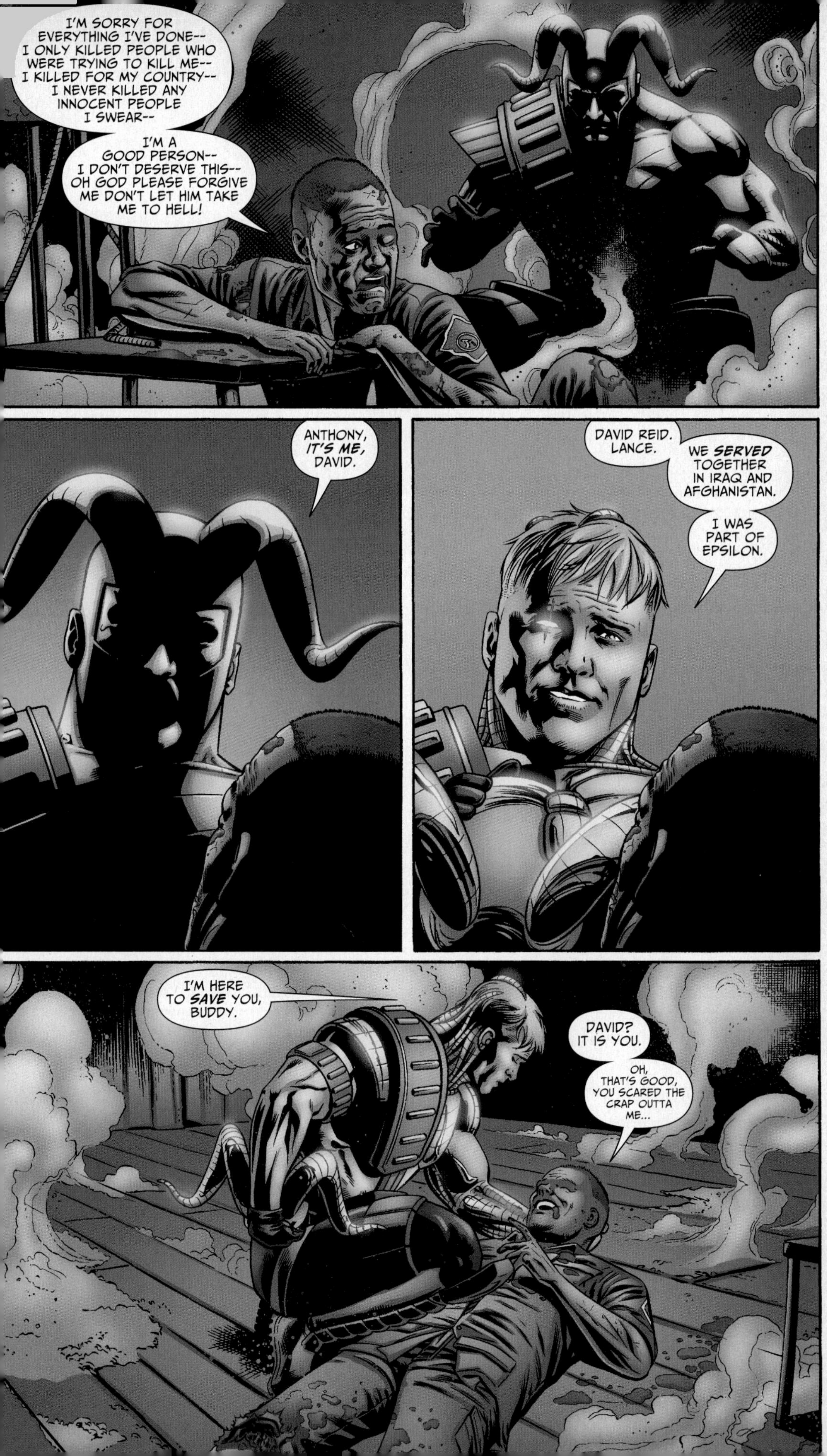
I'M SORRY FOR EVERYTHING I'VE DONE-- I ONLY KILLED PEOPLE WHO WERE TRYING TO KILL ME-- I KILLED FOR MY COUNTRY-- I NEVER KILLED ANY INNOCENT PEOPLE I SWEAR--
I'M A GOOD PERSON-- I DON'T DESERVE THIS-- OH GOD PLEASE FORGIVE ME DON'T LET HIM TAKE ME TO HELL!
ANTHONY, *IT'S ME,* DAVID.
DAVID REID. LANCE.
WE *SERVED* TOGETHER IN IRAQ AND AFGHANISTAN.
I WAS PART OF EPSILON.
I'M HERE TO *SAVE* YOU, BUDDY.
DAVID? IT IS YOU.
OH, THAT'S GOOD, YOU SCARED THE CRAP OUTTA ME...

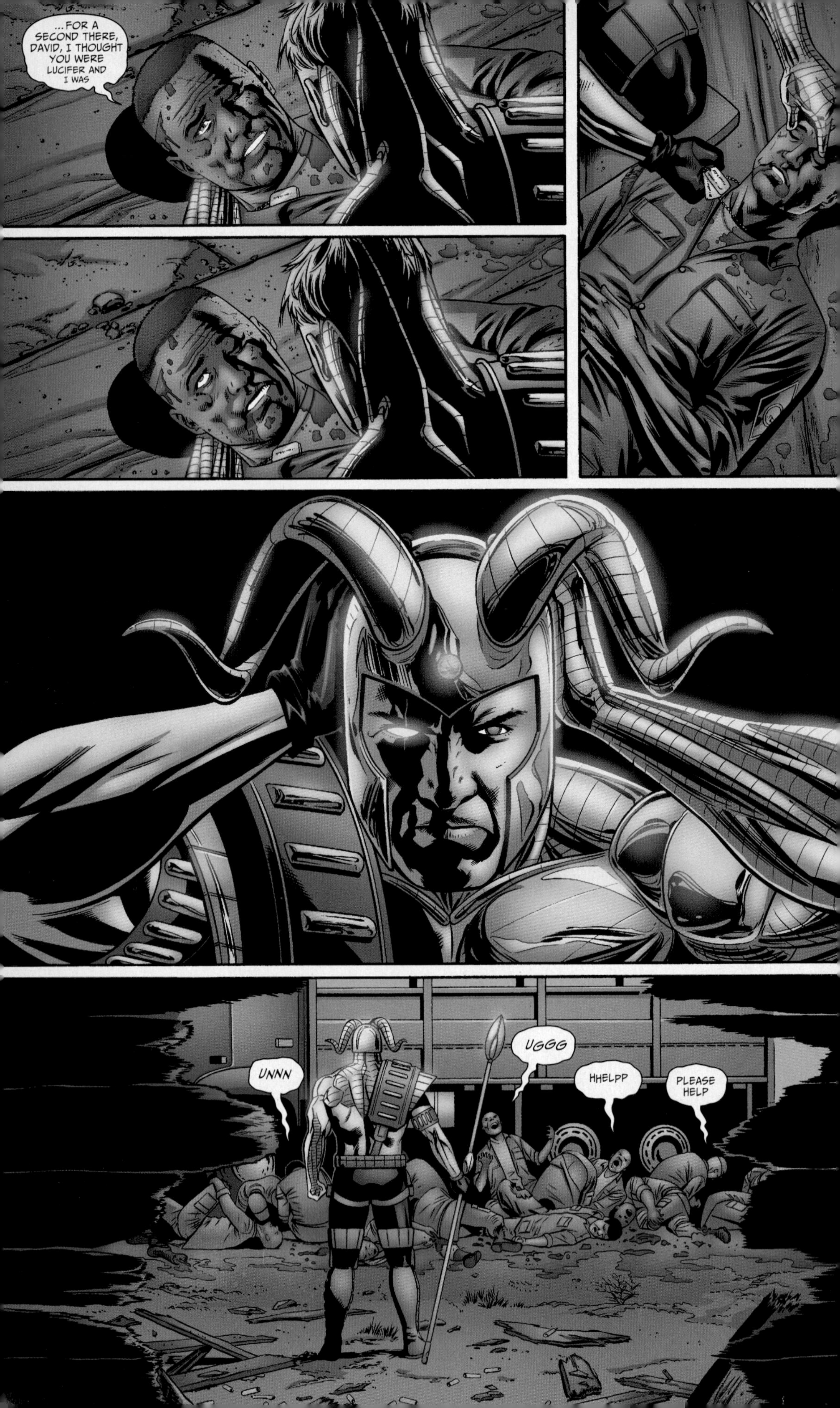
...FOR A SECOND THERE, DAVID, I THOUGHT YOU WERE LUCIFER AND I WAS
UNNN
UGGG
HHELPP
PLEASE HELP

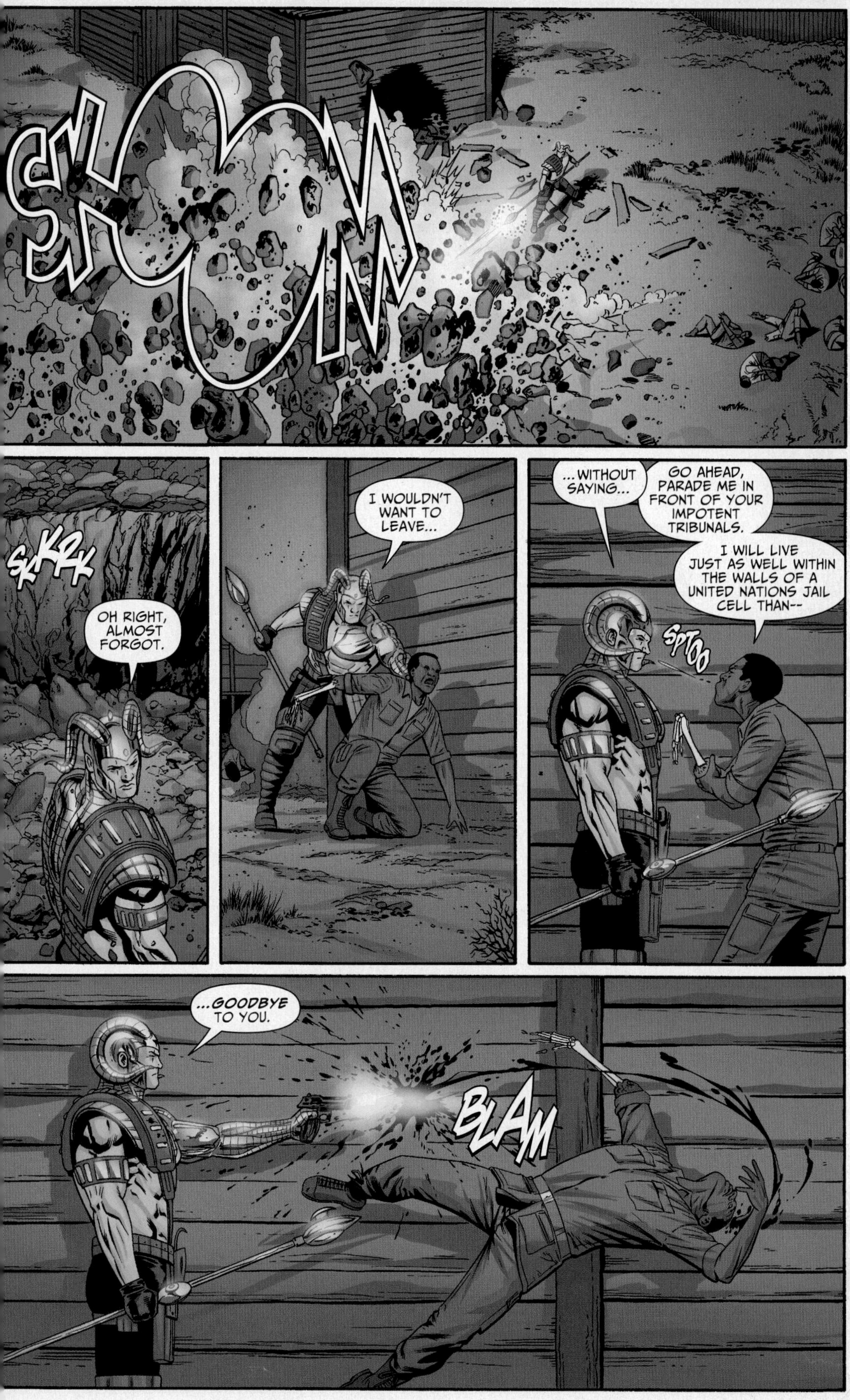
SKOOM
SKKRK
OH RIGHT, ALMOST FORGOT.
I WOULDN'T WANT TO LEAVE...
...WITHOUT SAYING...
GO AHEAD, PARADE ME IN FRONT OF YOUR IMPOTENT TRIBUNALS.
I WILL LIVE JUST AS WELL WITHIN THE WALLS OF A UNITED NATIONS JAIL CELL THAN--
SPTOO
...GOODBYE TO YOU.
BLAM

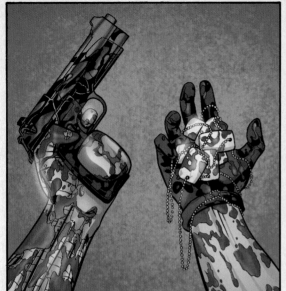

W-WHAT ABOUT US?

THE HOLE.

ROLL INTO IT.

I'M SURE IF YOU USE YOUR HEADS, SOME OF YOU'LL BE ABLE TO CRAWL OUT AND GET HELP.

...PLEASE DON'T LEAVE US HERE...

...THE SMELL OF BLOOD... THE WILD ANIMALS... THEY'LL EAT US ALIVE...

YES.

I HOPE SO.

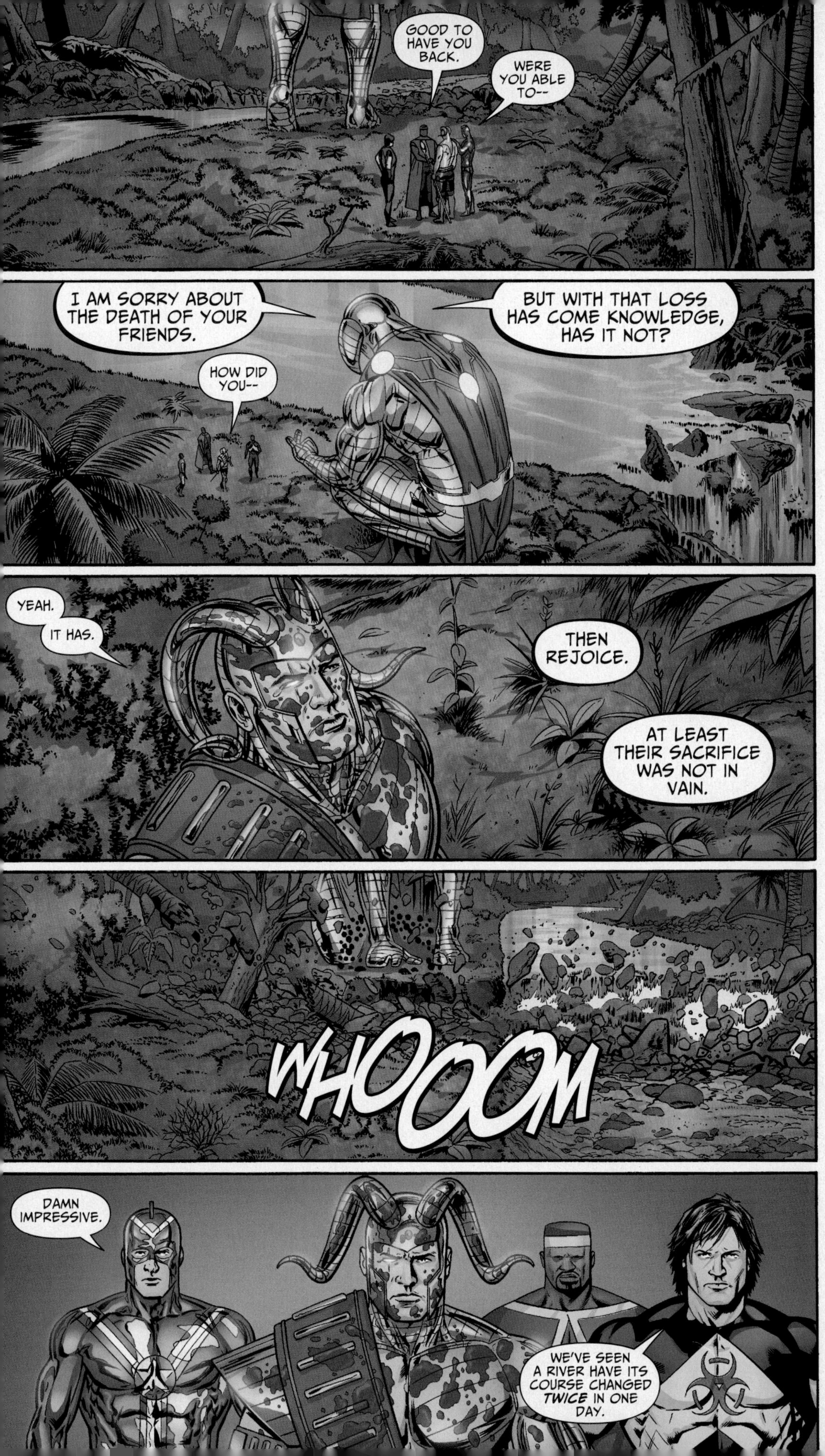
GOOD TO HAVE YOU BACK.
WERE YOU ABLE TO--
I AM SORRY ABOUT THE DEATH OF YOUR FRIENDS.
BUT WITH THAT LOSS HAS COME KNOWLEDGE, HAS IT NOT?
HOW DID YOU--
YEAH.
IT HAS.
THEN REJOICE.
AT LEAST THEIR SACRIFICE WAS NOT IN VAIN.
WHOOOOM
DAMN IMPRESSIVE.
WE'VE SEEN A RIVER HAVE ITS COURSE CHANGED *TWICE* IN ONE DAY.

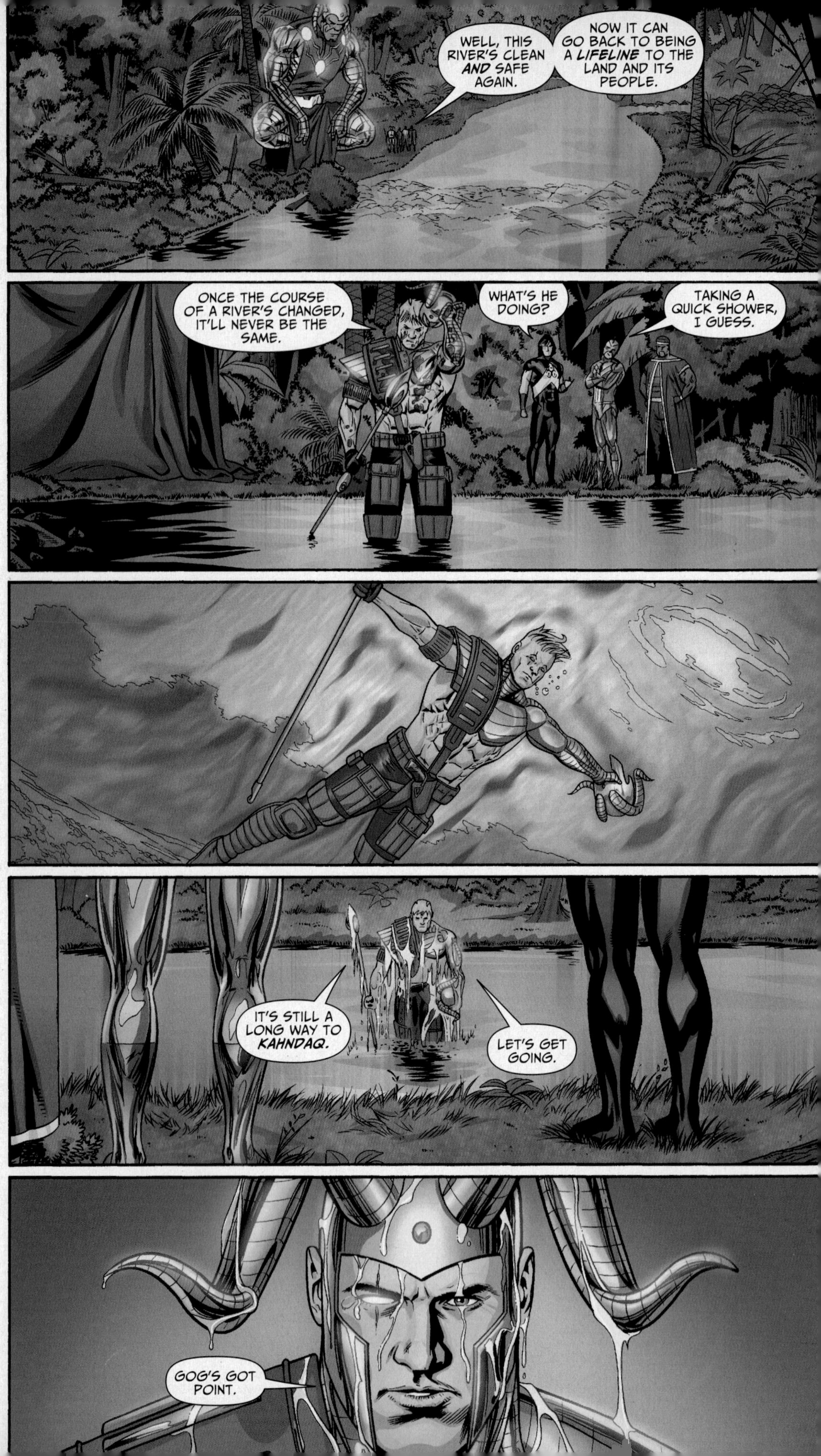
WELL, THIS RIVER'S CLEAN AND SAFE AGAIN.
NOW IT CAN GO BACK TO BEING A LIFELINE TO THE LAND AND ITS PEOPLE.
ONCE THE COURSE OF A RIVER'S CHANGED, IT'LL NEVER BE THE SAME.
WHAT'S HE DOING?
TAKING A QUICK SHOWER, I GUESS.
IT'S STILL A LONG WAY TO KAHNDAQ.
LET'S GET GOING.
GOG'S GOT POINT.

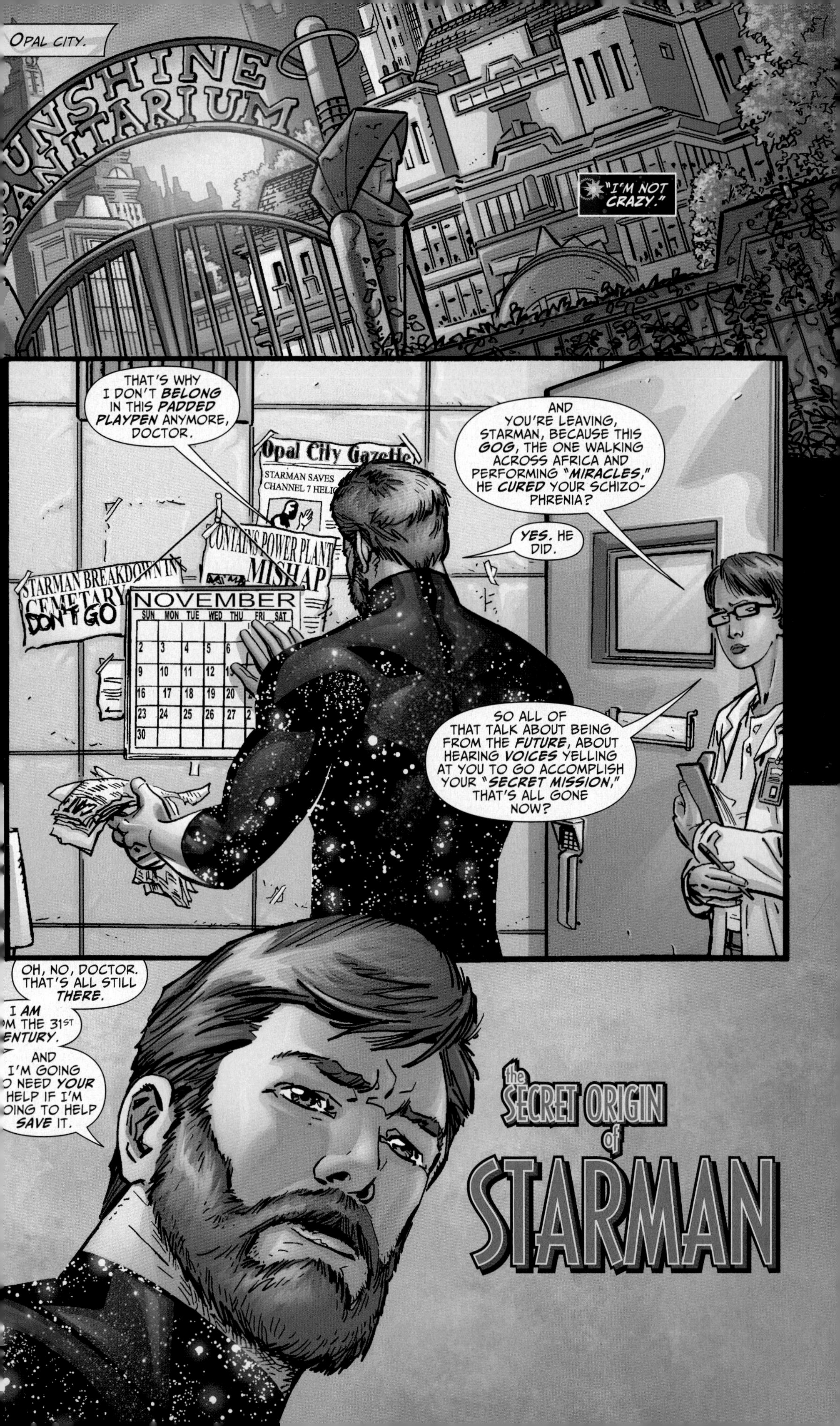
OPAL CITY.
SUNSHINE SANITARIUM
"I'M NOT CRAZY."
THAT'S WHY I DON'T BELONG IN THIS PADDED PLAYPEN ANYMORE, DOCTOR.
Opal City Gazette
STARMAN SAVES CHANNEL 7 HELIC
CONTAINS POWER PLANT MISHAP
STARMAN BREAKDOWN IN CEMETARY
DON'T GO
NOVEMBER
SUN MON TUE WED THU FRI SAT
AND YOU'RE LEAVING, STARMAN, BECAUSE THIS GOG, THE ONE WALKING ACROSS AFRICA AND PERFORMING "MIRACLES," HE CURED YOUR SCHIZOPHRENIA?
YES. HE DID.
SO ALL OF THAT TALK ABOUT BEING FROM THE FUTURE, ABOUT HEARING VOICES YELLING AT YOU TO GO ACCOMPLISH YOUR "SECRET MISSION," THAT'S ALL GONE NOW?
OH, NO, DOCTOR. THAT'S ALL STILL THERE.
I AM M THE 31ST ENTURY.
AND I'M GOING NEED YOUR HELP IF I'M OING TO HELP SAVE IT.
the SECRET ORIGIN of STARMAN

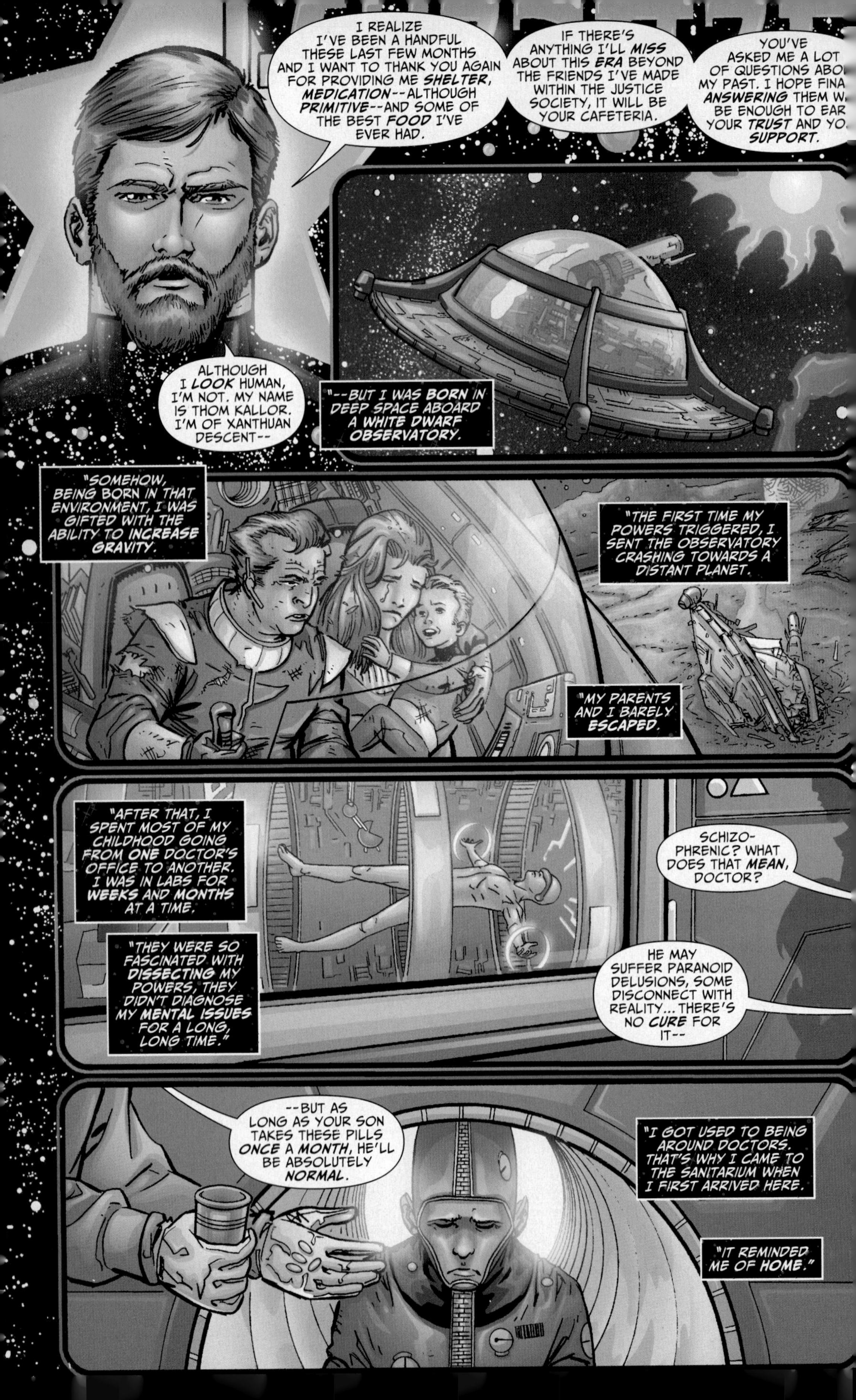
I REALIZE I'VE BEEN A HANDFUL THESE LAST FEW MONTHS AND I WANT TO THANK YOU AGAIN FOR PROVIDING ME SHELTER, MEDICATION--ALTHOUGH PRIMITIVE--AND SOME OF THE BEST FOOD I'VE EVER HAD.
IF THERE'S ANYTHING I'LL MISS ABOUT THIS ERA BEYOND THE FRIENDS I'VE MADE WITHIN THE JUSTICE SOCIETY, IT WILL BE YOUR CAFETERIA.
YOU'VE ASKED ME A LOT OF QUESTIONS ABO MY PAST. I HOPE FINA ANSWERING THEM W BE ENOUGH TO EAR YOUR TRUST AND YO SUPPORT.
ALTHOUGH I LOOK HUMAN, I'M NOT. MY NAME IS THOM KALLOR. I'M OF XANTHUAN DESCENT--
"--BUT I WAS BORN IN DEEP SPACE ABOARD A WHITE DWARF OBSERVATORY.
"SOMEHOW, BEING BORN IN THAT ENVIRONMENT, I WAS GIFTED WITH THE ABILITY TO INCREASE GRAVITY.
"THE FIRST TIME MY POWERS TRIGGERED, I SENT THE OBSERVATORY CRASHING TOWARDS A DISTANT PLANET.
"MY PARENTS AND I BARELY ESCAPED.
"AFTER THAT, I SPENT MOST OF MY CHILDHOOD GOING FROM ONE DOCTOR'S OFFICE TO ANOTHER. I WAS IN LABS FOR WEEKS AND MONTHS AT A TIME.
"THEY WERE SO FASCINATED WITH DISSECTING MY POWERS, THEY DIDN'T DIAGNOSE MY MENTAL ISSUES FOR A LONG, LONG TIME."
SCHIZO-PHRENIC? WHAT DOES THAT MEAN, DOCTOR?
HE MAY SUFFER PARANOID DELUSIONS, SOME DISCONNECT WITH REALITY... THERE'S NO CURE FOR IT--
--BUT AS LONG AS YOUR SON TAKES THESE PILLS ONCE A MONTH, HE'LL BE ABSOLUTELY NORMAL.
"I GOT USED TO BEING AROUND DOCTORS. THAT'S WHY I CAME TO THE SANITARIUM WHEN I FIRST ARRIVED HERE.
"IT REMINDED ME OF HOME."

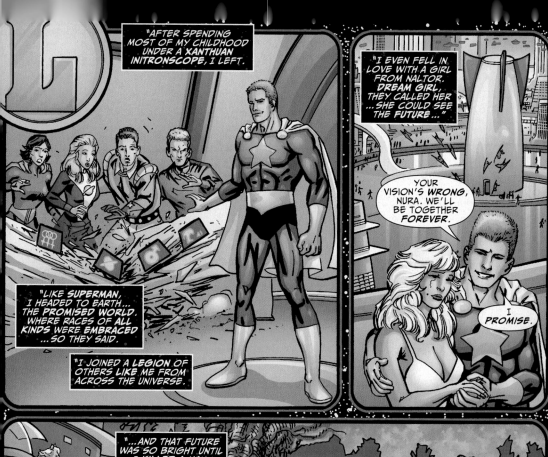

"AFTER SPENDING MOST OF MY CHILDHOOD UNDER A XANTHUAN INITRONSCOPE, I LEFT.

"LIKE SUPERMAN, I HEADED TO EARTH... THE PROMISED WORLD. WHERE RACES OF ALL KINDS WERE EMBRACED ...SO THEY SAID.

"I JOINED A LEGION OF OTHERS LIKE ME FROM ACROSS THE UNIVERSE.

"I EVEN FELL IN LOVE WITH A GIRL FROM NALTOR. DREAM GIRL, THEY CALLED HER ...SHE COULD SEE THE FUTURE..."

YOUR VISION'S WRONG, NURA. WE'LL BE TOGETHER FOREVER.

I PROMISE.

"...AND THAT FUTURE WAS SO BRIGHT UNTIL I KILLED A MAN.

"IT WAS SELF-DEFENSE, BUT THAT DIDN'T MATTER.

"I WAS VOTED OUT."

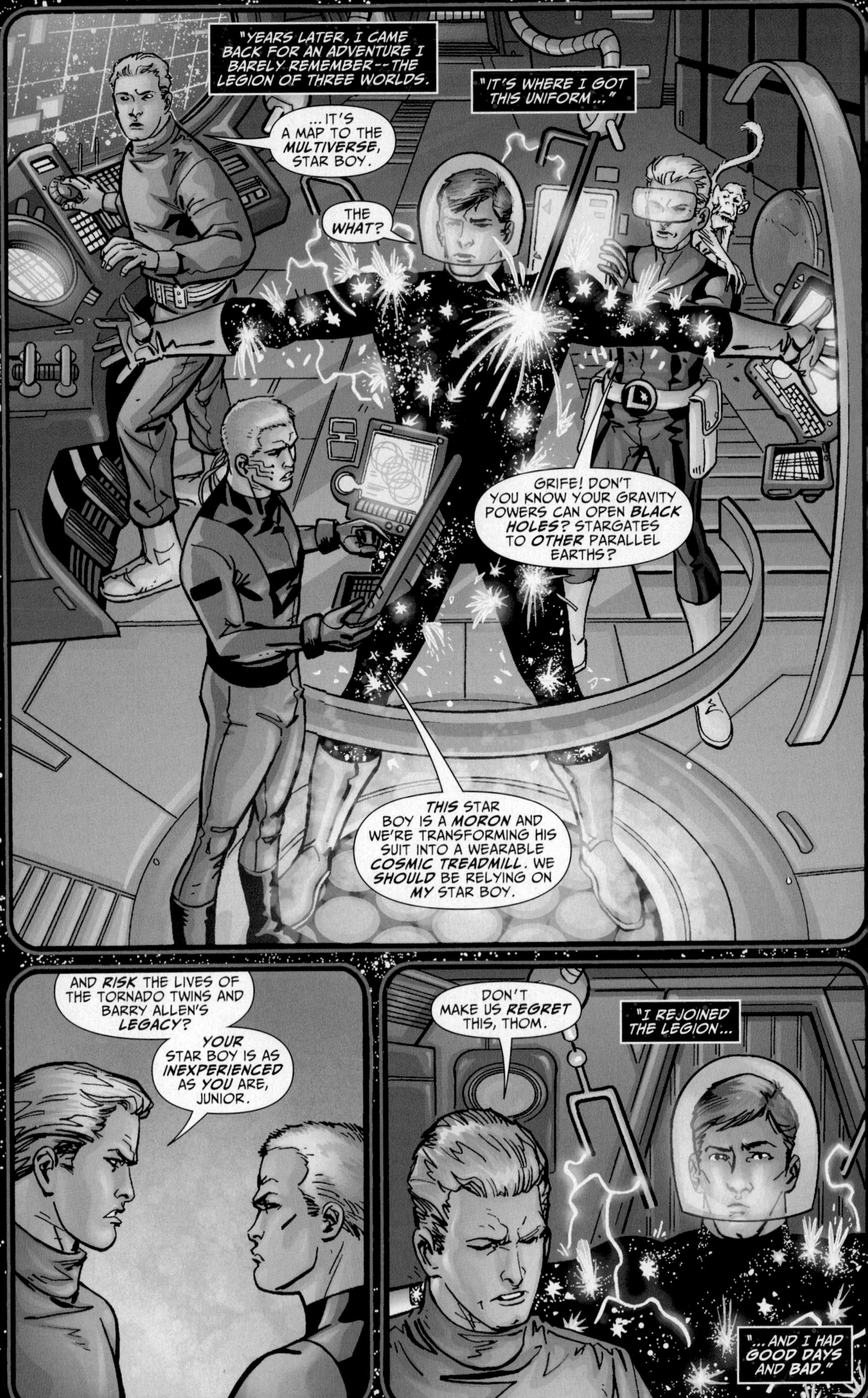
"YEARS LATER, I CAME BACK FOR AN ADVENTURE I BARELY REMEMBER--THE LEGION OF THREE WORLDS.
"IT'S WHERE I GOT THIS UNIFORM..."
...IT'S A MAP TO THE MULTIVERSE, STAR BOY.
THE WHAT?
GRIFE! DON'T YOU KNOW YOUR GRAVITY POWERS CAN OPEN BLACK HOLES? STARGATES TO OTHER PARALLEL EARTHS?
THIS STAR BOY IS A MORON AND WE'RE TRANSFORMING HIS SUIT INTO A WEARABLE COSMIC TREADMILL. WE SHOULD BE RELYING ON MY STAR BOY.
AND RISK THE LIVES OF THE TORNADO TWINS AND BARRY ALLEN'S LEGACY?
YOUR STAR BOY IS AS INEXPERIENCED AS YOU ARE, JUNIOR.
DON'T MAKE US REGRET THIS, THOM.
"I REJOINED THE LEGION...
"...AND I HAD GOOD DAYS AND BAD."

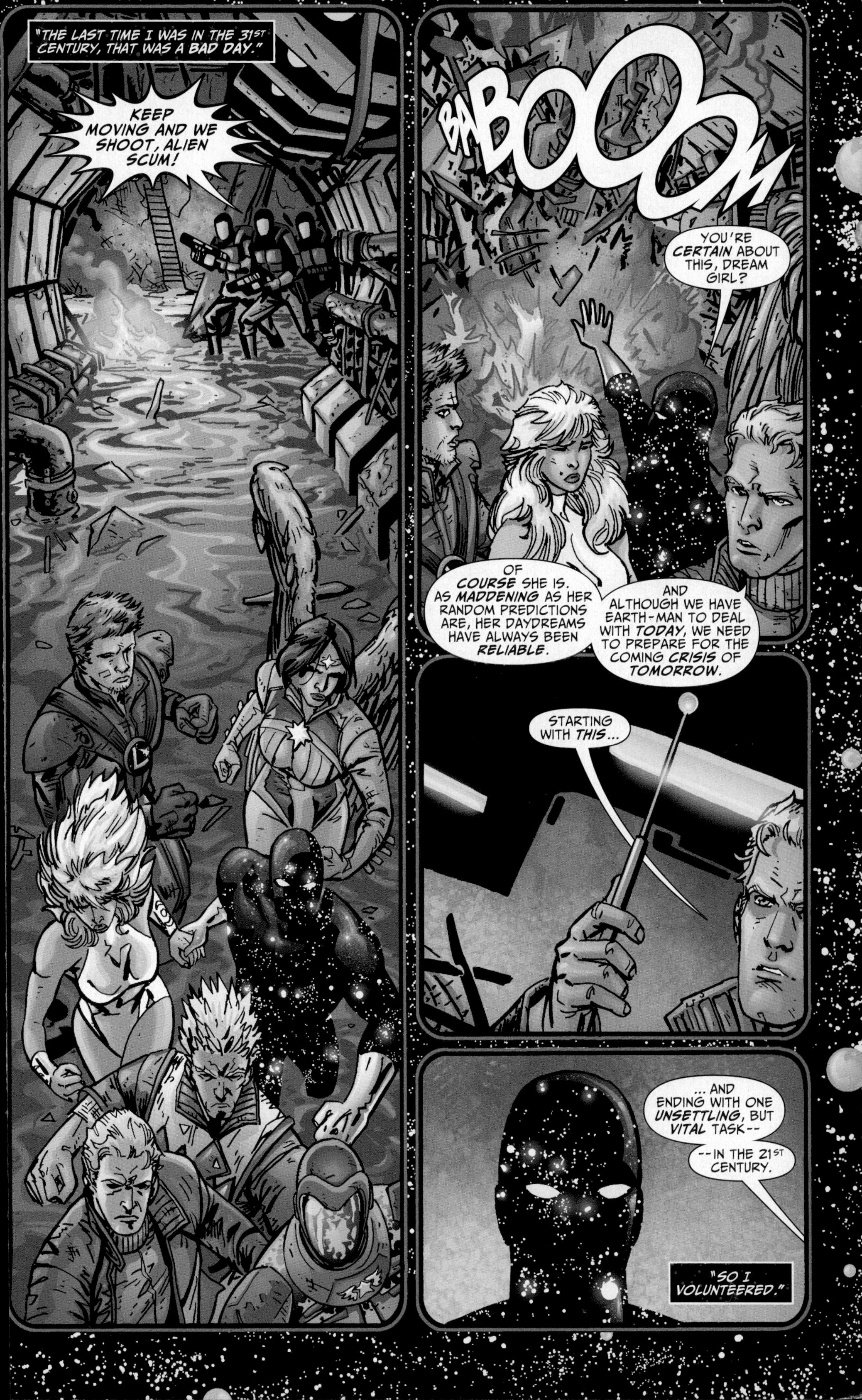
"THE LAST TIME I WAS IN THE 31ST CENTURY, THAT WAS A BAD DAY."
KEEP MOVING AND WE SHOOT, ALIEN SCUM!
BABOOOM
YOU'RE CERTAIN ABOUT THIS, DREAM GIRL?
OF COURSE SHE IS. AS MADDENING AS HER RANDOM PREDICTIONS ARE, HER DAYDREAMS HAVE ALWAYS BEEN RELIABLE.
AND ALTHOUGH WE HAVE EARTH-MAN TO DEAL WITH TODAY, WE NEED TO PREPARE FOR THE COMING CRISIS OF TOMORROW.
STARTING WITH THIS...
...AND ENDING WITH ONE UNSETTLING, BUT VITAL TASK--
--IN THE 21ST CENTURY.
"SO I VOLUNTEERED."

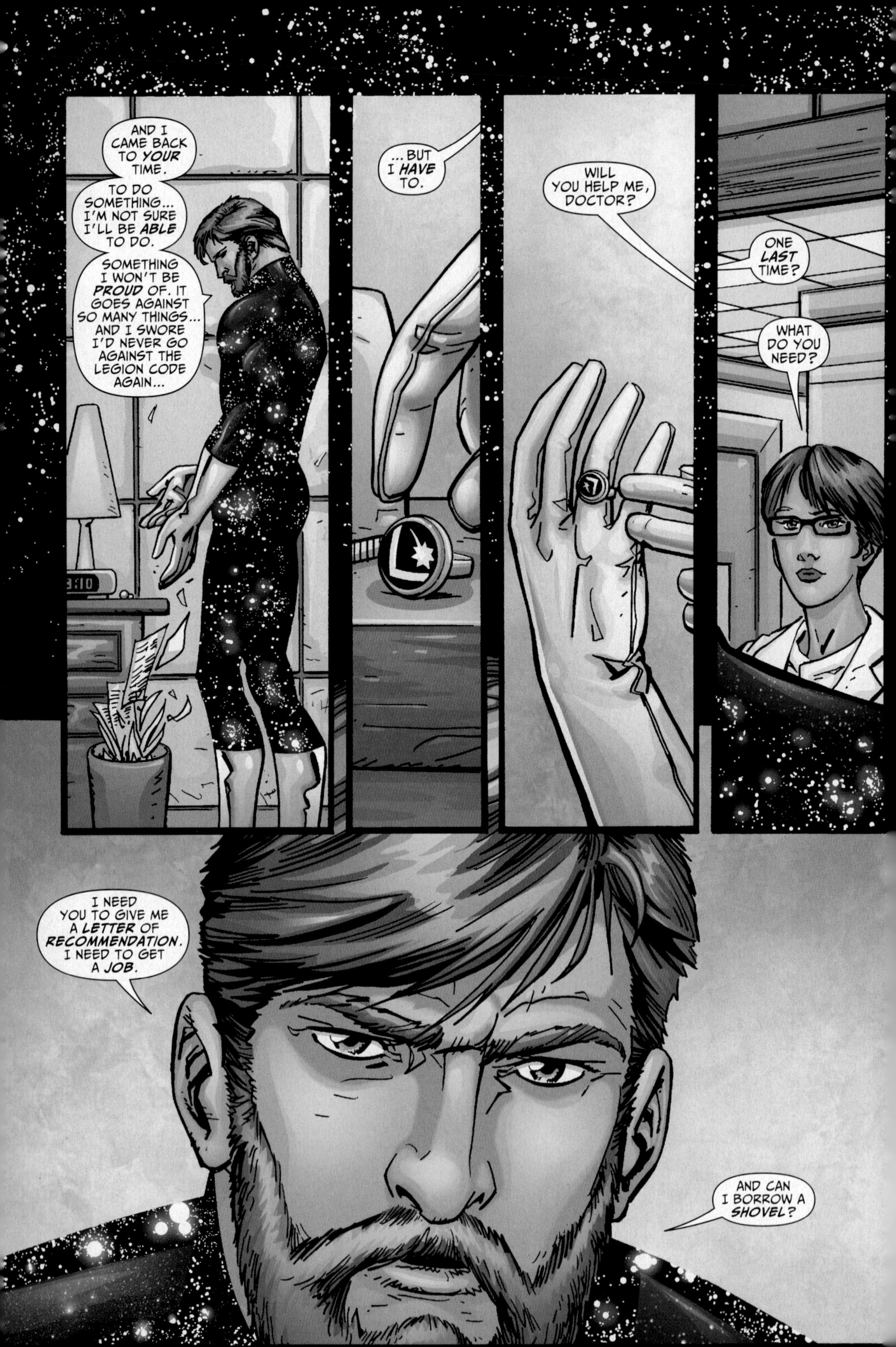
AND I CAME BACK TO YOUR TIME.
TO DO SOMETHING... I'M NOT SURE I'LL BE ABLE TO DO.
SOMETHING I WON'T BE PROUD OF. IT GOES AGAINST SO MANY THINGS... AND I SWORE I'D NEVER GO AGAINST THE LEGION CODE AGAIN...
...BUT I HAVE TO.
WILL YOU HELP ME, DOCTOR?
ONE LAST TIME?
WHAT DO YOU NEED?
I NEED YOU TO GIVE ME A LETTER OF RECOMMENDATION. I NEED TO GET A JOB.
AND CAN I BORROW A SHOVEL?

JUSTICE SOCIETY OF AMERICA KINGDOM COME SPECIAL: THE KINGDOM #1 cover A by Alex Ross

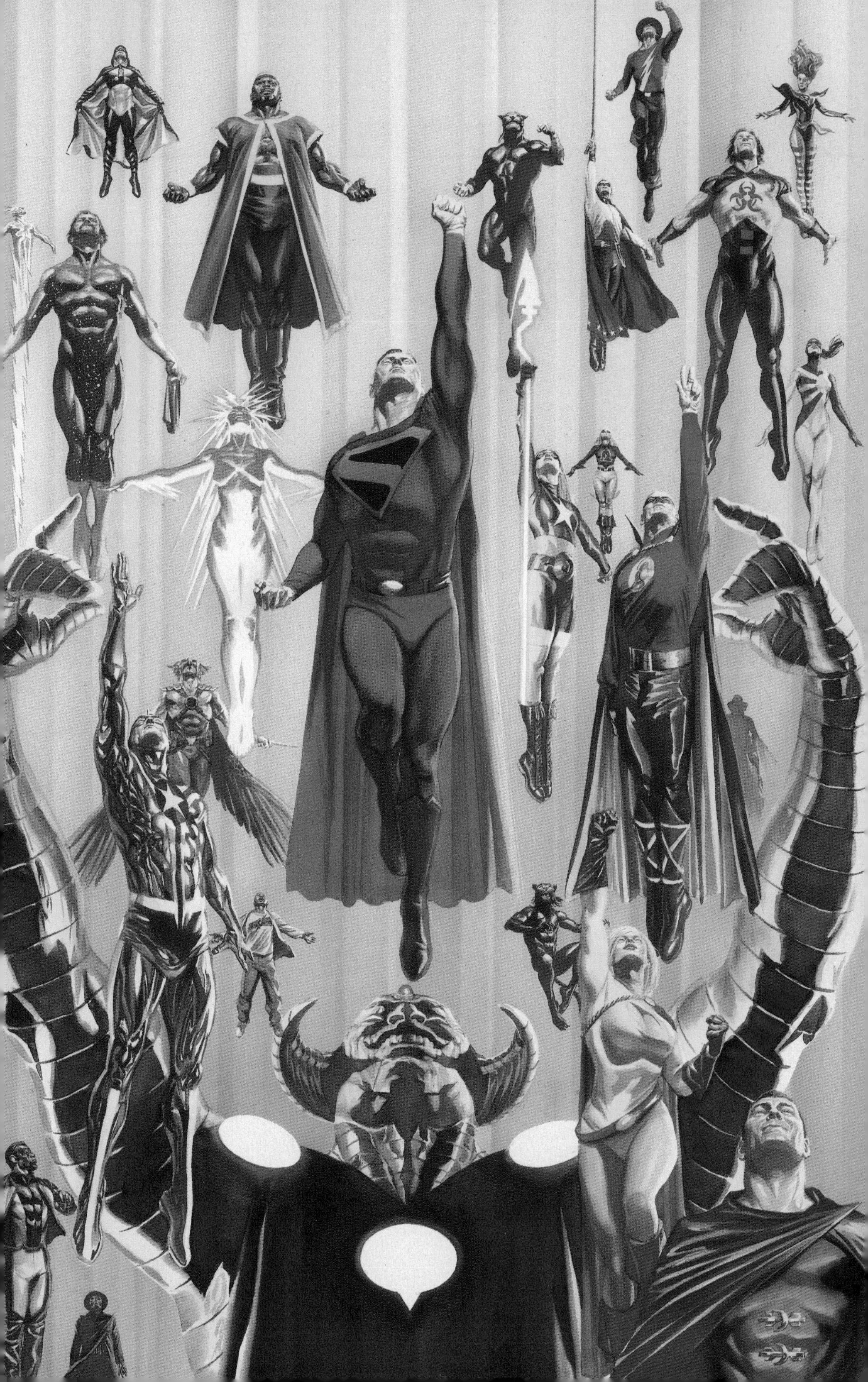

JUSTICE SOCIETY OF AMERICA KINGDOM COME SPECIAL: THE KINGDOM #1 Cover B by Fernando Pasarin
Written by Geoff Johns, with interior pencils by Fernando Pasarin and inks by Mick Gray, Jack Purcell, Norm Rapmund & Pasarin

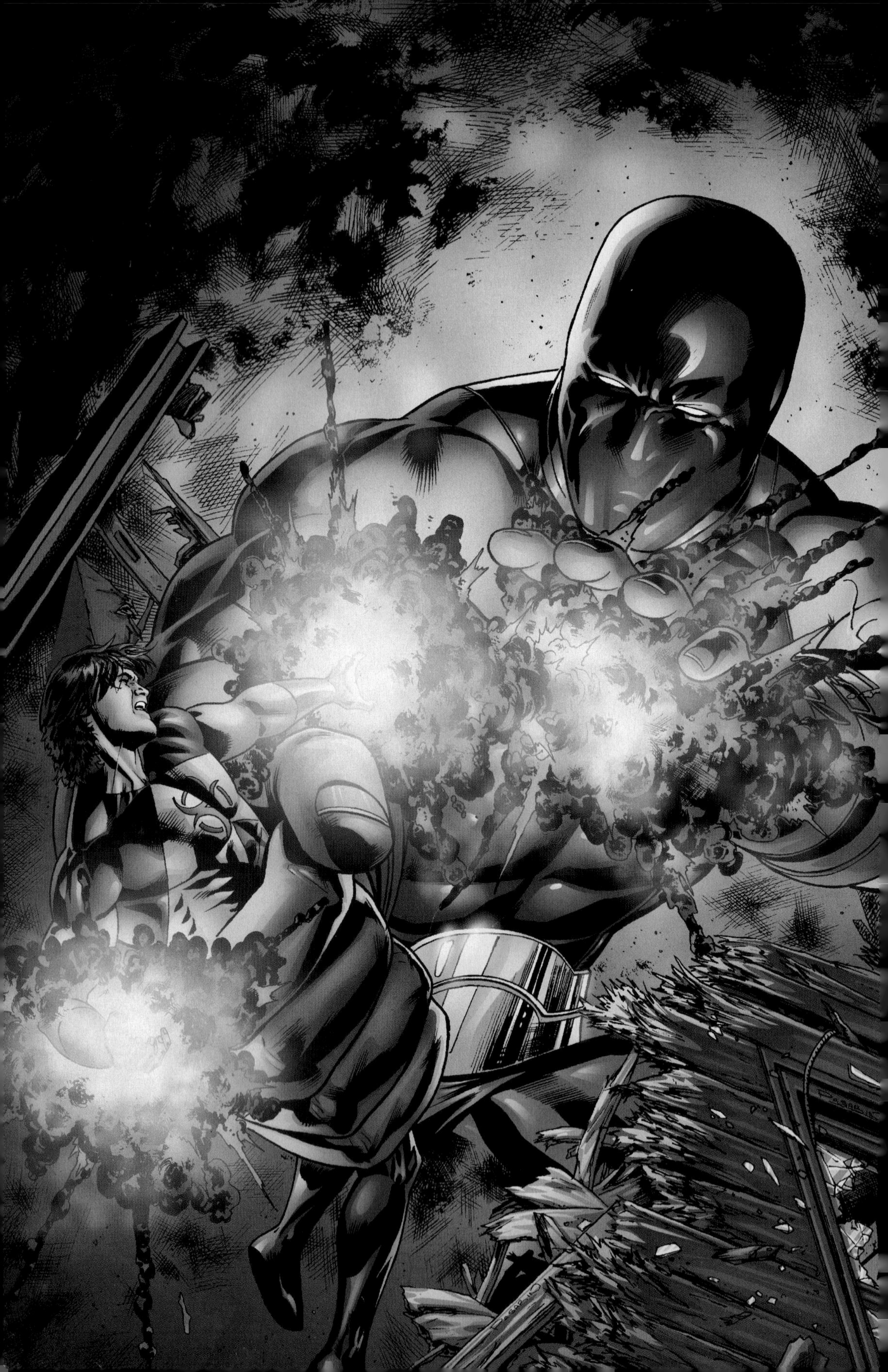

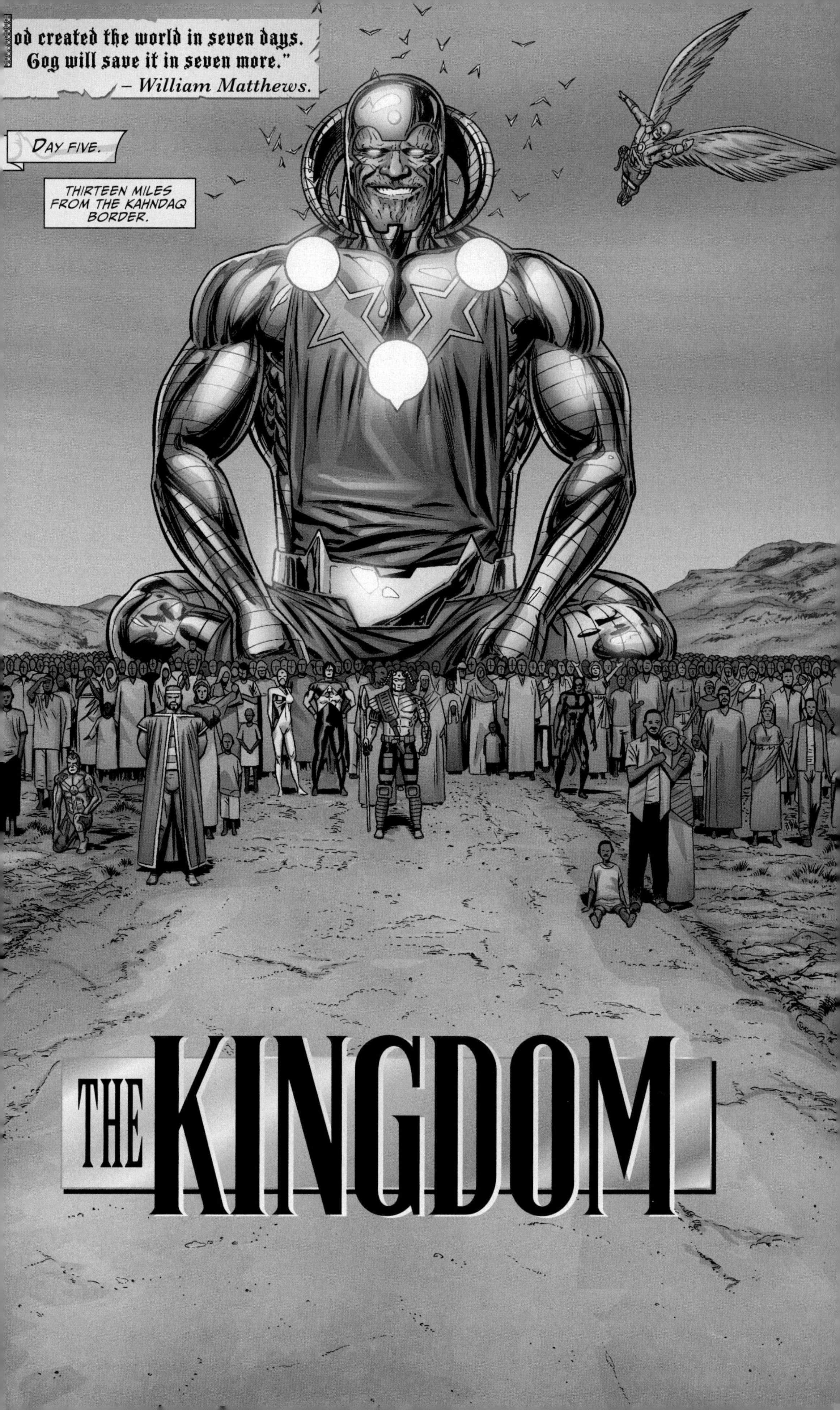

od created the world in seven days. Gog will save it in seven more."
– William Matthews.
DAY FIVE.
THIRTEEN MILES FROM THE KAHNDAQ BORDER.
THE KINGDOM

THE SUN SETS WITH BEAUTY ON THIS FIFTH DAY OF SERVICE.

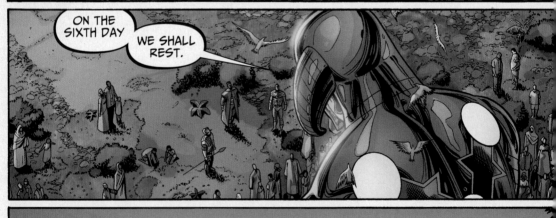

ON THE SIXTH DAY

WE SHALL REST.

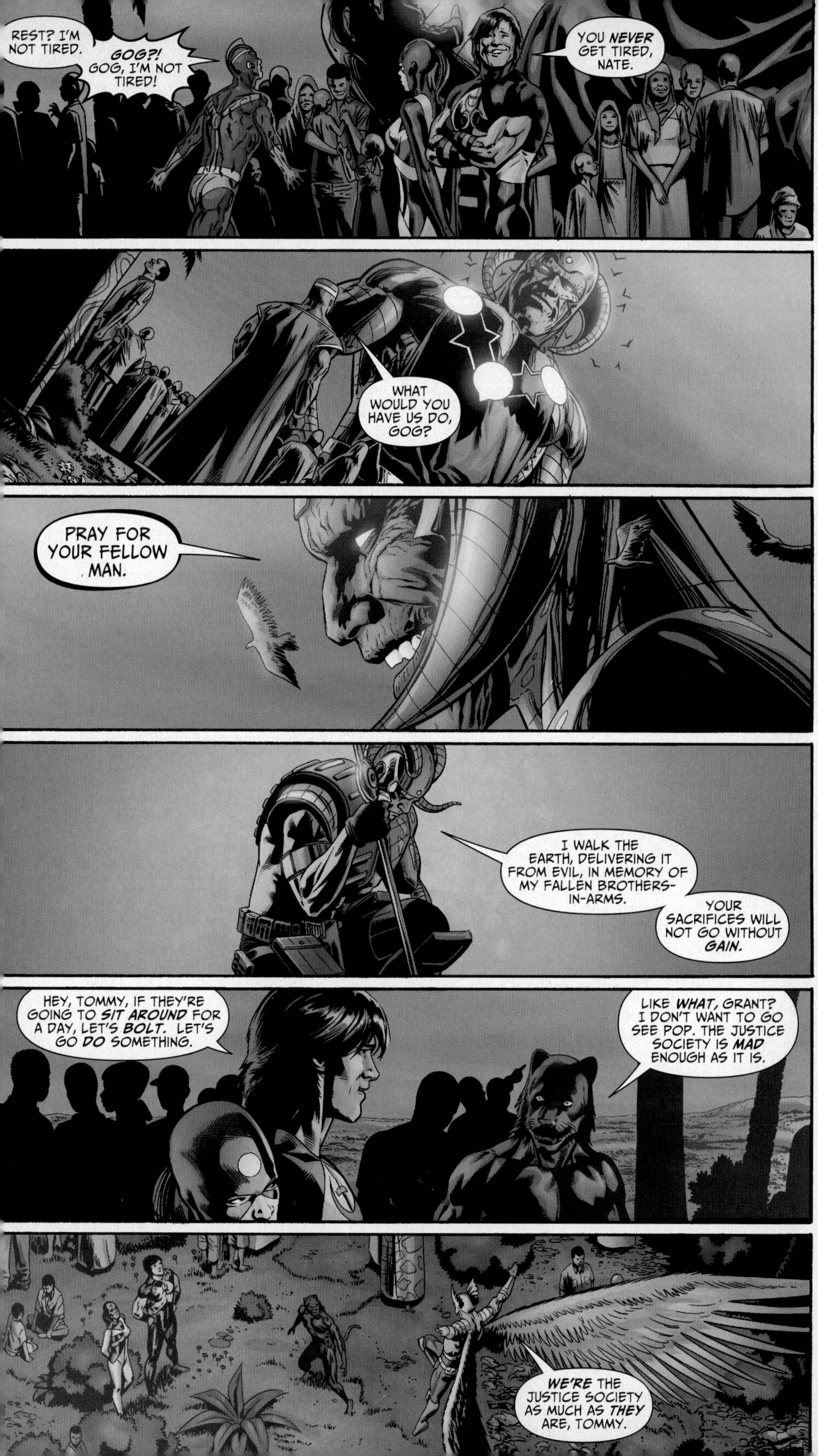

REST? I'M NOT TIRED.
GOG?! GOG, I'M NOT TIRED!
YOU NEVER GET TIRED, NATE.
WHAT WOULD YOU HAVE US DO, GOG?
PRAY FOR YOUR FELLOW MAN.
I WALK THE EARTH, DELIVERING IT FROM EVIL, IN MEMORY OF MY FALLEN BROTHERS-IN-ARMS.
YOUR SACRIFICES WILL NOT GO WITHOUT GAIN.
HEY, TOMMY, IF THEY'RE GOING TO SIT AROUND FOR A DAY, LET'S BOLT. LET'S GO DO SOMETHING.
LIKE WHAT, GRANT? I DON'T WANT TO GO SEE POP. THE JUSTICE SOCIETY IS MAD ENOUGH AS IT IS.
WE'RE THE JUSTICE SOCIETY AS MUCH AS THEY ARE, TOMMY.

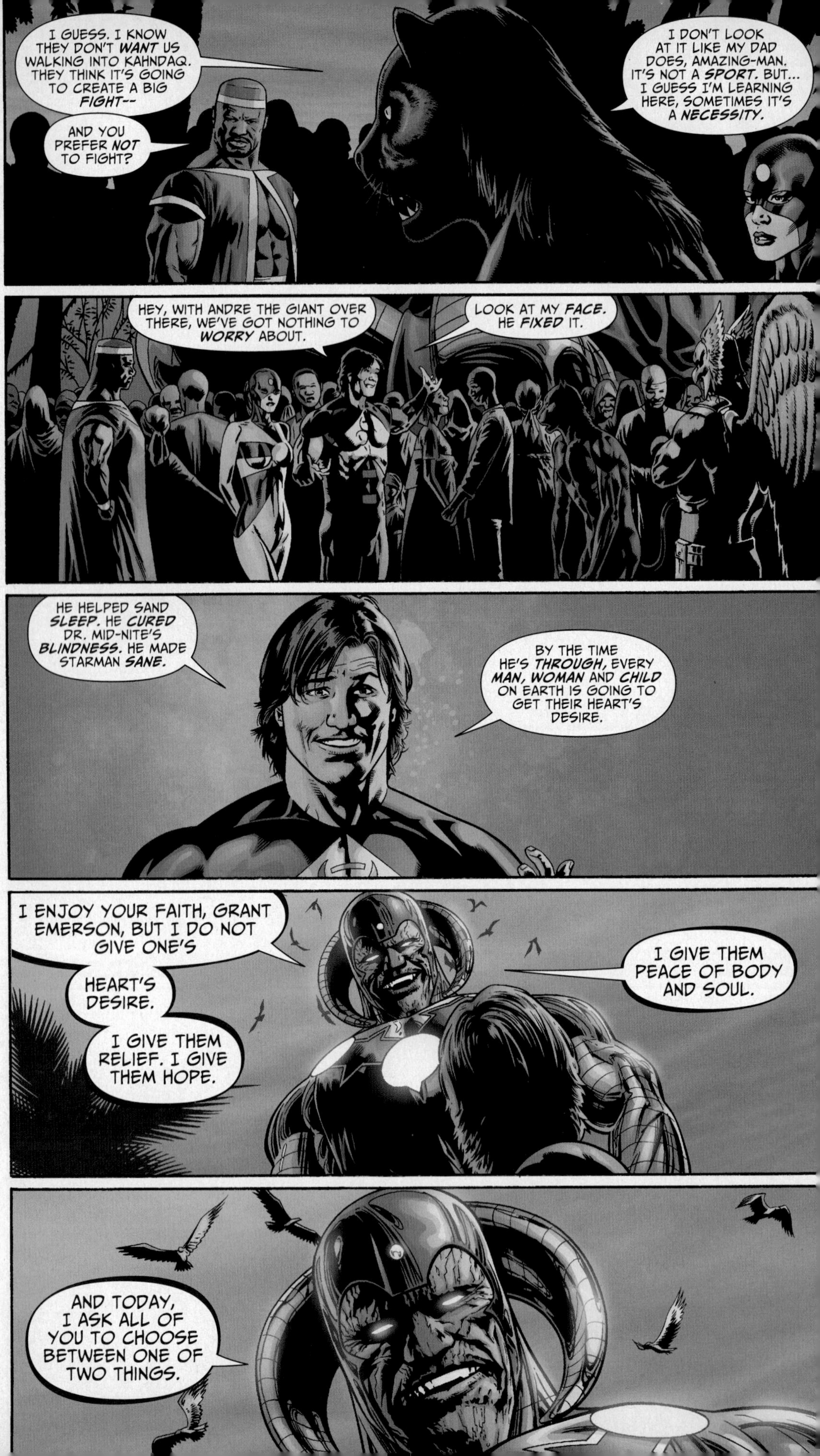

I GUESS. I KNOW THEY DON'T *WANT* US WALKING INTO KAHNDAQ. THEY THINK IT'S GOING TO CREATE A BIG *FIGHT*--
AND YOU PREFER *NOT* TO FIGHT?
I DON'T LOOK AT IT LIKE MY DAD DOES, AMAZING-MAN. IT'S NOT A *SPORT.* BUT... I GUESS I'M LEARNING HERE, SOMETIMES IT'S A *NECESSITY.*
HEY, WITH ANDRE THE GIANT OVER THERE, WE'VE GOT NOTHING TO *WORRY* ABOUT.
LOOK AT MY *FACE.* HE *FIXED* IT.
HE HELPED SAND *SLEEP.* HE *CURED* DR. MID-NITE'S *BLINDNESS.* HE MADE STARMAN *SANE.*
BY THE TIME HE'S *THROUGH,* EVERY *MAN, WOMAN* AND *CHILD* ON EARTH IS GOING TO GET THEIR HEART'S DESIRE.
I ENJOY YOUR FAITH, GRANT EMERSON, BUT I DO NOT GIVE ONE'S
HEART'S DESIRE.
I GIVE THEM RELIEF. I GIVE THEM HOPE.
I GIVE THEM PEACE OF BODY AND SOUL.
AND TODAY, I ASK ALL OF YOU TO CHOOSE BETWEEN ONE OF TWO THINGS.

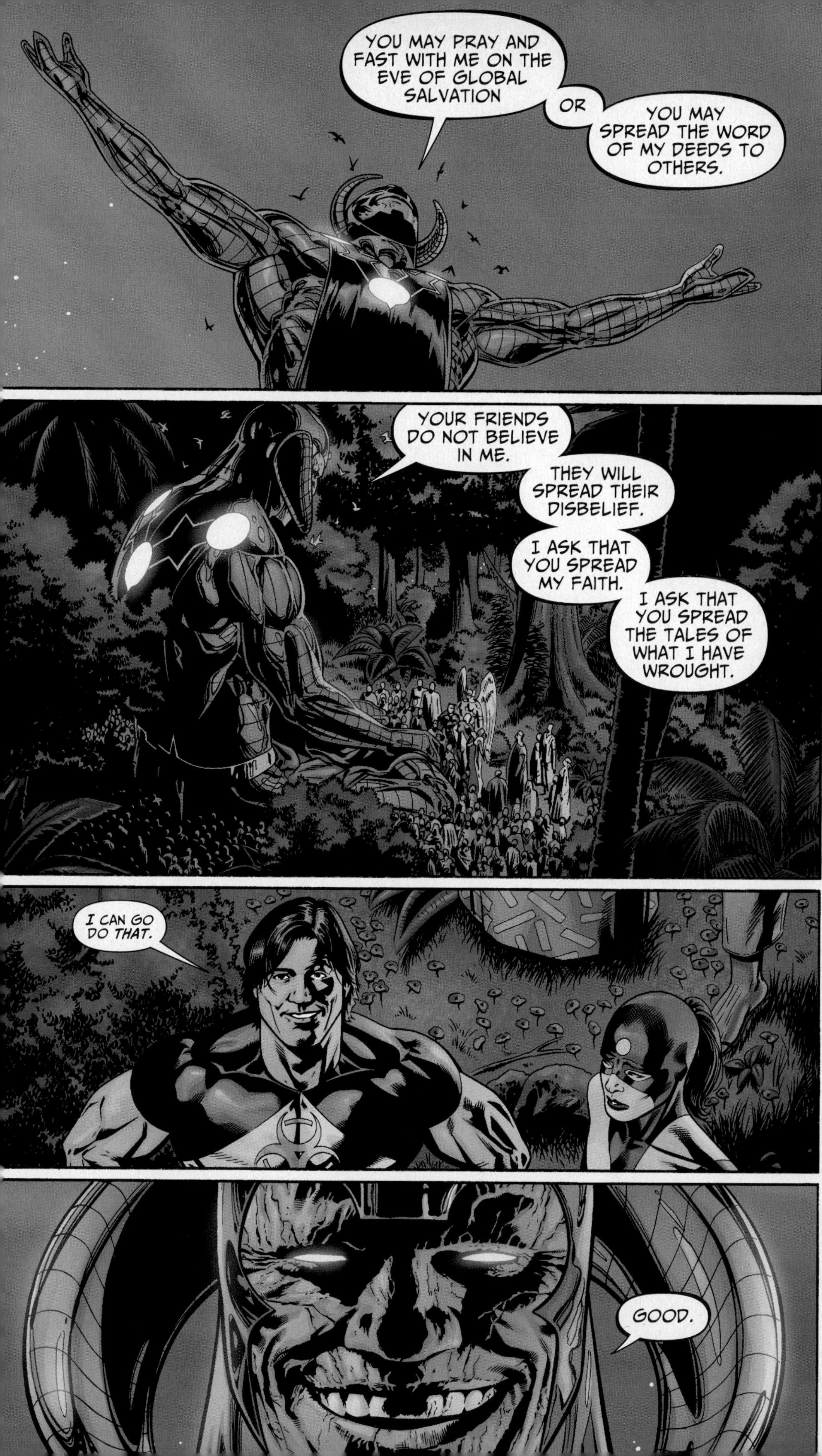

YOU MAY PRAY AND FAST WITH ME ON THE EVE OF GLOBAL SALVATION
OR
YOU MAY SPREAD THE WORD OF MY DEEDS TO OTHERS.
YOUR FRIENDS DO NOT BELIEVE IN ME.
THEY WILL SPREAD THEIR DISBELIEF.
I ASK THAT YOU SPREAD MY FAITH.
I ASK THAT YOU SPREAD THE TALES OF WHAT I HAVE WROUGHT.
I CAN GO DO THAT.
GOOD.

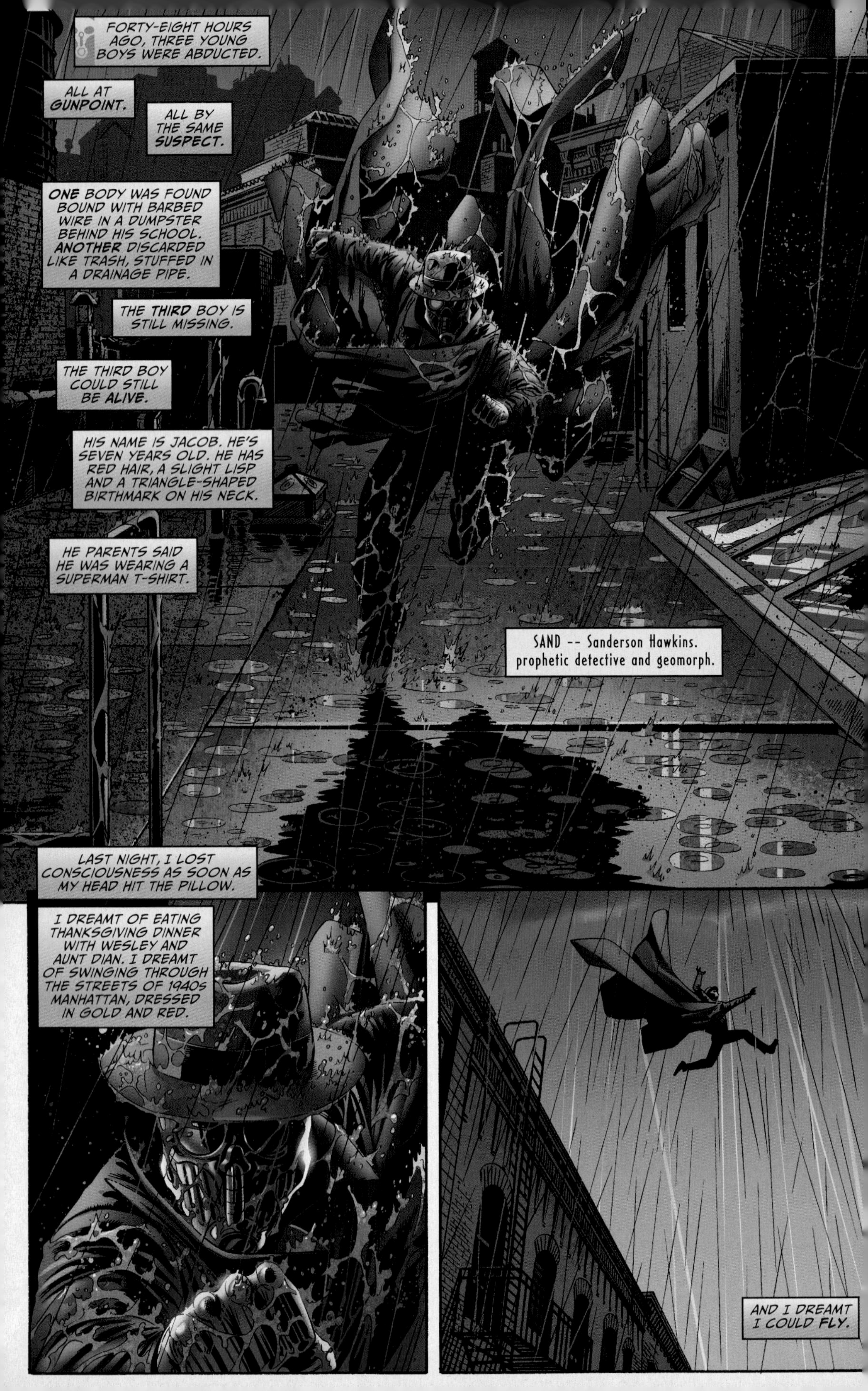
FORTY-EIGHT HOURS AGO, THREE YOUNG BOYS WERE ABDUCTED.
ALL AT GUNPOINT.
ALL BY THE SAME SUSPECT.
ONE BODY WAS FOUND BOUND WITH BARBED WIRE IN A DUMPSTER BEHIND HIS SCHOOL. ANOTHER DISCARDED LIKE TRASH, STUFFED IN A DRAINAGE PIPE.
THE THIRD BOY IS STILL MISSING.
THE THIRD BOY COULD STILL BE ALIVE.
HIS NAME IS JACOB. HE'S SEVEN YEARS OLD. HE HAS RED HAIR, A SLIGHT LISP AND A TRIANGLE-SHAPED BIRTHMARK ON HIS NECK.
HE PARENTS SAID HE WAS WEARING A SUPERMAN T-SHIRT.
SAND -- Sanderson Hawkins. prophetic detective and geomorph.
LAST NIGHT, I LOST CONSCIOUSNESS AS SOON AS MY HEAD HIT THE PILLOW.
I DREAMT OF EATING THANKSGIVING DINNER WITH WESLEY AND AUNT DIAN. I DREAMT OF SWINGING THROUGH THE STREETS OF 1940s MANHATTAN, DRESSED IN GOLD AND RED.
AND I DREAMT I COULD FLY.

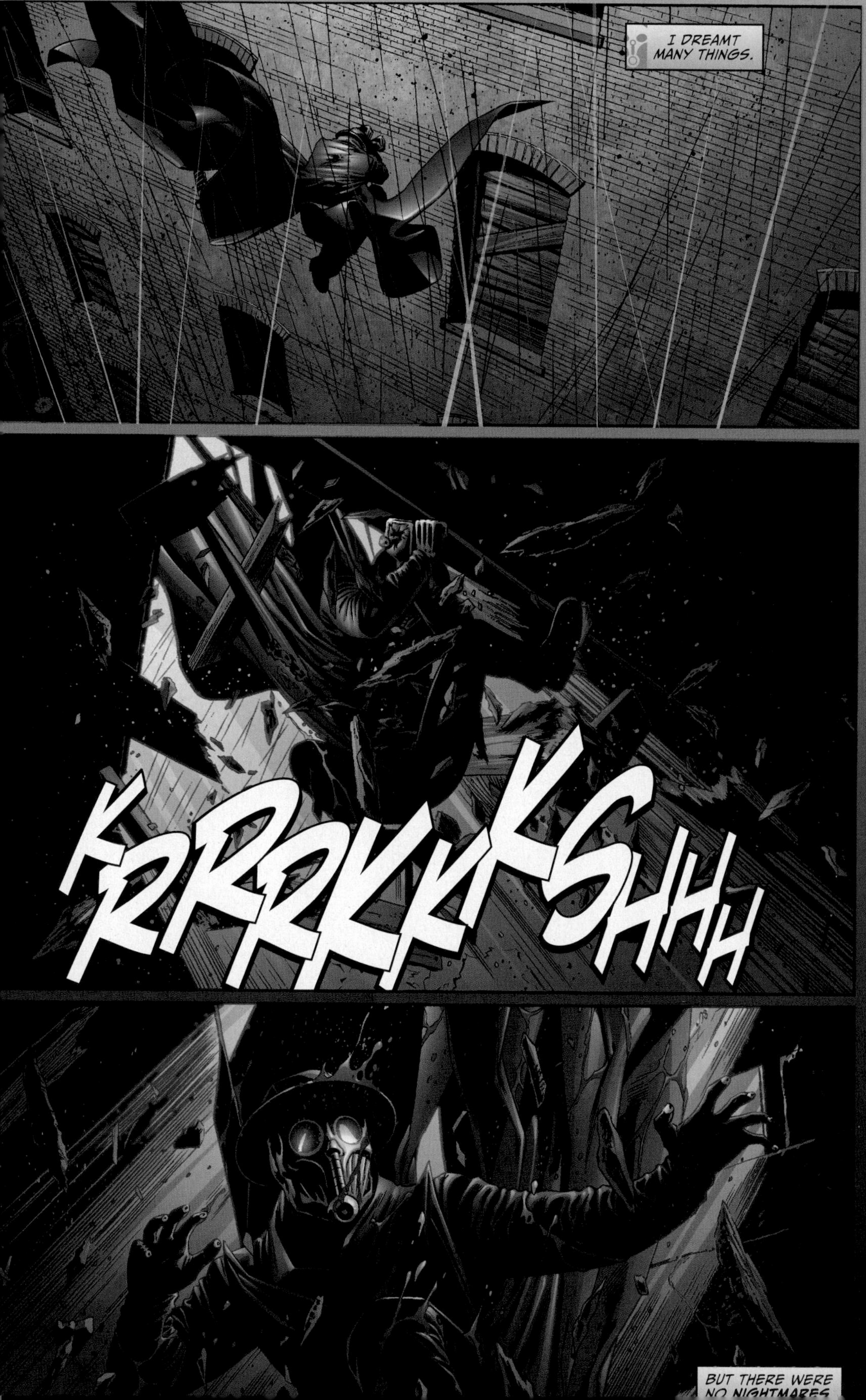
I DREAMT MANY THINGS.
KRRRKKKSHHH
BUT THERE WERE NO NIGHTMARES

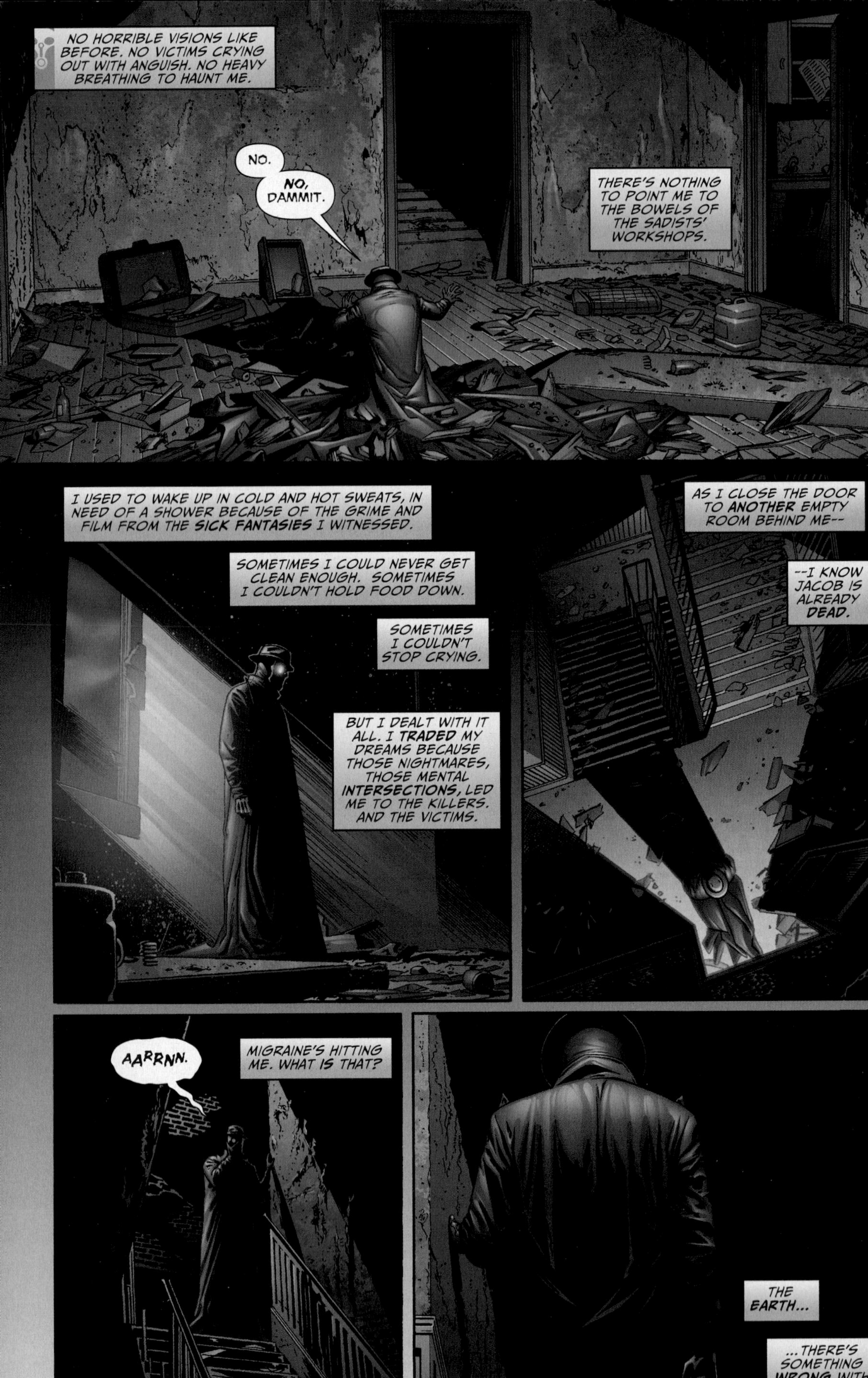
NO HORRIBLE VISIONS LIKE BEFORE. NO VICTIMS CRYING OUT WITH ANGUISH. NO HEAVY BREATHING TO HAUNT ME.
NO.
NO, DAMMIT.
THERE'S NOTHING TO POINT ME TO THE BOWELS OF THE SADISTS' WORKSHOPS.
I USED TO WAKE UP IN COLD AND HOT SWEATS, IN NEED OF A SHOWER BECAUSE OF THE GRIME AND FILM FROM THE SICK FANTASIES I WITNESSED.
SOMETIMES I COULD NEVER GET CLEAN ENOUGH. SOMETIMES I COULDN'T HOLD FOOD DOWN.
SOMETIMES I COULDN'T STOP CRYING.
BUT I DEALT WITH IT ALL. I TRADED MY DREAMS BECAUSE THOSE NIGHTMARES, THOSE MENTAL INTERSECTIONS, LED ME TO THE KILLERS. AND THE VICTIMS.
AS I CLOSE THE DOOR TO ANOTHER EMPTY ROOM BEHIND ME--
--I KNOW JACOB IS ALREADY DEAD.
AARRNN.
MIGRAINE'S HITTING ME. WHAT IS THAT?
THE EARTH...
...THERE'S SOMETHING

THIS IS WHAT A *GOD* LOOKS LIKE.

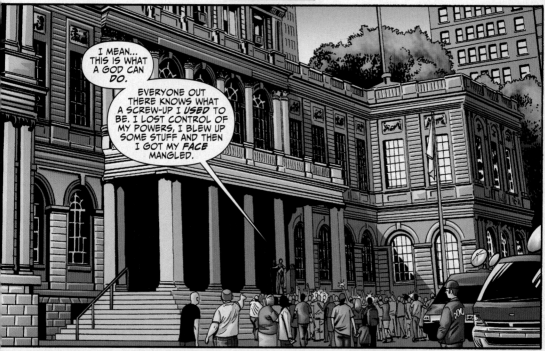

I MEAN... THIS IS WHAT A *GOD* CAN *DO.*

EVERYONE OUT THERE KNOWS WHAT A SCREW-UP I *USED* TO BE. I LOST CONTROL OF MY POWERS, I BLEW UP SOME STUFF AND THEN I GOT MY *FACE* MANGLED.

I HAD TO WEAR THIS *MASK* TO HIDE IT.

NOW? I DON'T *NEED* TO.

I WAS *TOUCHED* BY THIS *GIANT* THAT'S BEEN WALKING ACROSS AFRICA AND *HEALING* EVERYONE IN *SIGHT.*

I WAS TOUCHED BY *GOG.*

BWOOSHH

YOU'RE GOING TO HEAR PEOPLE SAY THIS IS *WRONG.*

I'M HERE TO TELL YOU, TO *SHOW* EVERYONE *SUFFERING* OUT THERE...

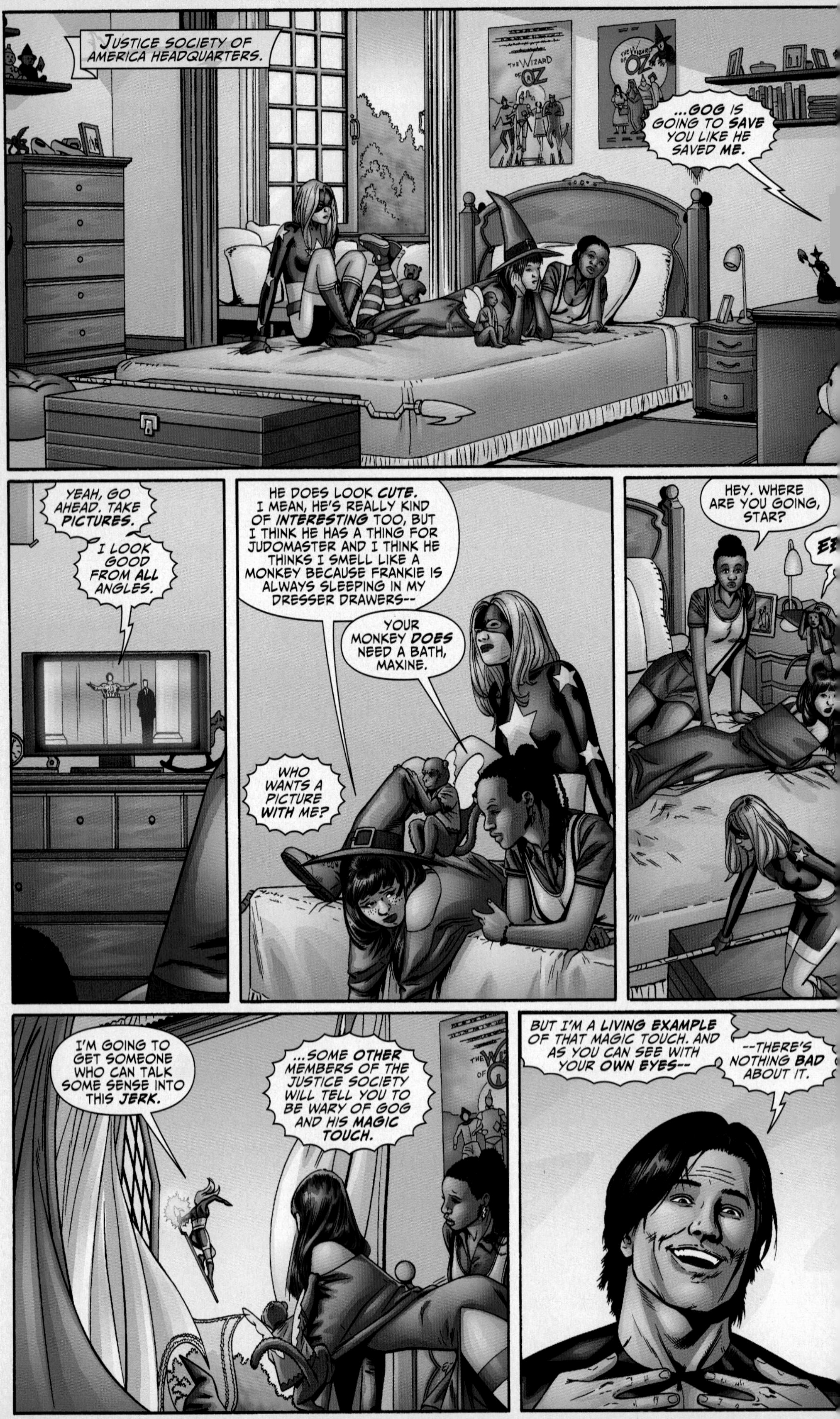
JUSTICE SOCIETY OF AMERICA HEADQUARTERS.
...GOG IS GOING TO SAVE YOU LIKE HE SAVED ME.
YEAH, GO AHEAD. TAKE PICTURES.
I LOOK GOOD FROM ALL ANGLES.
HE DOES LOOK CUTE. I MEAN, HE'S REALLY KIND OF INTERESTING TOO, BUT I THINK HE HAS A THING FOR JUDOMASTER AND I THINK HE THINKS I SMELL LIKE A MONKEY BECAUSE FRANKIE IS ALWAYS SLEEPING IN MY DRESSER DRAWERS--
YOUR MONKEY DOES NEED A BATH, MAXINE.
WHO WANTS A PICTURE WITH ME?
HEY. WHERE ARE YOU GOING, STAR?
I'M GOING TO GET SOMEONE WHO CAN TALK SOME SENSE INTO THIS JERK.
...SOME OTHER MEMBERS OF THE JUSTICE SOCIETY WILL TELL YOU TO BE WARY OF GOG AND HIS MAGIC TOUCH.
BUT I'M A LIVING EXAMPLE OF THAT MAGIC TOUCH. AND AS YOU CAN SEE WITH YOUR OWN EYES--
--THERE'S NOTHING BAD ABOUT IT.

DR. MID-NITE -- Dr. Pieter Cross.
Super-hero surgeon.

WHEN DID YOU PAINT THE WALLS *BLUE?*

Uh, A FEW YEARS AGO, DOC.

I ASKED YOU IF IT MATTERED WHAT COLOR IT WAS, BUT YOU SAID--

"I WOULDN'T HAVE TO LOOK AT IT." YES. I REMEMBER NOW.

WE CAN CHANGE IT IF--

IT'S FINE, NITE-LITE. BESIDES, WE'VE GOT MORE IMPORTANT THINGS TO ATTEND TO.

WITH MY SIGHT BACK, WE NEED TO GET THE MRI AND CT SCANNERS UP AND RUNNING AGAIN.

...MAY NOT HAVE BEEN ABLE TO ...AD A PAPER OR *WATCH* A FILM ...OR *SEE* THE COLOR OF MY ...ALLS, BUT I COULD TELL IF ...A BONE WAS *BROKEN* WITH A GLANCE.

I CAUGHT AND REMOVED *HUNDREDS* OF TUMORS JUST AS THEY BEGAN TO GROW.

I SAVED *LIVES* BECAUSE I WAS *BLIND.*

YOU ALWAYS TELL US, IF THERE'S SOMETHING YOU CAN'T CONTROL, YOU ACCEPT IT AND YOU START DEALING WITH IT.

WHETHER IT'S ABOUT BEIN' *SICK* OR BEIN' *HEALTHY,* THAT WAS GOOD ADVICE.

NOW COME ON. WE GOT A *LONG LINE* OF PATIENTS TONIGHT, DOC.

NO WAY ARE WE GETTING THROUGH EVERYONE TONIGHT.

YOU BEST TAKE A *LOOK* OUTSIDE, DOCTOR CROSS.

SHINK

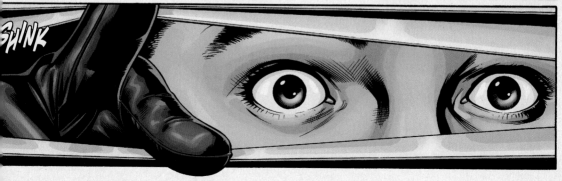

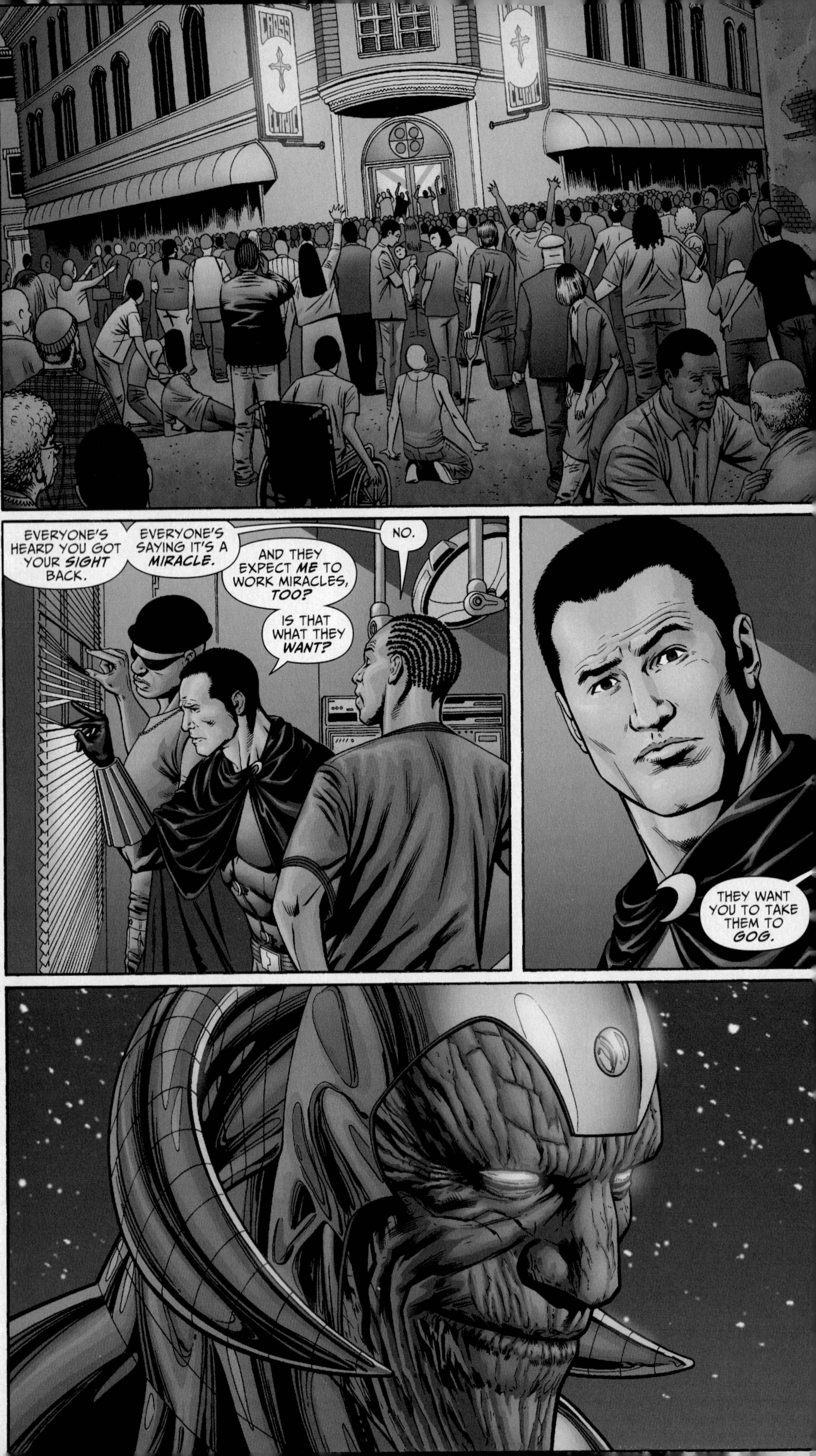

EVERYONE'S HEARD YOU GOT YOUR SIGHT BACK.
EVERYONE'S SAYING IT'S A MIRACLE.
NO.
AND THEY EXPECT ME TO WORK MIRACLES, TOO?
IS THAT WHAT THEY WANT?
THEY WANT YOU TO TAKE THEM TO GOG.

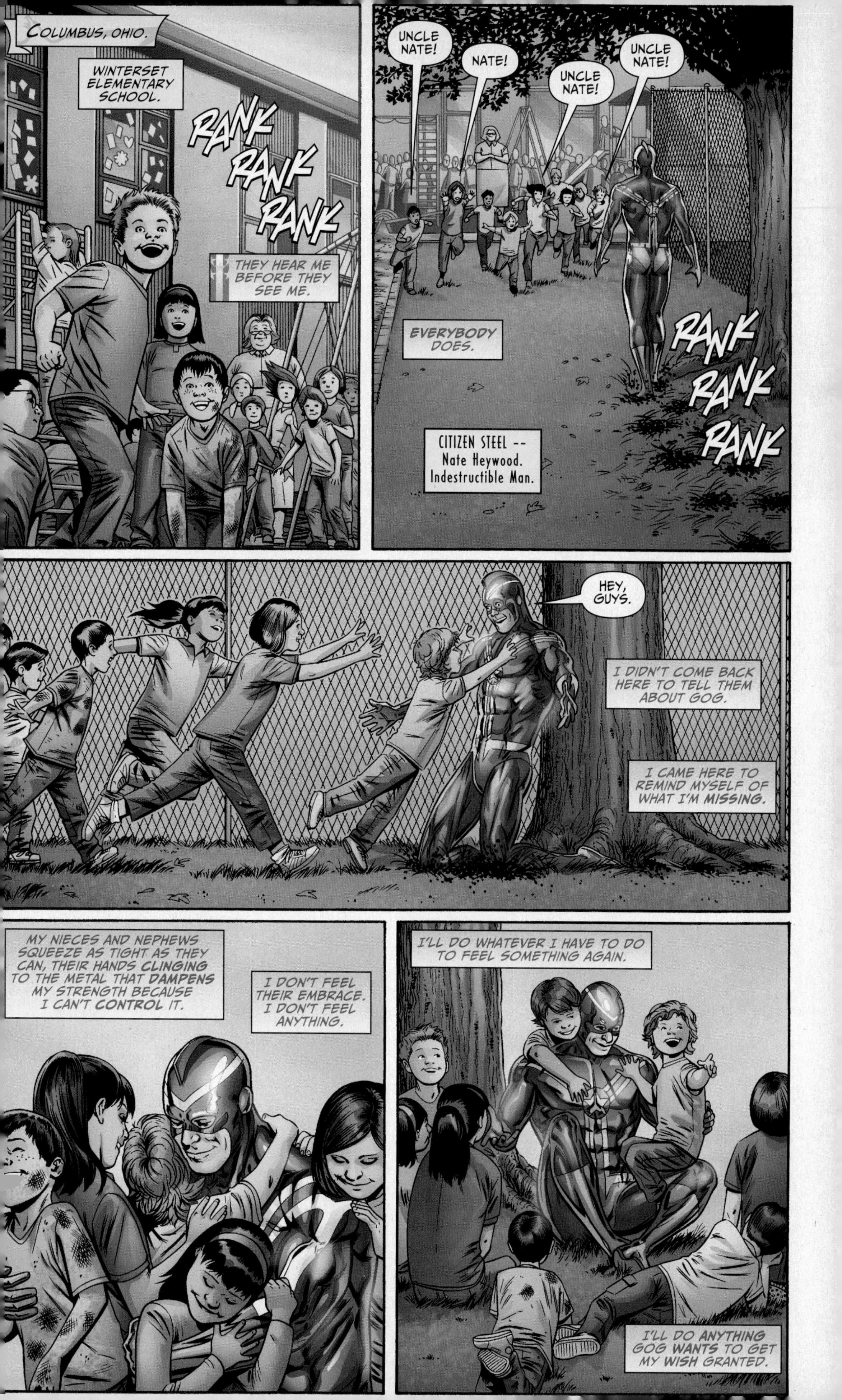
COLUMBUS, OHIO.
WINTERSET ELEMENTARY SCHOOL.
RANK RANK RANK
THEY HEAR ME BEFORE THEY SEE ME.
UNCLE NATE!
NATE!
UNCLE NATE!
UNCLE NATE!
EVERYBODY DOES.
RANK RANK RANK
CITIZEN STEEL -- Nate Heywood. Indestructible Man.
HEY, GUYS.
I DIDN'T COME BACK HERE TO TELL THEM ABOUT GOG.
I CAME HERE TO REMIND MYSELF OF WHAT I'M MISSING.
MY NIECES AND NEPHEWS SQUEEZE AS TIGHT AS THEY CAN, THEIR HANDS CLINGING TO THE METAL THAT DAMPENS MY STRENGTH BECAUSE I CAN'T CONTROL IT.
I DON'T FEEL THEIR EMBRACE. I DON'T FEEL ANYTHING.
I'LL DO WHATEVER I HAVE TO DO TO FEEL SOMETHING AGAIN.
I'LL DO ANYTHING GOG WANTS TO GET MY WISH GRANTED.

METROPOLIS.

NEW CARRERS STARTS HERE

EMPLOYMENT OPPORTUNITIES!

YES. THAT'S ME! I'M DANNY BLAINE.

JOB! JOB! JOB!

FIND RIGHT JOB FOR YOU TODAY!

STARMAN -- Thom Kallor. Cosmic cowboy from the future.

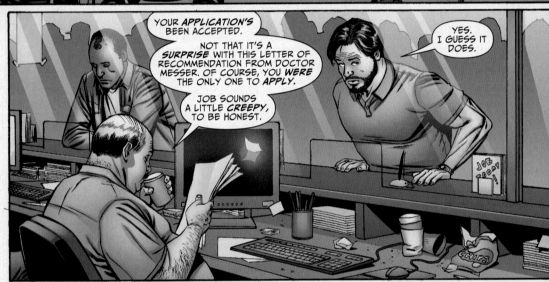

YOUR APPLICATION'S BEEN ACCEPTED.

NOT THAT IT'S A SURPRISE WITH THIS LETTER OF RECOMMENDATION FROM DOCTOR MESSER. OF COURSE, YOU WERE THE ONLY ONE TO APPLY.

JOB SOUNDS A LITTLE CREEPY, TO BE HONEST.

YES. I GUESS IT DOES.

YOU MUST BE DESPERATE TO TAKE A GIG LIKE THIS.

TIMES LIKE THIS, BEGGARS CAN'T BE CHOOSERS.

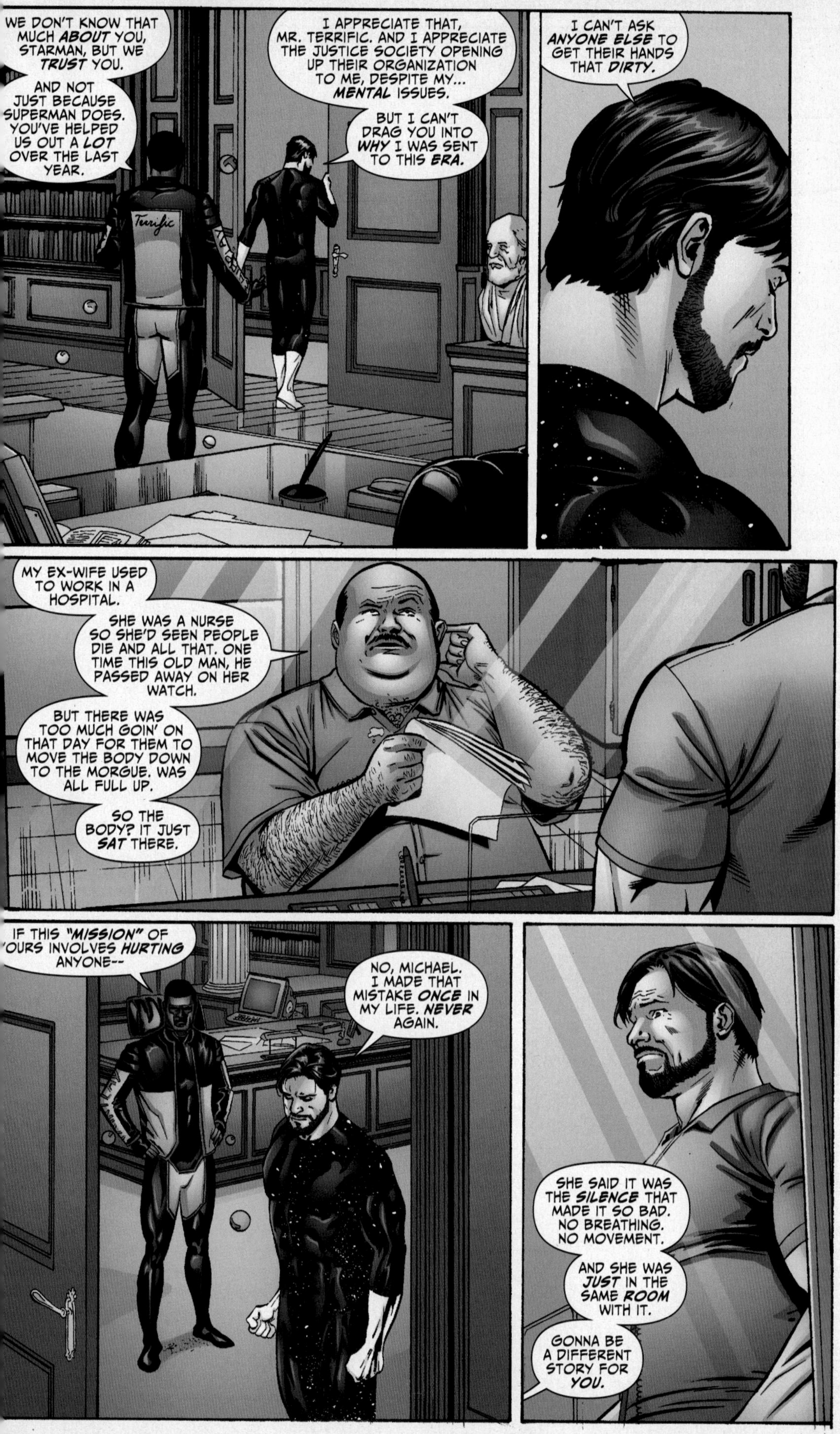

WE DON'T KNOW THAT MUCH ABOUT YOU, STARMAN, BUT WE TRUST YOU.
AND NOT JUST BECAUSE SUPERMAN DOES. YOU'VE HELPED US OUT A LOT OVER THE LAST YEAR.
I APPRECIATE THAT, MR. TERRIFIC. AND I APPRECIATE THE JUSTICE SOCIETY OPENING UP THEIR ORGANIZATION TO ME, DESPITE MY... MENTAL ISSUES.
BUT I CAN'T DRAG YOU INTO WHY I WAS SENT TO THIS ERA.
Terrific
I CAN'T ASK ANYONE ELSE TO GET THEIR HANDS THAT DIRTY.
MY EX-WIFE USED TO WORK IN A HOSPITAL.
SHE WAS A NURSE SO SHE'D SEEN PEOPLE DIE AND ALL THAT. ONE TIME THIS OLD MAN, HE PASSED AWAY ON HER WATCH.
BUT THERE WAS TOO MUCH GOIN' ON THAT DAY FOR THEM TO MOVE THE BODY DOWN TO THE MORGUE. WAS ALL FULL UP.
SO THE BODY? IT JUST SAT THERE.
IF THIS "MISSION" OF YOURS INVOLVES HURTING ANYONE--
NO, MICHAEL. I MADE THAT MISTAKE ONCE IN MY LIFE. NEVER AGAIN.
SHE SAID IT WAS THE SILENCE THAT MADE IT SO BAD. NO BREATHING. NO MOVEMENT.
AND SHE WAS JUST IN THE SAME ROOM WITH IT.
GONNA BE A DIFFERENT STORY FOR YOU.

I KNOW IT'S A *LOT* TO ASK, *MICHAEL,* BUT PLEASE *KEEP* TRUSTING ME. AND PLEASE KEEP THIS BETWEEN *US.*

IF I DON'T *SUCCEED,* THERE MIGHT NOT BE A *31ST CENTURY* FOR ME TO GET *BACK* TO.

SO...WHEN, *uh, WHEN DO* I START?

DAY *AFTER* TOMORROW.

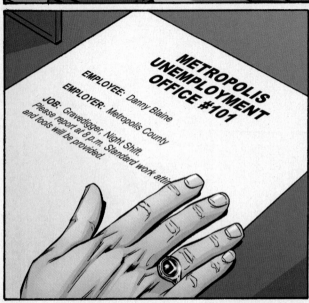

METROPOLIS UNEMPLOYMENT OFFICE #101

EMPLOYEE: Danny Blaine
EMPLOYER: Metropolis County
JOB: Gravedigger, Night Shift.
Please report at 8 p.m. Standard work attire and tools will be provided.

GOOD LUCK, PAL.

NEXT!

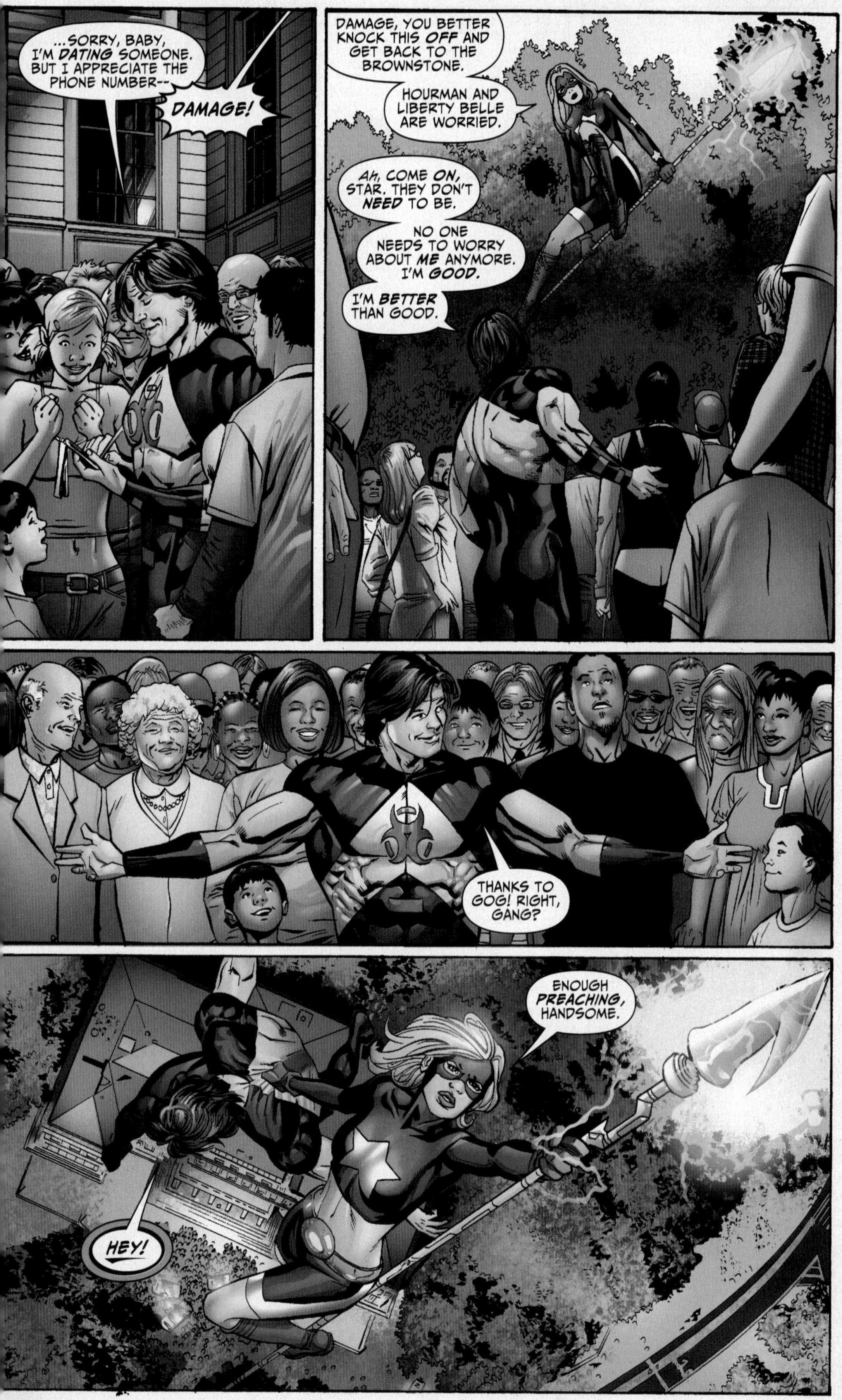
...SORRY, BABY, I'M DATING SOMEONE. BUT I APPRECIATE THE PHONE NUMBER--
DAMAGE!
DAMAGE, YOU BETTER KNOCK THIS OFF AND GET BACK TO THE BROWNSTONE.
HOURMAN AND LIBERTY BELLE ARE WORRIED.
Ah, COME ON, STAR. THEY DON'T NEED TO BE.
NO ONE NEEDS TO WORRY ABOUT ME ANYMORE. I'M GOOD.
I'M BETTER THAN GOOD.
THANKS TO GOG! RIGHT, GANG?
ENOUGH PREACHING, HANDSOME.
HEY!

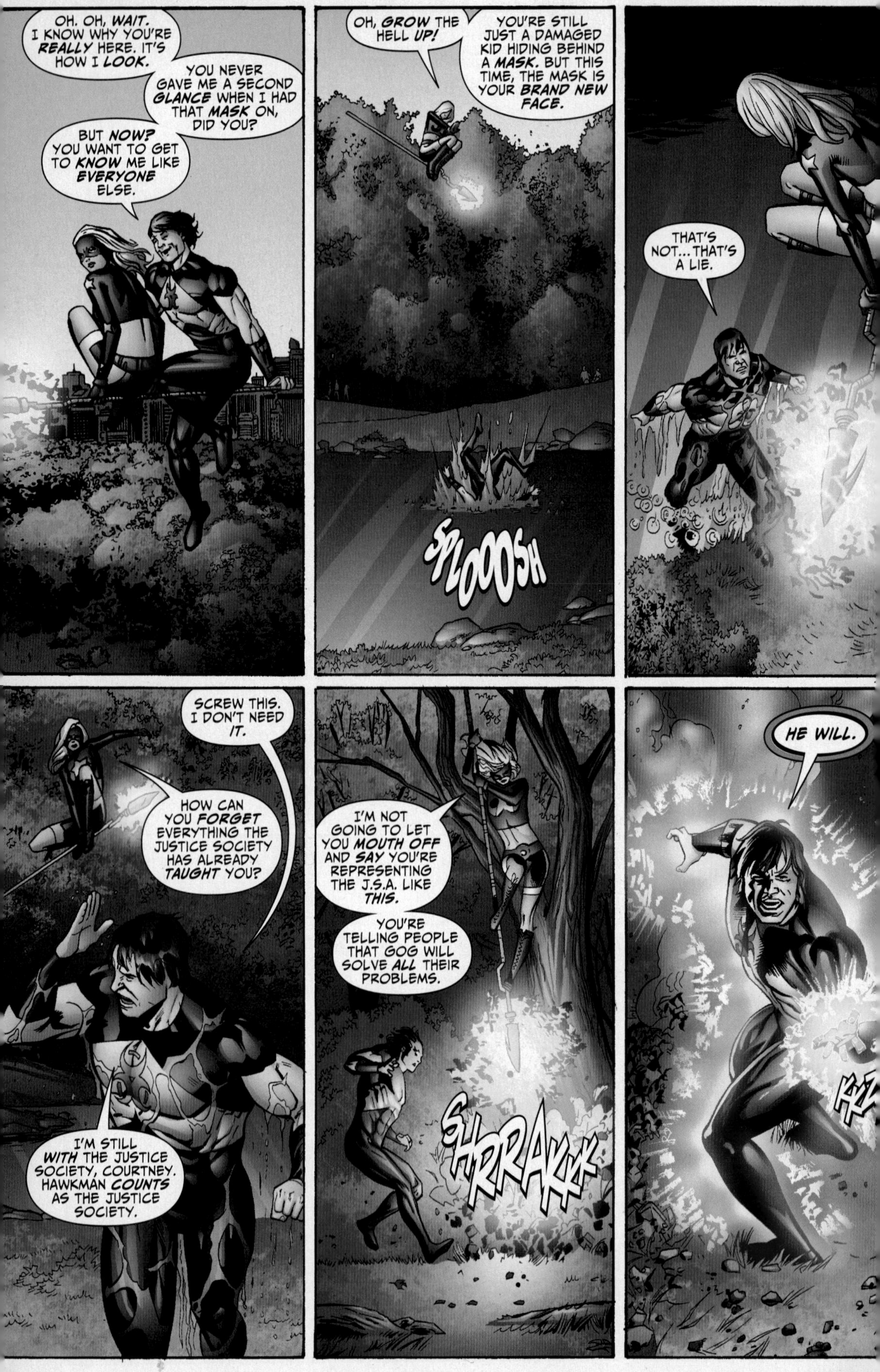
OH. OH, WAIT. I KNOW WHY YOU'RE REALLY HERE. IT'S HOW I LOOK.
YOU NEVER GAVE ME A SECOND GLANCE WHEN I HAD THAT MASK ON, DID YOU?
BUT NOW? YOU WANT TO GET TO KNOW ME LIKE EVERYONE ELSE.
OH, GROW THE HELL UP!
YOU'RE STILL JUST A DAMAGED KID HIDING BEHIND A MASK. BUT THIS TIME, THE MASK IS YOUR BRAND NEW FACE.
SPLOOOSH
THAT'S NOT... THAT'S A LIE.
SCREW THIS. I DON'T NEED IT.
HOW CAN YOU FORGET EVERYTHING THE JUSTICE SOCIETY HAS ALREADY TAUGHT YOU?
I'M STILL WITH THE JUSTICE SOCIETY, COURTNEY. HAWKMAN COUNTS AS THE JUSTICE SOCIETY.
I'M NOT GOING TO LET YOU MOUTH OFF AND SAY YOU'RE REPRESENTING THE J.S.A. LIKE THIS.
YOU'RE TELLING PEOPLE THAT GOG WILL SOLVE ALL THEIR PROBLEMS.
SHRRAKKK
HE WILL.

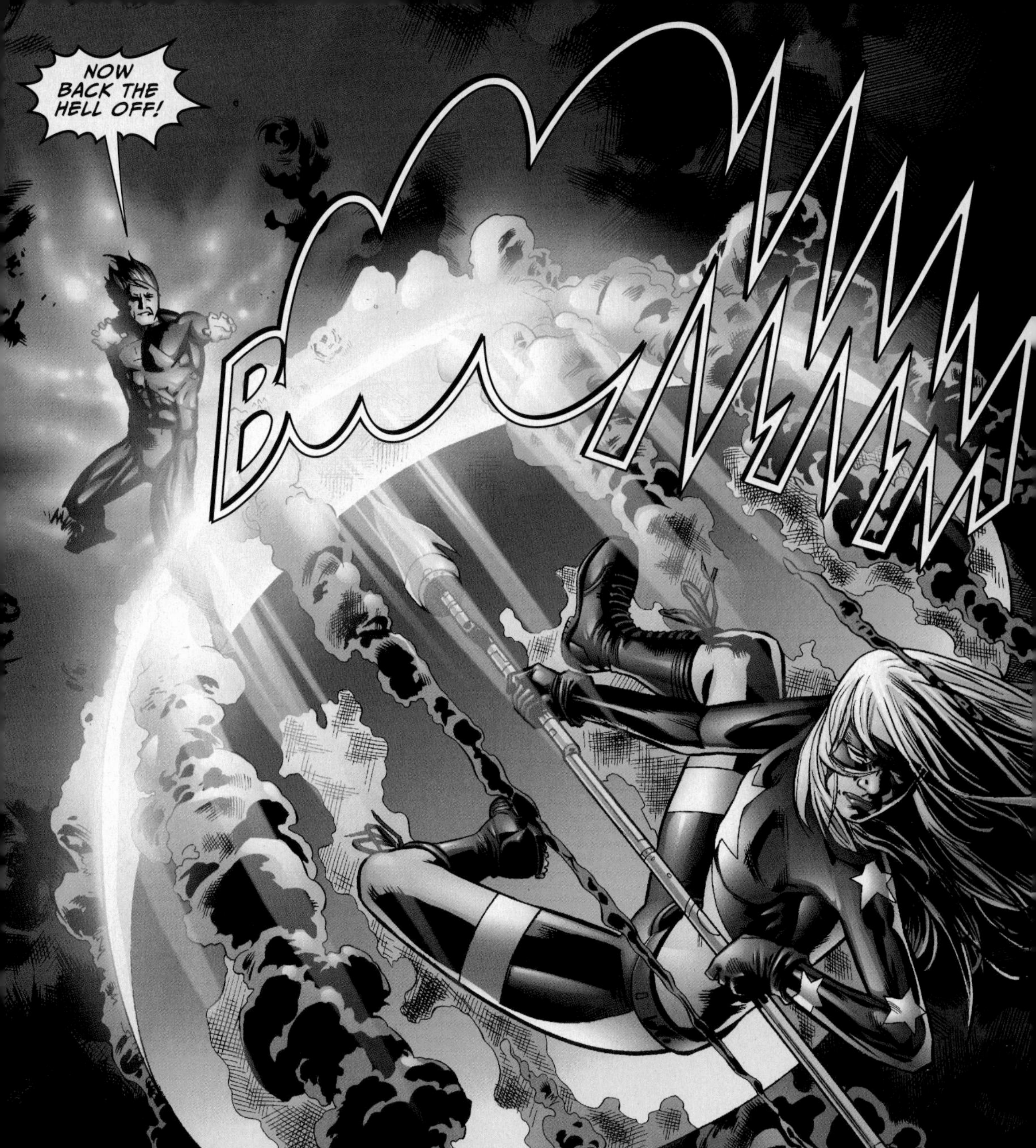
NOW BACK THE HELL OFF!
BRAMMM

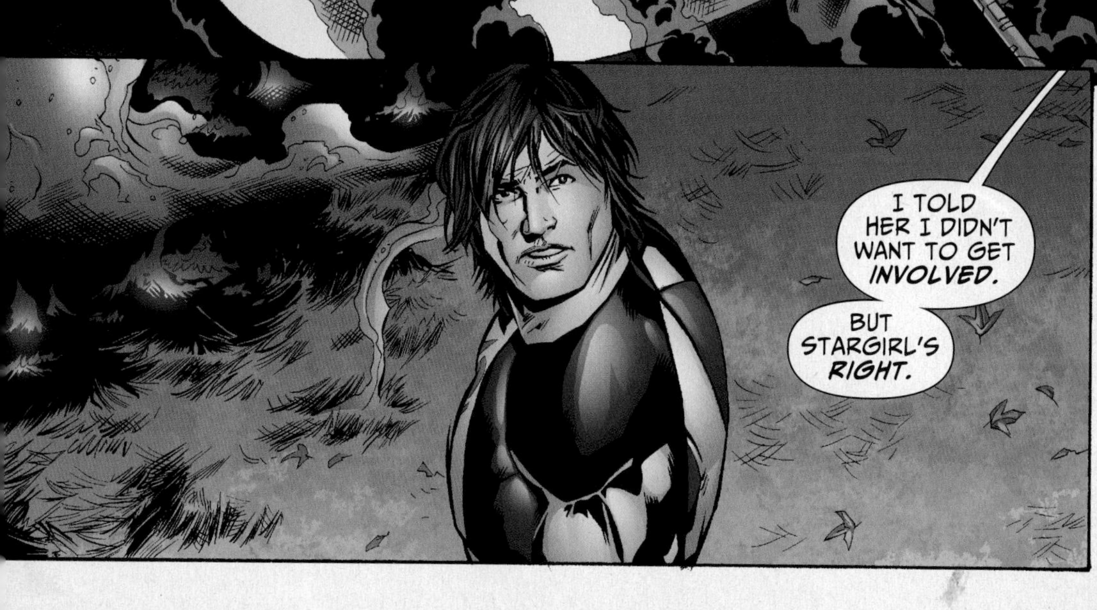
I TOLD HER I DIDN'T WANT TO GET *INVOLVED.*
BUT STARGIRL'S *RIGHT.*

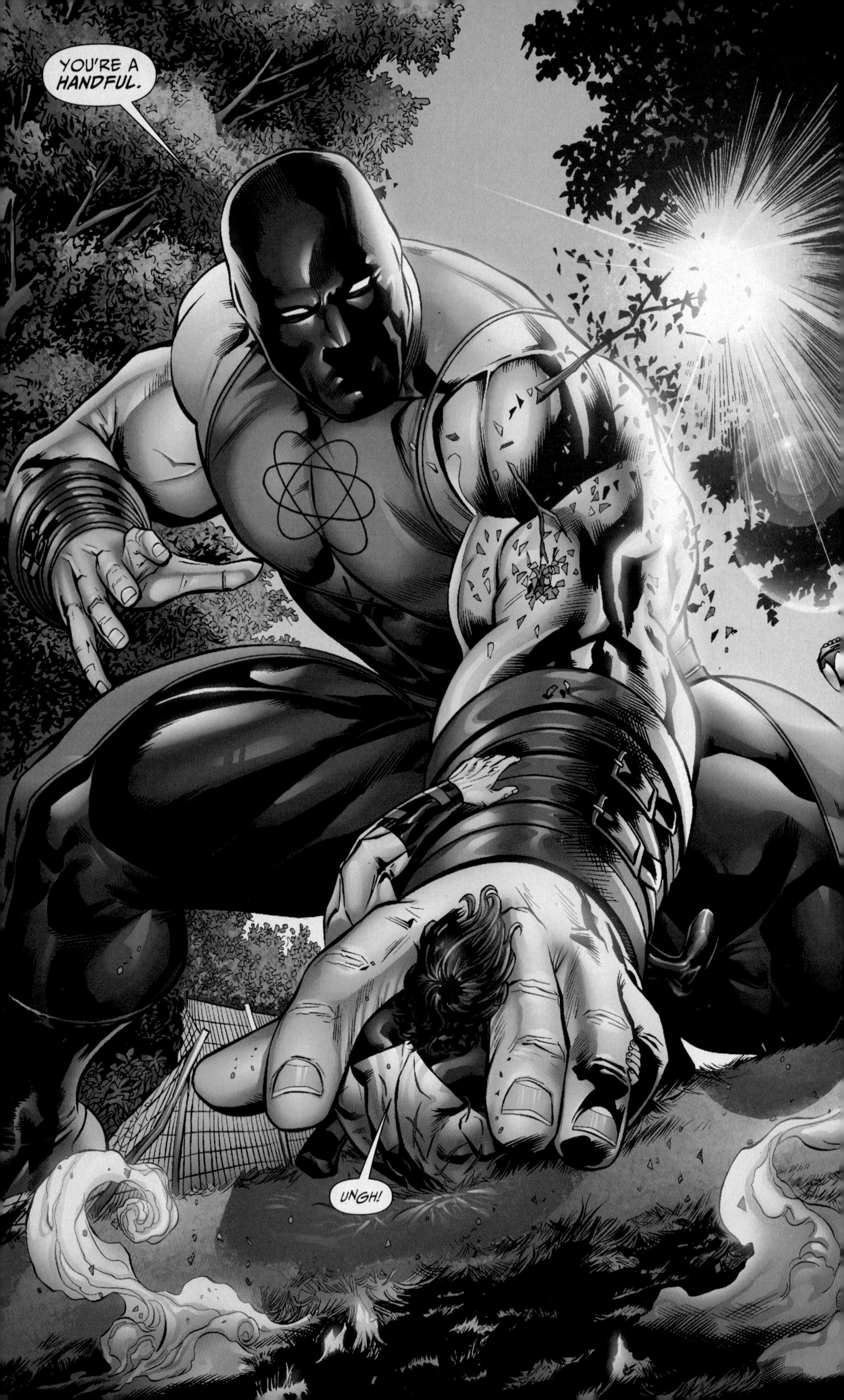
YOU'RE A HANDFUL.
UNGH!

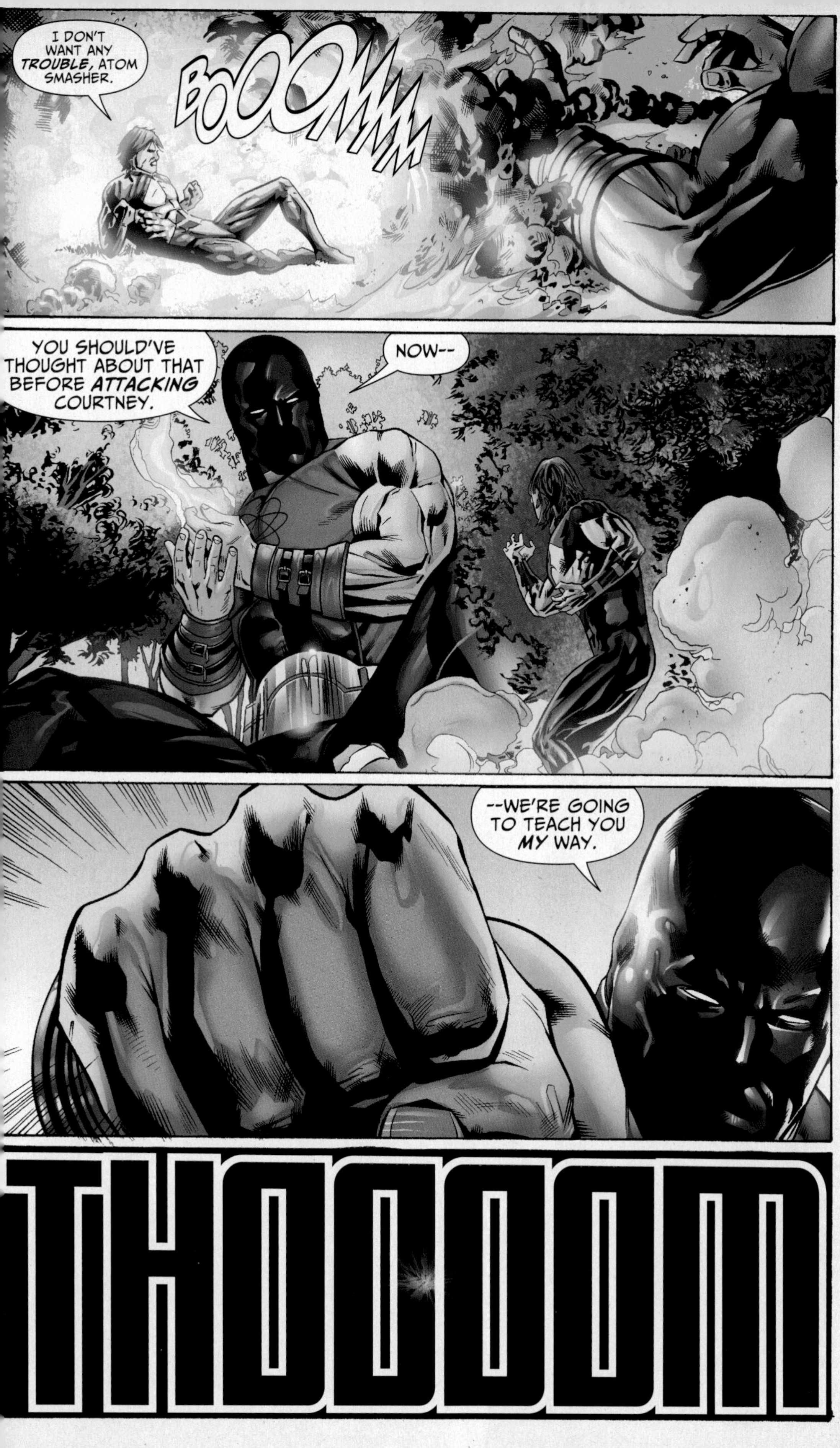

I DON'T WANT ANY *TROUBLE*, ATOM SMASHER.
BOOOMMM
YOU SHOULD'VE THOUGHT ABOUT THAT BEFORE *ATTACKING* COURTNEY.
NOW--
--WE'RE GOING TO TEACH YOU *MY* WAY.
THOOOM

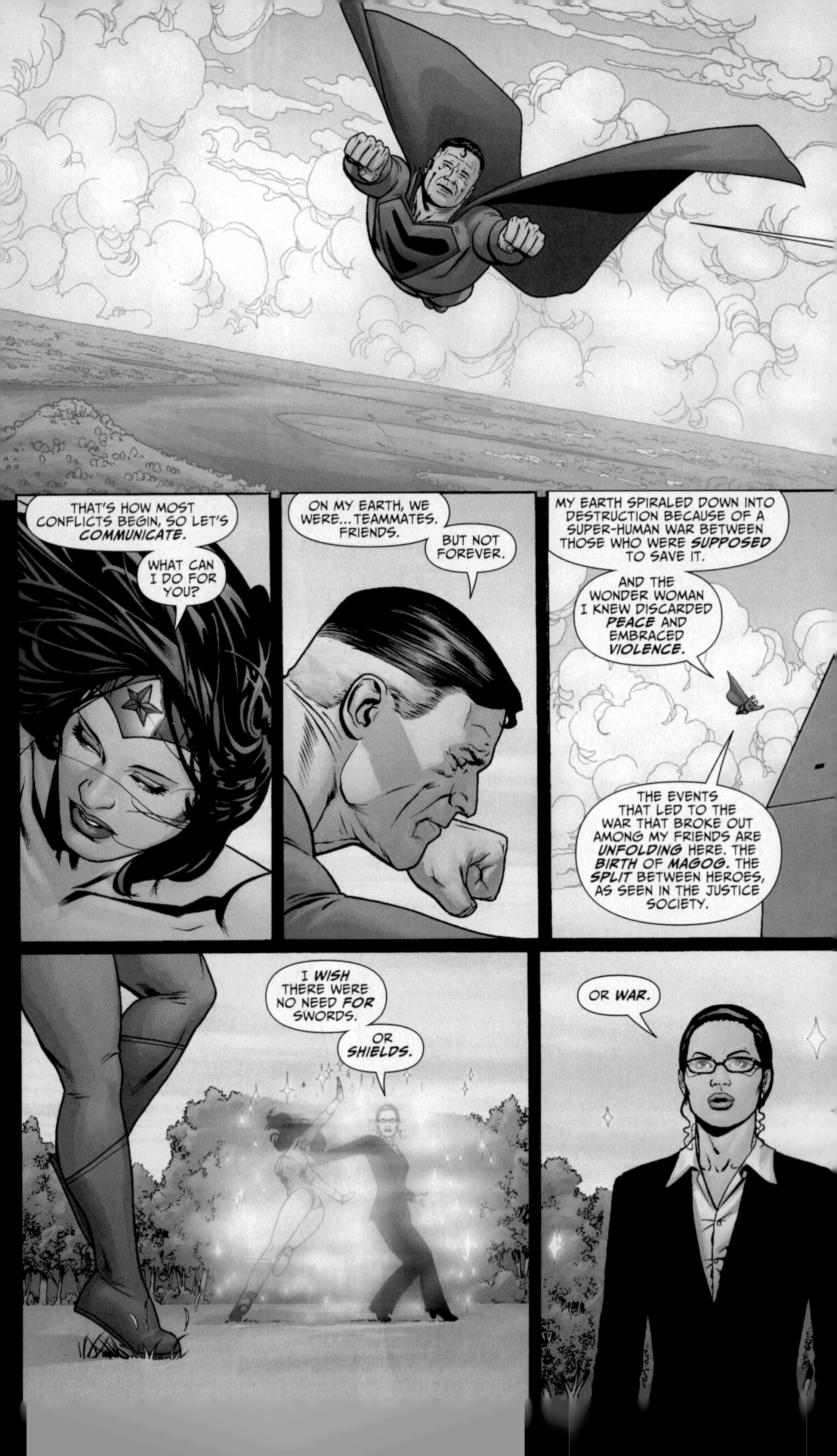
THAT'S HOW MOST CONFLICTS BEGIN, SO LET'S COMMUNICATE.
WHAT CAN I DO FOR YOU?
ON MY EARTH, WE WERE... TEAMMATES. FRIENDS.
BUT NOT FOREVER.
MY EARTH SPIRALED DOWN INTO DESTRUCTION BECAUSE OF A SUPER-HUMAN WAR BETWEEN THOSE WHO WERE SUPPOSED TO SAVE IT.
AND THE WONDER WOMAN I KNEW DISCARDED PEACE AND EMBRACED VIOLENCE.
THE EVENTS THAT LED TO THE WAR THAT BROKE OUT AMONG MY FRIENDS ARE UNFOLDING HERE. THE BIRTH OF MAGOG. THE SPLIT BETWEEN HEROES, AS SEEN IN THE JUSTICE SOCIETY.
I WISH THERE WERE NO NEED FOR SWORDS.
OR SHIELDS.
OR WAR.

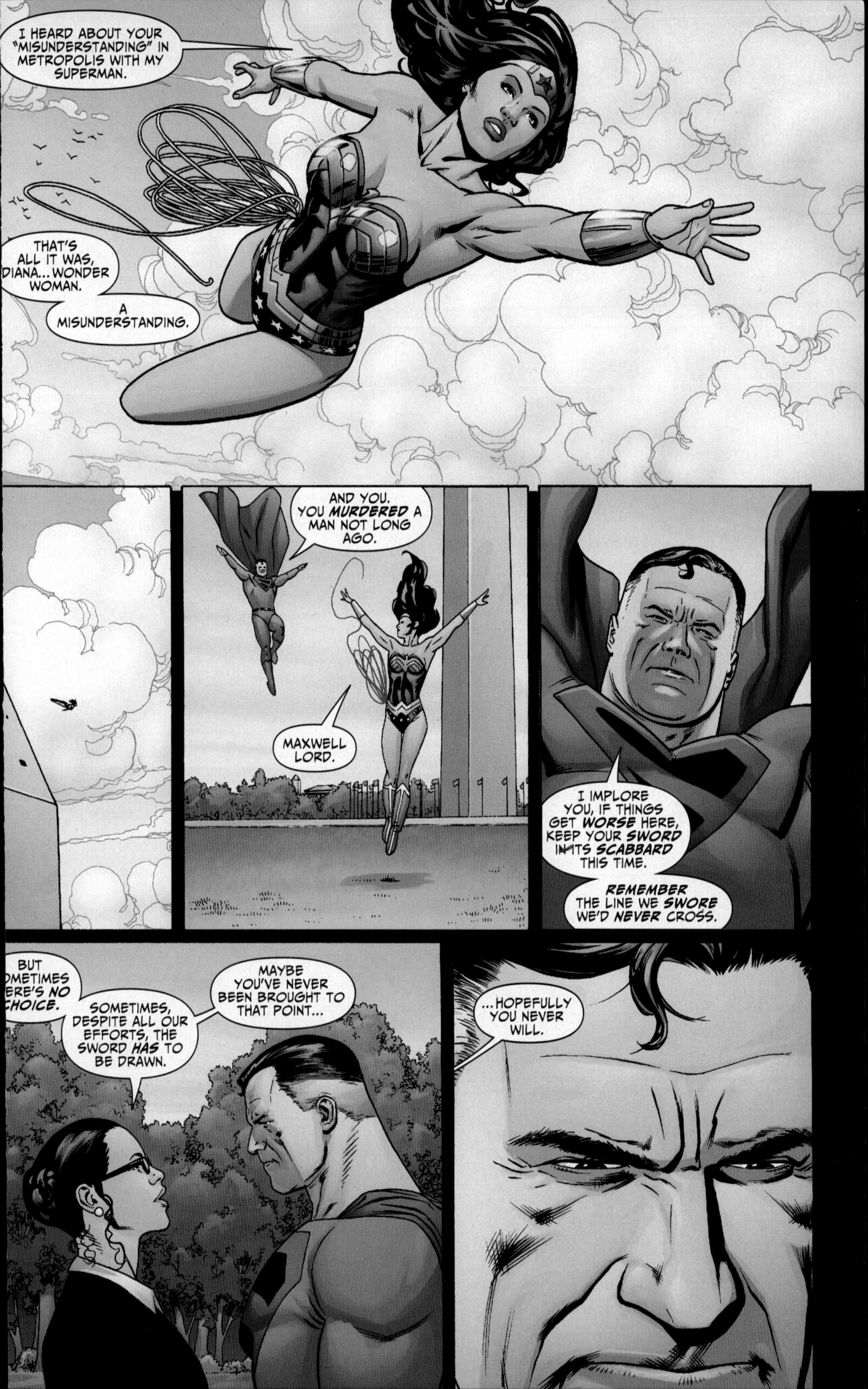
I HEARD ABOUT YOUR "MISUNDERSTANDING" IN METROPOLIS WITH MY SUPERMAN.
THAT'S ALL IT WAS, DIANA... WONDER WOMAN.
A MISUNDERSTANDING.
AND YOU. YOU MURDERED A MAN NOT LONG AGO.
MAXWELL LORD.
I IMPLORE YOU, IF THINGS GET WORSE HERE, KEEP YOUR SWORD IN ITS SCABBARD THIS TIME.
REMEMBER THE LINE WE SWORE WE'D NEVER CROSS.
BUT SOMETIMES THERE'S NO CHOICE.
SOMETIMES, DESPITE ALL OUR EFFORTS, THE SWORD HAS TO BE DRAWN.
MAYBE YOU'VE NEVER BEEN BROUGHT TO THAT POINT...
...HOPEFULLY YOU NEVER WILL.

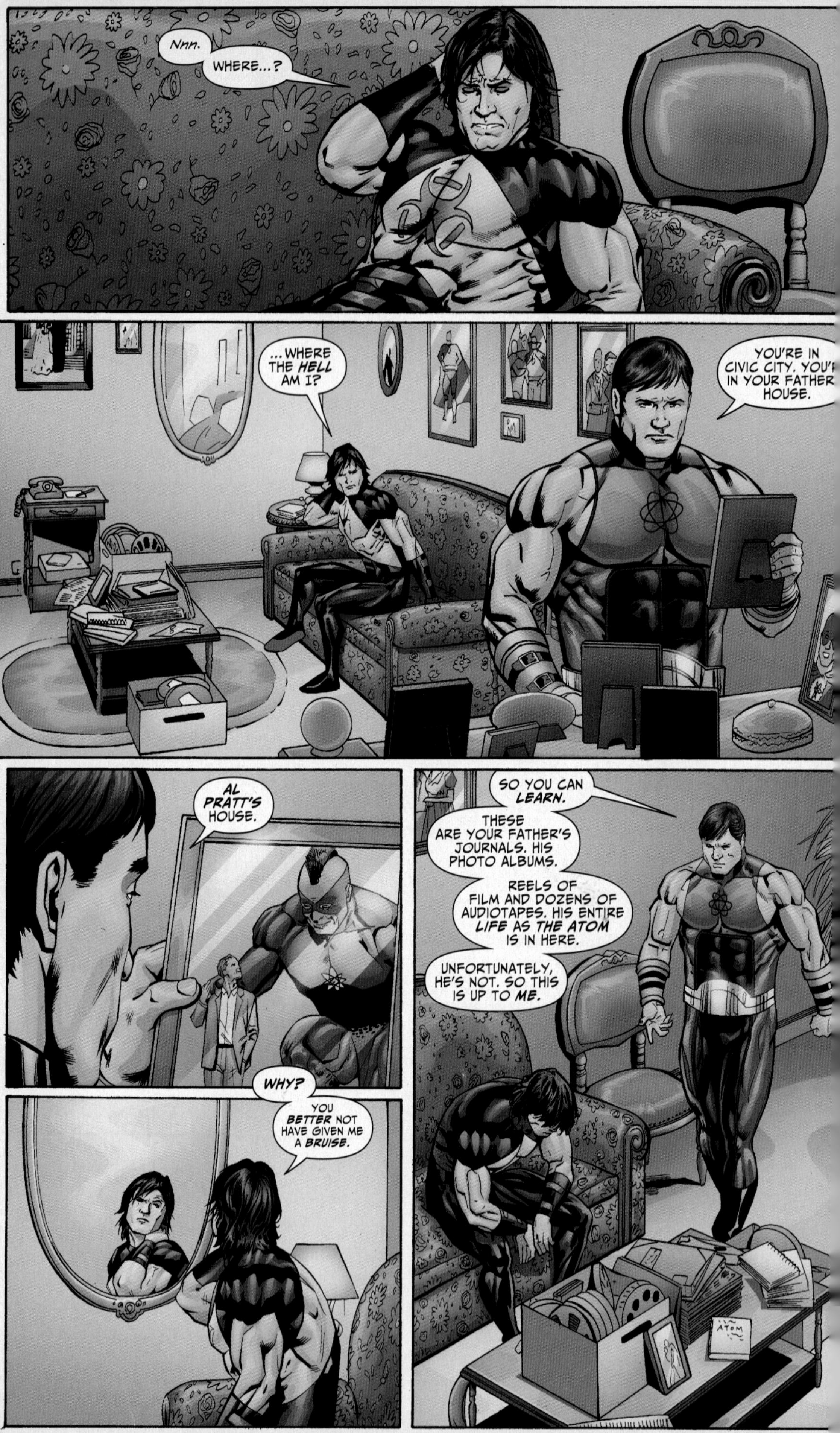

Nnn.
WHERE...?
...WHERE THE HELL AM I?
YOU'RE IN CIVIC CITY. YOU'R IN YOUR FATHER HOUSE.
AL PRATT'S HOUSE.
WHY?
YOU BETTER NOT HAVE GIVEN ME A BRUISE.
SO YOU CAN LEARN.
THESE ARE YOUR FATHER'S JOURNALS. HIS PHOTO ALBUMS.
REELS OF FILM AND DOZENS OF AUDIOTAPES. HIS ENTIRE LIFE AS THE ATOM IS IN HERE.
UNFORTUNATELY, HE'S NOT. SO THIS IS UP TO ME.
ATOM

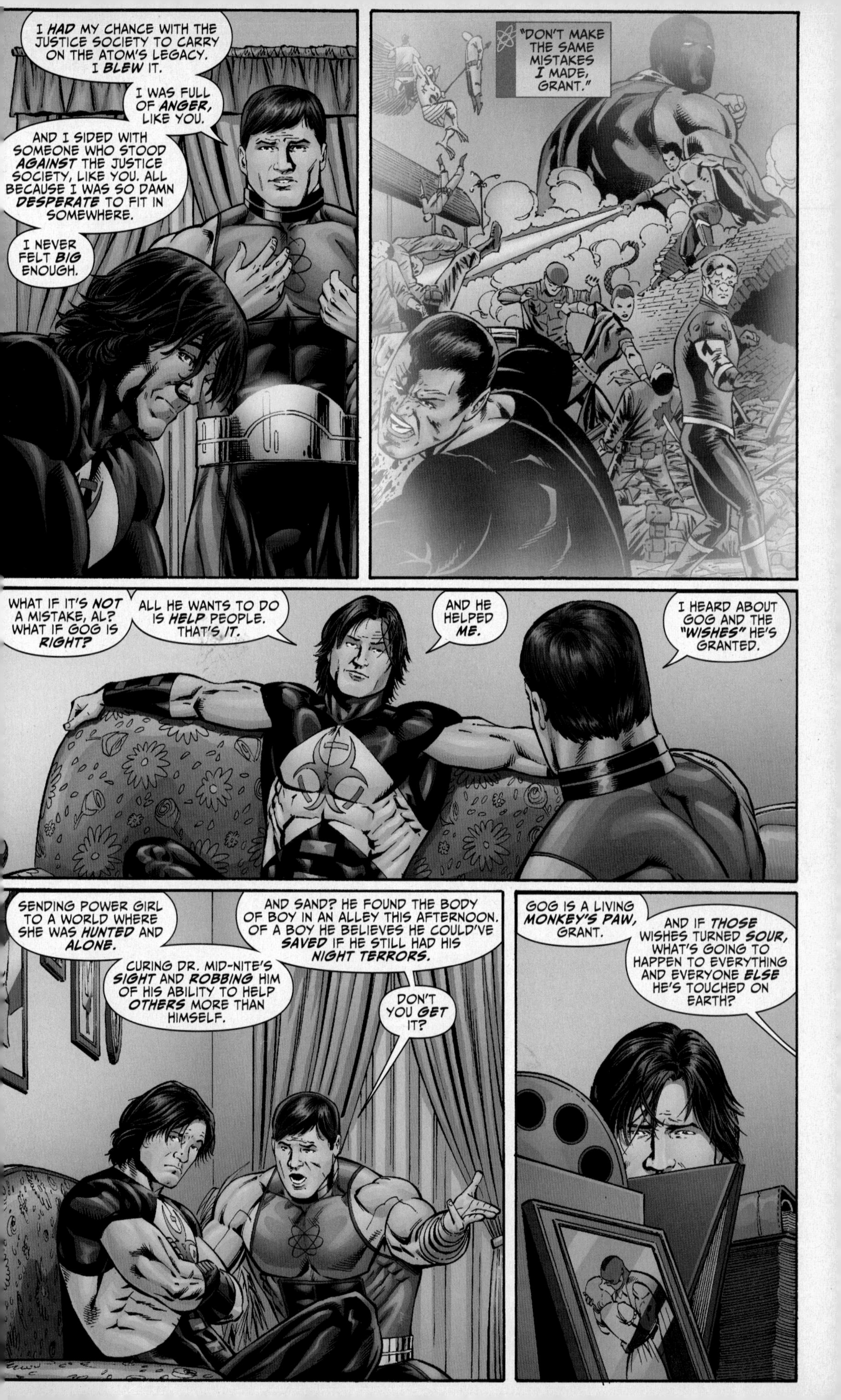
I HAD MY CHANCE WITH THE JUSTICE SOCIETY TO CARRY ON THE ATOM'S LEGACY. I BLEW IT.
I WAS FULL OF ANGER, LIKE YOU.
AND I SIDED WITH SOMEONE WHO STOOD AGAINST THE JUSTICE SOCIETY, LIKE YOU. ALL BECAUSE I WAS SO DAMN DESPERATE TO FIT IN SOMEWHERE.
I NEVER FELT BIG ENOUGH.
"DON'T MAKE THE SAME MISTAKES I MADE, GRANT."
WHAT IF IT'S NOT A MISTAKE, AL? WHAT IF GOG IS RIGHT?
ALL HE WANTS TO DO IS HELP PEOPLE. THAT'S IT.
AND HE HELPED ME.
I HEARD ABOUT GOG AND THE "WISHES" HE'S GRANTED.
SENDING POWER GIRL TO A WORLD WHERE SHE WAS HUNTED AND ALONE.
CURING DR. MID-NITE'S SIGHT AND ROBBING HIM OF HIS ABILITY TO HELP OTHERS MORE THAN HIMSELF.
AND SAND? HE FOUND THE BODY OF BOY IN AN ALLEY THIS AFTERNOON. OF A BOY HE BELIEVES HE COULD'VE SAVED IF HE STILL HAD HIS NIGHT TERRORS.
DON'T YOU GET IT?
GOG IS A LIVING MONKEY'S PAW, GRANT.
AND IF THOSE WISHES TURNED SOUR, WHAT'S GOING TO HAPPEN TO EVERYTHING AND EVERYONE ELSE HE'S TOUCHED ON EARTH?

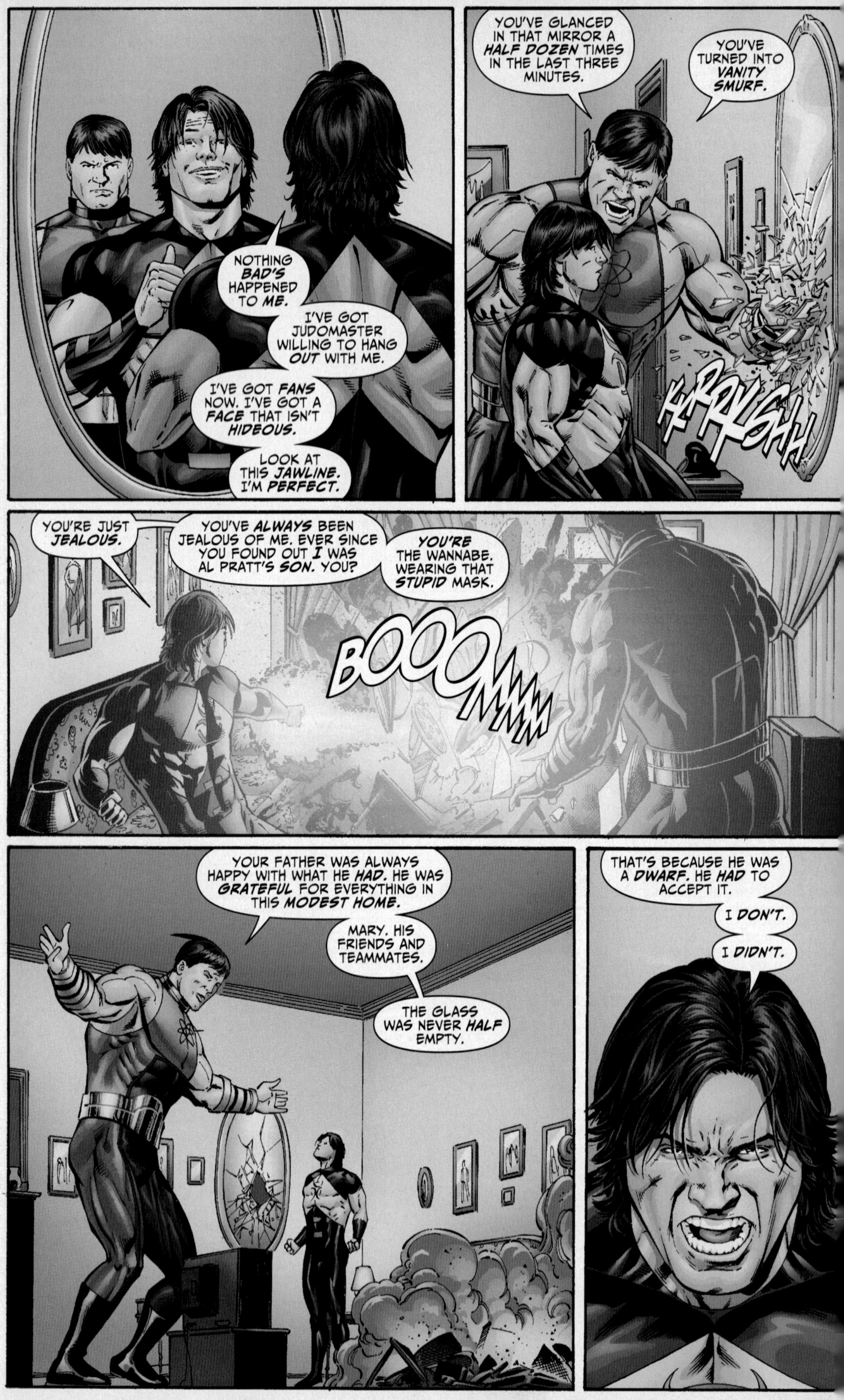

NOTHING BAD'S HAPPENED TO ME.
I'VE GOT JUDOMASTER WILLING TO HANG OUT WITH ME.
I'VE GOT FANS NOW. I'VE GOT A FACE THAT ISN'T HIDEOUS.
LOOK AT THIS JAWLINE. I'M PERFECT.
YOU'VE GLANCED IN THAT MIRROR A HALF DOZEN TIMES IN THE LAST THREE MINUTES.
YOU'VE TURNED INTO VANITY SMURF.
KRRRUSHH
YOU'RE JUST JEALOUS.
YOU'VE ALWAYS BEEN JEALOUS OF ME. EVER SINCE YOU FOUND OUT I WAS AL PRATT'S SON. YOU?
YOU'RE THE WANNABE. WEARING THAT STUPID MASK.
BOOOMMM
YOUR FATHER WAS ALWAYS HAPPY WITH WHAT HE HAD. HE WAS GRATEFUL FOR EVERYTHING IN THIS MODEST HOME.
MARY. HIS FRIENDS AND TEAMMATES.
THE GLASS WAS NEVER HALF EMPTY.
THAT'S BECAUSE HE WAS A DWARF. HE HAD TO ACCEPT IT.
I DON'T.
I DIDN'T.

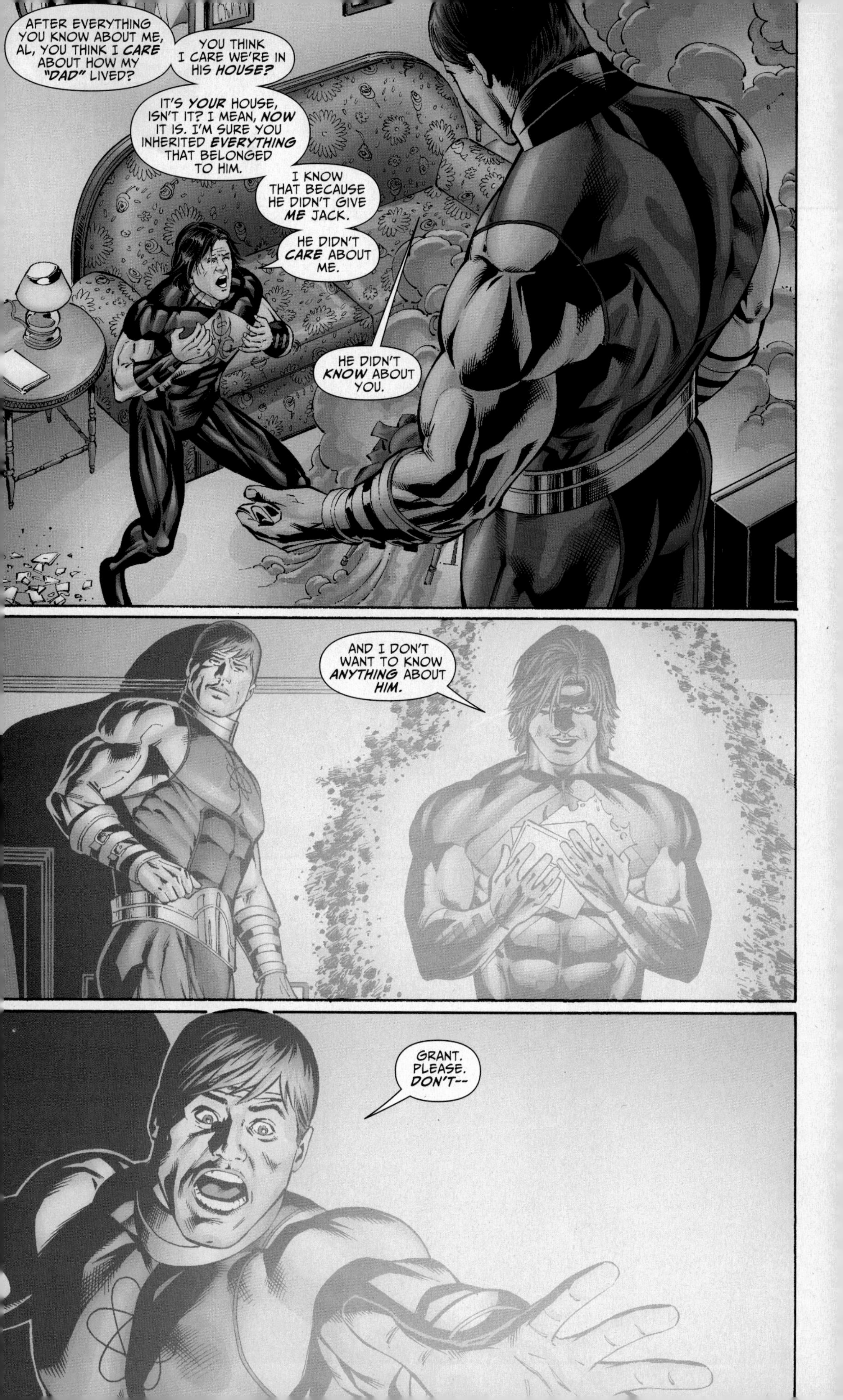
AFTER EVERYTHING YOU KNOW ABOUT ME, AL, YOU THINK I CARE ABOUT HOW MY "DAD" LIVED?
YOU THINK I CARE WE'RE IN HIS HOUSE?
IT'S YOUR HOUSE, ISN'T IT? I MEAN, NOW IT IS. I'M SURE YOU INHERITED EVERYTHING THAT BELONGED TO HIM.
I KNOW THAT BECAUSE HE DIDN'T GIVE ME JACK.
HE DIDN'T CARE ABOUT ME.
HE DIDN'T KNOW ABOUT YOU.
AND I DON'T WANT TO KNOW ANYTHING ABOUT HIM.
GRANT. PLEASE. DON'T--

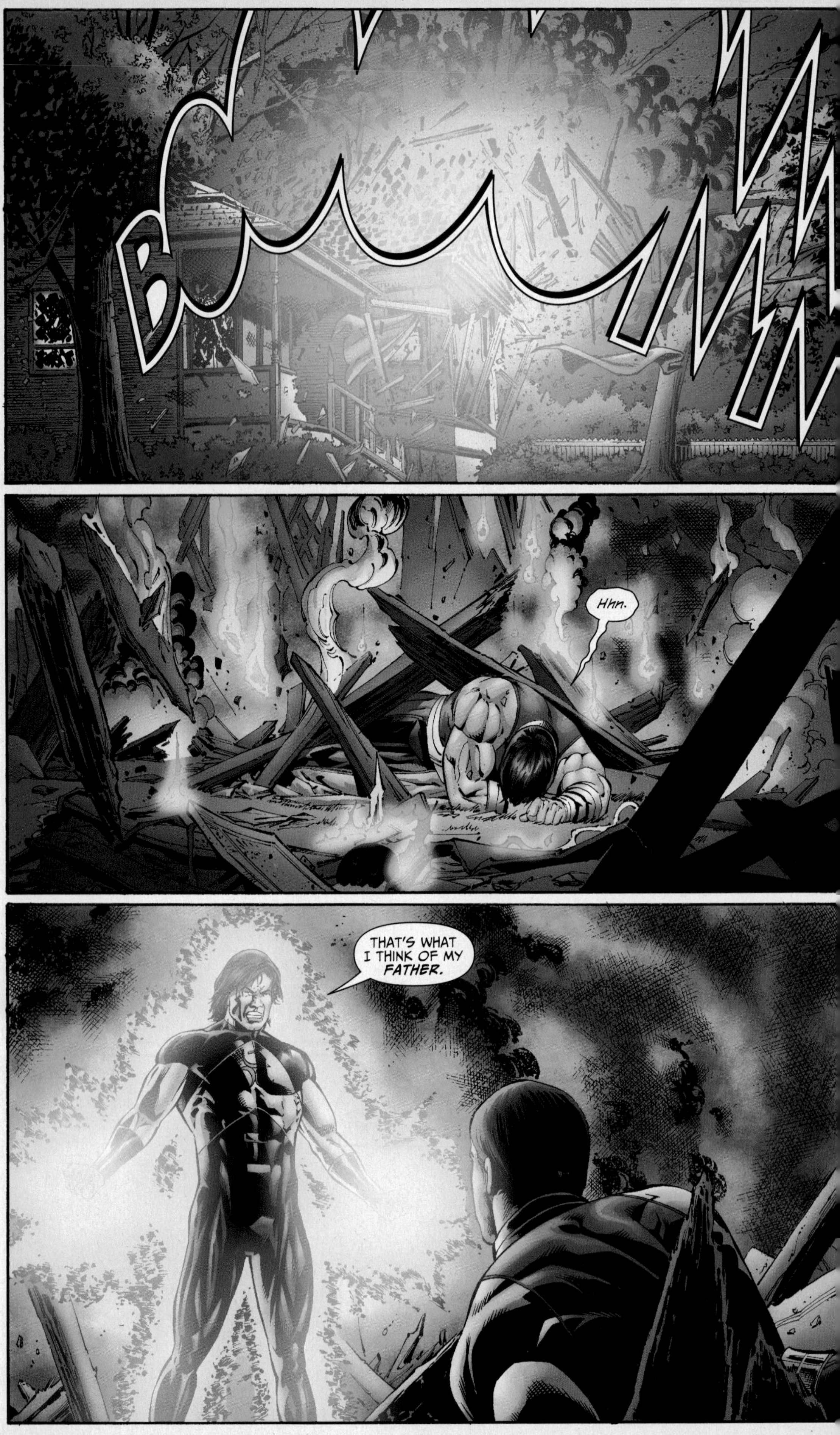
BOOM
Hhn.
THAT'S WHAT I THINK OF MY *FATHER.*

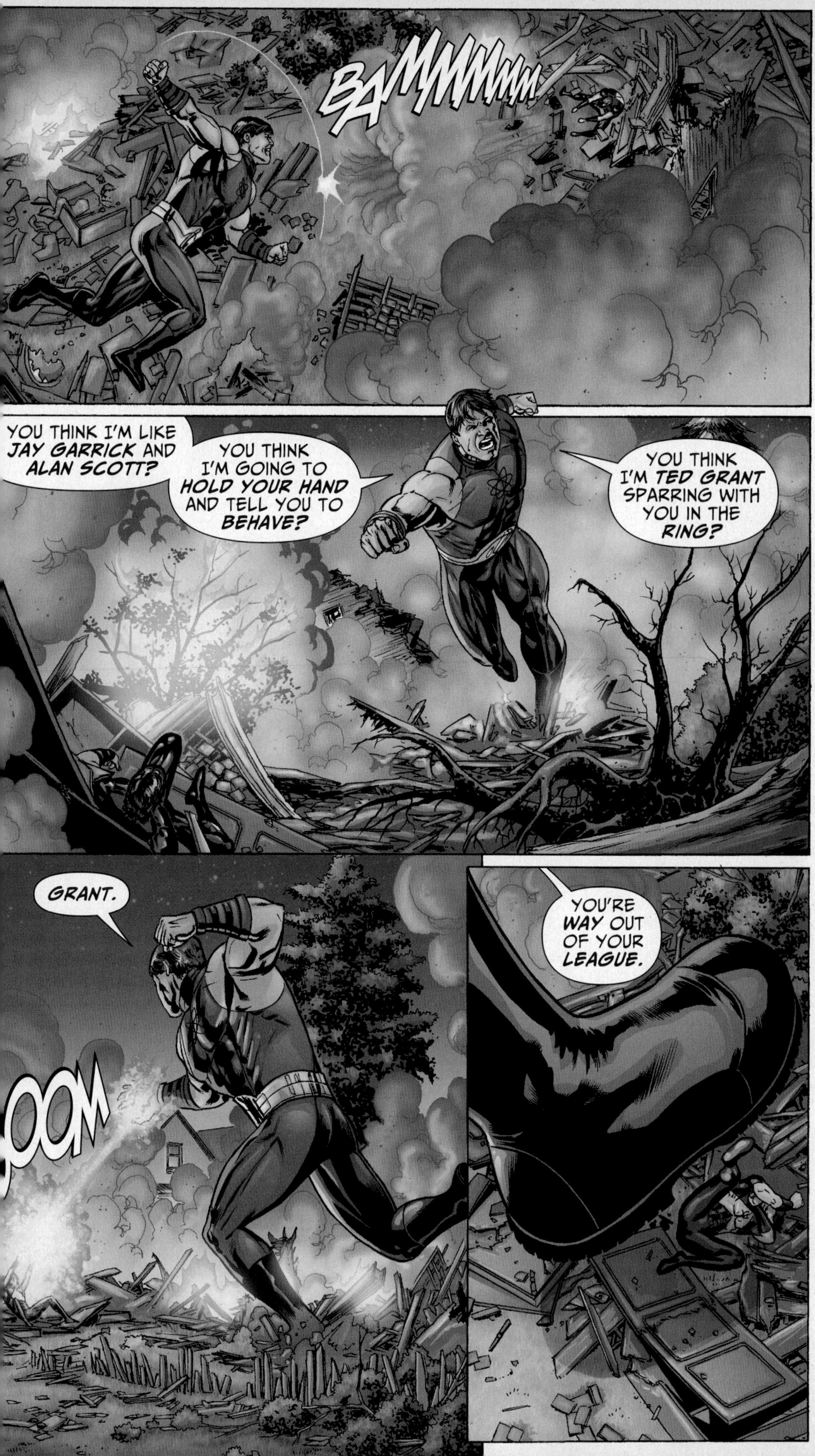
BAMMMMMM
YOU THINK I'M LIKE JAY GARRICK AND ALAN SCOTT?
YOU THINK I'M GOING TO HOLD YOUR HAND AND TELL YOU TO BEHAVE?
YOU THINK I'M TED GRANT SPARRING WITH YOU IN THE RING?
GRANT.
OOM
YOU'RE WAY OUT OF YOUR LEAGUE.

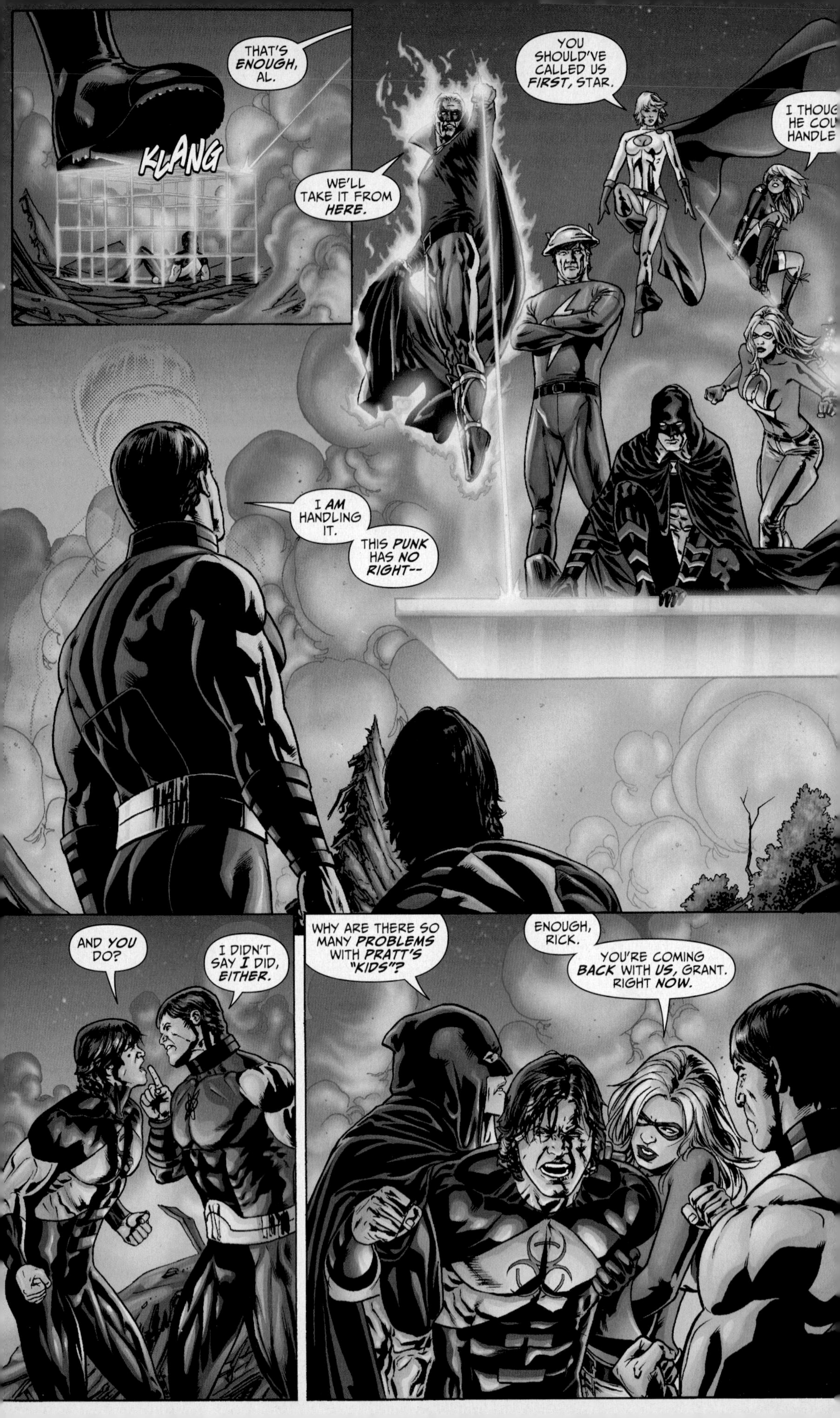
THAT'S *ENOUGH*, AL.
KLANG
YOU SHOULD'VE CALLED US *FIRST*, STAR.
WE'LL TAKE IT FROM *HERE*.
I THOUG HE COU HANDLE
I *AM* HANDLING IT.
THIS *PUNK* HAS *NO RIGHT*--
AND *YOU* DO?
I DIDN'T SAY *I* DID, *EITHER*.
WHY ARE THERE SO MANY *PROBLEMS* WITH *PRATT'S "KIDS"*?
ENOUGH, RICK.
YOU'RE COMING *BACK* WITH *US*, GRANT. RIGHT *NOW*.

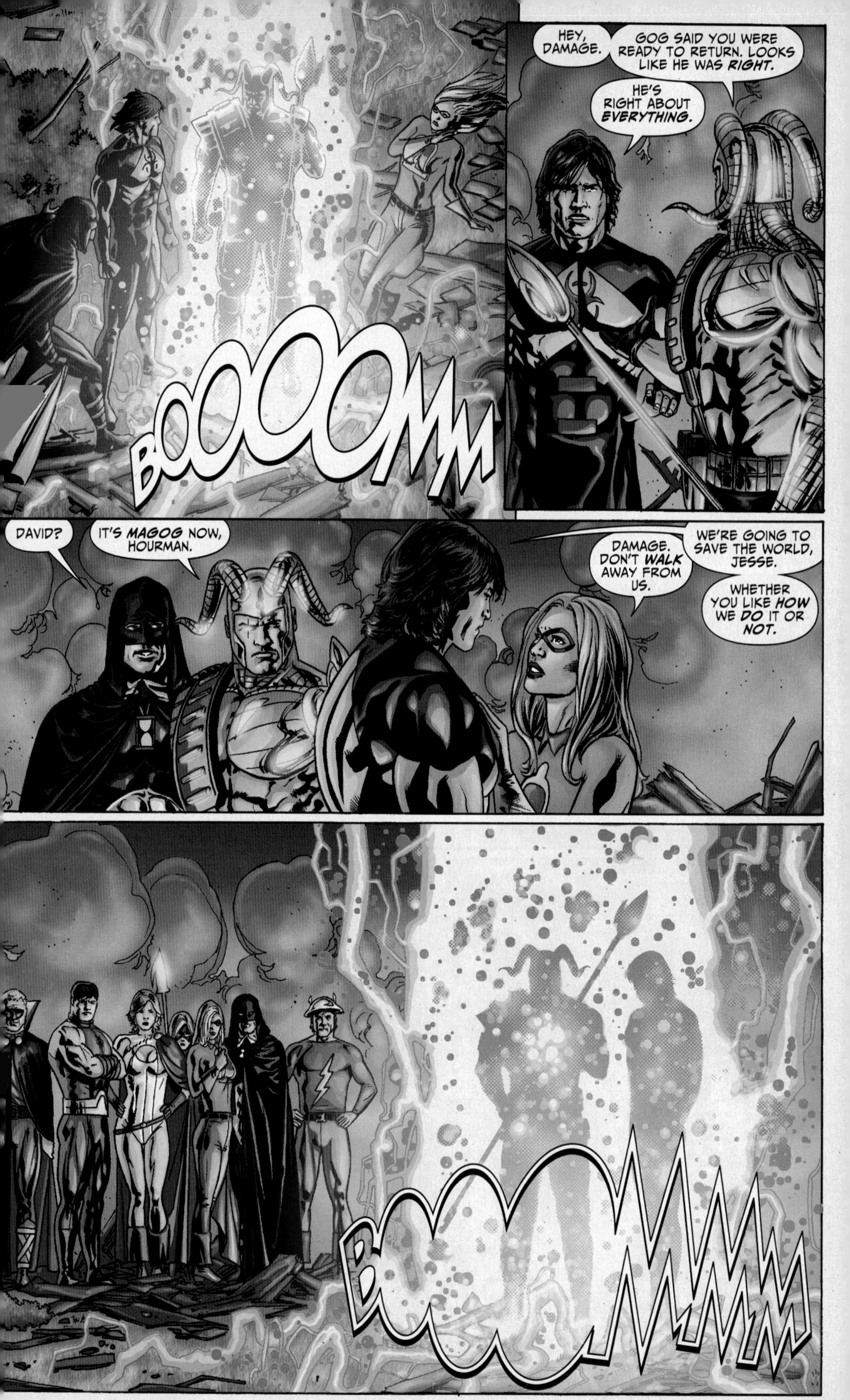
BOOOOMM
HEY, DAMAGE.
GOG SAID YOU WERE READY TO RETURN. LOOKS LIKE HE WAS RIGHT.
HE'S RIGHT ABOUT EVERYTHING.
DAVID?
IT'S MAGOG NOW, HOURMAN.
DAMAGE. DON'T WALK AWAY FROM US.
WE'RE GOING TO SAVE THE WORLD, JESSE.
WHETHER YOU LIKE HOW WE DO IT OR NOT.
BOOOMMM

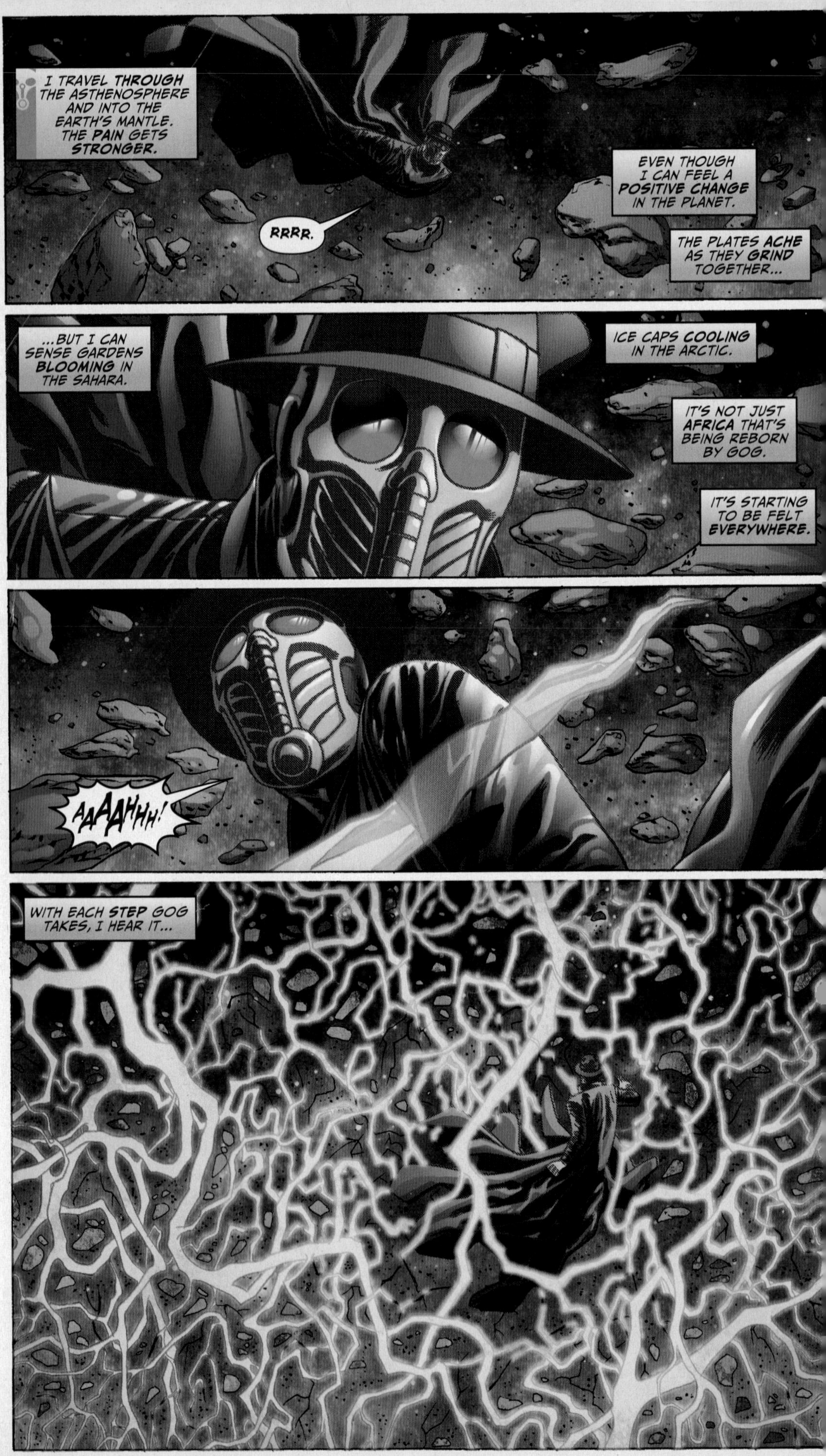
I TRAVEL THROUGH THE ASTHENOSPHERE AND INTO THE EARTH'S MANTLE. THE PAIN GETS STRONGER.
RRRR.
EVEN THOUGH I CAN FEEL A POSITIVE CHANGE IN THE PLANET.
THE PLATES ACHE AS THEY GRIND TOGETHER...
...BUT I CAN SENSE GARDENS BLOOMING IN THE SAHARA.
ICE CAPS COOLING IN THE ARCTIC.
IT'S NOT JUST AFRICA THAT'S BEING REBORN BY GOG.
IT'S STARTING TO BE FELT EVERYWHERE.
AAAAHHH!
WITH EACH STEP GOG TAKES, I HEAR IT...

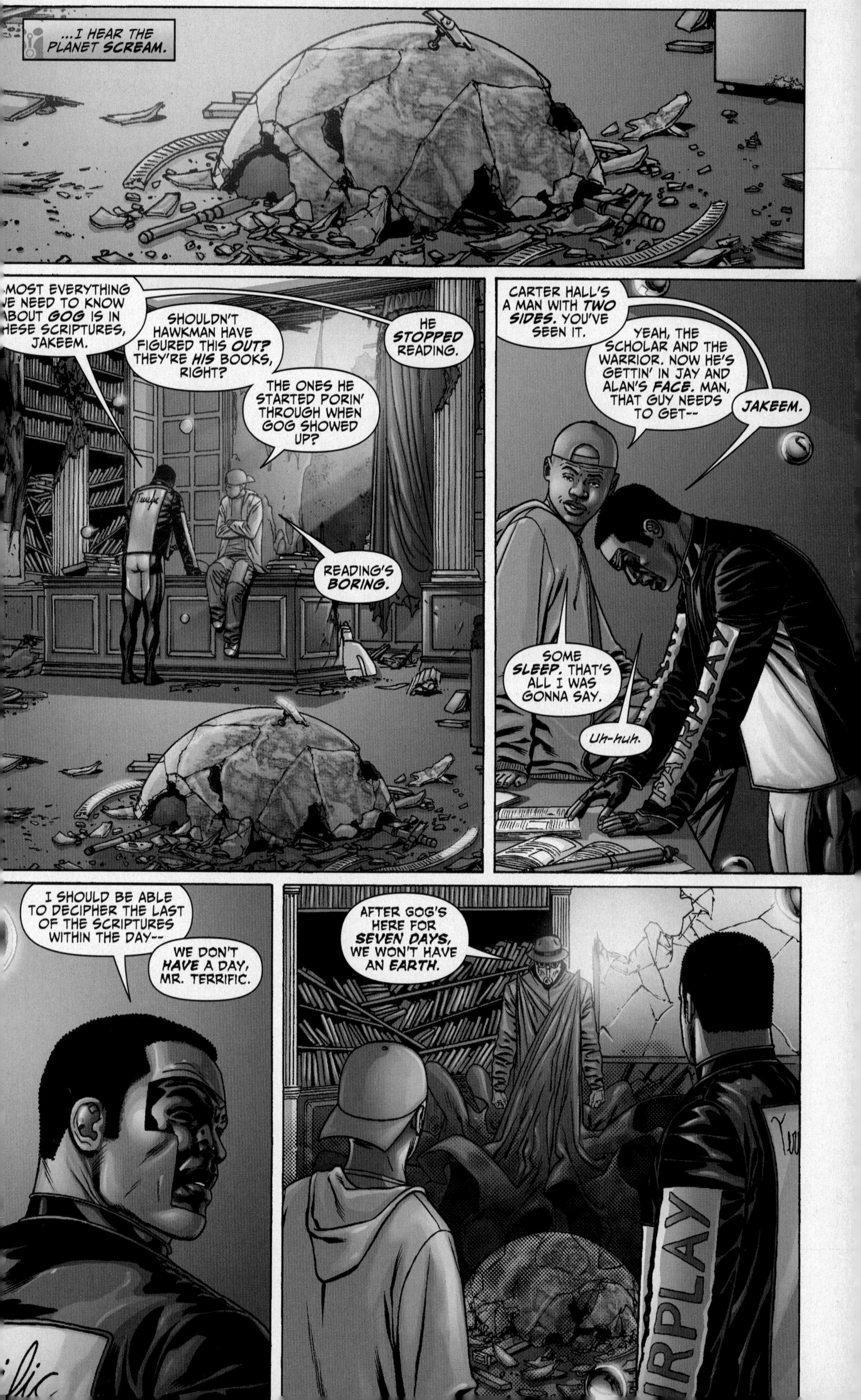
...I HEAR THE PLANET SCREAM.
MOST EVERYTHING WE NEED TO KNOW ABOUT GOG IS IN THESE SCRIPTURES, JAKEEM.
SHOULDN'T HAWKMAN HAVE FIGURED THIS OUT? THEY'RE HIS BOOKS, RIGHT?
HE STOPPED READING.
THE ONES HE STARTED PORIN' THROUGH WHEN GOG SHOWED UP?
READING'S BORING.
CARTER HALL'S A MAN WITH TWO SIDES. YOU'VE SEEN IT.
YEAH, THE SCHOLAR AND THE WARRIOR. NOW HE'S GETTIN' IN JAY AND ALAN'S FACE. MAN, THAT GUY NEEDS TO GET--
JAKEEM.
SOME SLEEP. THAT'S ALL I WAS GONNA SAY.
Uh-huh.
I SHOULD BE ABLE TO DECIPHER THE LAST OF THE SCRIPTURES WITHIN THE DAY--
WE DON'T HAVE A DAY, MR. TERRIFIC.
AFTER GOG'S HERE FOR SEVEN DAYS, WE WON'T HAVE AN EARTH.

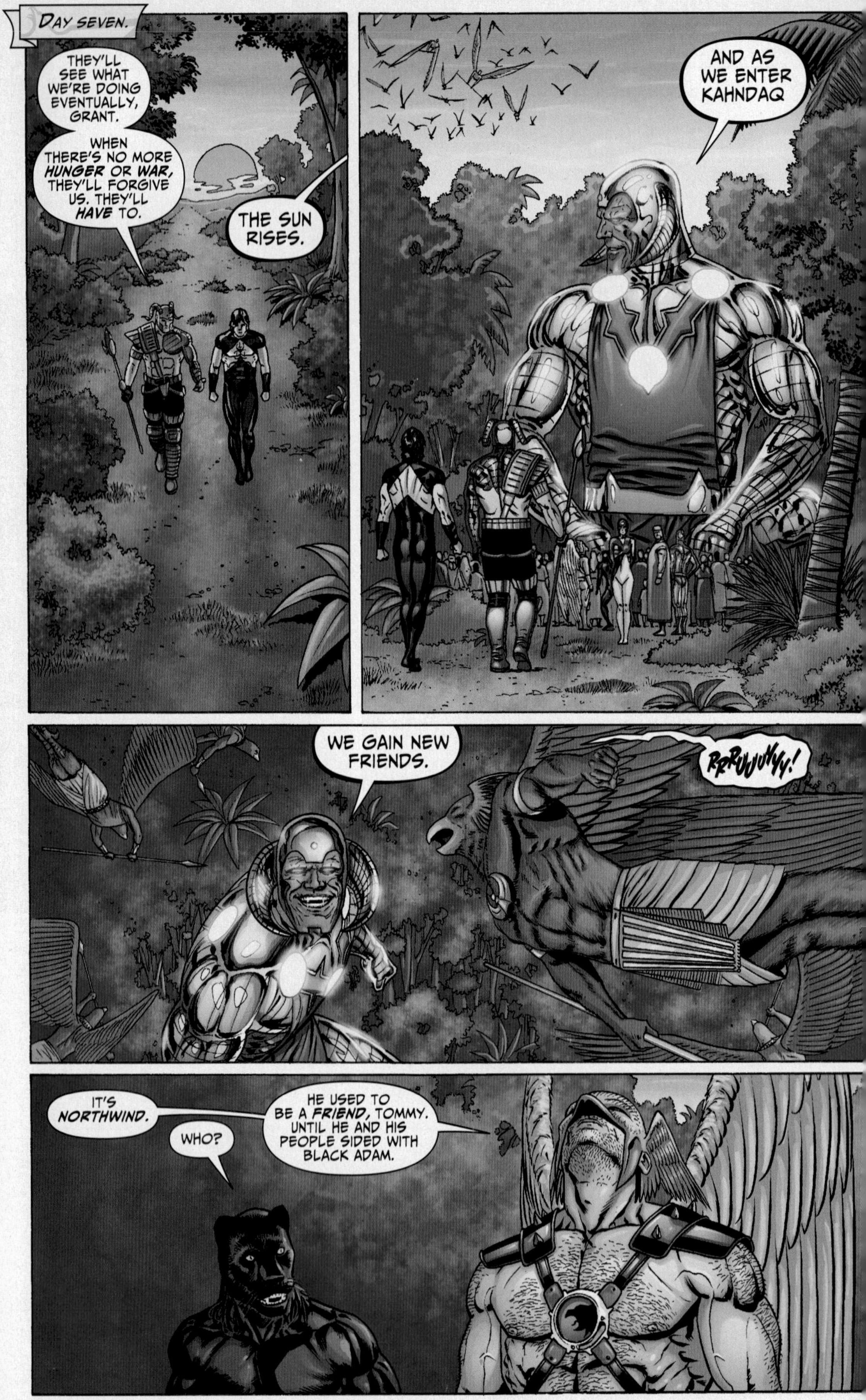
DAY SEVEN.
THEY'LL SEE WHAT WE'RE DOING EVENTUALLY, GRANT.
WHEN THERE'S NO MORE HUNGER OR WAR, THEY'LL FORGIVE US. THEY'LL HAVE TO.
THE SUN RISES.
AND AS WE ENTER KAHNDAQ
WE GAIN NEW FRIENDS.
RRRUUUHYY!
IT'S NORTHWIND.
WHO?
HE USED TO BE A FRIEND, TOMMY. UNTIL HE AND HIS PEOPLE SIDED WITH BLACK ADAM.

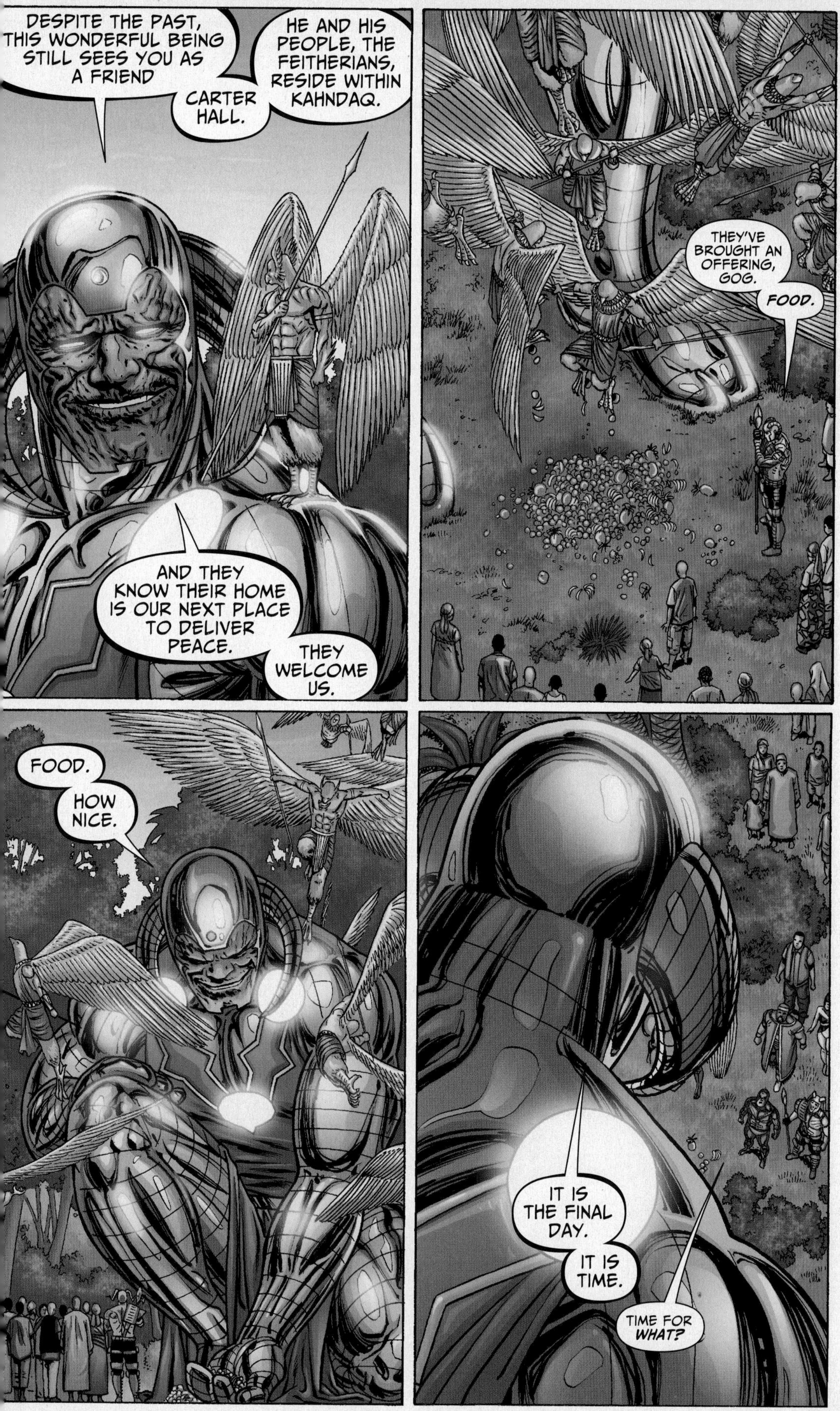
DESPITE THE PAST, THIS WONDERFUL BEING STILL SEES YOU AS A FRIEND
CARTER HALL.
HE AND HIS PEOPLE, THE FEITHERIANS, RESIDE WITHIN KAHNDAQ.
AND THEY KNOW THEIR HOME IS OUR NEXT PLACE TO DELIVER PEACE.
THEY WELCOME US.
THEY'VE BROUGHT AN OFFERING, GOG.
FOOD.
FOOD.
HOW NICE.
IT IS THE FINAL DAY.
IT IS TIME.
TIME FOR WHAT?

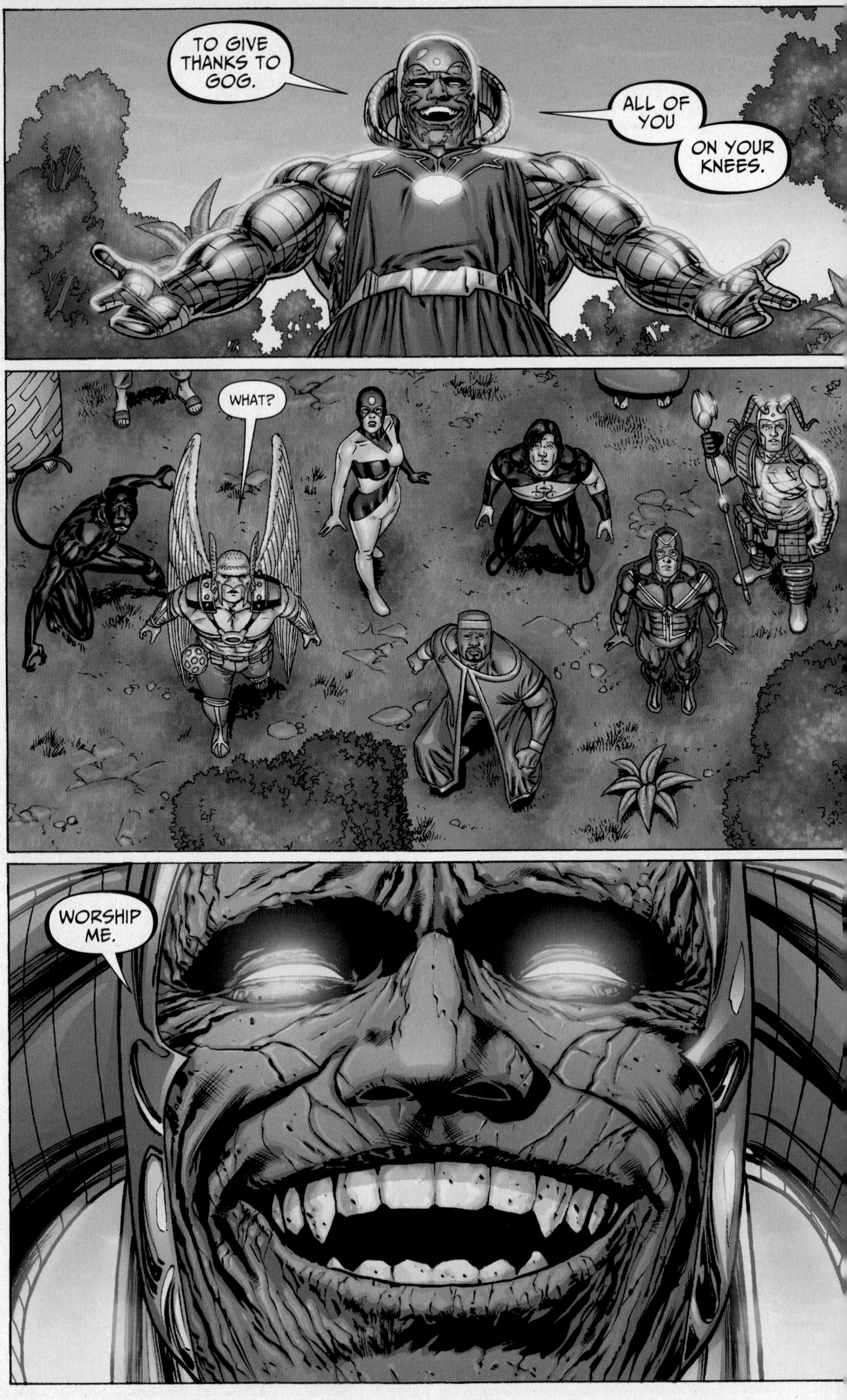
TO GIVE THANKS TO GOG.
ALL OF YOU
ON YOUR KNEES.
WHAT?
WORSHIP ME.

JUSTICE SOCIETY OF AMERICA #21 cover A by Alex Ross

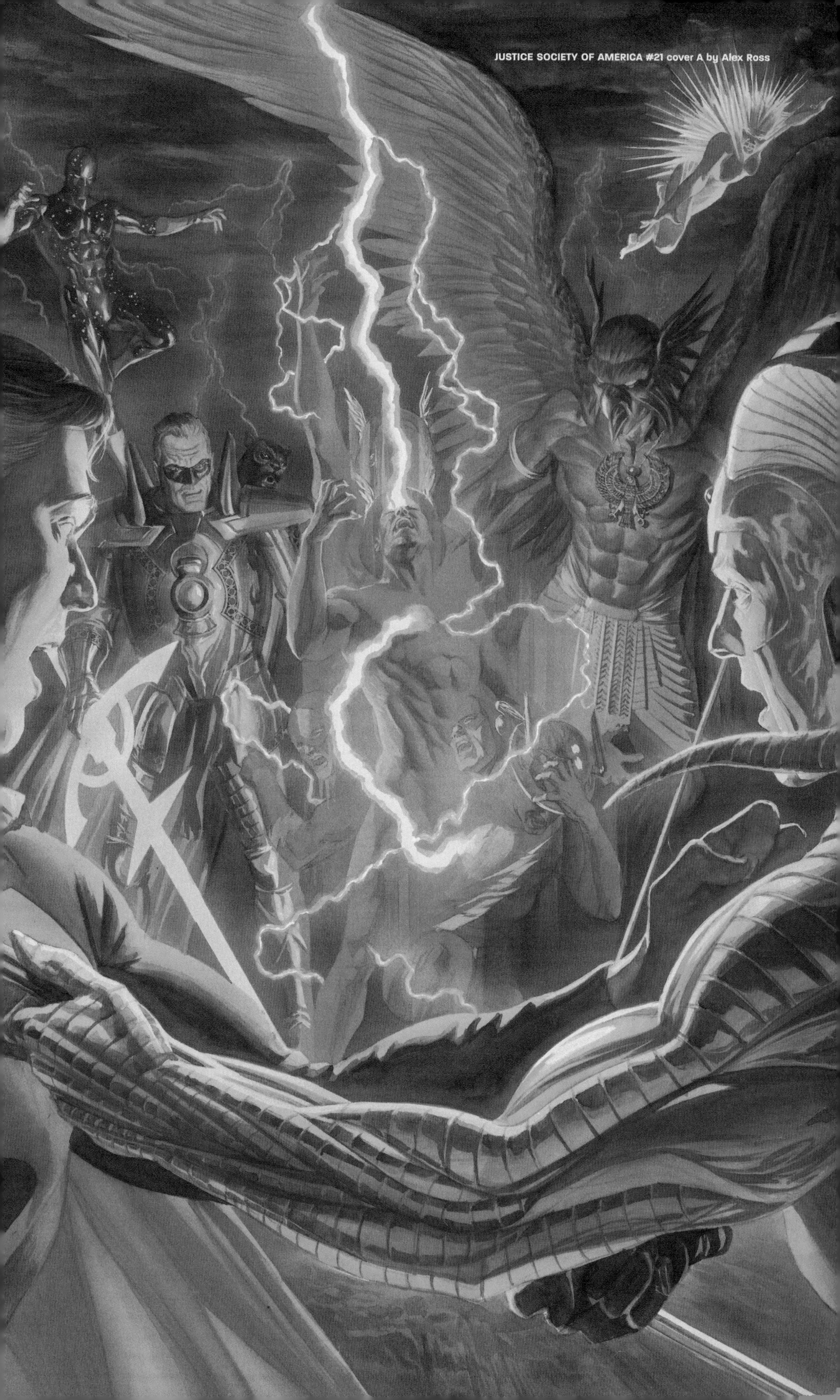

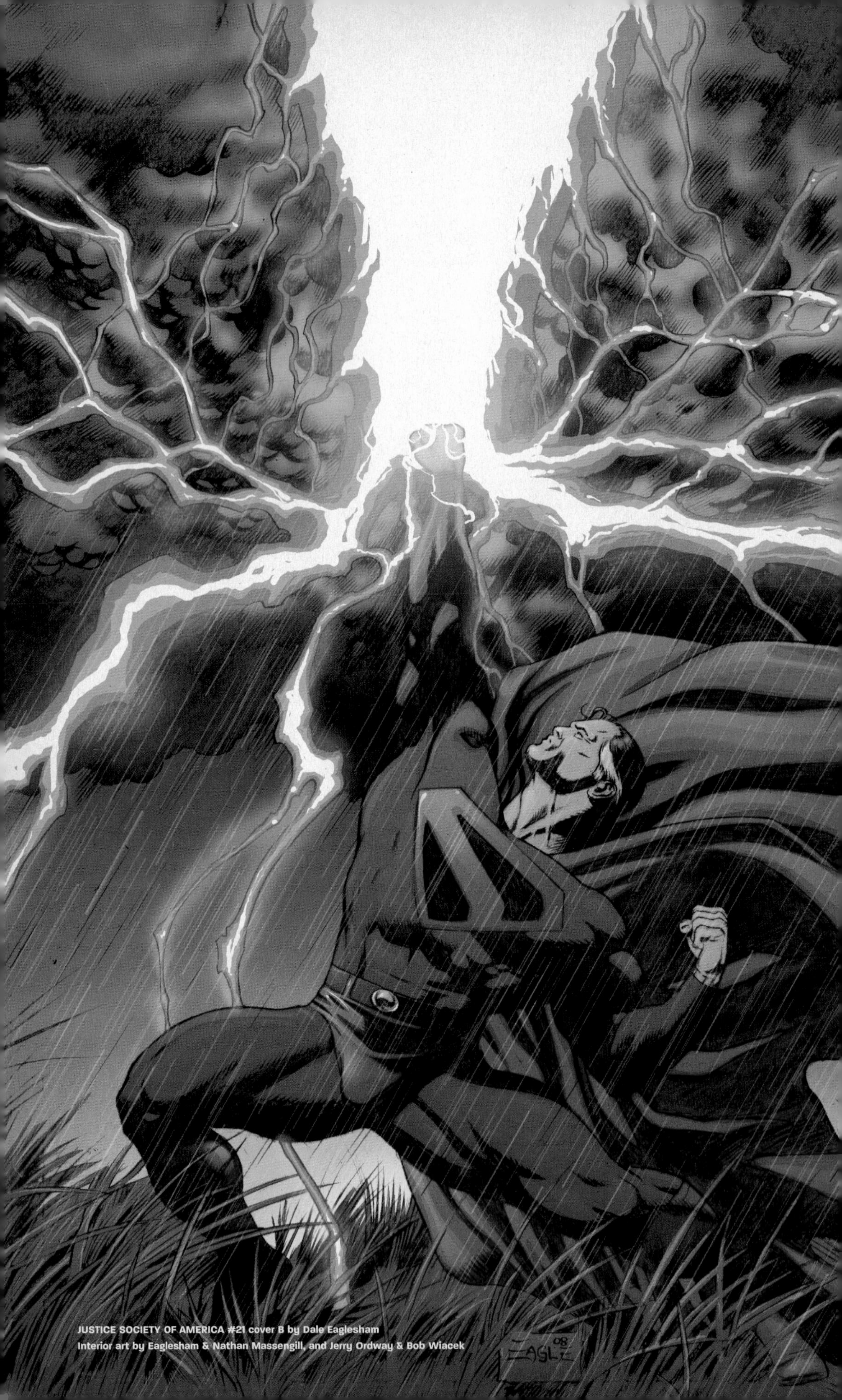

JUSTICE SOCIETY OF AMERICA #21 cover B by Dale Eaglesham
Interior art by Eaglesham & Nathan Massengill, and Jerry Ordway & Bob Wiacek

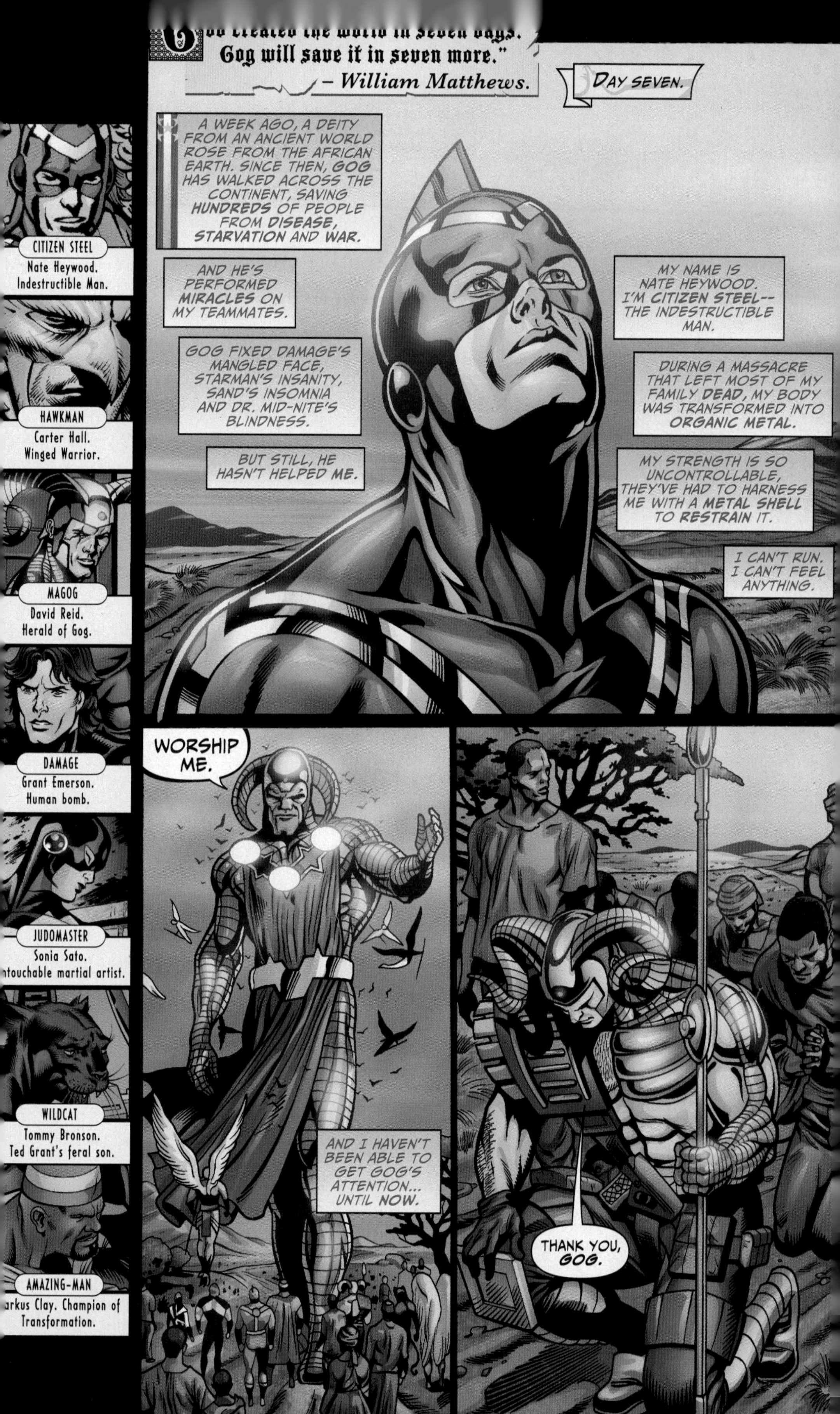
"God created the world in seven days. Gog will save it in seven more."
– William Matthews.
DAY SEVEN.
CITIZEN STEEL
Nate Heywood. Indestructible Man.
HAWKMAN
Carter Hall. Winged Warrior.
MAGOG
David Reid. Herald of Gog.
DAMAGE
Grant Emerson. Human bomb.
JUDOMASTER
Sonia Sato. ntouchable martial artist.
WILDCAT
Tommy Bronson. Ted Grant's feral son.
AMAZING-MAN
arkus Clay. Champion of Transformation.
A WEEK AGO, A DEITY FROM AN ANCIENT WORLD ROSE FROM THE AFRICAN EARTH. SINCE THEN, GOG HAS WALKED ACROSS THE CONTINENT, SAVING HUNDREDS OF PEOPLE FROM DISEASE, STARVATION AND WAR.
AND HE'S PERFORMED MIRACLES ON MY TEAMMATES.
GOG FIXED DAMAGE'S MANGLED FACE, STARMAN'S INSANITY, SAND'S INSOMNIA AND DR. MID-NITE'S BLINDNESS.
BUT STILL, HE HASN'T HELPED ME.
MY NAME IS NATE HEYWOOD. I'M CITIZEN STEEL-- THE INDESTRUCTIBLE MAN.
DURING A MASSACRE THAT LEFT MOST OF MY FAMILY DEAD, MY BODY WAS TRANSFORMED INTO ORGANIC METAL.
MY STRENGTH IS SO UNCONTROLLABLE, THEY'VE HAD TO HARNESS ME WITH A METAL SHELL TO RESTRAIN IT.
I CAN'T RUN. I CAN'T FEEL ANYTHING.
WORSHIP ME.
AND I HAVEN'T BEEN ABLE TO GET GOG'S ATTENTION... UNTIL NOW.
THANK YOU, GOG.

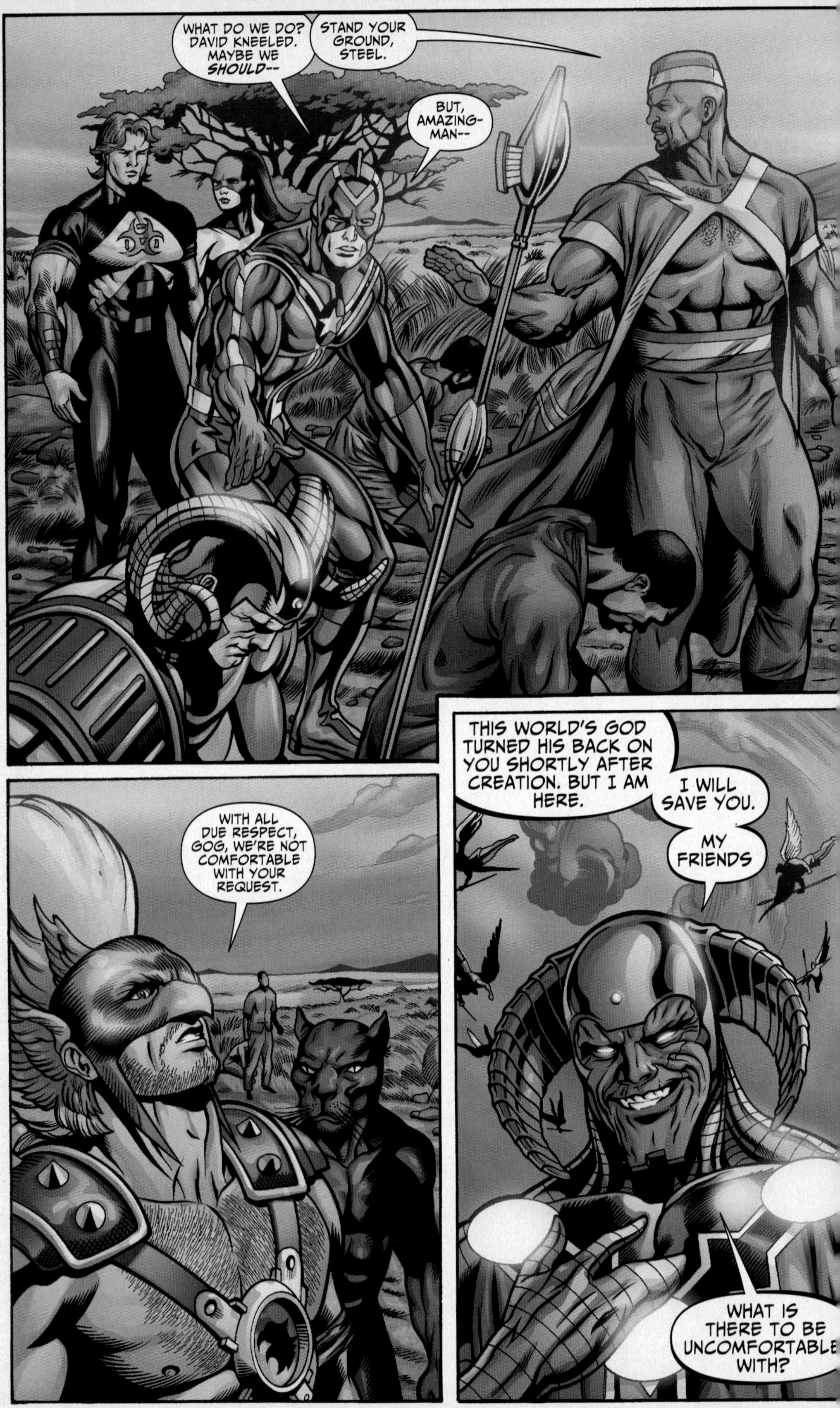

WHAT DO WE DO? DAVID KNEELED. MAYBE WE SHOULD--
STAND YOUR GROUND, STEEL.
BUT, AMAZING-MAN--
WITH ALL DUE RESPECT, GOG, WE'RE NOT COMFORTABLE WITH YOUR REQUEST.
THIS WORLD'S GOD TURNED HIS BACK ON YOU SHORTLY AFTER CREATION. BUT I AM HERE.
I WILL SAVE YOU.
MY FRIENDS
WHAT IS THERE TO BE UNCOMFORTABLE WITH?

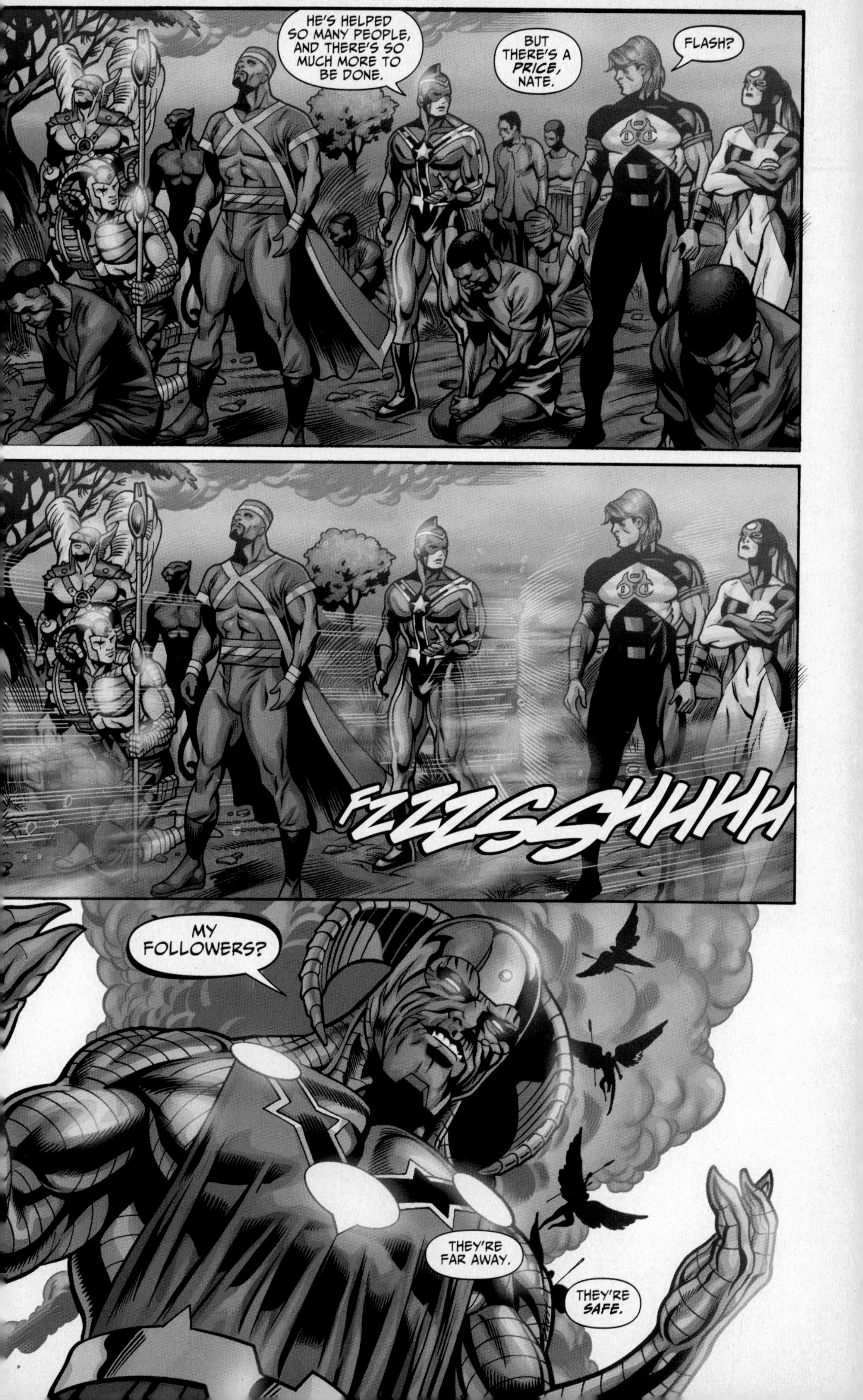

HE'S HELPED SO MANY PEOPLE, AND THERE'S SO MUCH MORE TO BE DONE.
BUT THERE'S A *PRICE*, NATE.
FLASH?
FZZZSSHHHH
MY FOLLOWERS?
THEY'RE FAR AWAY.
THEY'RE *SAFE*.

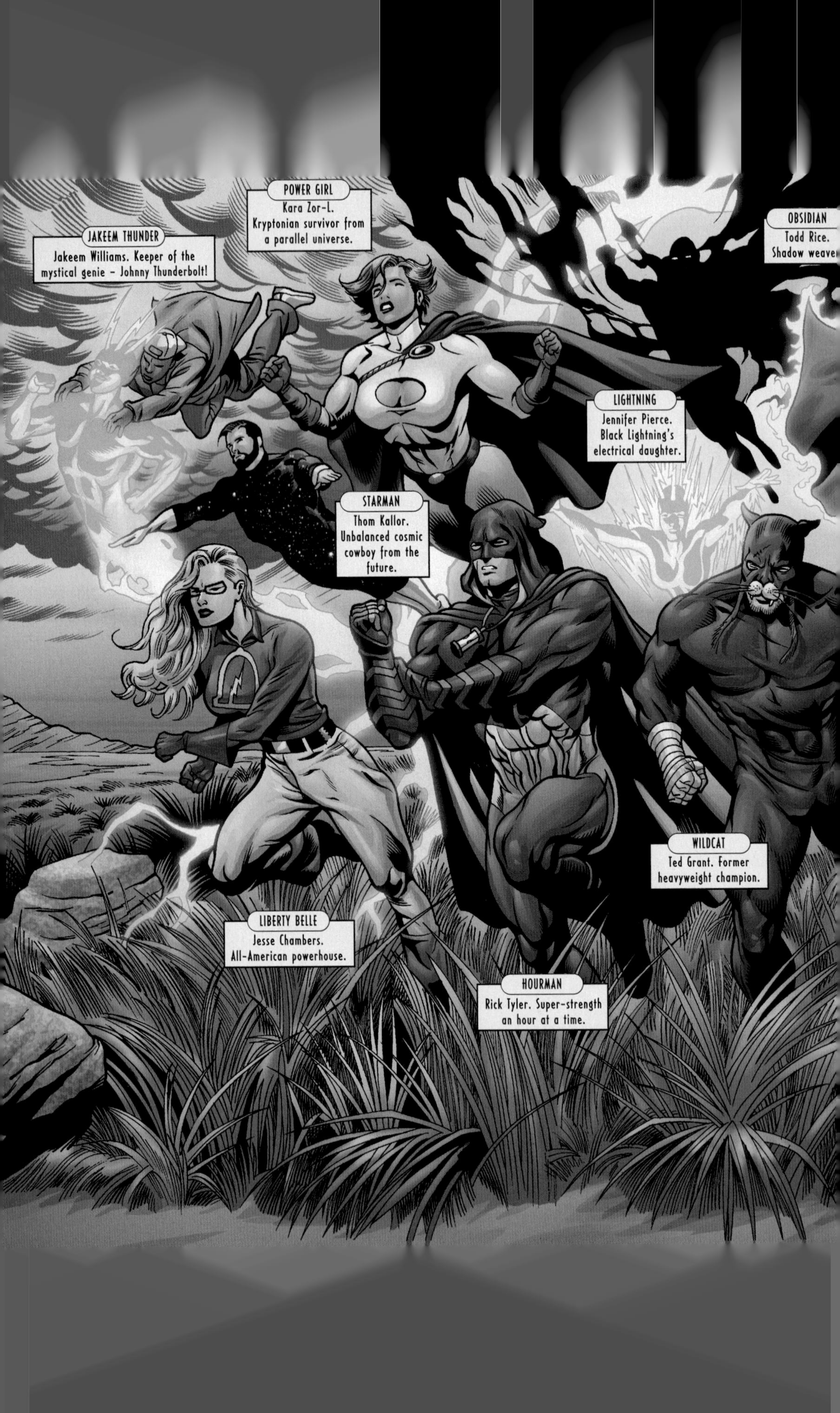
JAKEEM THUNDER
Jakeem Williams. Keeper of the mystical genie - Johnny Thunderbolt!
POWER GIRL
Kara Zor-L. Kryptonian survivor from a parallel universe.
OBSIDIAN
Todd Rice. Shadow weave
LIGHTNING
Jennifer Pierce. Black Lightning's electrical daughter.
STARMAN
Thom Kallor. Unbalanced cosmic cowboy from the future.
WILDCAT
Ted Grant. Former heavyweight champion.
LIBERTY BELLE
Jesse Chambers. All-American powerhouse.
HOURMAN
Rick Tyler. Super-strength an hour at a time.

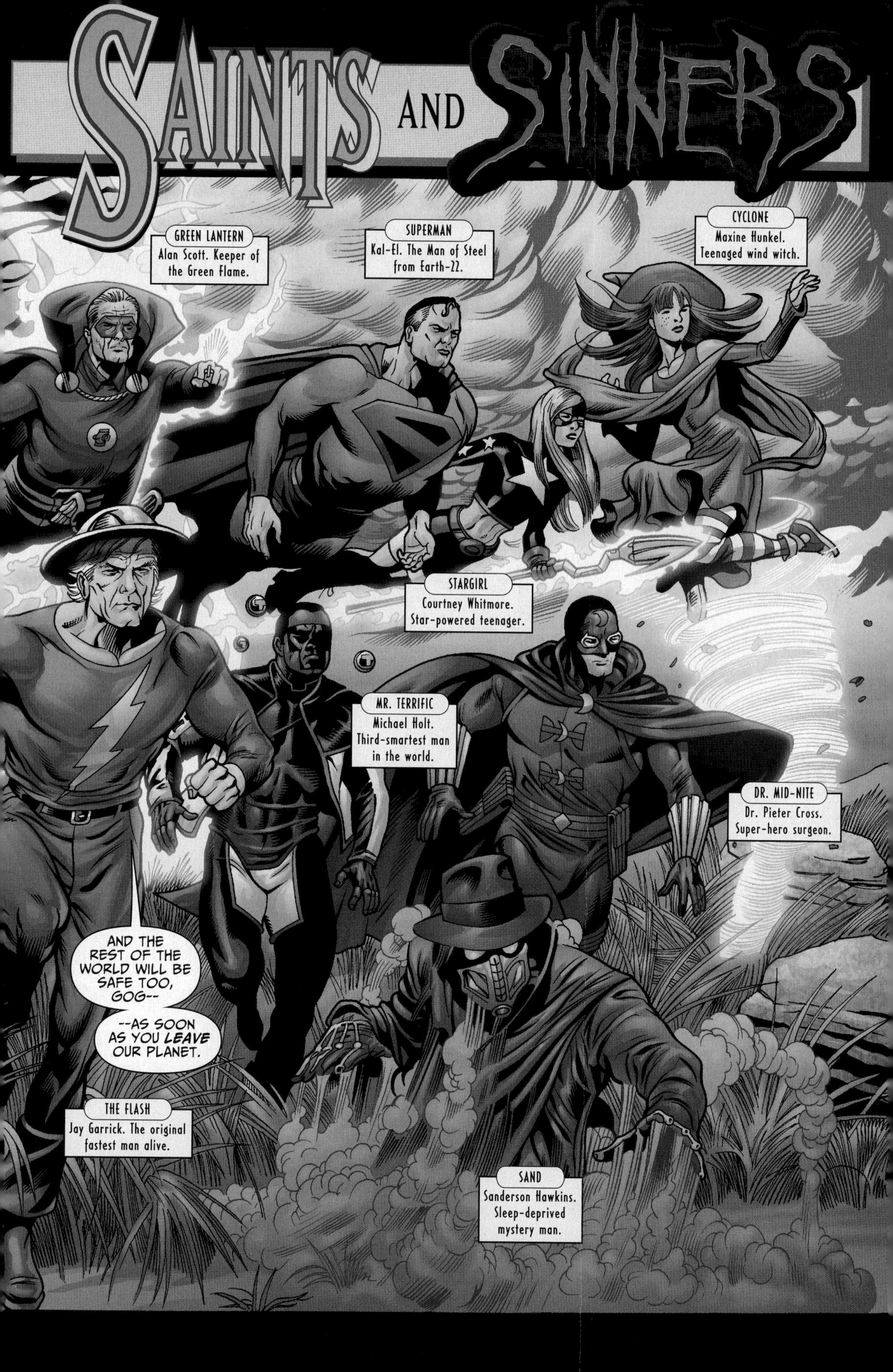

SAINTS AND SINNERS
GREEN LANTERN
Alan Scott. Keeper of the Green Flame.
SUPERMAN
Kal-El. The Man of Steel from Earth-22.
CYCLONE
Maxine Hunkel. Teenaged wind witch.
STARGIRL
Courtney Whitmore. Star-powered teenager.
MR. TERRIFIC
Michael Holt. Third-smartest man in the world.
DR. MID-NITE
Dr. Pieter Cross. Super-hero surgeon.
AND THE REST OF THE WORLD WILL BE SAFE TOO, GOG--
--AS SOON AS YOU LEAVE OUR PLANET.
THE FLASH
Jay Garrick. The original fastest man alive.
SAND
Sanderson Hawkins. Sleep-deprived mystery man.

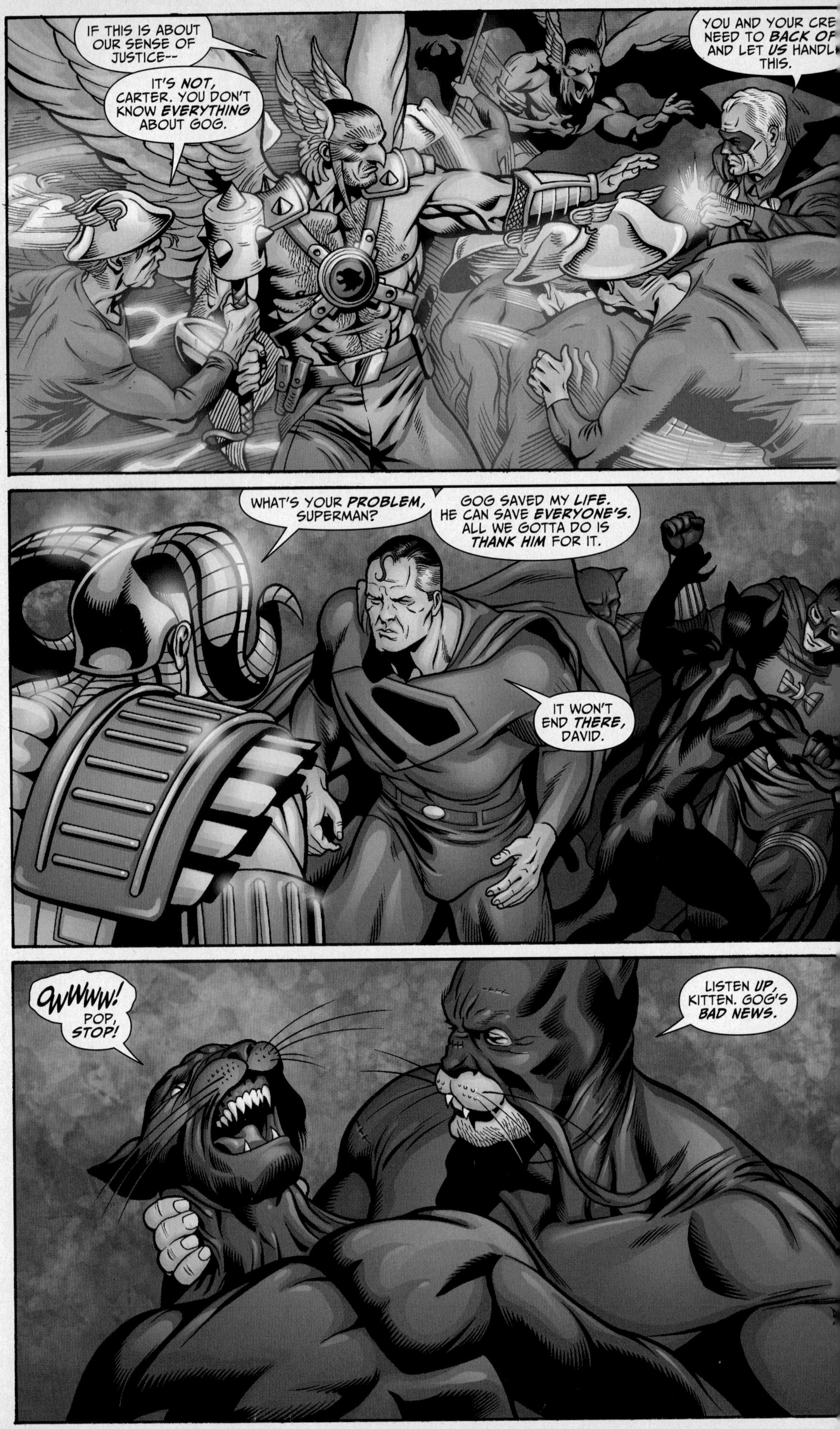

IF THIS IS ABOUT OUR SENSE OF JUSTICE--
IT'S NOT, CARTER. YOU DON'T KNOW EVERYTHING ABOUT GOG.
YOU AND YOUR CRE NEED TO BACK OF AND LET US HANDL THIS.
WHAT'S YOUR PROBLEM, SUPERMAN?
GOG SAVED MY LIFE. HE CAN SAVE EVERYONE'S. ALL WE GOTTA DO IS THANK HIM FOR IT.
IT WON'T END THERE, DAVID.
OWWWW! POP, STOP!
LISTEN UP, KITTEN. GOG'S BAD NEWS.

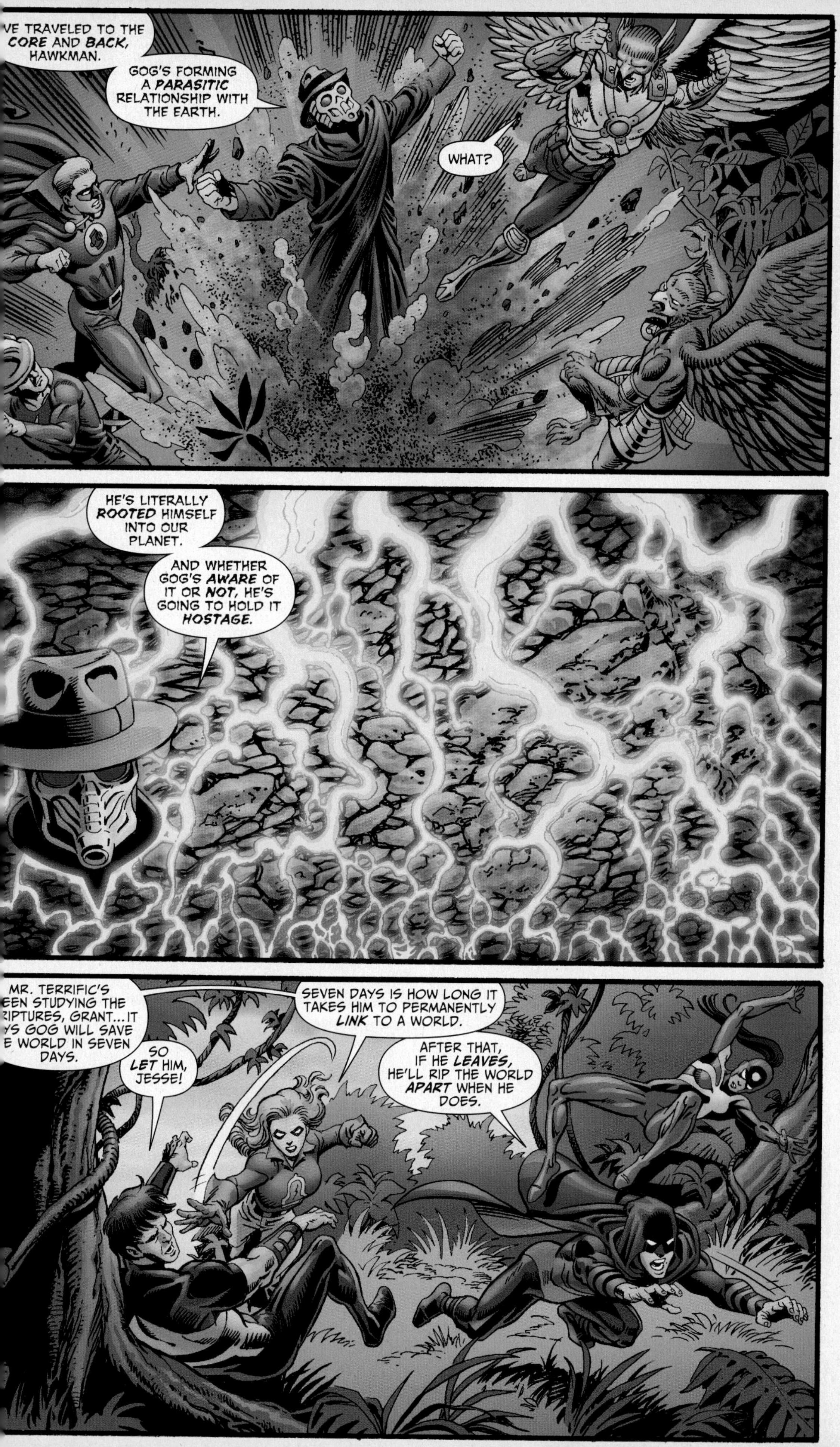
VE TRAVELED TO THE CORE AND BACK, HAWKMAN.
GOG'S FORMING A PARASITIC RELATIONSHIP WITH THE EARTH.
WHAT?
HE'S LITERALLY ROOTED HIMSELF INTO OUR PLANET.
AND WHETHER GOG'S AWARE OF IT OR NOT, HE'S GOING TO HOLD IT HOSTAGE.
MR. TERRIFIC'S EEN STUDYING THE RIPTURES, GRANT... IT YS GOG WILL SAVE E WORLD IN SEVEN DAYS.
SO LET HIM, JESSE!
SEVEN DAYS IS HOW LONG IT TAKES HIM TO PERMANENTLY LINK TO A WORLD.
AFTER THAT, IF HE LEAVES, HE'LL RIP THE WORLD APART WHEN HE DOES.

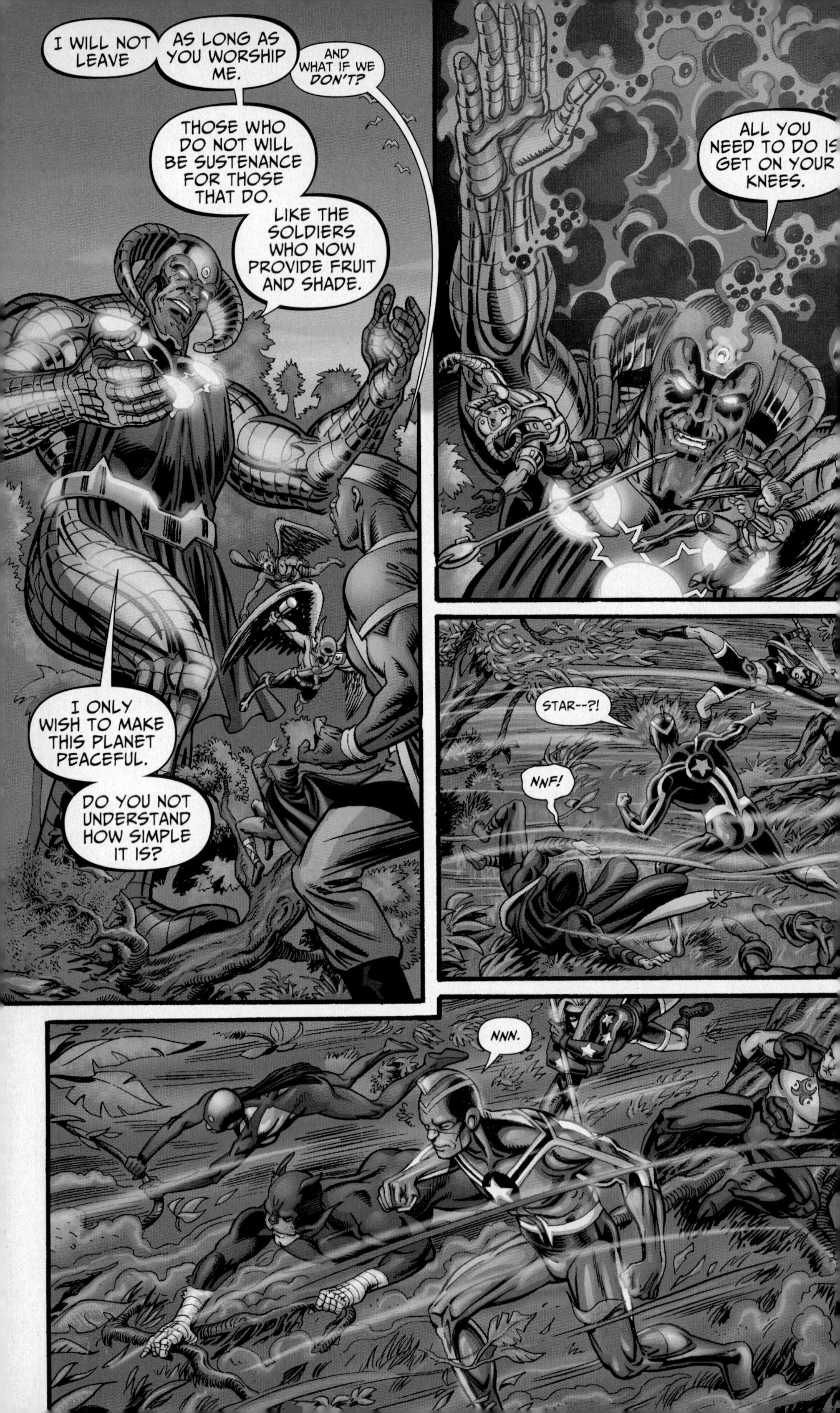
I WILL NOT LEAVE
AS LONG AS YOU WORSHIP ME.
AND WHAT IF WE *DON'T?*
THOSE WHO DO NOT WILL BE SUSTENANCE FOR THOSE THAT DO.
LIKE THE SOLDIERS WHO NOW PROVIDE FRUIT AND SHADE.
I ONLY WISH TO MAKE THIS PLANET PEACEFUL.
DO YOU NOT UNDERSTAND HOW SIMPLE IT IS?
ALL YOU NEED TO DO IS GET ON YOUR KNEES.
STAR--?!
NNF!
NNN.

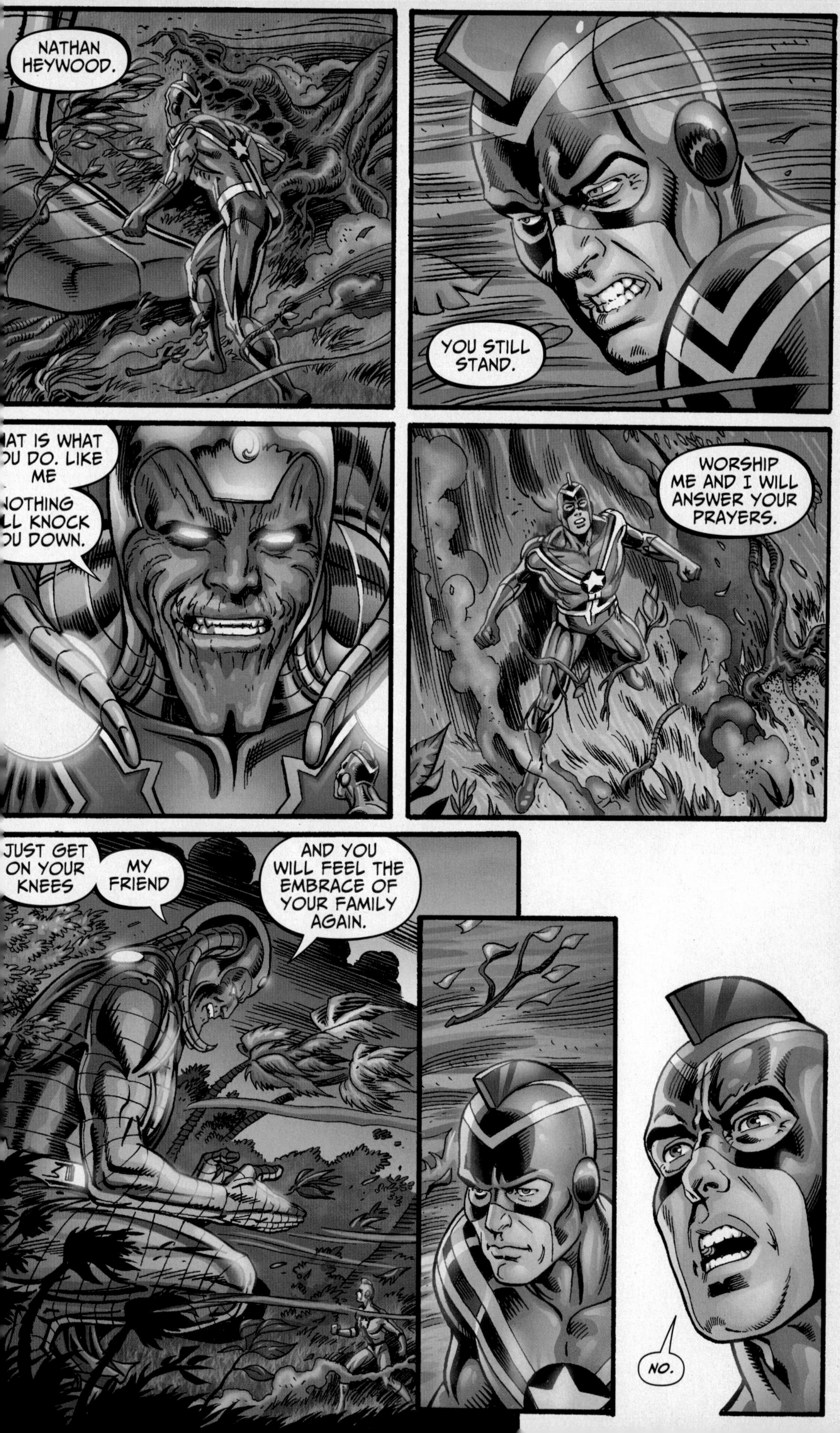
NATHAN HEYWOOD.
YOU STILL STAND.
AT IS WHAT OU DO. LIKE ME
NOTHING LL KNOCK OU DOWN.
WORSHIP ME AND I WILL ANSWER YOUR PRAYERS.
JUST GET ON YOUR KNEES
MY FRIEND
AND YOU WILL FEEL THE EMBRACE OF YOUR FAMILY AGAIN.
NO.

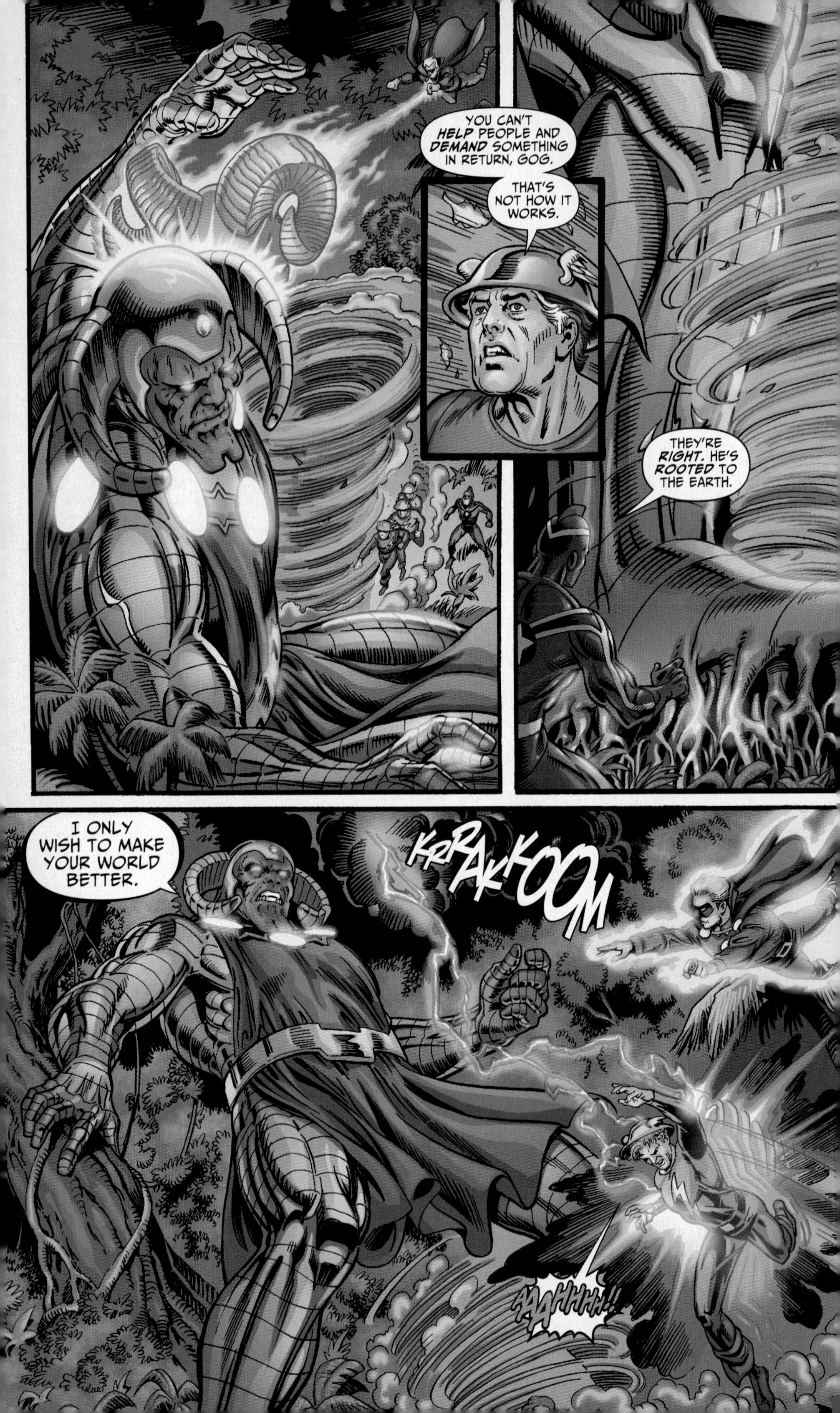

YOU CAN'T HELP PEOPLE AND DEMAND SOMETHING IN RETURN, GOG.
THAT'S NOT HOW IT WORKS.
THEY'RE RIGHT. HE'S ROOTED TO THE EARTH.
I ONLY WISH TO MAKE YOUR WORLD BETTER.
KRRAKKOOM
AAAHHHH!!

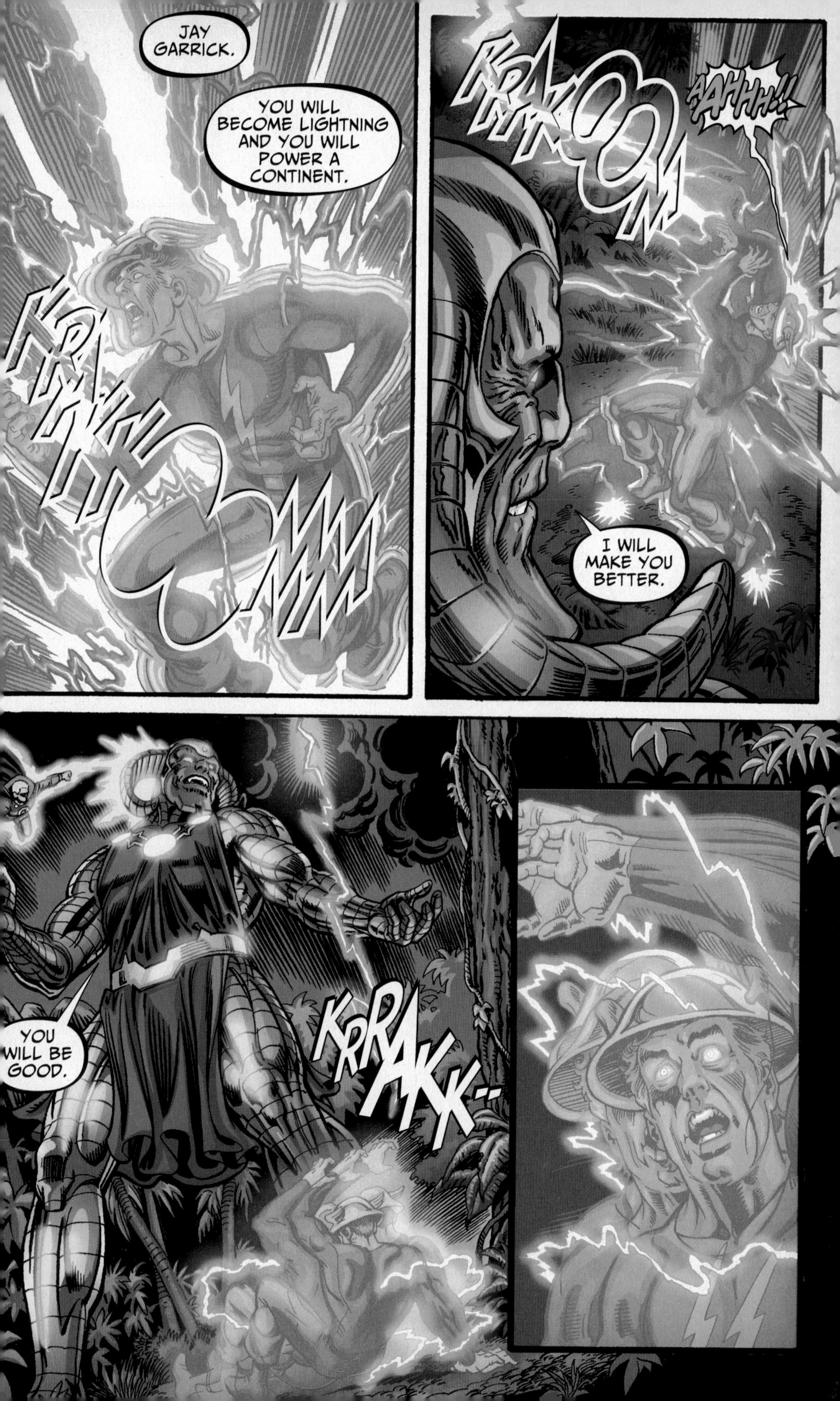
JAY GARRICK.
YOU WILL BECOME LIGHTNING AND YOU WILL POWER A CONTINENT.
KRAKKATHOOM
KRAKATOOM
AAHHH!!
I WILL MAKE YOU BETTER.
YOU WILL BE GOOD.
KRRAKK--

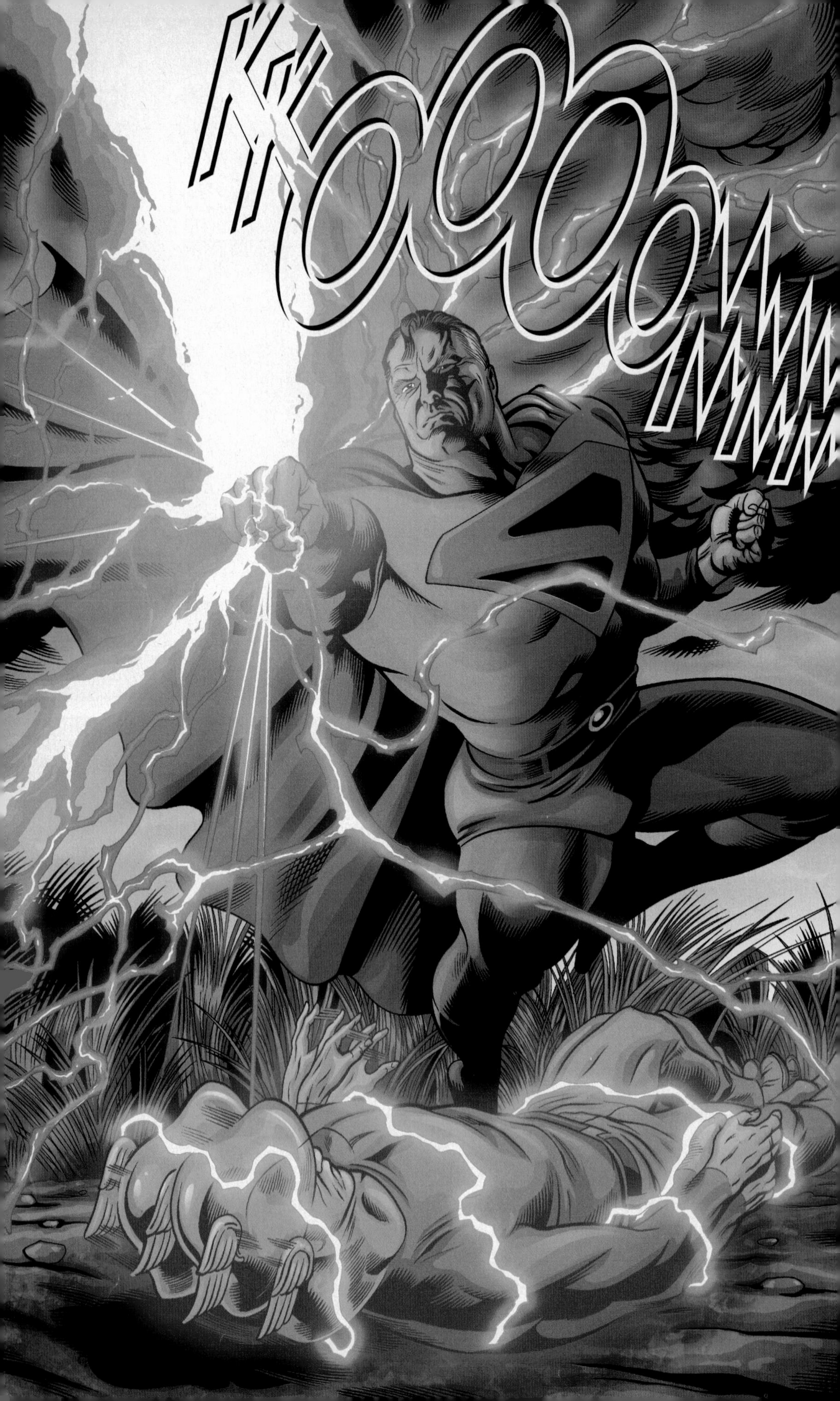

KROOOOOMM

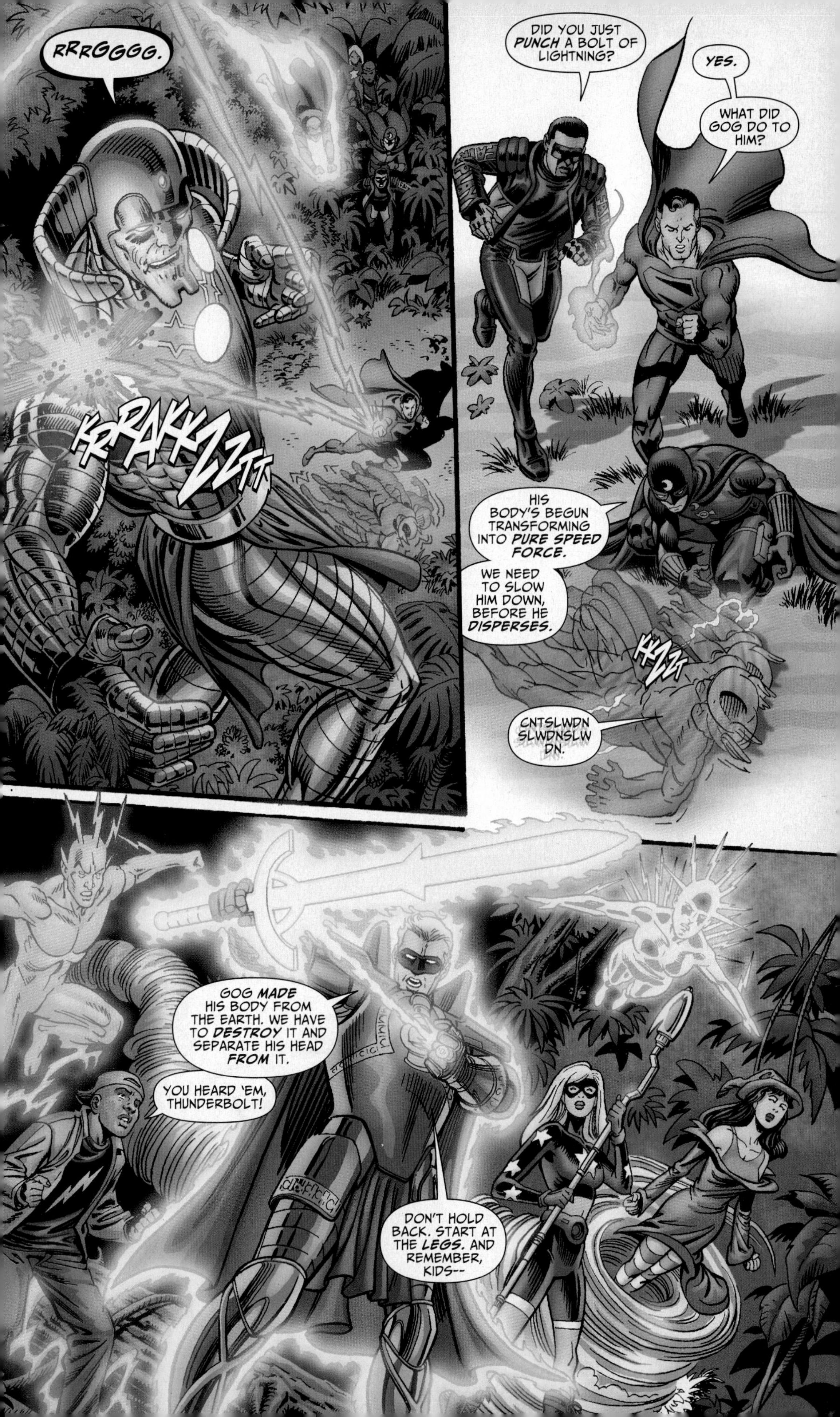
RRRGGGG.
KRRAKKZZTT
DID YOU JUST PUNCH A BOLT OF LIGHTNING?
YES.
WHAT DID GOG DO TO HIM?
HIS BODY'S BEGUN TRANSFORMING INTO PURE SPEED FORCE.
WE NEED TO SLOW HIM DOWN, BEFORE HE DISPERSES.
KKZZT
CNTSLWDN SLWDNSLW DN.
GOG MADE HIS BODY FROM THE EARTH. WE HAVE TO DESTROY IT AND SEPARATE HIS HEAD FROM IT.
YOU HEARD 'EM, THUNDERBOLT!
DON'T HOLD BACK. START AT THE LEGS. AND REMEMBER, KIDS--

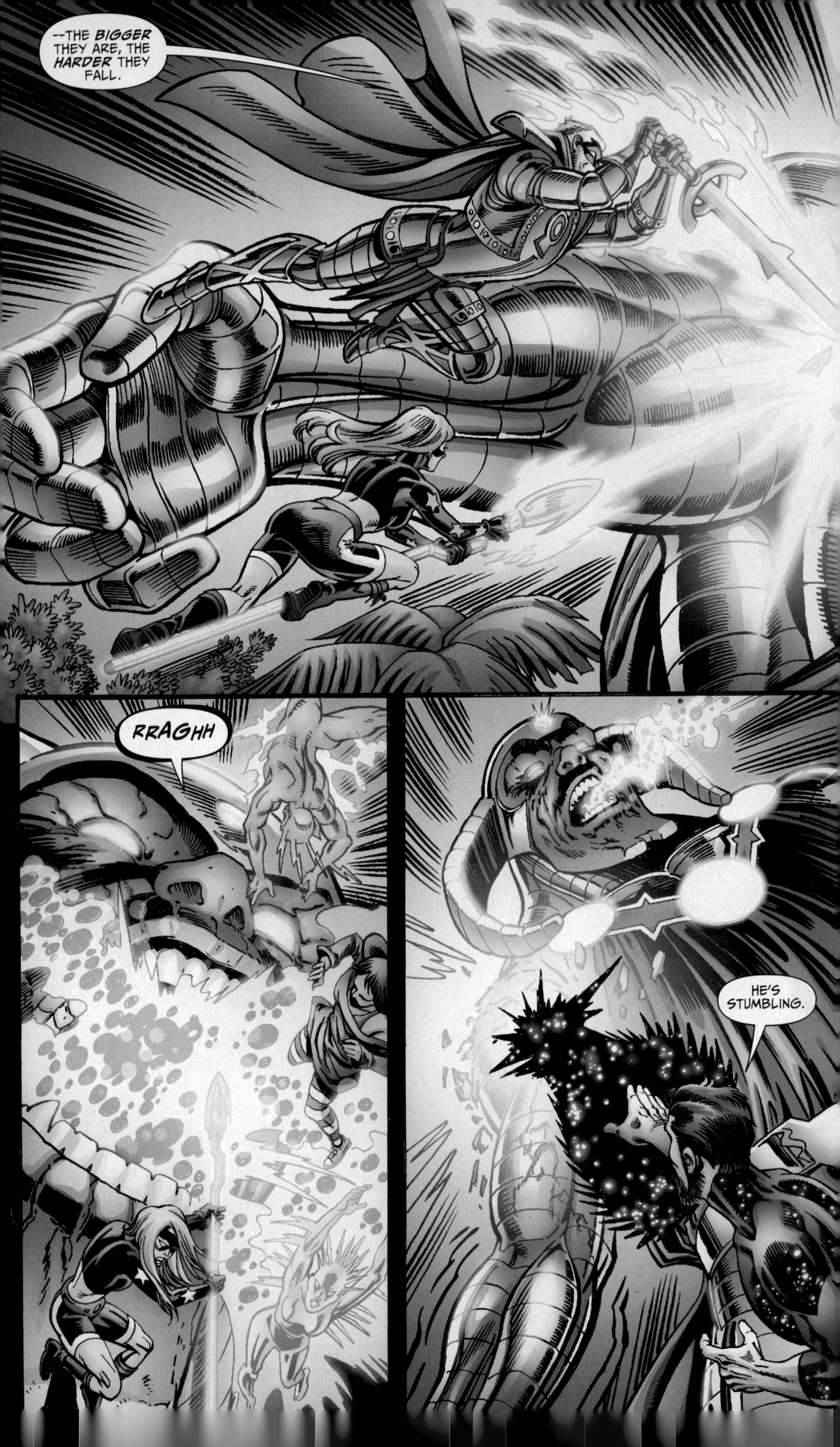
--THE BIGGER THEY ARE, THE HARDER THEY FALL.
RRAGHH
HE'S STUMBLING.

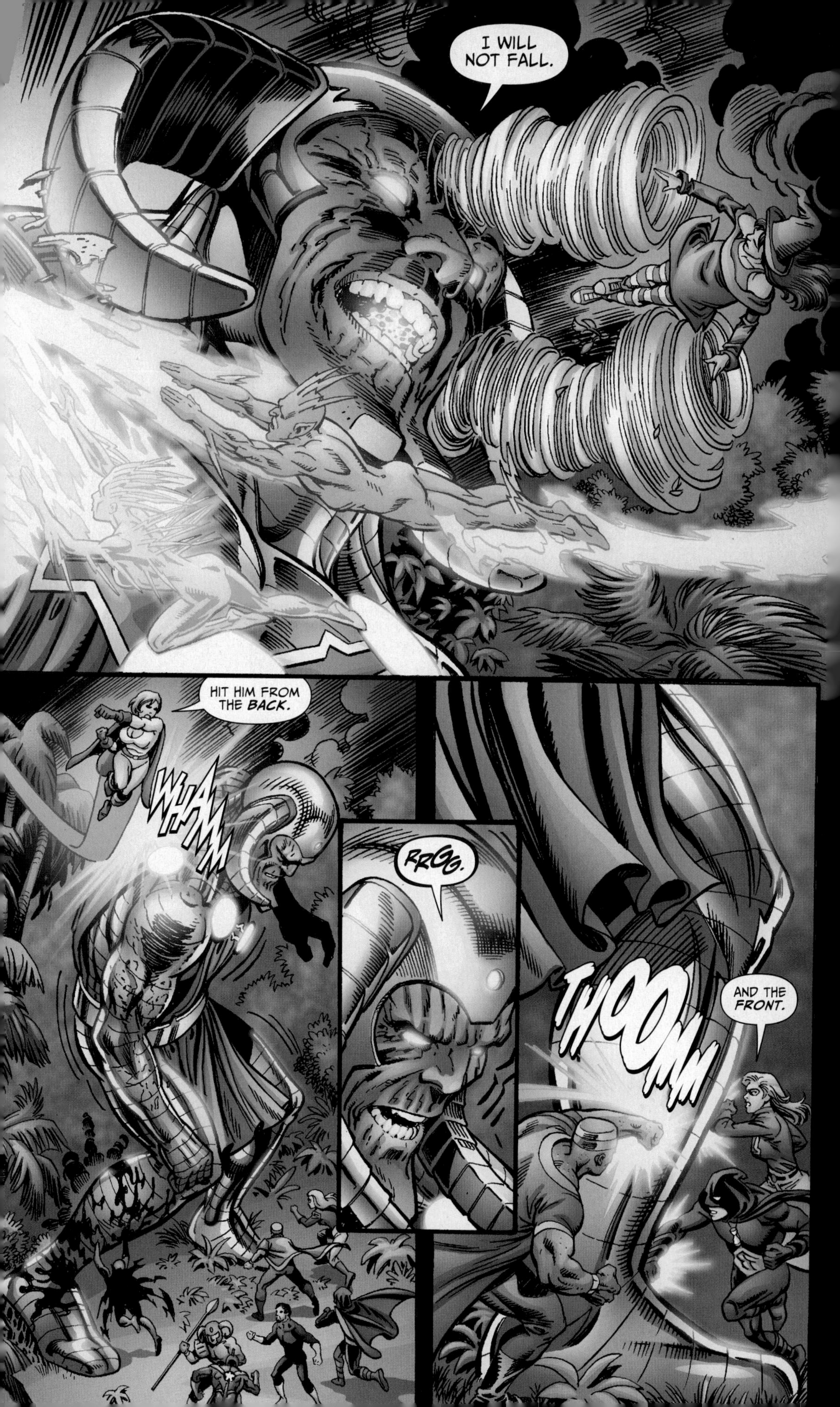
I WILL NOT FALL.
HIT HIM FROM THE BACK.
WHAMM
RRGG.
THOOMM
AND THE FRONT.

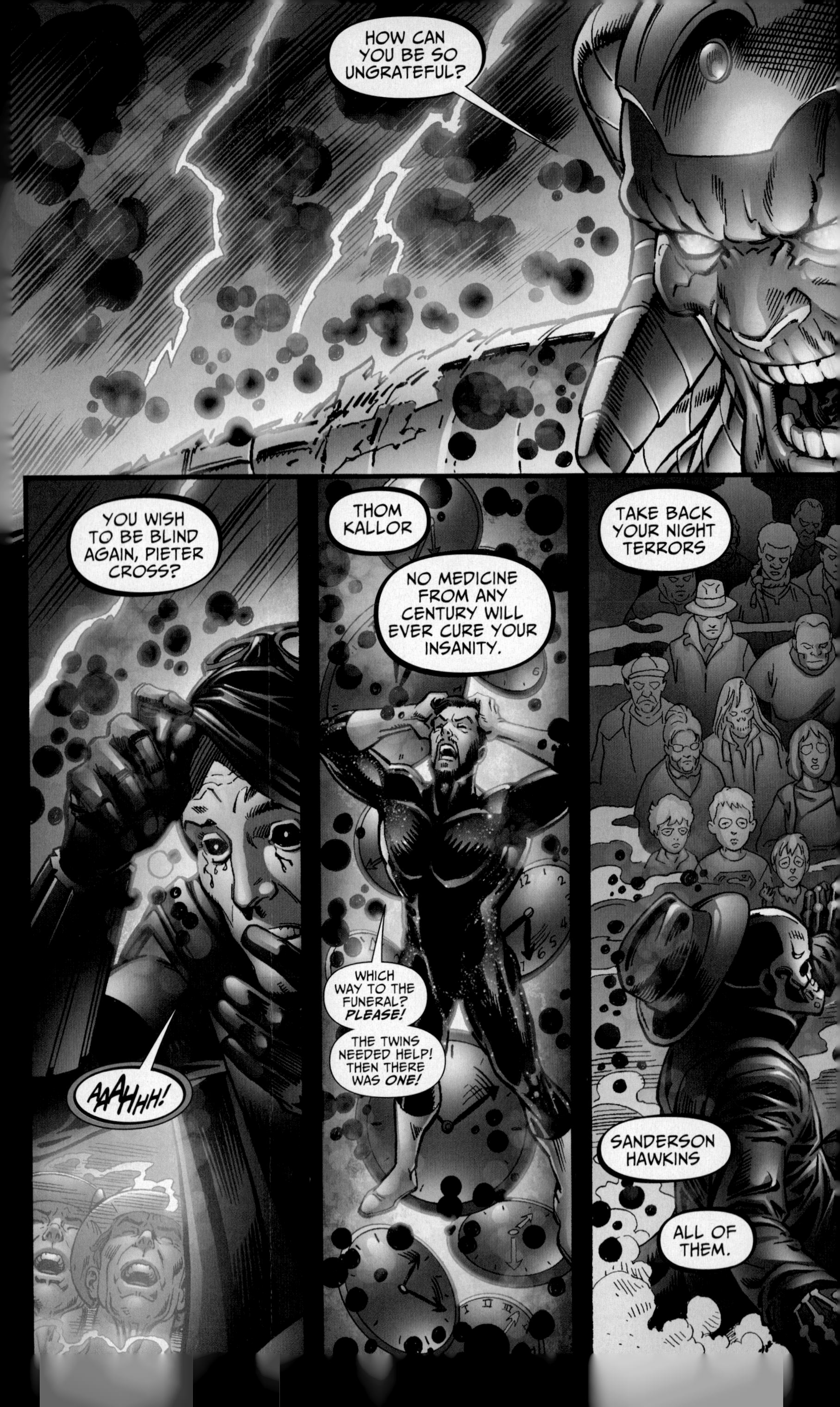
HOW CAN YOU BE SO UNGRATEFUL?
YOU WISH TO BE BLIND AGAIN, PIETER CROSS?
AAAHHH!
THOM KALLOR
NO MEDICINE FROM ANY CENTURY WILL EVER CURE YOUR INSANITY.
WHICH WAY TO THE FUNERAL? *PLEASE!*
THE TWINS NEEDED HELP! THEN THERE WAS *ONE!*
TAKE BACK YOUR NIGHT TERRORS
SANDERSON HAWKINS
ALL OF THEM.

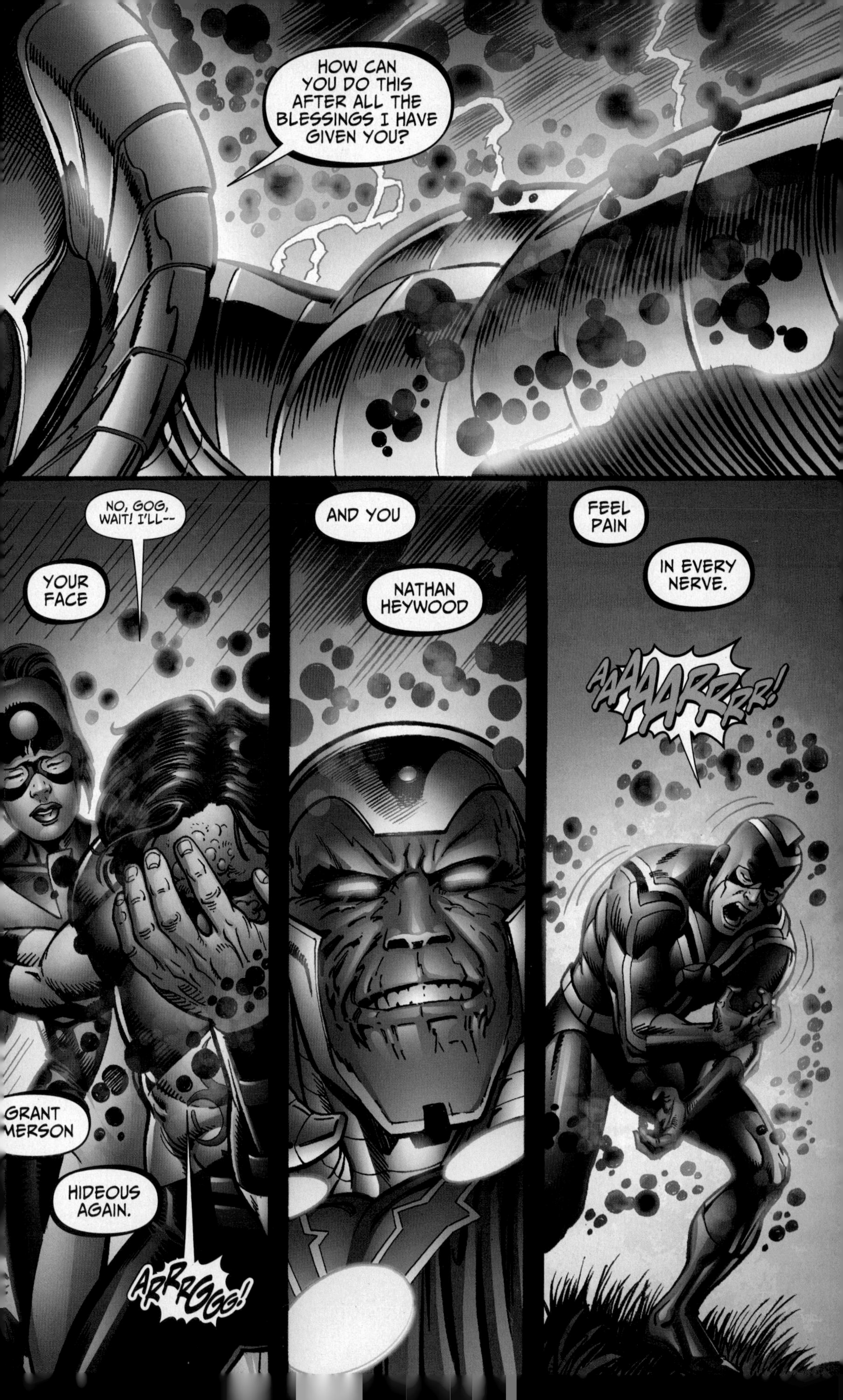
HOW CAN YOU DO THIS AFTER ALL THE BLESSINGS I HAVE GIVEN YOU?
NO, GOG, WAIT! I'LL--
YOUR FACE
GRANT
MERSON
HIDEOUS AGAIN.
ARRRGGG!
AND YOU
NATHAN HEYWOOD
FEEL PAIN
IN EVERY NERVE.
AAAAARRRRR!

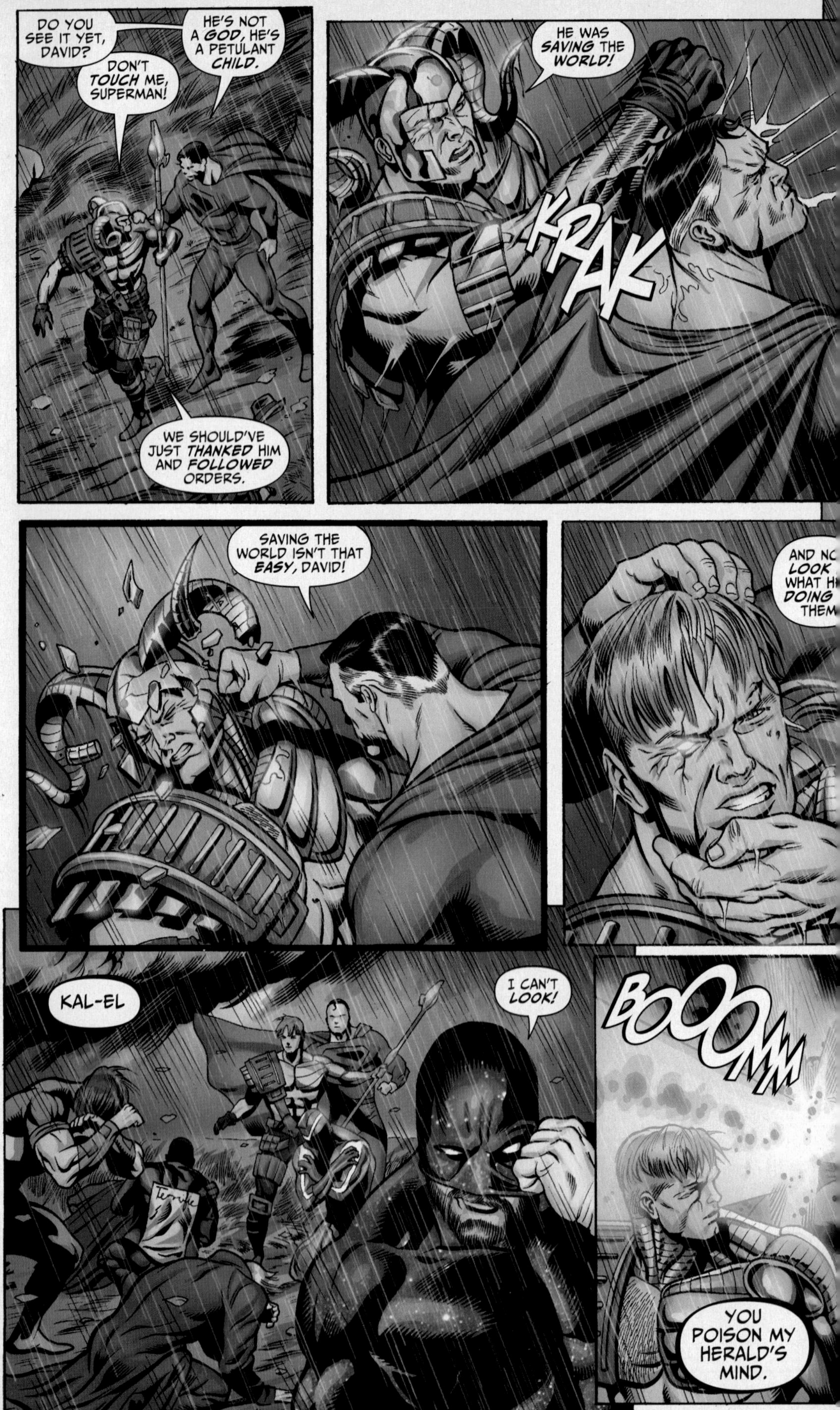
DO YOU SEE IT YET, DAVID?
DON'T TOUCH ME, SUPERMAN!
HE'S NOT A GOD, HE'S A PETULANT CHILD.
WE SHOULD'VE JUST THANKED HIM AND FOLLOWED ORDERS.
HE WAS SAVING THE WORLD!
KRAK
SAVING THE WORLD ISN'T THAT EASY, DAVID!
AND NO LOOK WHAT H DOING THEM
KAL-EL
I CAN'T LOOK!
BOOOMM
YOU POISON MY HERALD'S MIND.

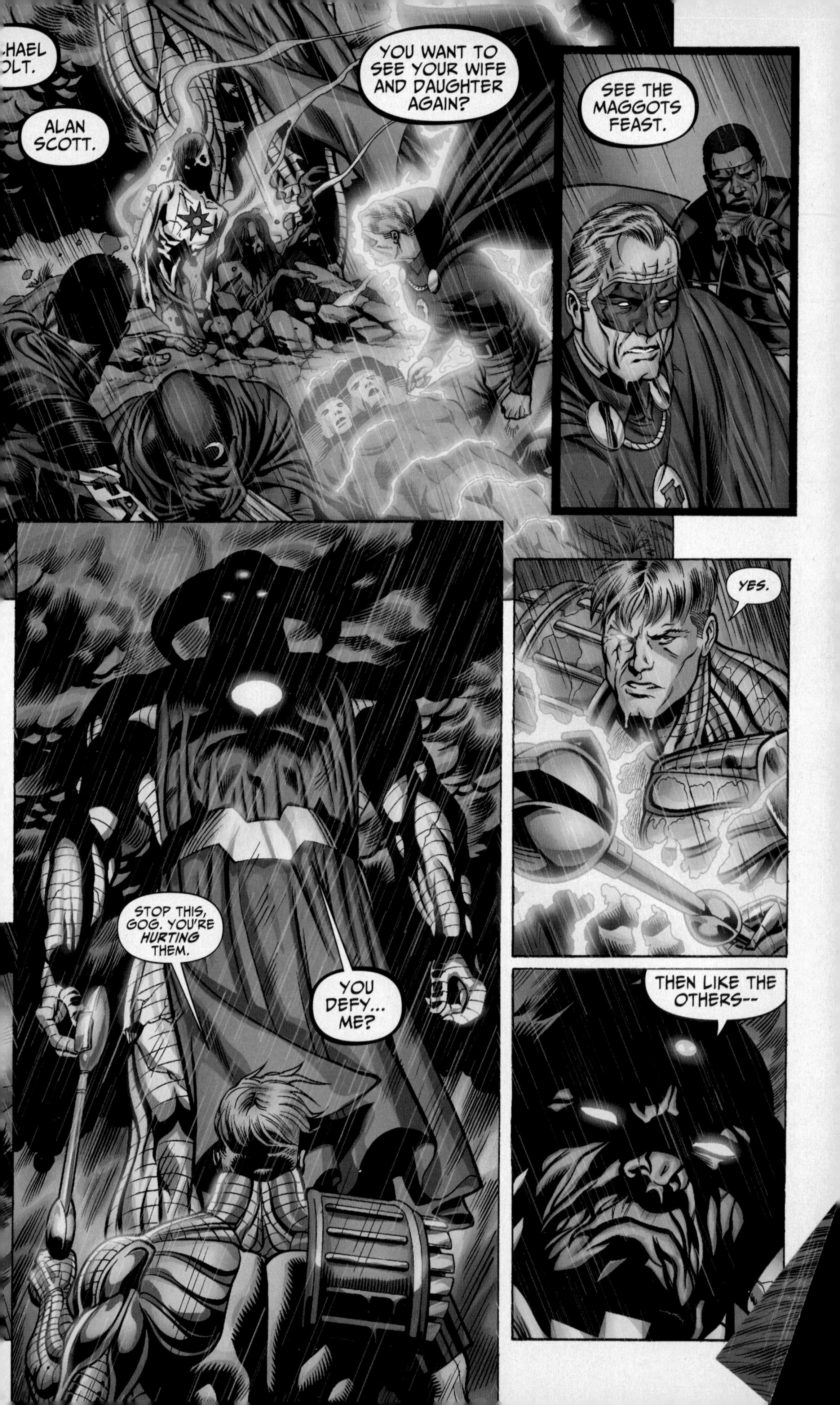

-CHAEL
-OLT.
ALAN SCOTT.
YOU WANT TO SEE YOUR WIFE AND DAUGHTER AGAIN?
SEE THE MAGGOTS FEAST.
STOP THIS, GOG. YOU'RE *HURTING* THEM.
YOU DEFY... ME?
YES.
THEN LIKE THE OTHERS--

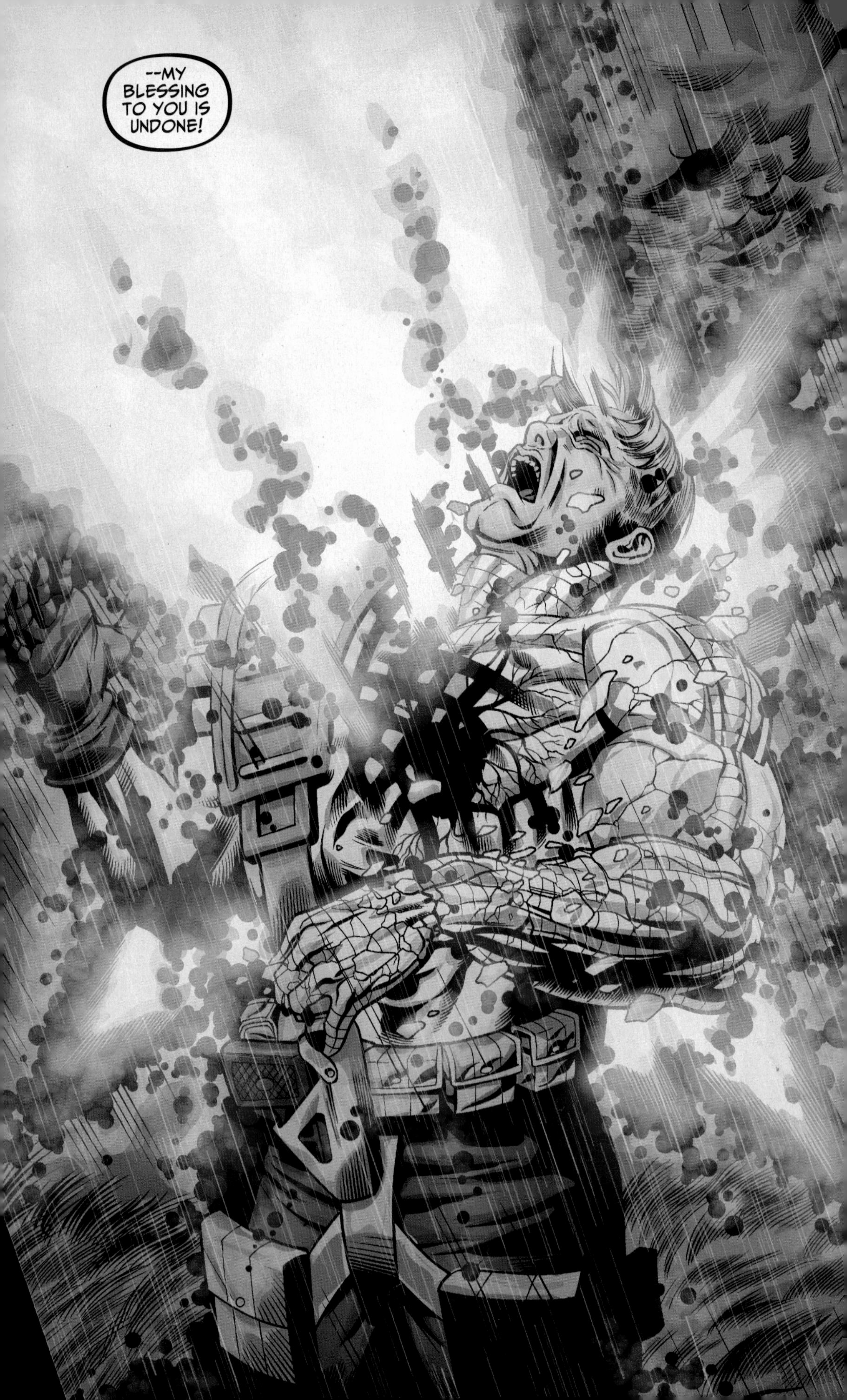
--MY BLESSING TO YOU IS UNDONE!

JUSTICE SOCIETY OF AMERICA #22 cover A by Alex Ross

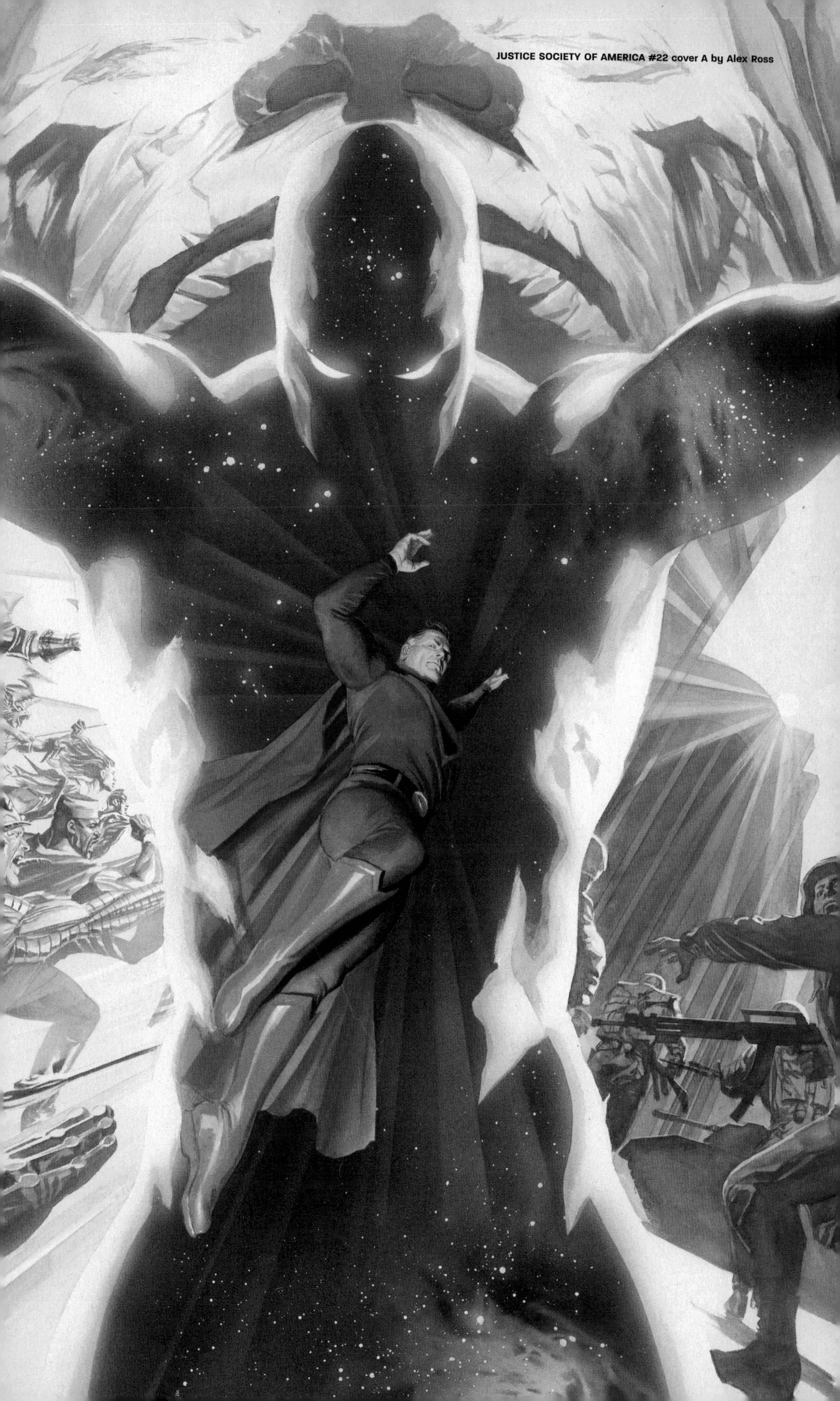

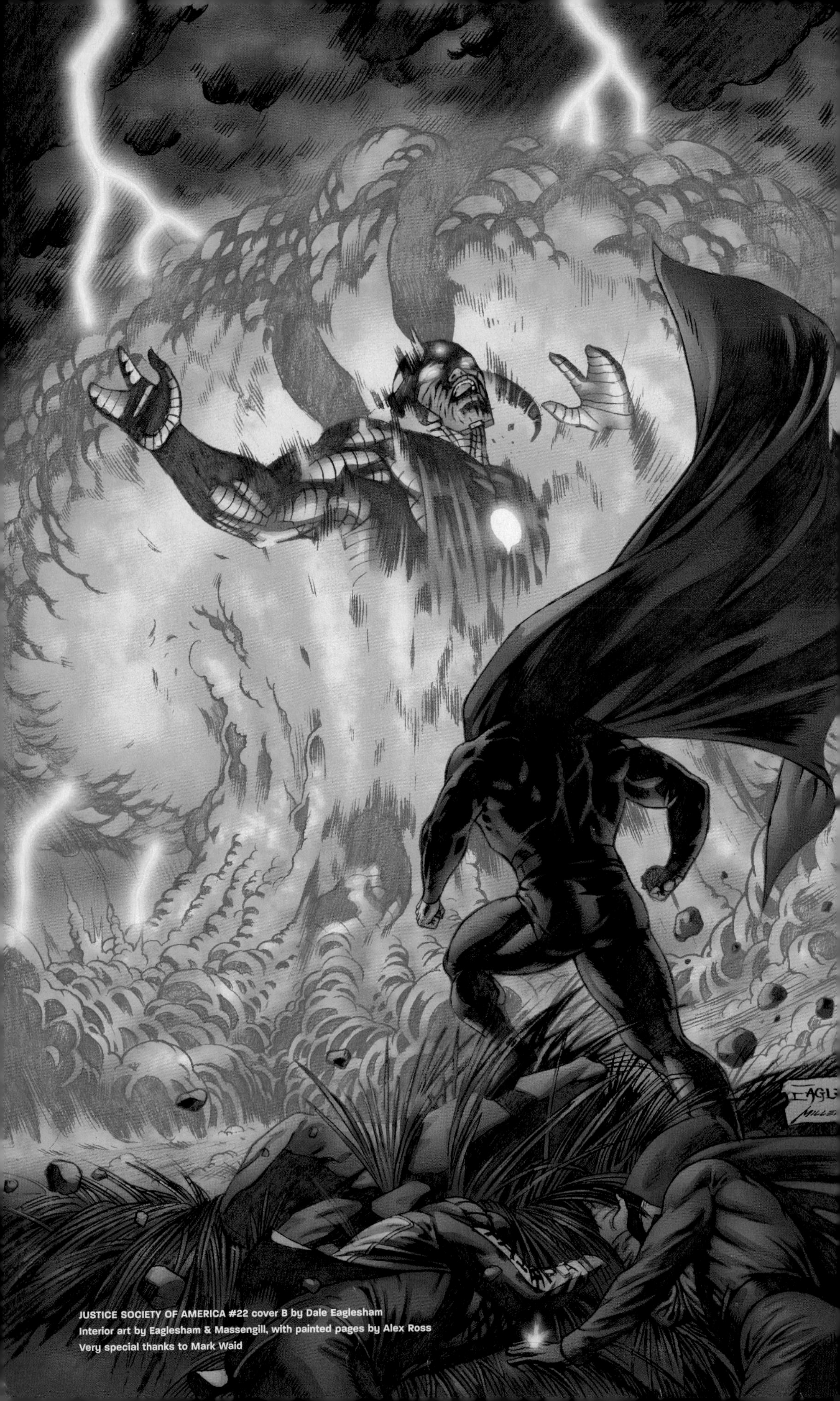

JUSTICE SOCIETY OF AMERICA #22 cover B by Dale Eaglesham
Interior art by Eaglesham & Massengill, with painted pages by Alex Ross
Very special thanks to Mark Waid

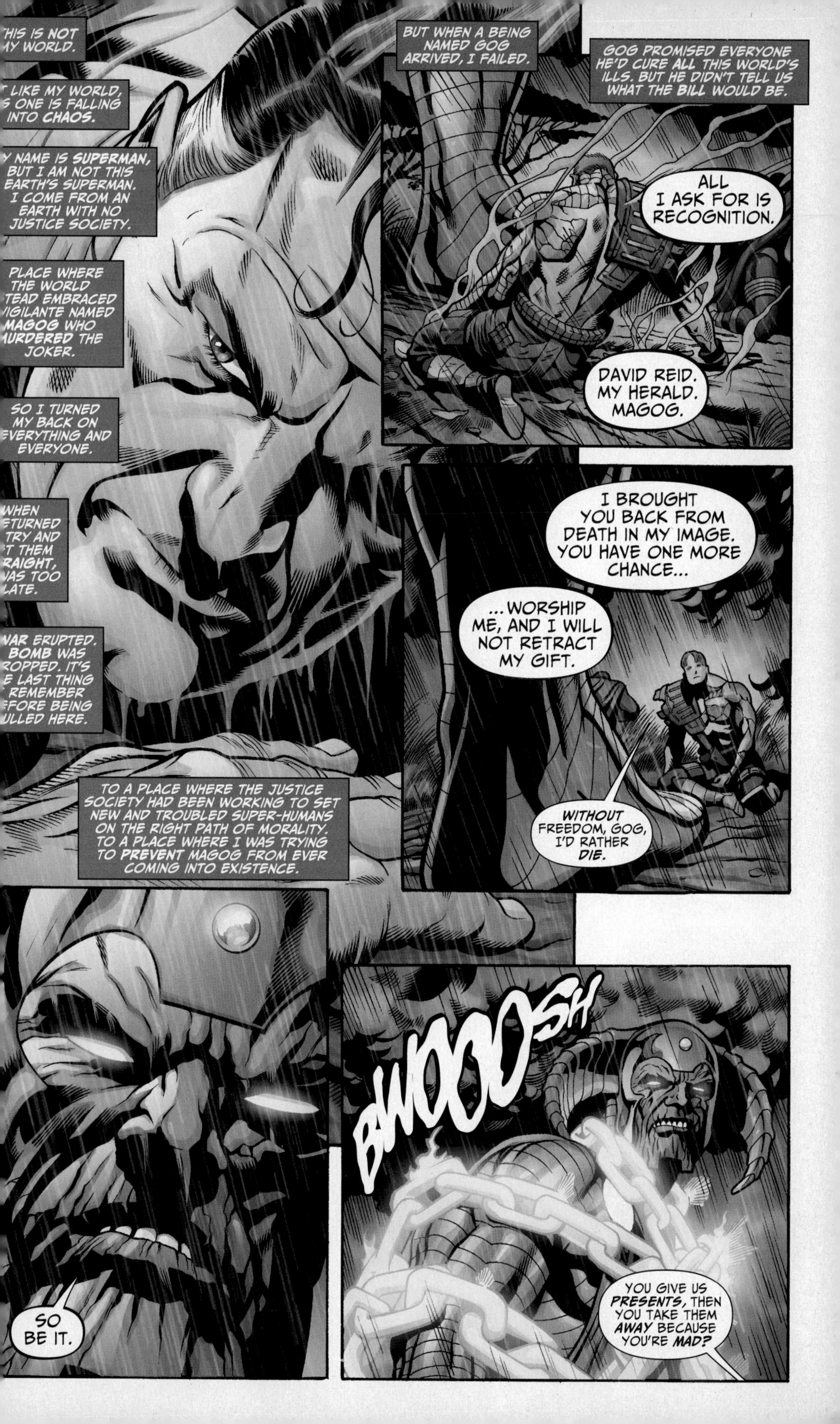
THIS IS NOT MY WORLD.
T LIKE MY WORLD, S ONE IS FALLING INTO CHAOS.
Y NAME IS SUPERMAN, BUT I AM NOT THIS EARTH'S SUPERMAN. I COME FROM AN EARTH WITH NO JUSTICE SOCIETY.
PLACE WHERE THE WORLD TEAD EMBRACED VIGILANTE NAMED MAGOG WHO URDERED THE JOKER.
SO I TURNED MY BACK ON EVERYTHING AND EVERYONE.
WHEN ETURNED TRY AND T THEM RAIGHT, AS TOO LATE.
VAR ERUPTED. BOMB WAS ROPPED. IT'S E LAST THING REMEMBER EFORE BEING ULLED HERE.
TO A PLACE WHERE THE JUSTICE SOCIETY HAD BEEN WORKING TO SET NEW AND TROUBLED SUPER-HUMANS ON THE RIGHT PATH OF MORALITY. TO A PLACE WHERE I WAS TRYING TO PREVENT MAGOG FROM EVER COMING INTO EXISTENCE.
BUT WHEN A BEING NAMED GOG ARRIVED, I FAILED.
GOG PROMISED EVERYONE HE'D CURE ALL THIS WORLD'S ILLS. BUT HE DIDN'T TELL US WHAT THE BILL WOULD BE.
ALL I ASK FOR IS RECOGNITION.
DAVID REID. MY HERALD. MAGOG.
I BROUGHT YOU BACK FROM DEATH IN MY IMAGE. YOU HAVE ONE MORE CHANCE...
...WORSHIP ME, AND I WILL NOT RETRACT MY GIFT.
WITHOUT FREEDOM, GOG, I'D RATHER DIE.
SO BE IT.
BWOOOSH
YOU GIVE US PRESENTS, THEN YOU TAKE THEM AWAY BECAUSE YOU'RE MAD?

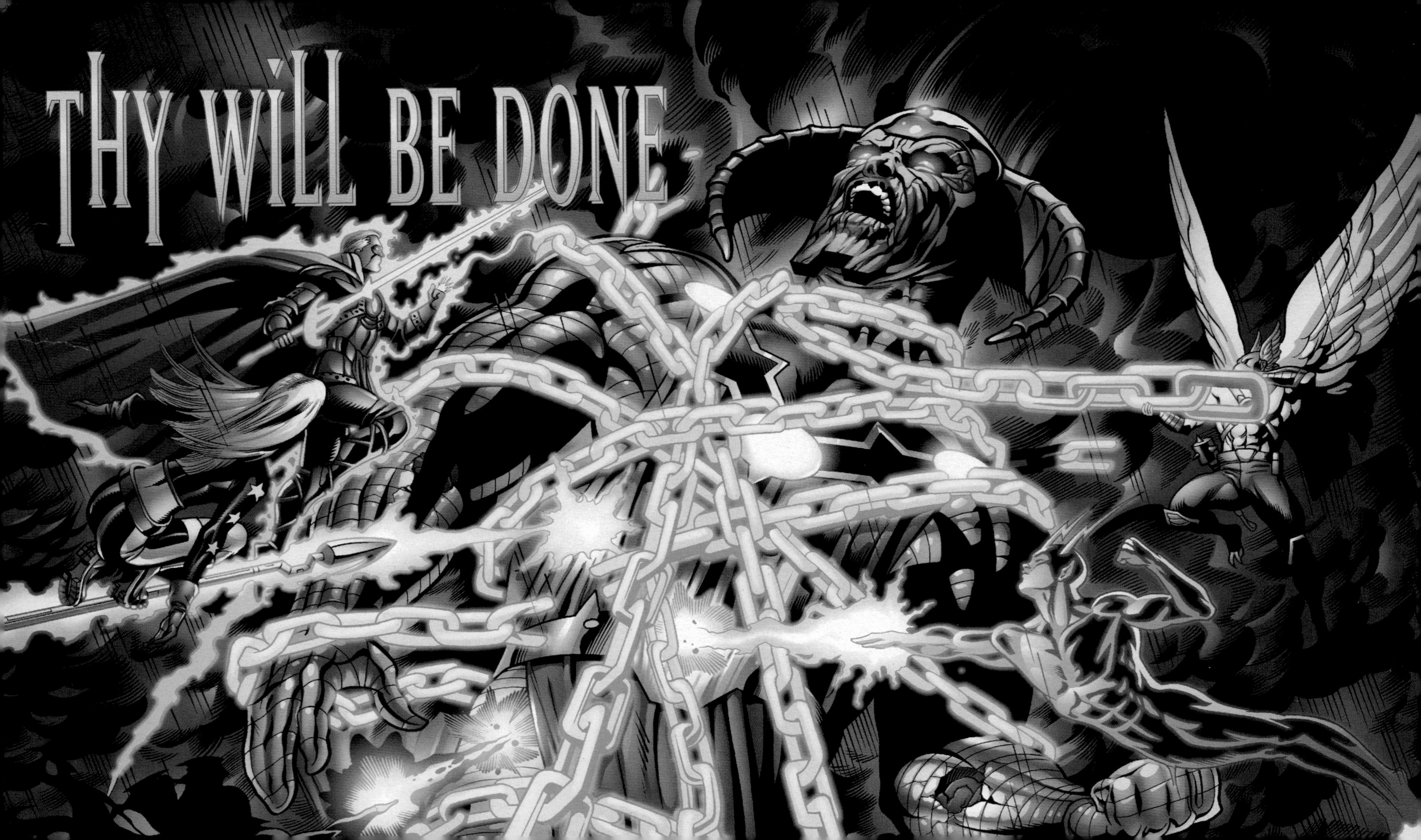
THY WILL BE DONE

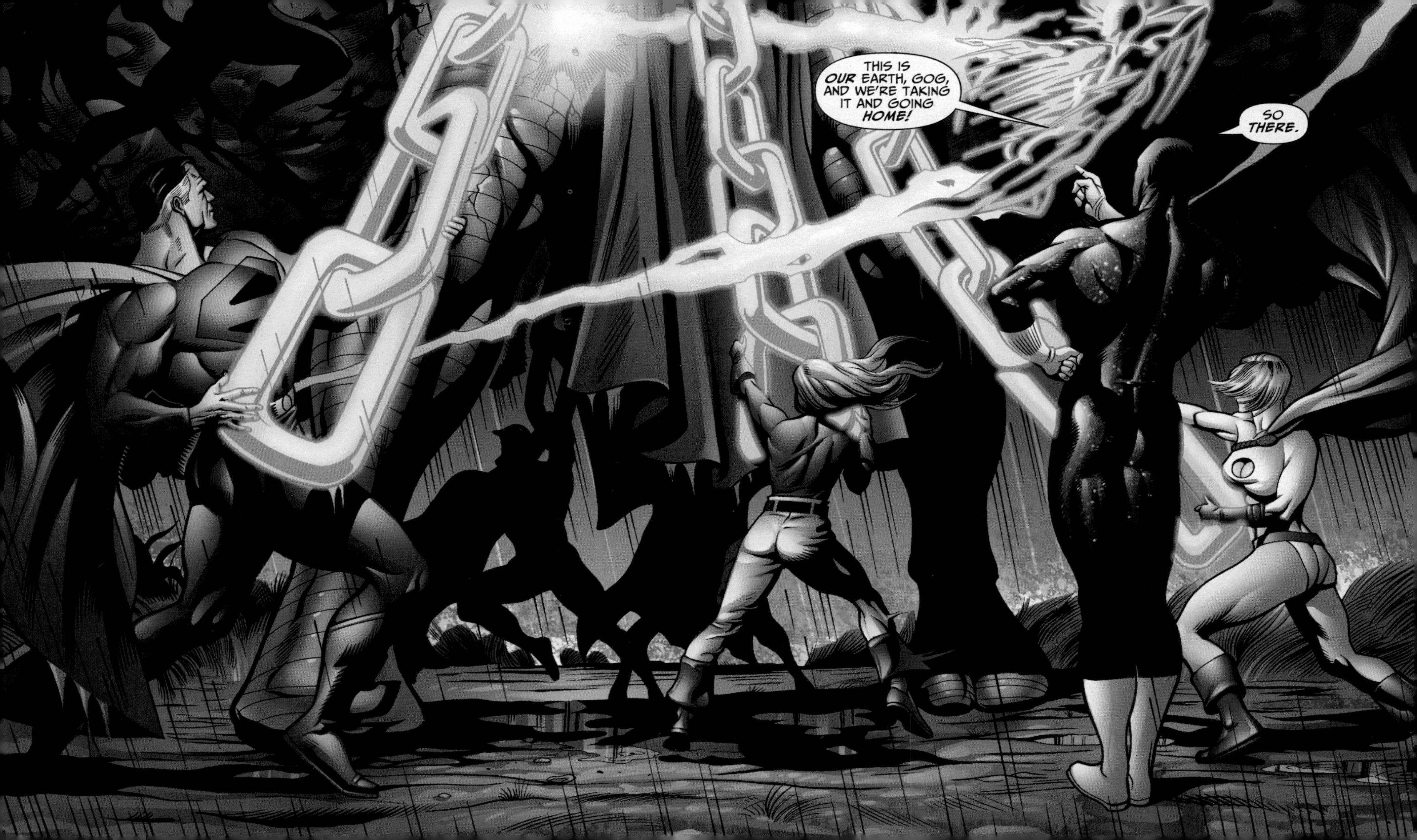
THIS IS *OUR* EARTH, GOG, AND WE'RE TAKING IT AND GOING *HOME!*
SO THERE.

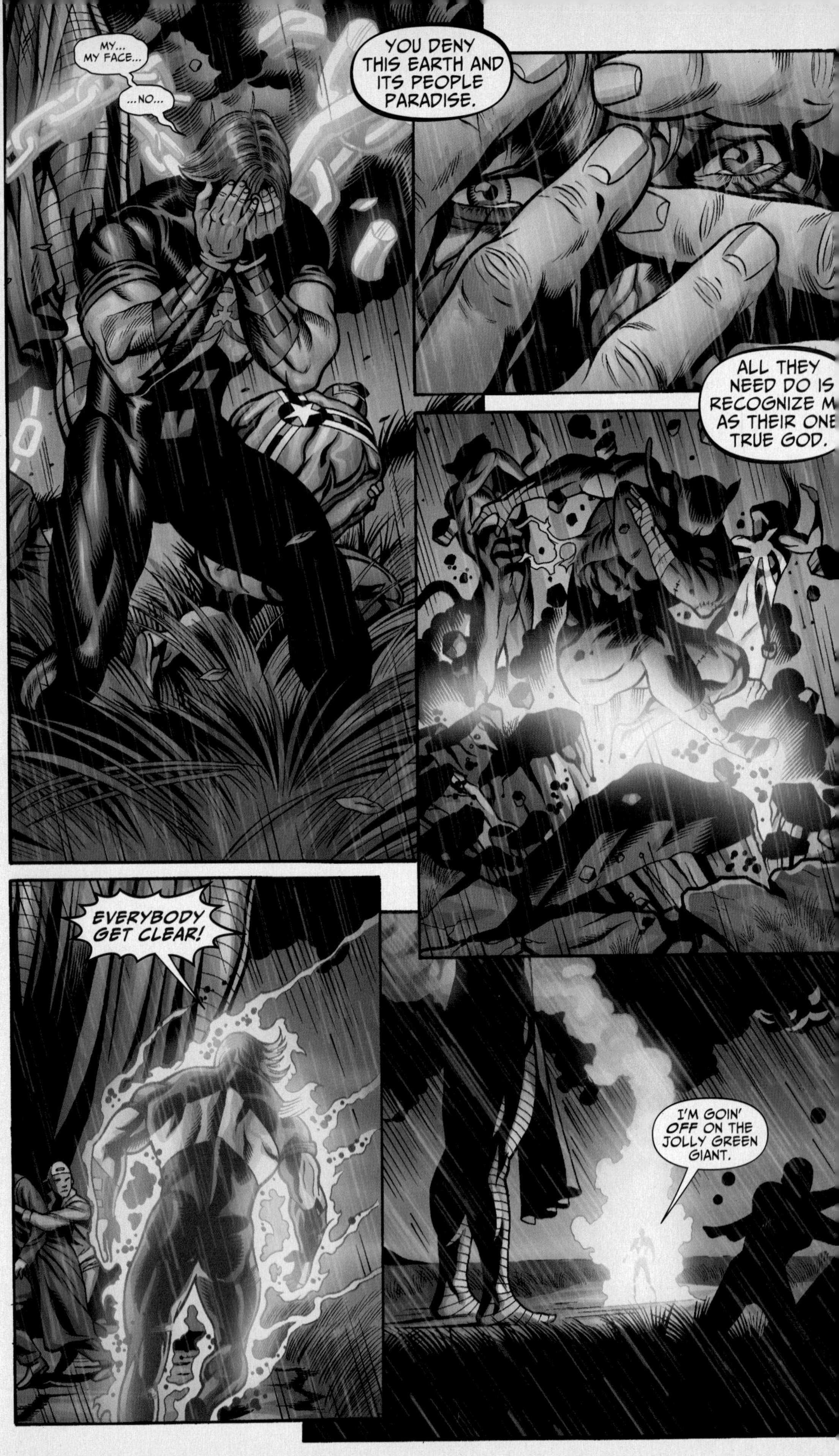
MY... MY FACE...
...NO...
YOU DENY THIS EARTH AND ITS PEOPLE PARADISE.
ALL THEY NEED DO IS RECOGNIZE M AS THEIR ONE TRUE GOD.
EVERYBODY GET CLEAR!
I'M GOIN' OFF ON THE JOLLY GREEN GIANT.

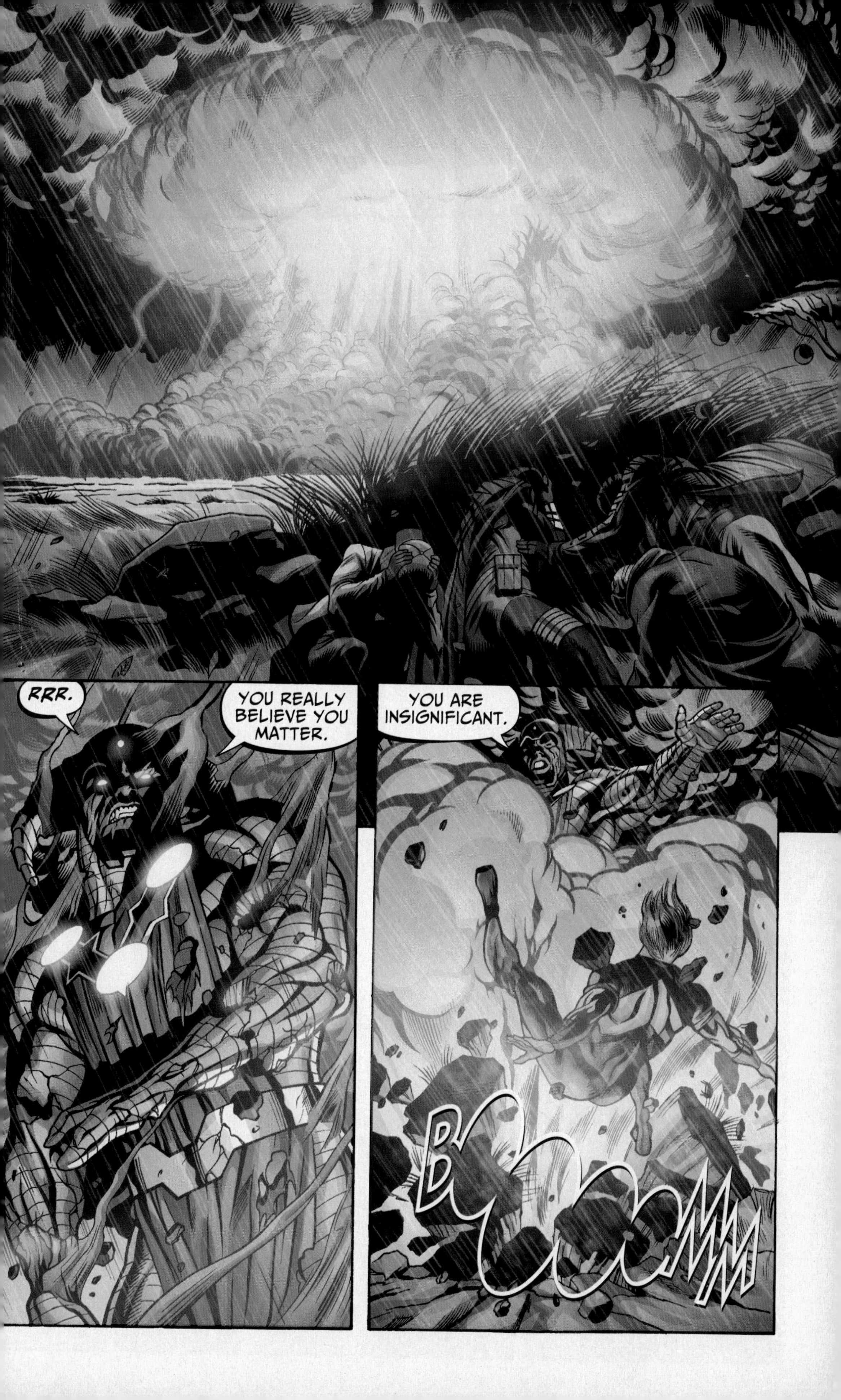
RRR.
YOU REALLY BELIEVE YOU MATTER.
YOU ARE INSIGNIFICANT.
BOOOOMM

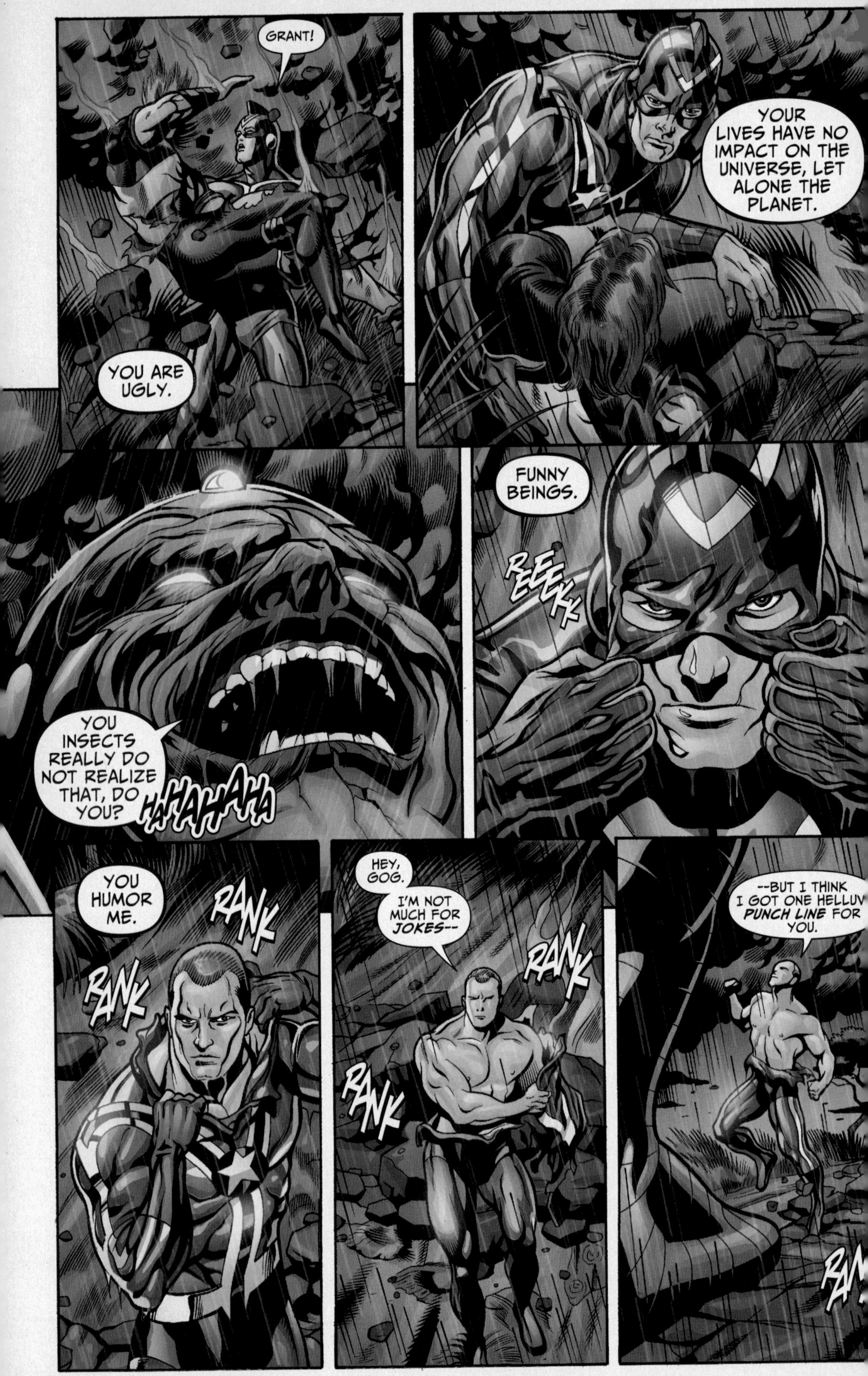
GRANT!
YOU ARE UGLY.
YOUR LIVES HAVE NO IMPACT ON THE UNIVERSE, LET ALONE THE PLANET.
YOU INSECTS REALLY DO NOT REALIZE THAT, DO YOU?
HAHAHAHAHA
FUNNY BEINGS.
REEEKK
YOU HUMOR ME.
RANK
RANK
HEY, GOG.
I'M NOT MUCH FOR *JOKES*--
RANK
RANK
--BUT I THINK I GOT ONE HELLUVA *PUNCH LINE* FOR YOU.

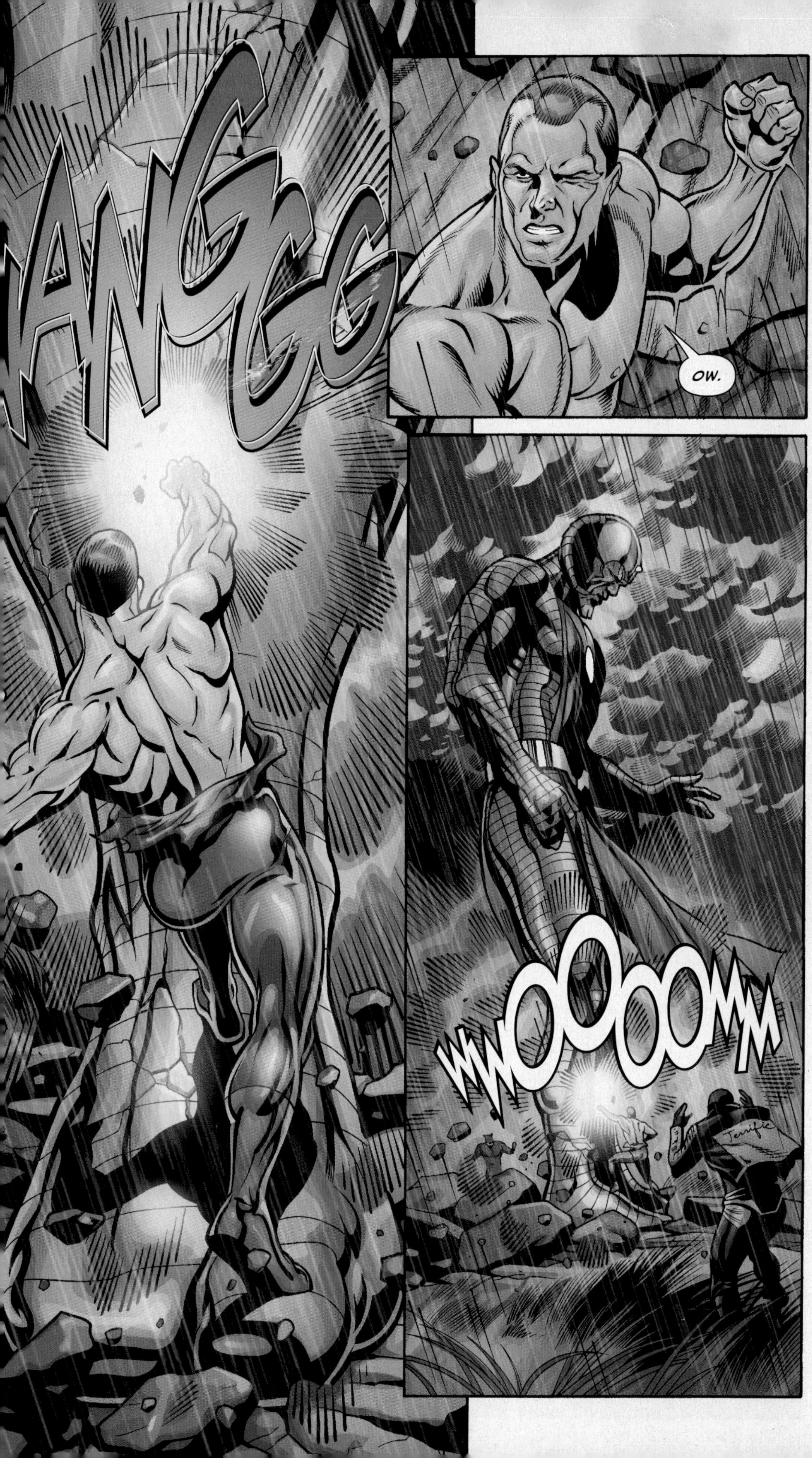
ANGGG
OW.
WWOOOOMM

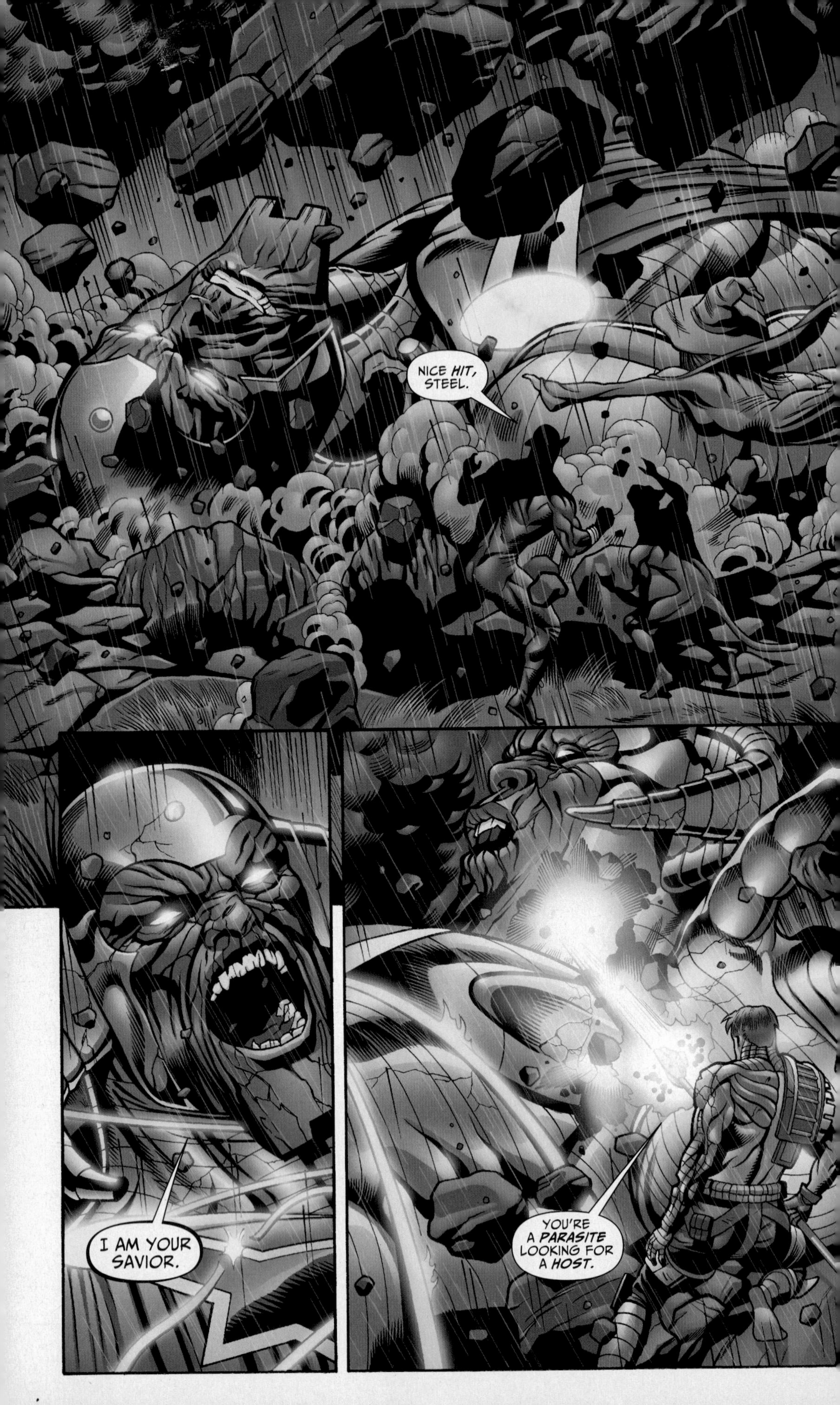
NICE HIT, STEEL.
I AM YOUR SAVIOR.
YOU'RE A PARASITE LOOKING FOR A HOST.

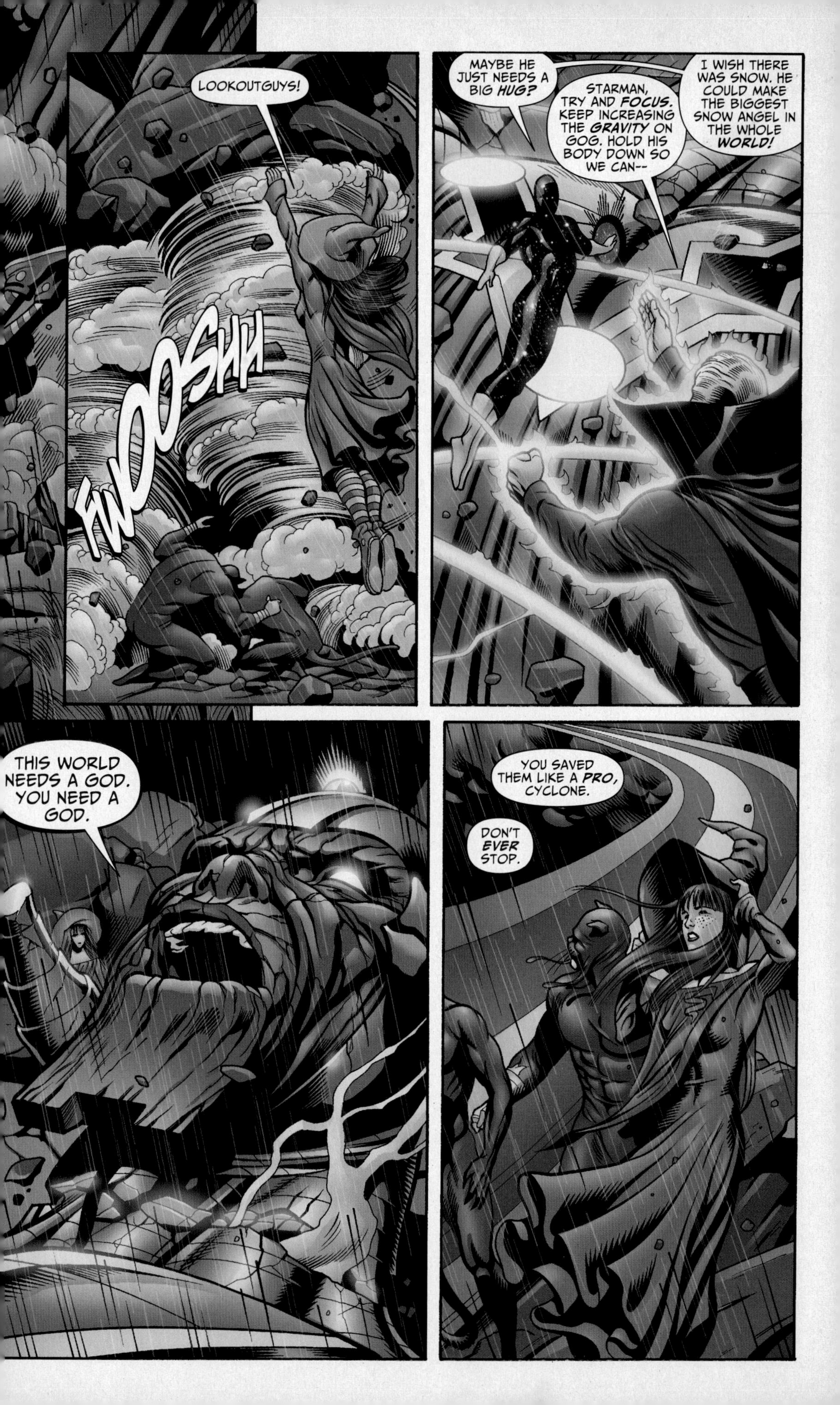
LOOKOUTGUYS!
FWOOSHH
MAYBE HE JUST NEEDS A BIG HUG?
STARMAN, TRY AND FOCUS. KEEP INCREASING THE GRAVITY ON GOG. HOLD HIS BODY DOWN SO WE CAN--
I WISH THERE WAS SNOW. HE COULD MAKE THE BIGGEST SNOW ANGEL IN THE WHOLE WORLD!
THIS WORLD NEEDS A GOD. YOU NEED A GOD.
YOU SAVED THEM LIKE A PRO, CYCLONE.
DON'T EVER STOP.

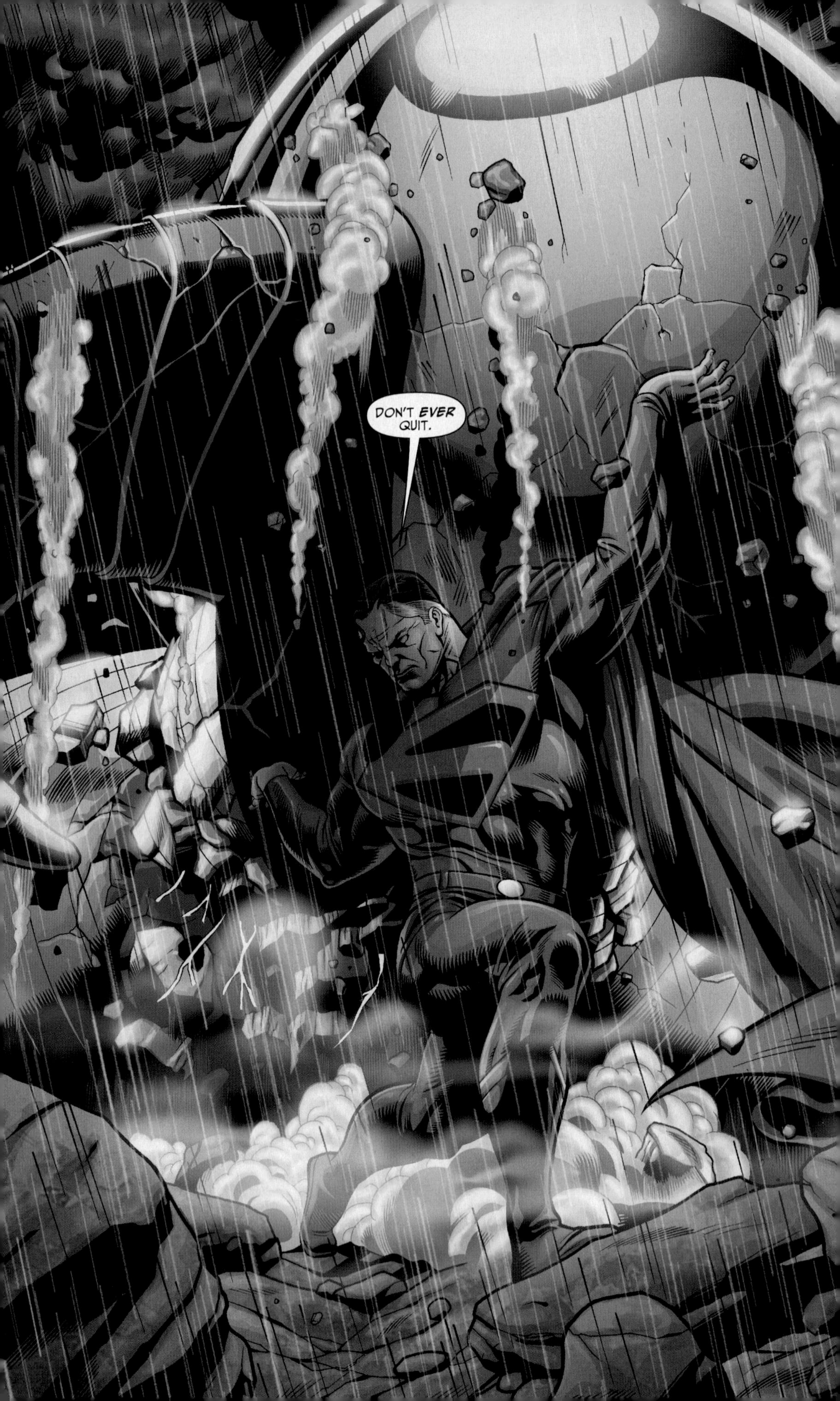
DON'T EVER QUIT.

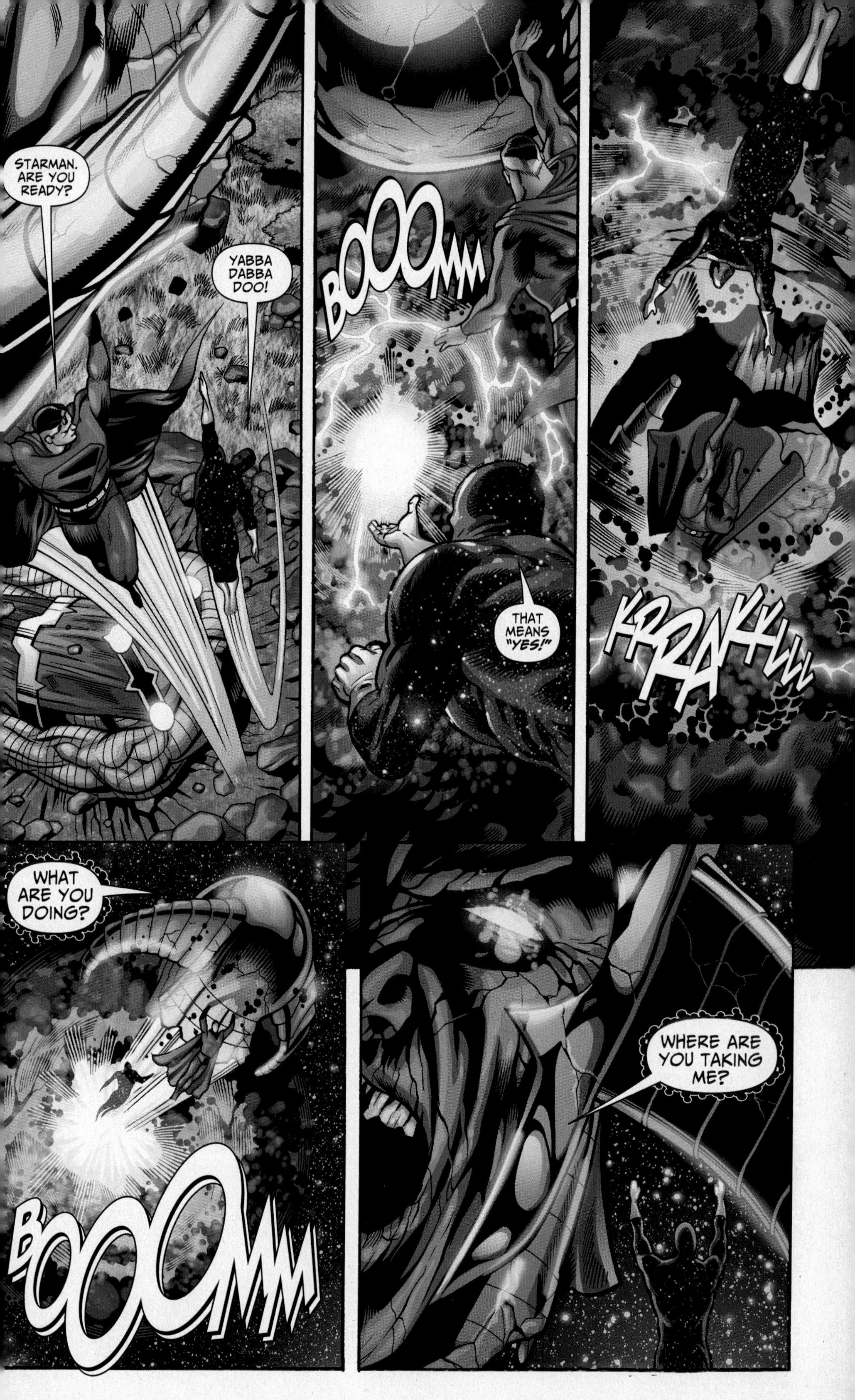
STARMAN. ARE YOU READY?
YABBA DABBA DOO!
BOOOMMM
THAT MEANS "YES!"
KRRAKKLLL
WHAT ARE YOU DOING?
BOOOMMM
WHERE ARE YOU TAKING ME?

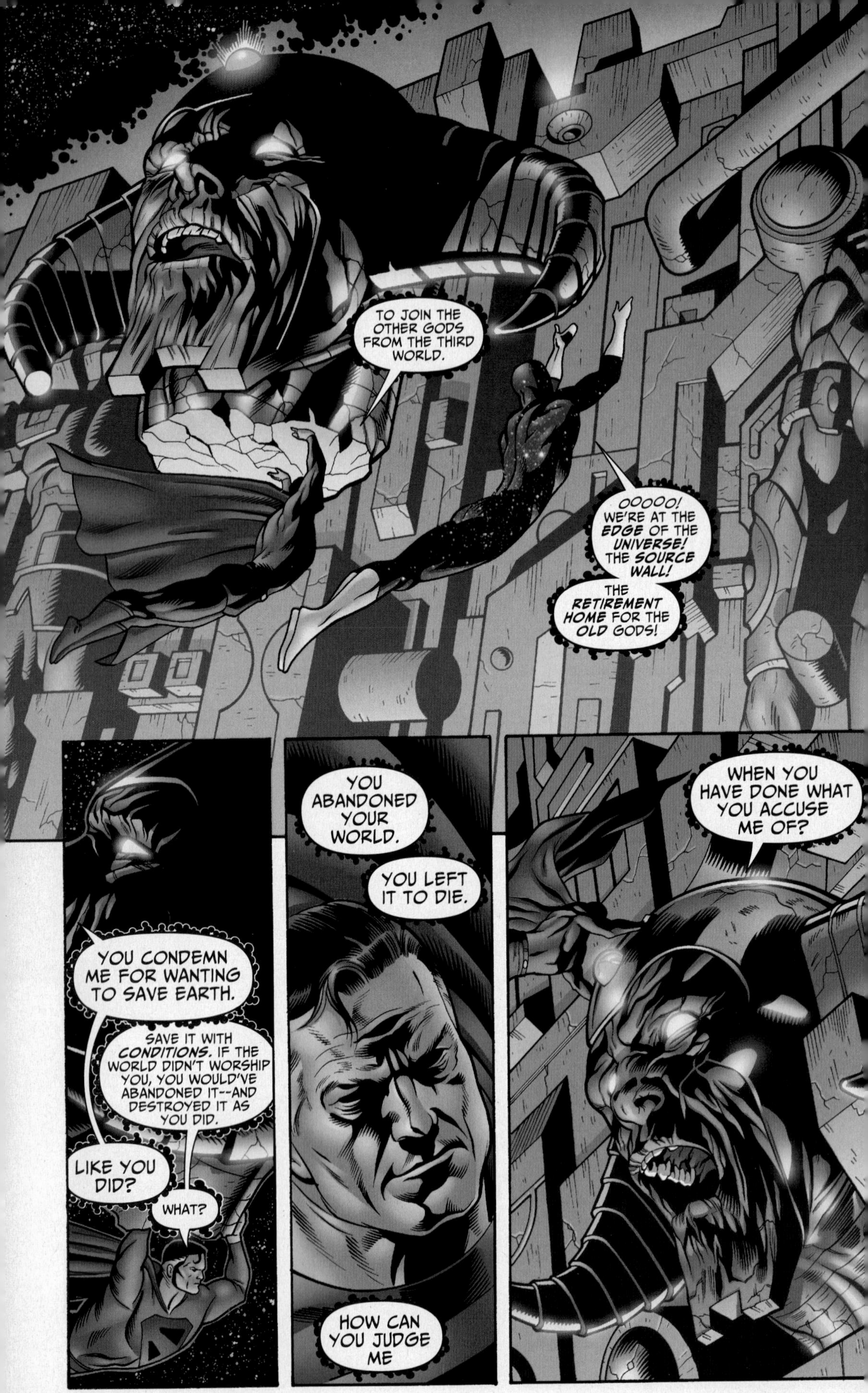

TO JOIN THE OTHER GODS FROM THE THIRD WORLD.
OOOOO! WE'RE AT THE EDGE OF THE UNIVERSE! THE SOURCE WALL!
THE RETIREMENT HOME FOR THE OLD GODS!
YOU CONDEMN ME FOR WANTING TO SAVE EARTH.
SAVE IT WITH CONDITIONS. IF THE WORLD DIDN'T WORSHIP YOU, YOU WOULD'VE ABANDONED IT--AND DESTROYED IT AS YOU DID.
LIKE YOU DID?
WHAT?
YOU ABANDONED YOUR WORLD.
YOU LEFT IT TO DIE.
HOW CAN YOU JUDGE ME
WHEN YOU HAVE DONE WHAT YOU ACCUSE ME OF?

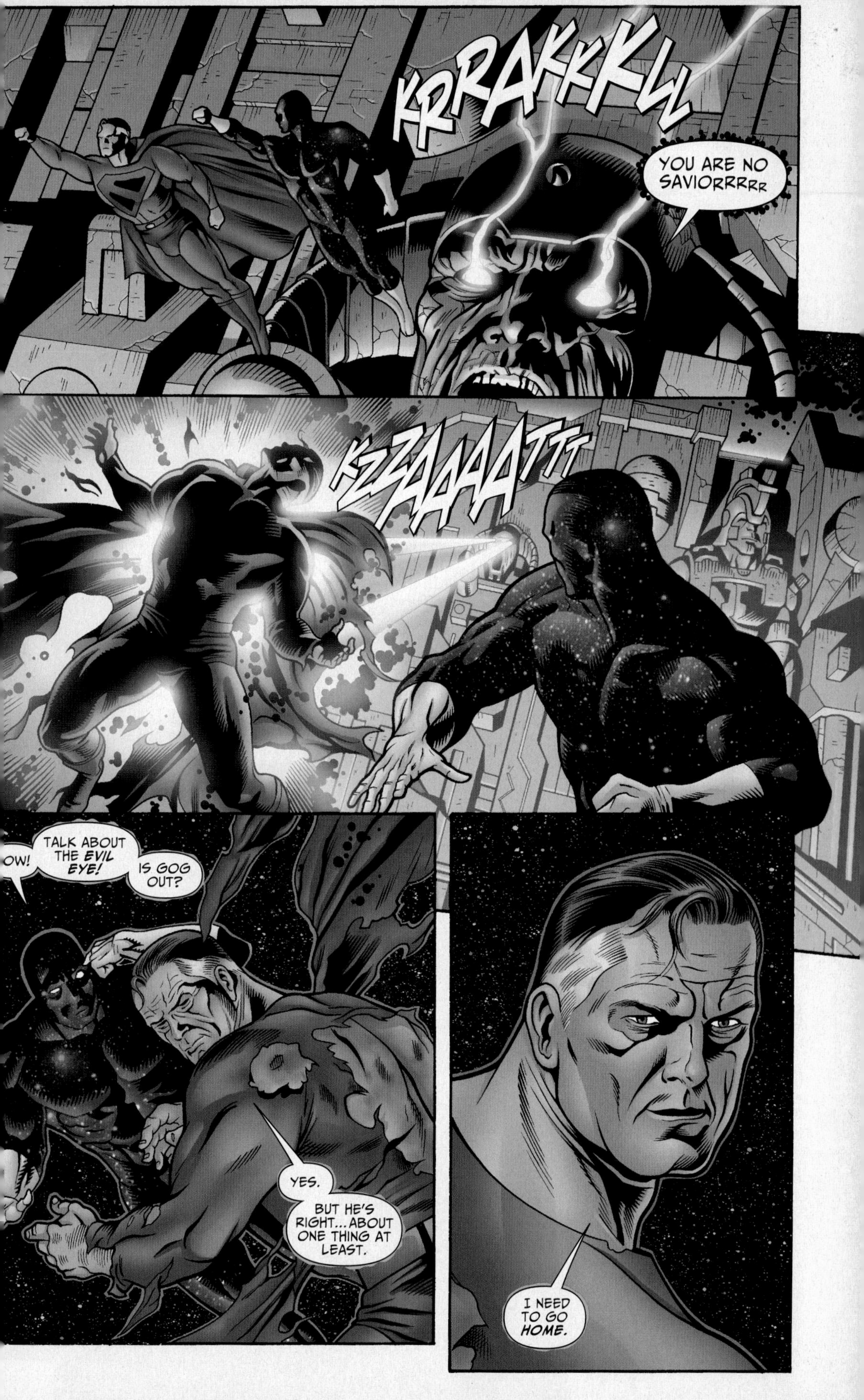
KRRAKKKLL
YOU ARE NO SAVIORRRRr
KZZAAAATTT
OW!
TALK ABOUT THE *EVIL EYE!*
IS GOG OUT?
YES.
BUT HE'S RIGHT... ABOUT ONE THING AT LEAST.
I NEED TO GO *HOME.*

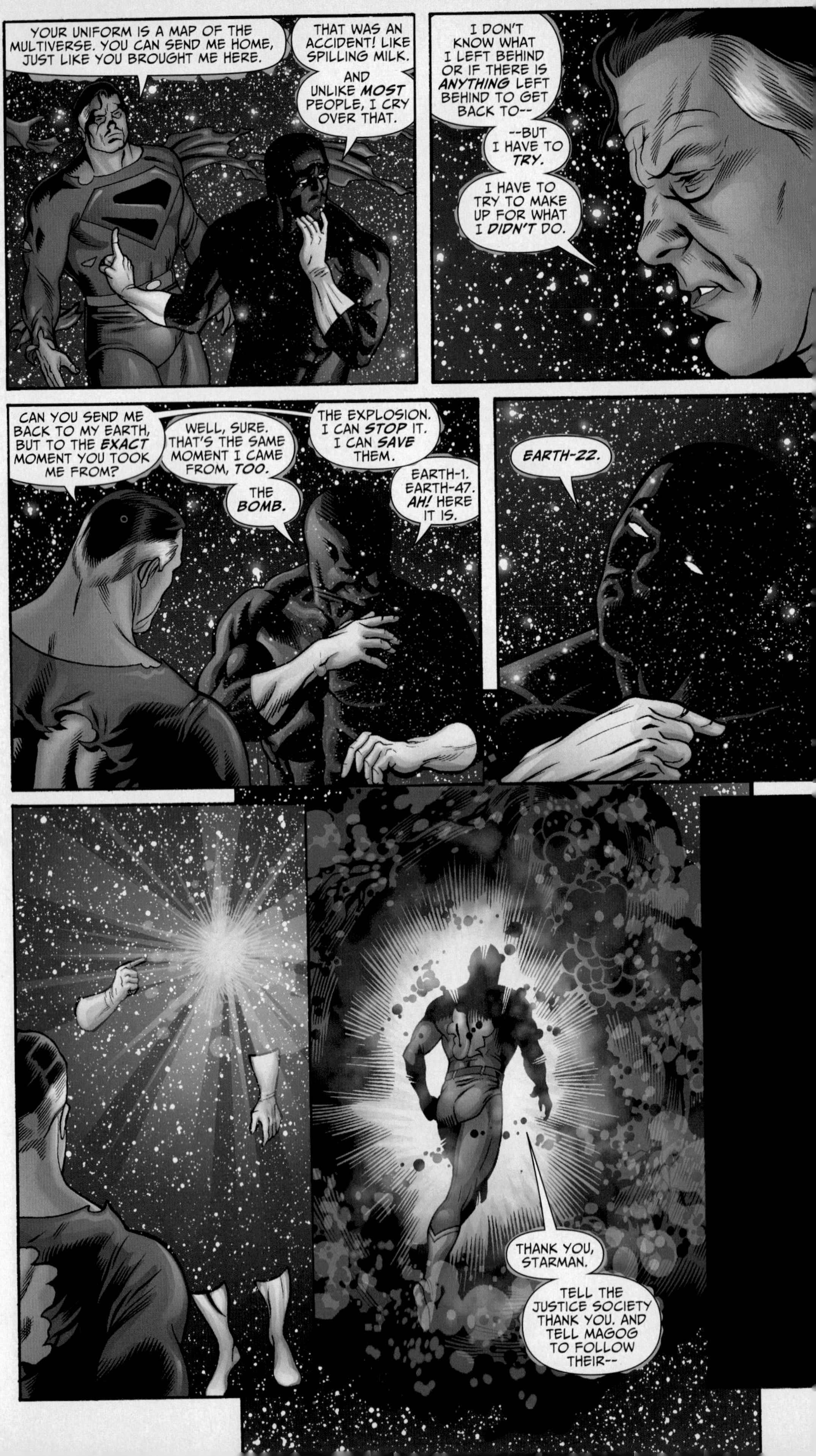

YOUR UNIFORM IS A MAP OF THE MULTIVERSE. YOU CAN SEND ME HOME, JUST LIKE YOU BROUGHT ME HERE.
THAT WAS AN ACCIDENT! LIKE SPILLING MILK.
AND UNLIKE MOST PEOPLE, I CRY OVER THAT.
I DON'T KNOW WHAT I LEFT BEHIND OR IF THERE IS ANYTHING LEFT BEHIND TO GET BACK TO--
--BUT I HAVE TO TRY.
I HAVE TO TRY TO MAKE UP FOR WHAT I DIDN'T DO.
CAN YOU SEND ME BACK TO MY EARTH, BUT TO THE EXACT MOMENT YOU TOOK ME FROM?
WELL, SURE. THAT'S THE SAME MOMENT I CAME FROM, TOO.
THE BOMB.
THE EXPLOSION. I CAN STOP IT. I CAN SAVE THEM.
EARTH-1. EARTH-47. AH! HERE IT IS.
EARTH-22.
THANK YOU, STARMAN.
TELL THE JUSTICE SOCIETY THANK YOU. AND TELL MAGOG TO FOLLOW THEIR--

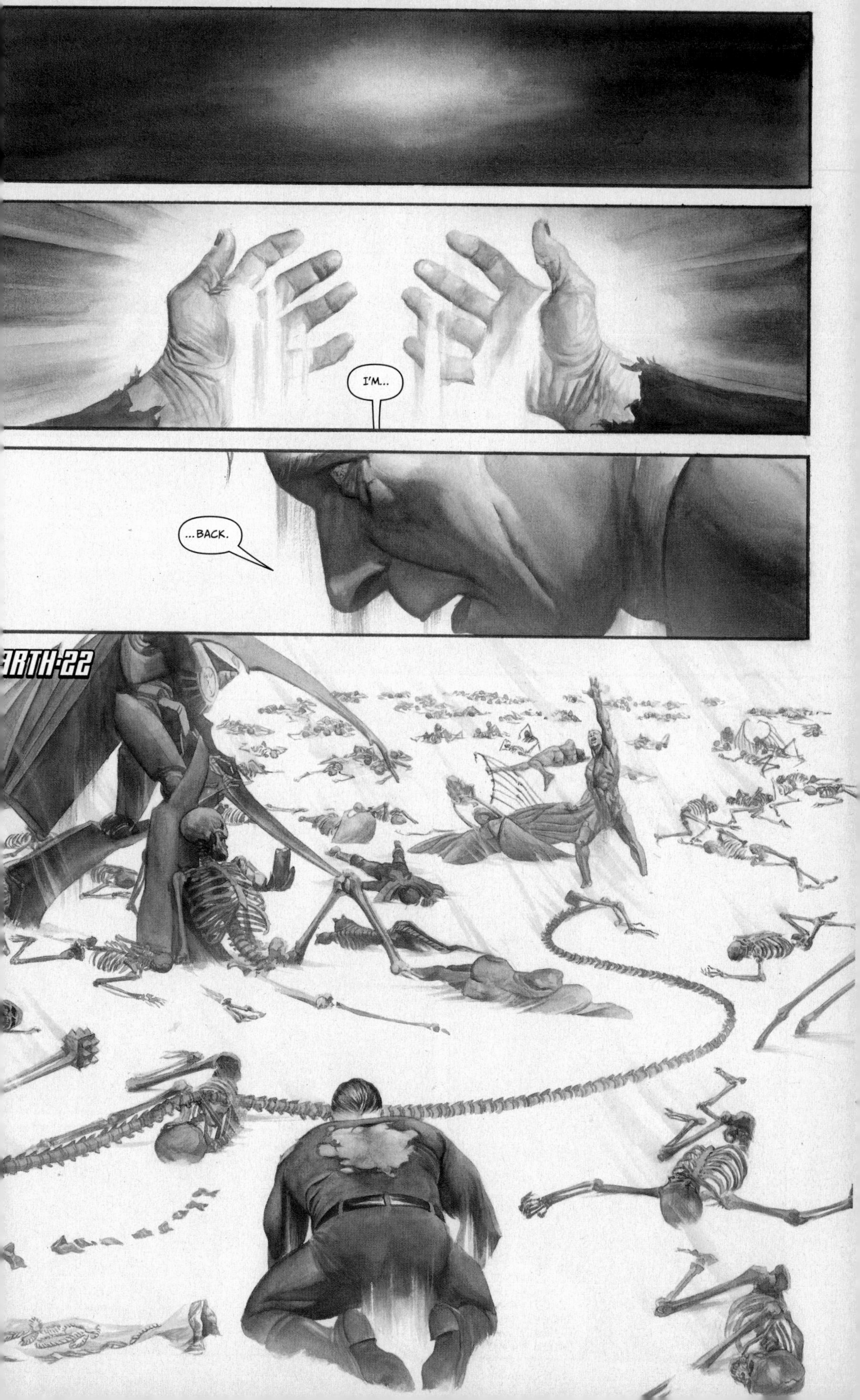
I'M...
...BACK.
ARTH-22

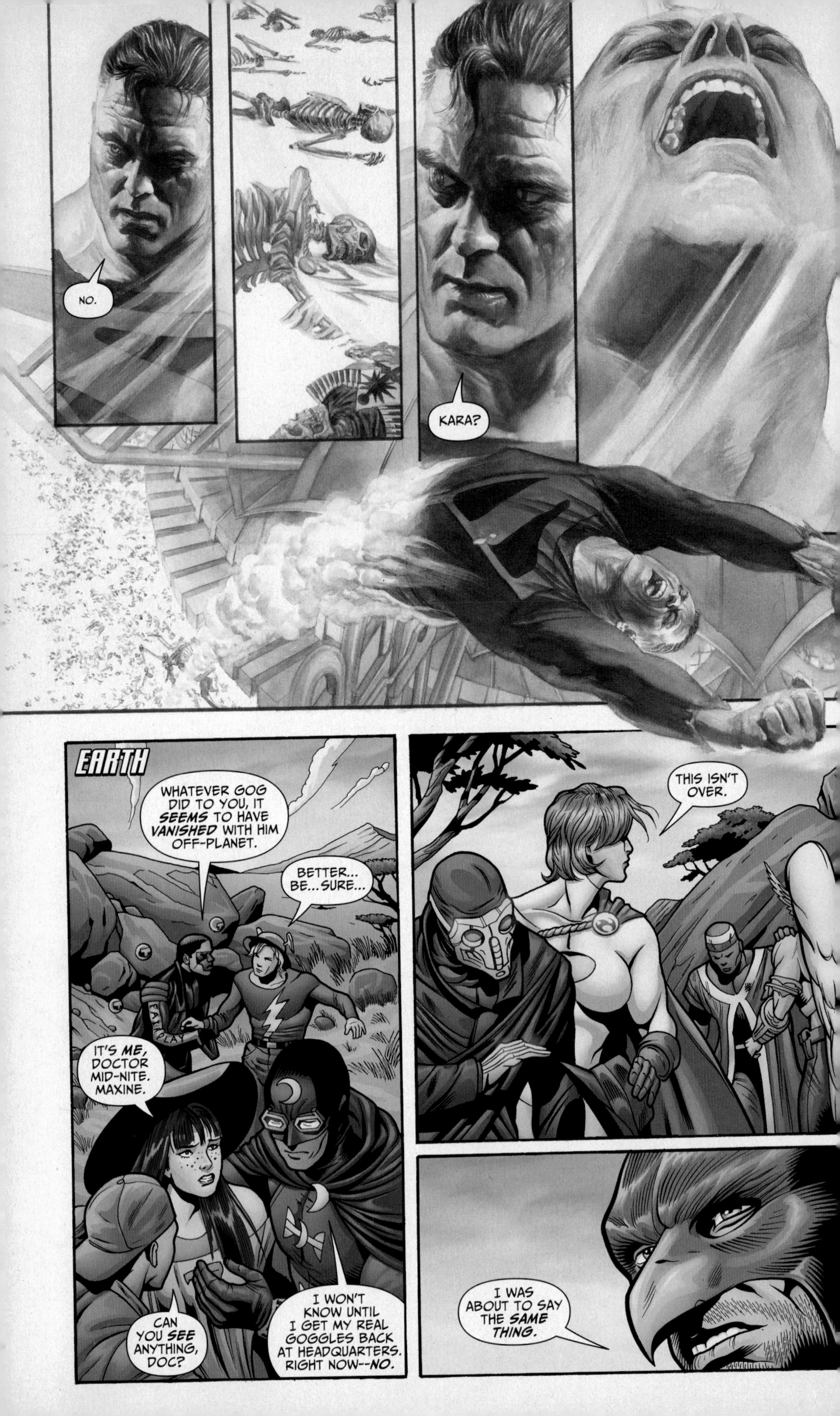
NO.
KARA?
EARTH
WHATEVER GOG DID TO YOU, IT SEEMS TO HAVE VANISHED WITH HIM OFF-PLANET.
BETTER... BE... SURE...
IT'S ME, DOCTOR MID-NITE. MAXINE.
CAN YOU SEE ANYTHING, DOC?
I WON'T KNOW UNTIL I GET MY REAL GOGGLES BACK AT HEADQUARTERS. RIGHT NOW--NO.
THIS ISN'T OVER.
I WAS ABOUT TO SAY THE SAME THING.

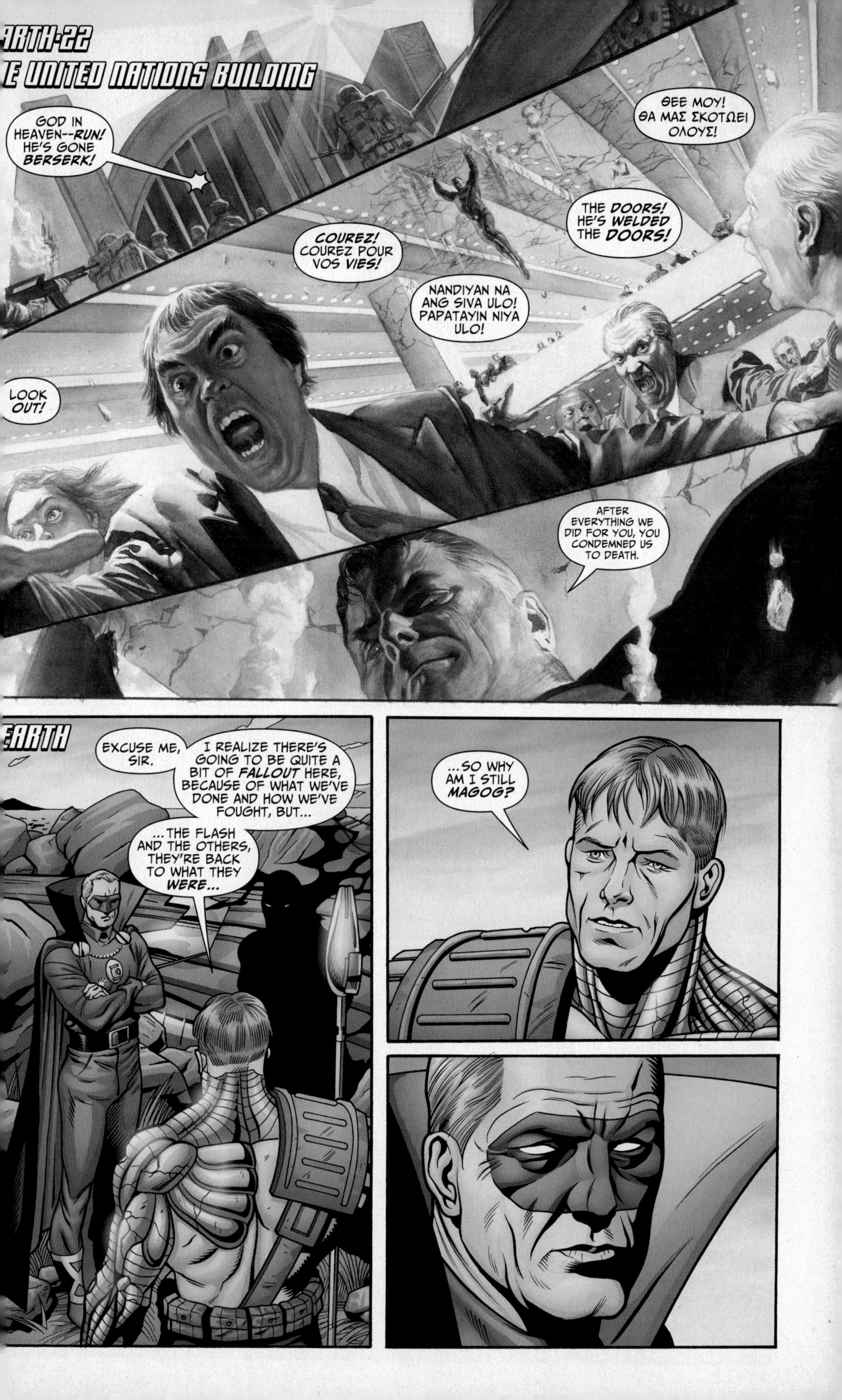
ARTH-22
E UNITED NATIONS BUILDING
GOD IN HEAVEN--RUN! HE'S GONE BERSERK!
ΘΕΕ ΜΟΥ! ΘΑ ΜΑΣ ΣΚΟΤΩΕΙ ΟΛΟΥΣ!
THE DOORS! HE'S WELDED THE DOORS!
COUREZ! COUREZ POUR VOS VIES!
NANDIYAN NA ANG SIVA ULO! PAPATAYIN NIYA ULO!
LOOK OUT!
AFTER EVERYTHING WE DID FOR YOU, YOU CONDEMNED US TO DEATH.
EARTH
EXCUSE ME, SIR.
I REALIZE THERE'S GOING TO BE QUITE A BIT OF FALLOUT HERE, BECAUSE OF WHAT WE'VE DONE AND HOW WE'VE FOUGHT, BUT...
...THE FLASH AND THE OTHERS, THEY'RE BACK TO WHAT THEY WERE...
...SO WHY AM I STILL MAGOG?

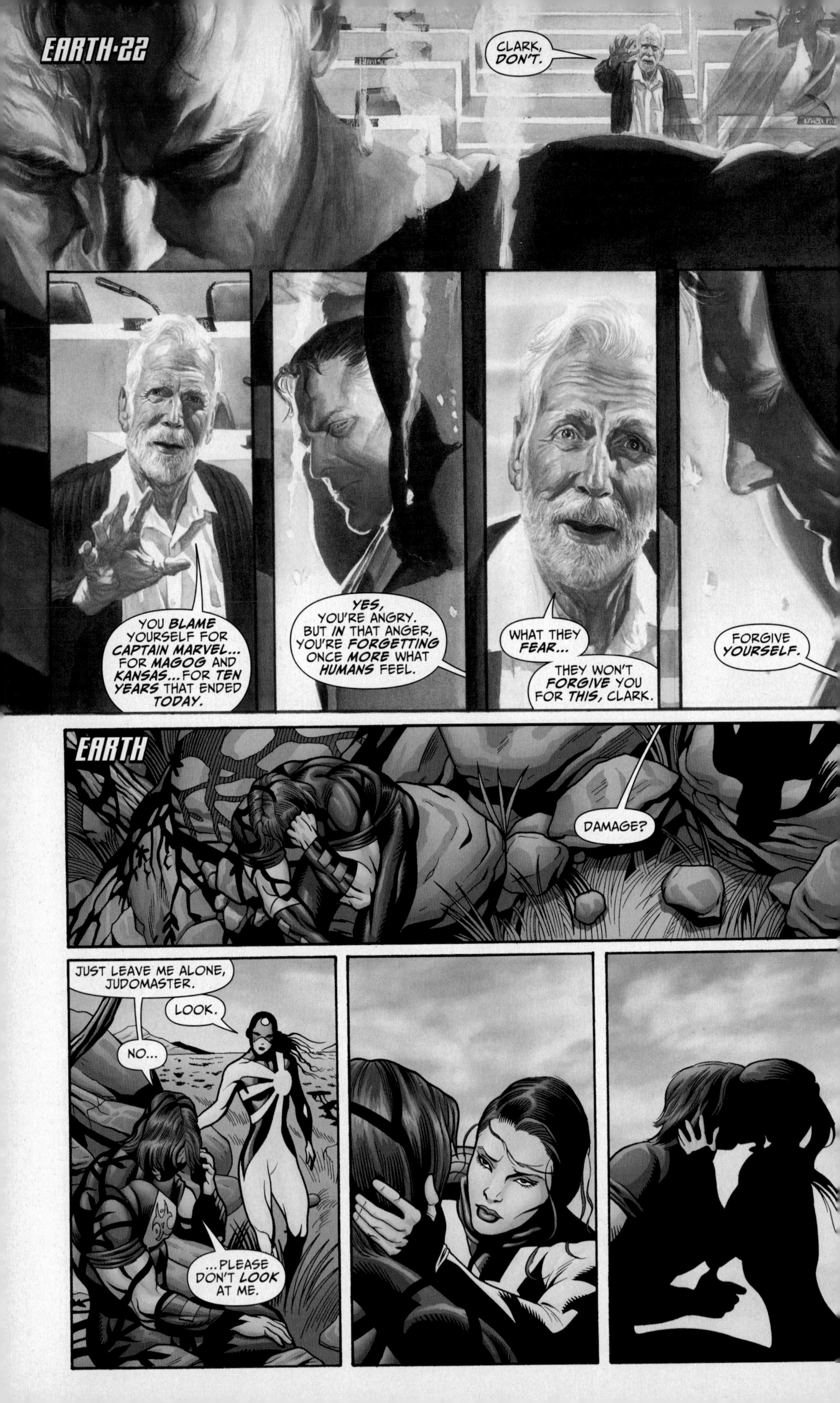
EARTH-22
CLARK, DON'T.
YOU BLAME YOURSELF FOR CAPTAIN MARVEL... FOR MAGOG AND KANSAS... FOR TEN YEARS THAT ENDED TODAY.
YES, YOU'RE ANGRY. BUT IN THAT ANGER, YOU'RE FORGETTING ONCE MORE WHAT HUMANS FEEL.
WHAT THEY FEAR...
THEY WON'T FORGIVE YOU FOR THIS, CLARK.
FORGIVE YOURSELF.
EARTH
DAMAGE?
JUST LEAVE ME ALONE, JUDOMASTER.
LOOK.
NO...
...PLEASE DON'T LOOK AT ME.

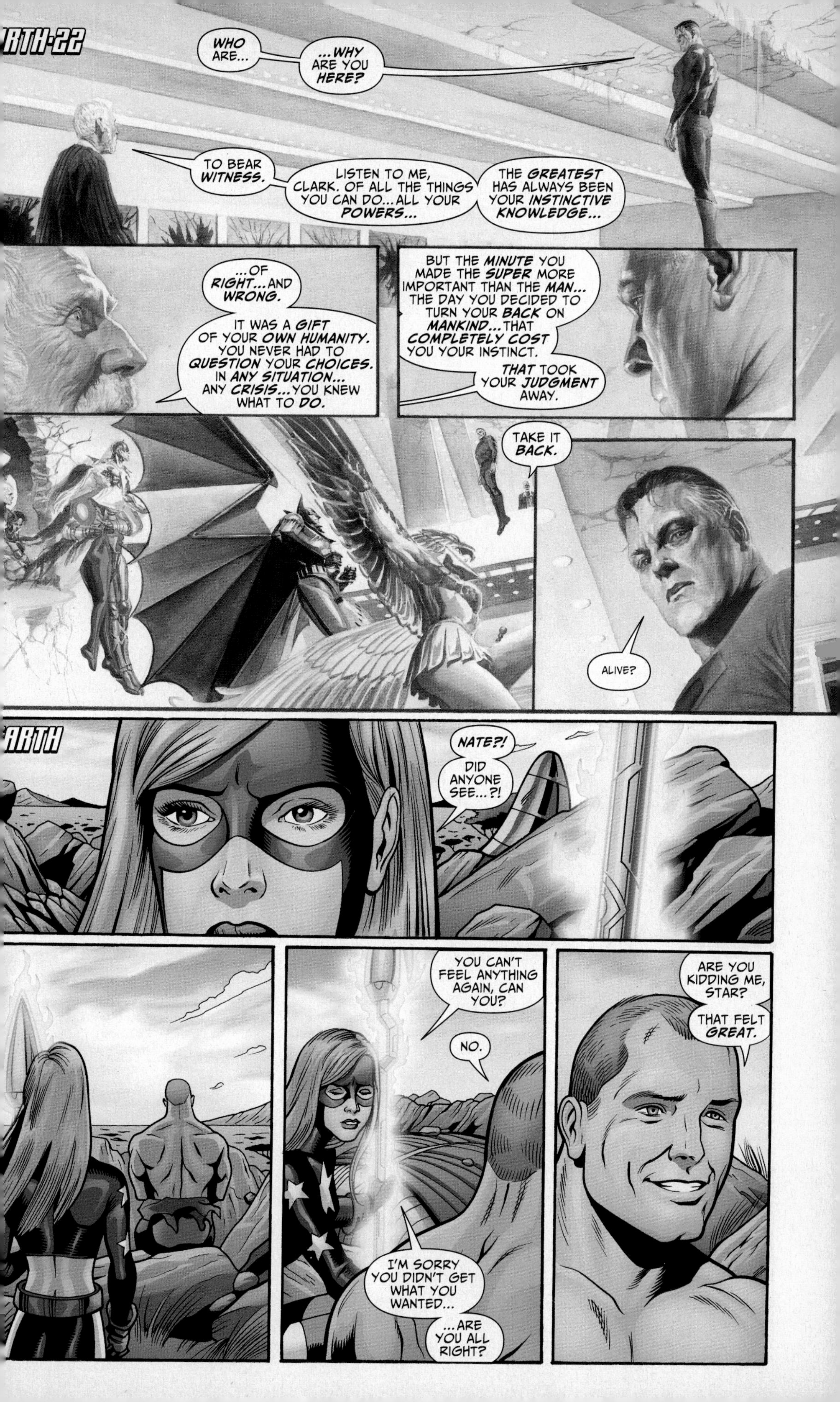

RTH-22
WHO ARE...
...WHY ARE YOU HERE?
TO BEAR WITNESS.
LISTEN TO ME, CLARK. OF ALL THE THINGS YOU CAN DO...ALL YOUR POWERS...
THE GREATEST HAS ALWAYS BEEN YOUR INSTINCTIVE KNOWLEDGE...
...OF RIGHT...AND WRONG.
IT WAS A GIFT OF YOUR OWN HUMANITY. YOU NEVER HAD TO QUESTION YOUR CHOICES. IN ANY SITUATION... ANY CRISIS...YOU KNEW WHAT TO DO.
BUT THE MINUTE YOU MADE THE SUPER MORE IMPORTANT THAN THE MAN... THE DAY YOU DECIDED TO TURN YOUR BACK ON MANKIND...THAT COMPLETELY COST YOU YOUR INSTINCT.
THAT TOOK YOUR JUDGMENT AWAY.
TAKE IT BACK.
ALIVE?
ARTH
NATE?!
DID ANYONE SEE...?!
YOU CAN'T FEEL ANYTHING AGAIN, CAN YOU?
NO.
I'M SORRY YOU DIDN'T GET WHAT YOU WANTED...
...ARE YOU ALL RIGHT?
ARE YOU KIDDING ME, STAR?
THAT FELT GREAT.

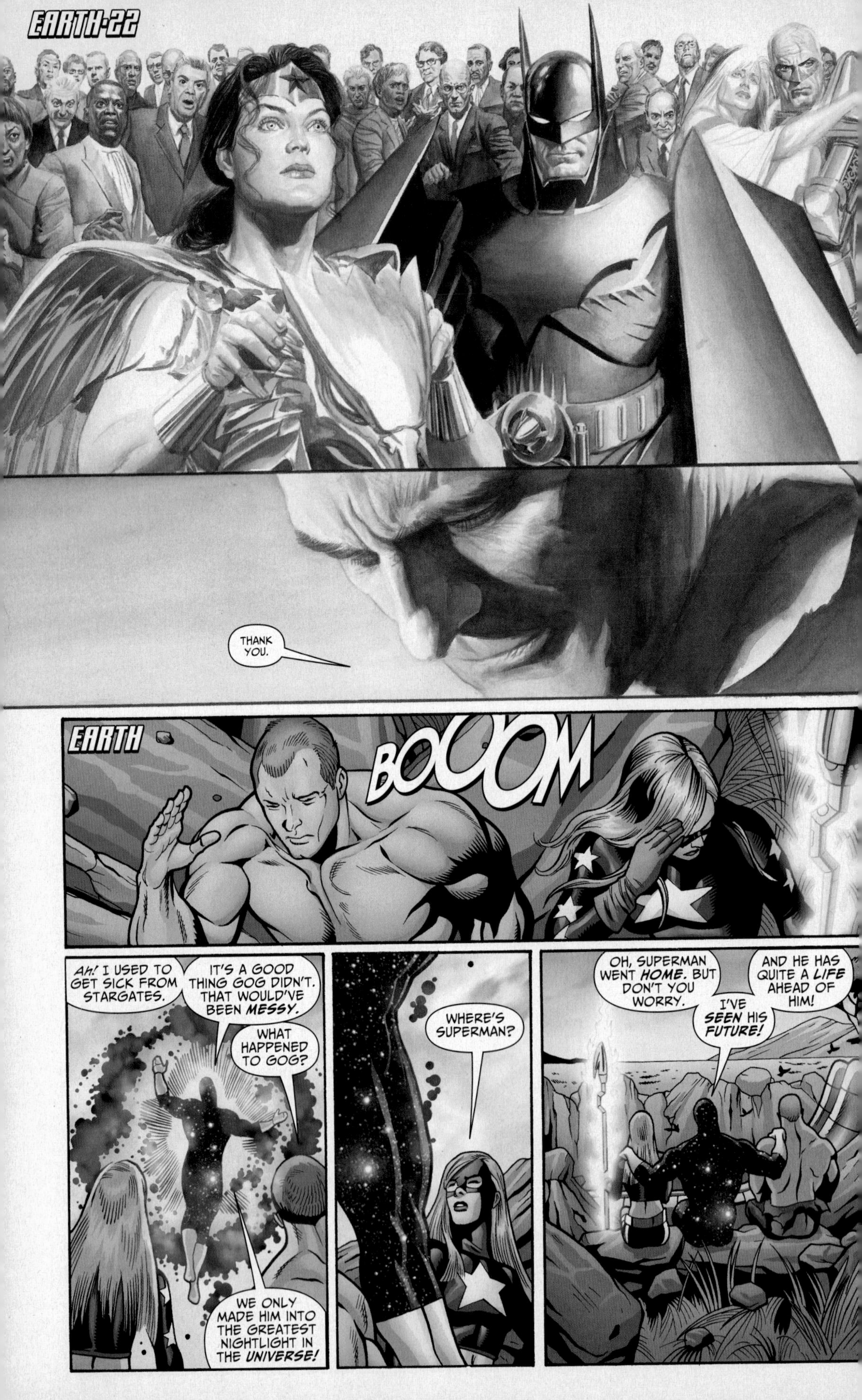
EARTH-22
THANK YOU.
EARTH
BOOOOM
Ah! I USED TO GET SICK FROM STARGATES.
IT'S A GOOD THING GOG DIDN'T. THAT WOULD'VE BEEN MESSY.
WHAT HAPPENED TO GOG?
WE ONLY MADE HIM INTO THE GREATEST NIGHTLIGHT IN THE UNIVERSE!
WHERE'S SUPERMAN?
OH, SUPERMAN WENT HOME. BUT DON'T YOU WORRY.
I'VE SEEN HIS FUTURE!
AND HE HAS QUITE A LIFE AHEAD OF HIM!

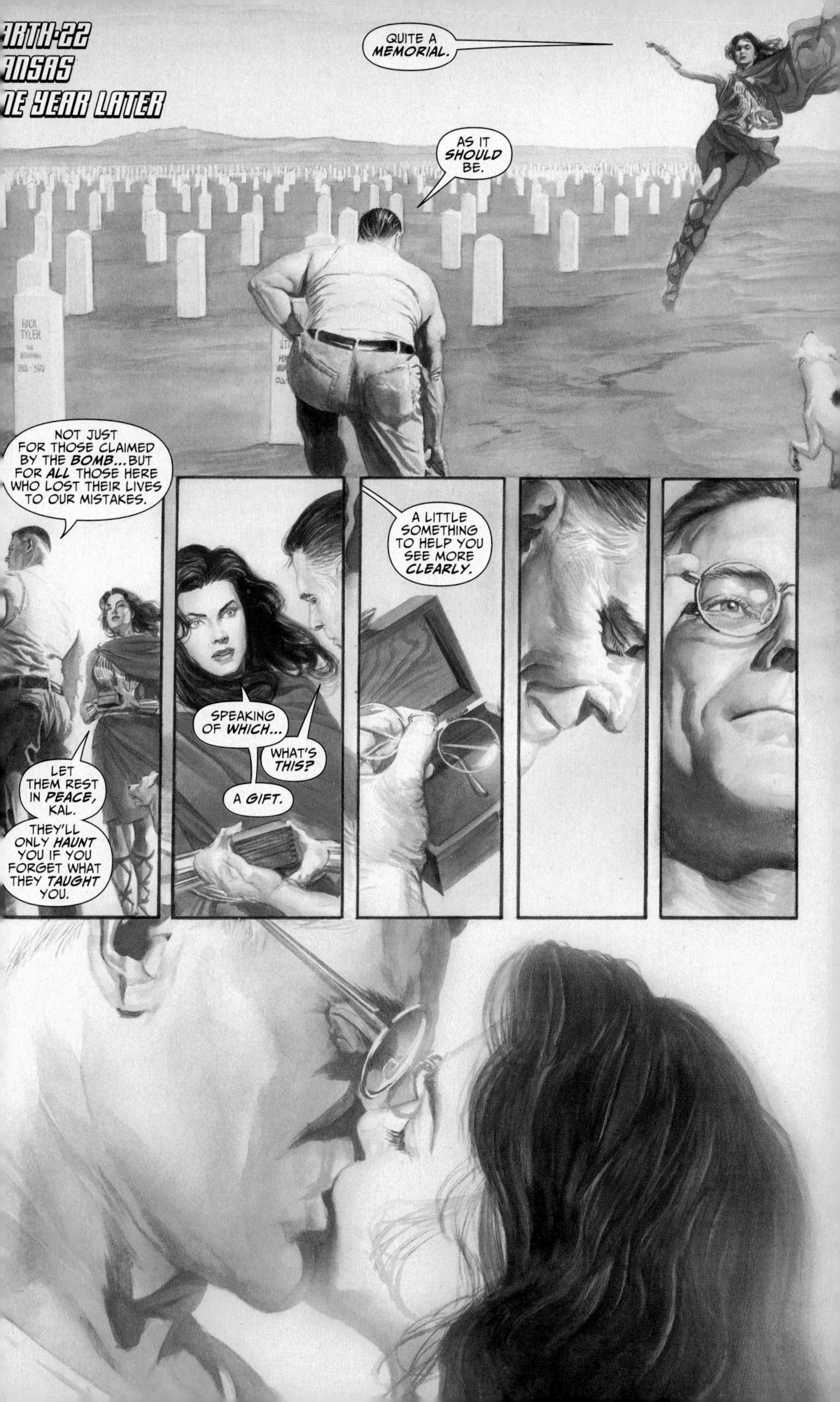

ARTH-22
ANSAS
NE YEAR LATER
QUITE A MEMORIAL.
AS IT SHOULD BE.
HICK TYLER
NOT JUST FOR THOSE CLAIMED BY THE BOMB...BUT FOR ALL THOSE HERE WHO LOST THEIR LIVES TO OUR MISTAKES.
LET THEM REST IN PEACE, KAL.
THEY'LL ONLY HAUNT YOU IF YOU FORGET WHAT THEY TAUGHT YOU.
SPEAKING OF WHICH...
WHAT'S THIS?
A GIFT.
A LITTLE SOMETHING TO HELP YOU SEE MORE CLEARLY.

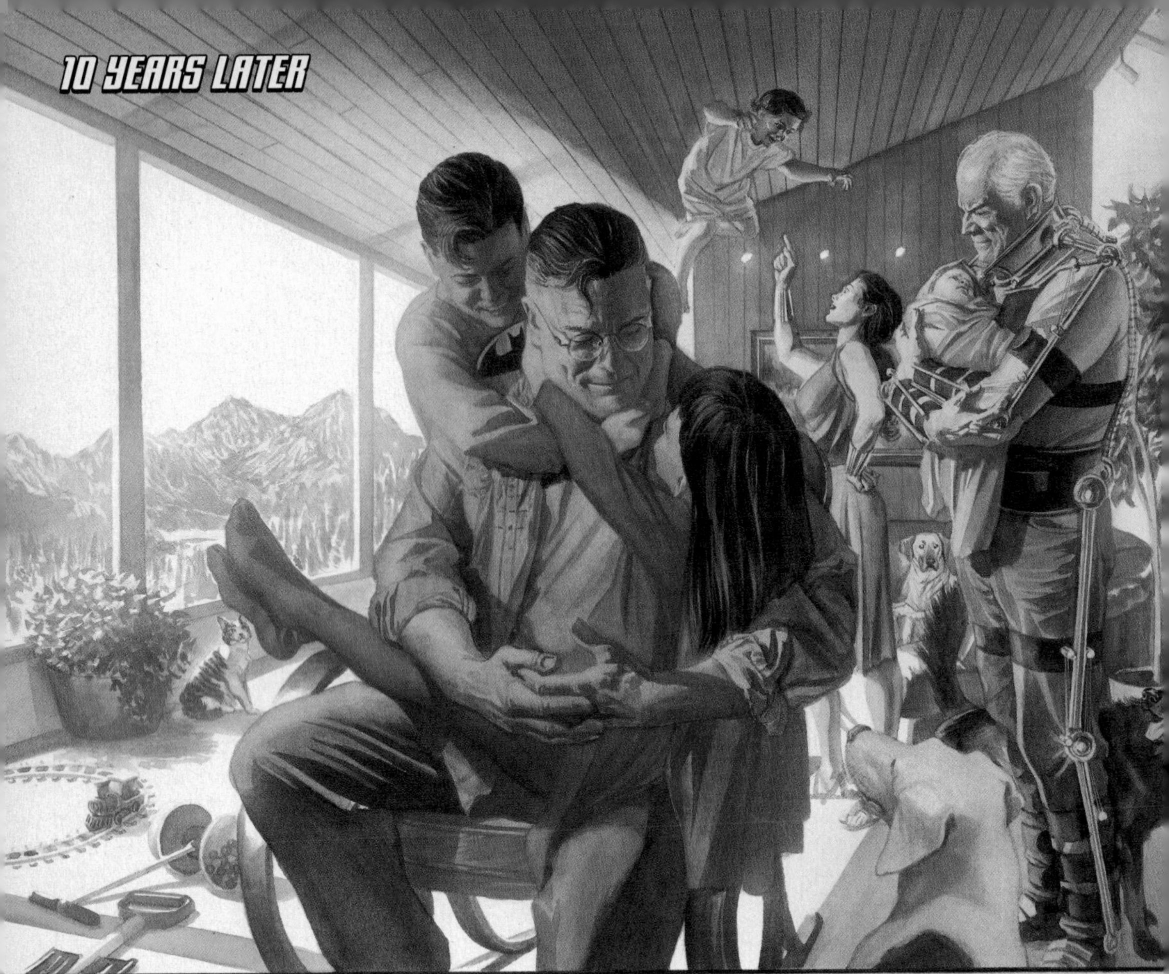
10 YEARS LATER
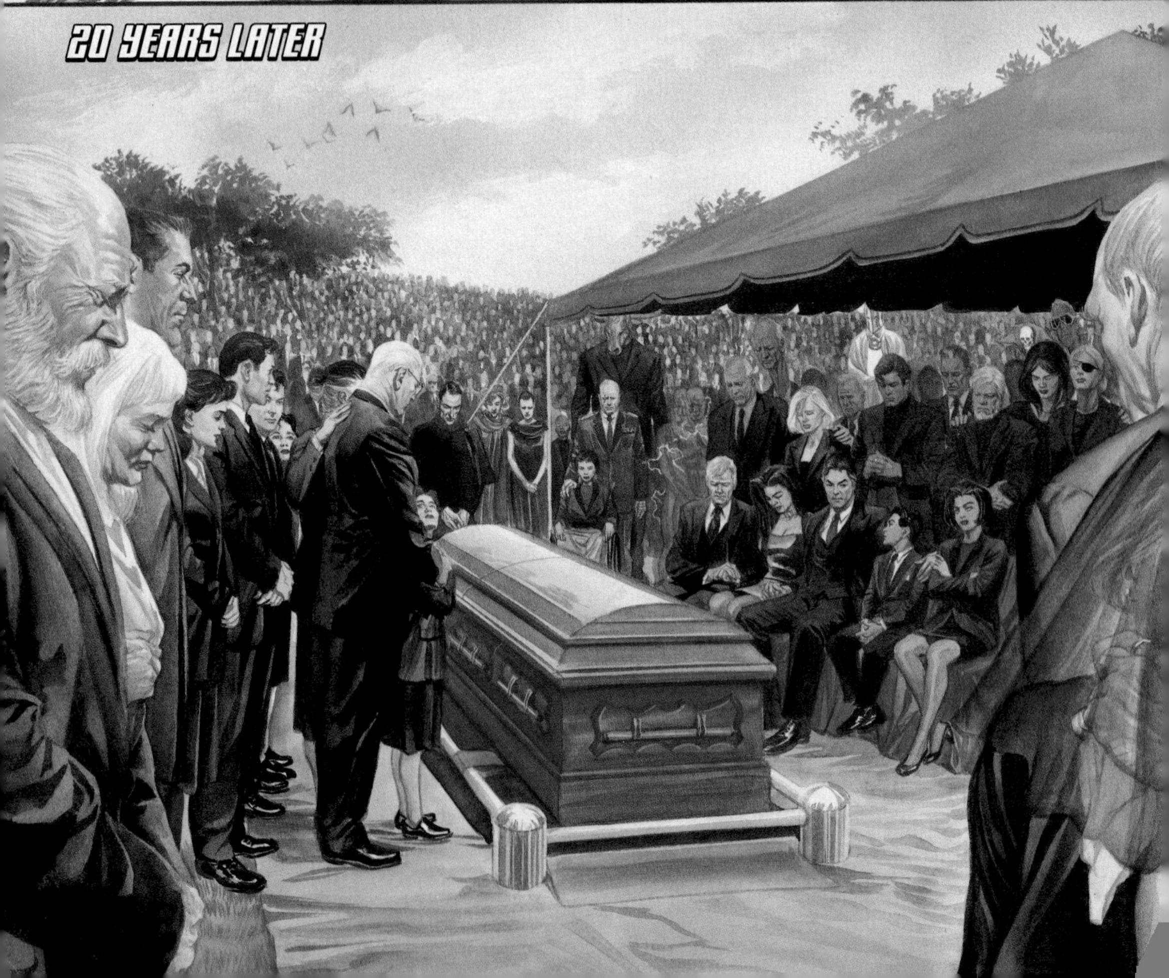
20 YEARS LATER

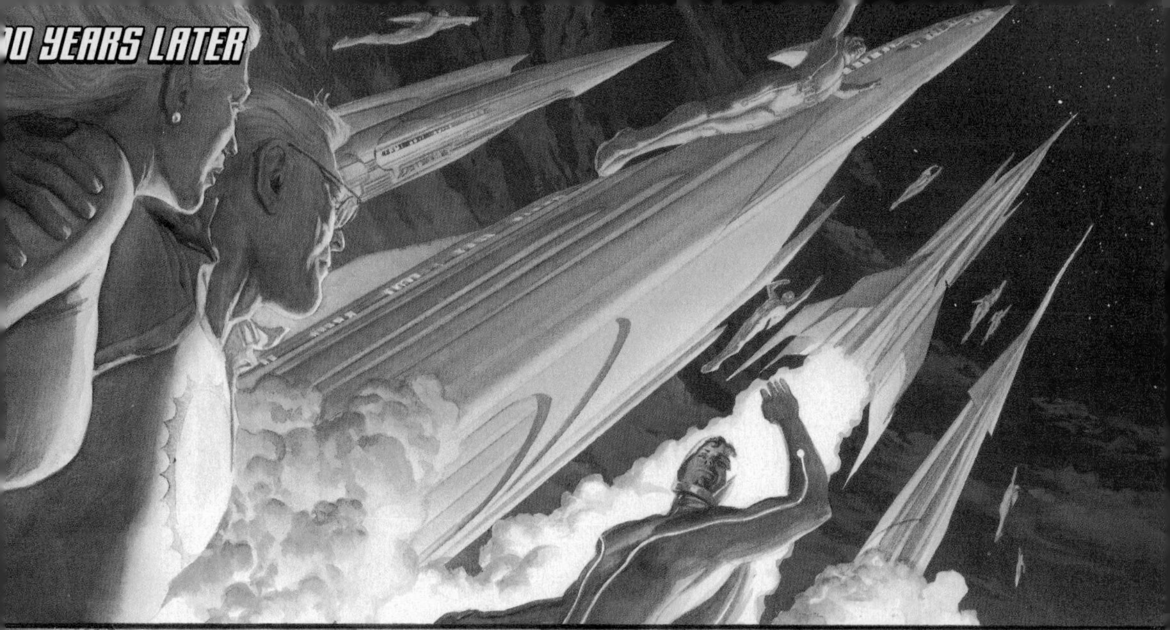
0 YEARS LATER

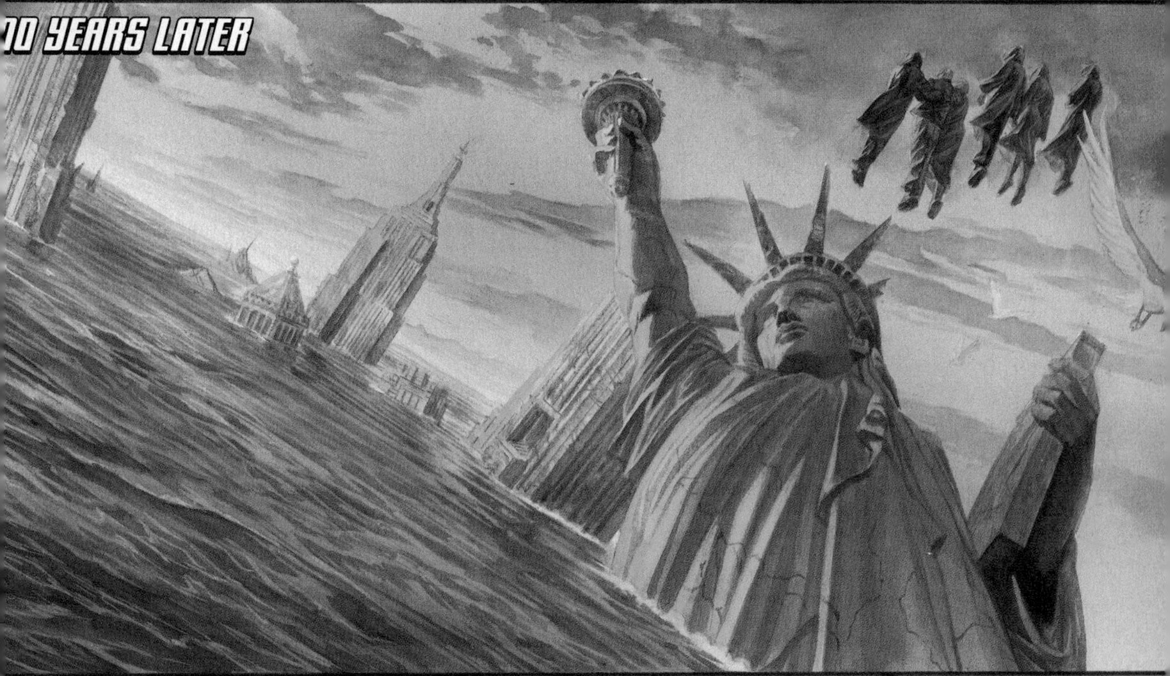
0 YEARS LATER

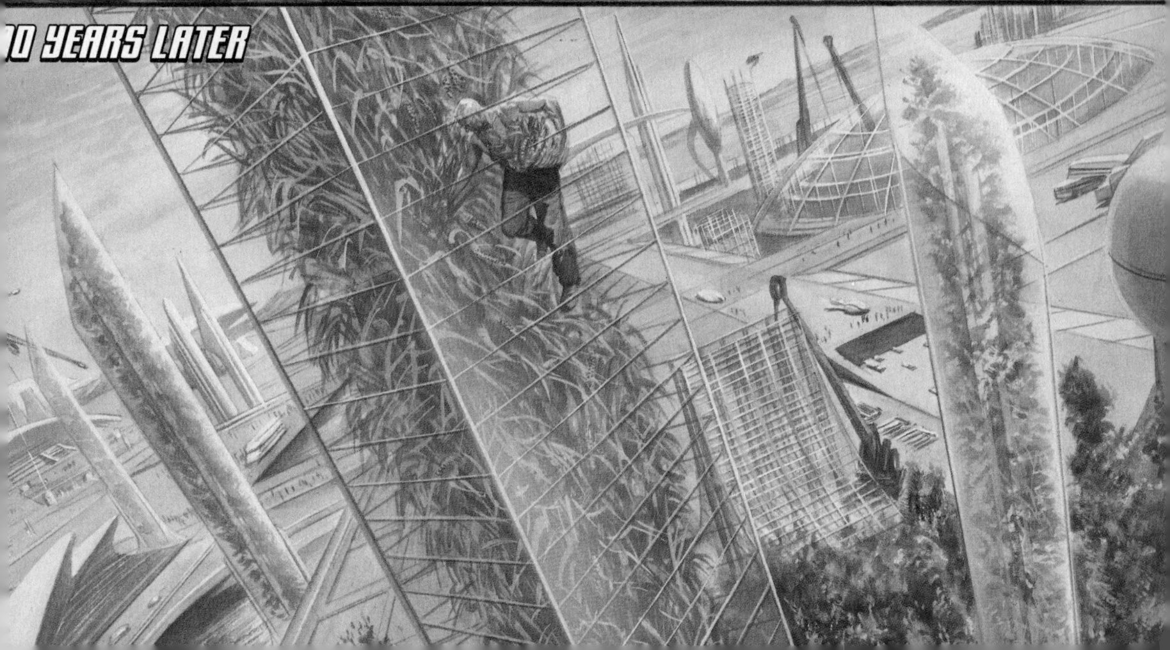
0 YEARS LATER

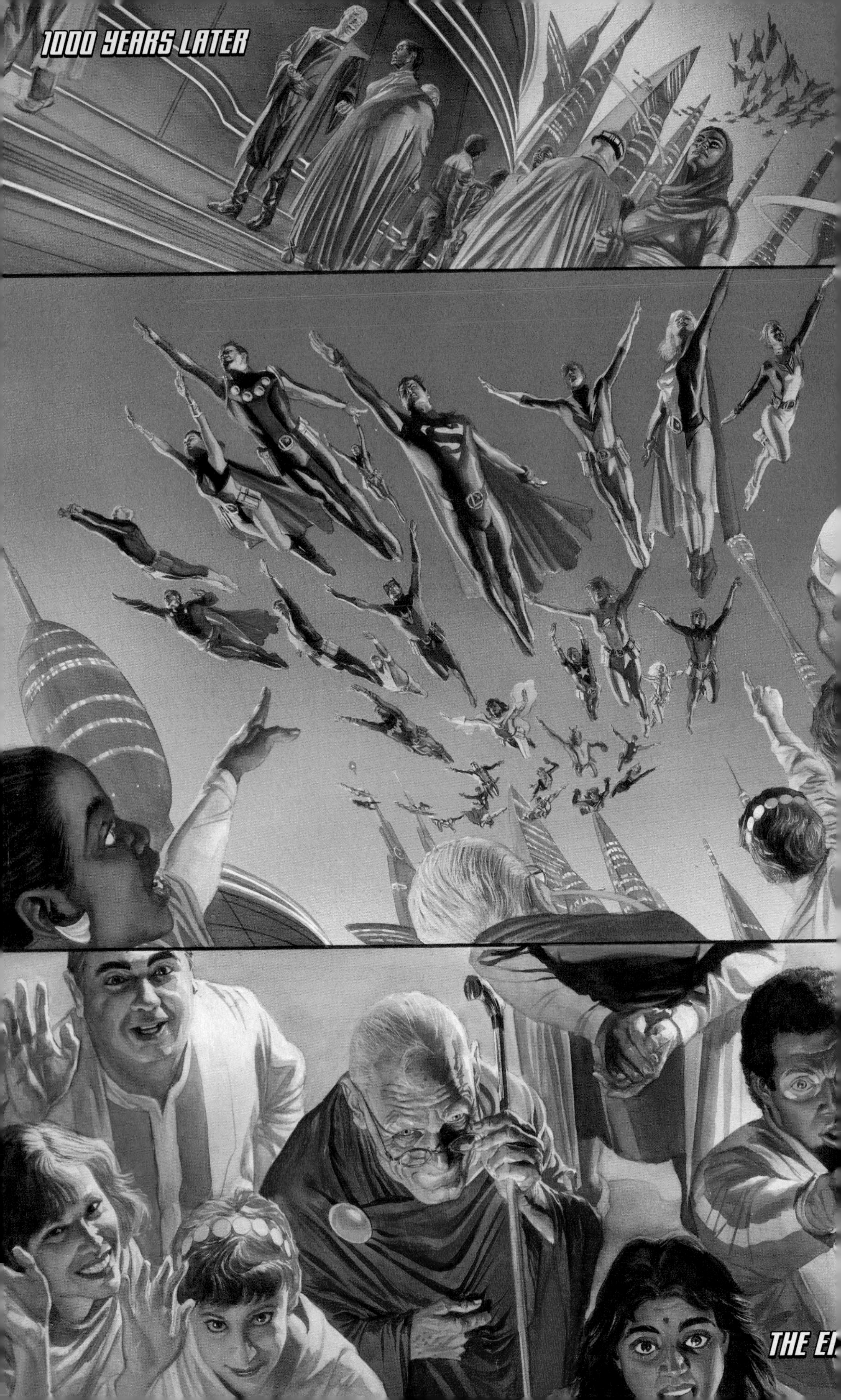

1000 YEARS LATER
THE EI

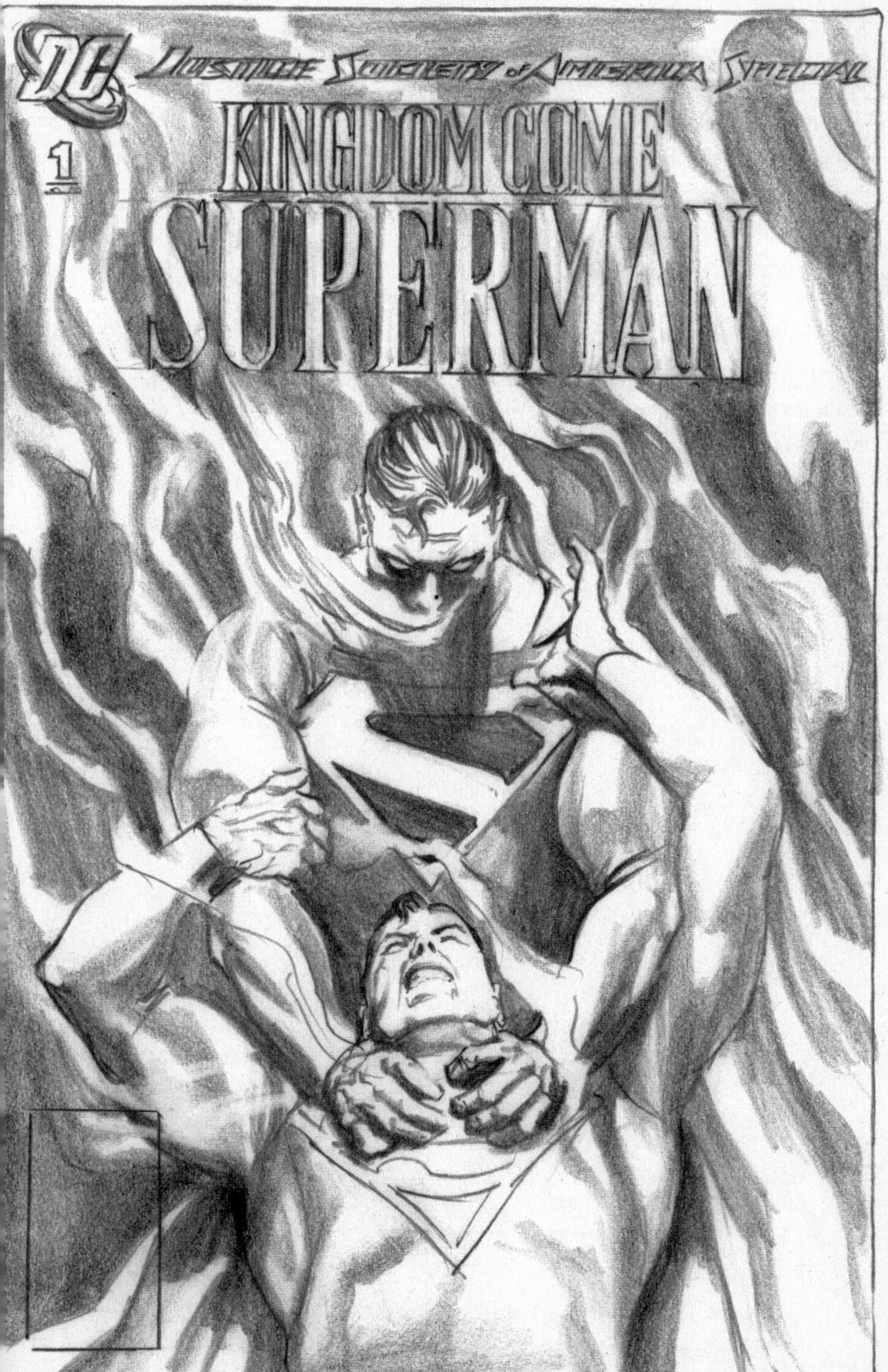
DC
JUSTICE SOCIETY of AMERICA SPECIAL
KINGDOM COME
SUPERMAN
1

MY KINGDOM COME

A look into KINGDOM COME SPECIAL: SUPERMAN

by Alex Ross

After such a cheery tale, we thought it might be interesting to show some of the process of how I wrote, drew, and inked my first comic book and personal sequel to Kingdom Come. First of all, I wouldn't really intend a true sequel with this storyline because I feel a need to protect the original series as a finite and complete drama. If it didn't try to be the final tale of the Age of Superheroes, then its purpose would be undone. The work we've done in Justice Society of America, with Geoff's indulgence, borrows Superman from Kingdom Come to play out a drama that doubles as a hopefully worthy epic in its own right, and a fun revisitation of a beloved character.

Well, like with this issue you've just read, not always fun, but passionate. Over the last ten years since I worked on the Kingdom Come series, I've imagined various details of what I would do to add to its backstory and ultimate definition. The story of how the KC Lois died was chief among these ideas.

2   3

BACK TO REALITY: AGAIN REMINISCENT OF CAPTAIN MARVEL FIGHTING SUPERMAN FROM KC. HIS NARRATION PONDERS, "HOW DID I WIND UP THE BAD GUY?"

TALKING ABOUT LOOKING UP THE PREACHER, SUDDENLY DISTRACTED BY FAR OFF VISION.

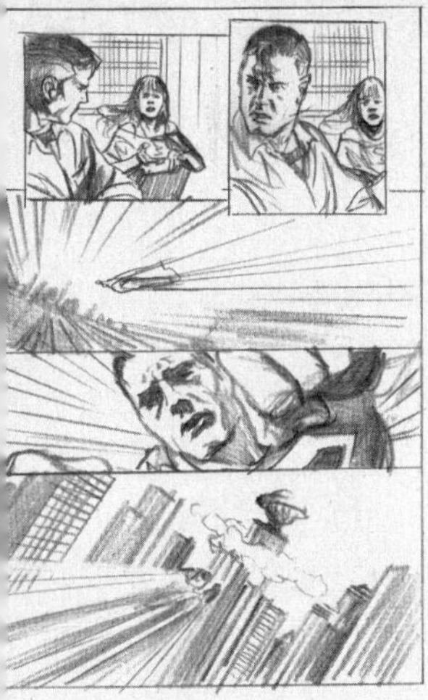

7

SPEEDS TO METROPOLIS FROM NEW YORK TO FIND PLANET'S TOP OFFICES SURROUNDED BY GREEN SMOKE CLOUD.

PAINTED IMAGES OF JOKER PULLING BACK AND STRIKING FORWARD.

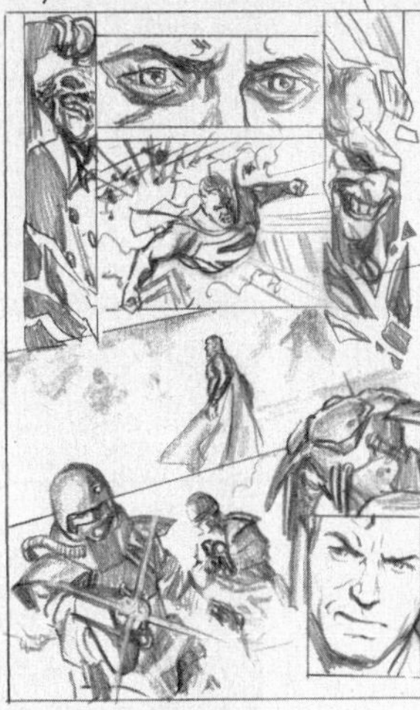

8

SUPERMAN BURSTS INTO SMOKE-FILLED NEWSROOM. SHADOWY FIGURES EMERGE OF A HIT SQUAD USING KRYPTONITE. HE SMILES SLIGHTLY.

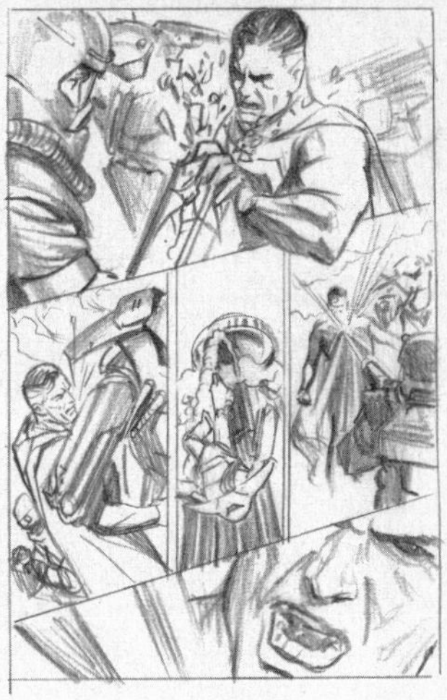

9

HE CRUSHES THE KRYPTONITE GUN OVER THE MERCENARY'S HAND. WHEN STRUCK BY ANOTHER, MORE HEAVILY-ARMORED FIGURE HE KNOCKS HIM OUT OF THE BUILDING. THEY FIRE KRYPTONITE LASERS AT HIM WHILE HE YELLS "WHAT DID YOU DO WITH THE PEOPLE!"

THE SMOKE BEGINS TO GET TO HIS EYES, HAVING AT LEAST THAT MUCH POTENCY. HE CAN STILL SENSE WHERE THE MEN ARE.

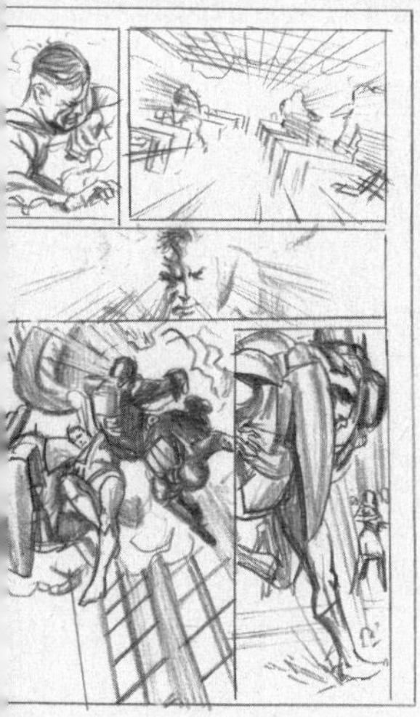

10

HE ADVANCES ON THEM WITH EYES CLOSED AND CARRIES THREE ARMORED FIGURES DOWN TO THE STREET BELOW.

PAINTED IMAGE

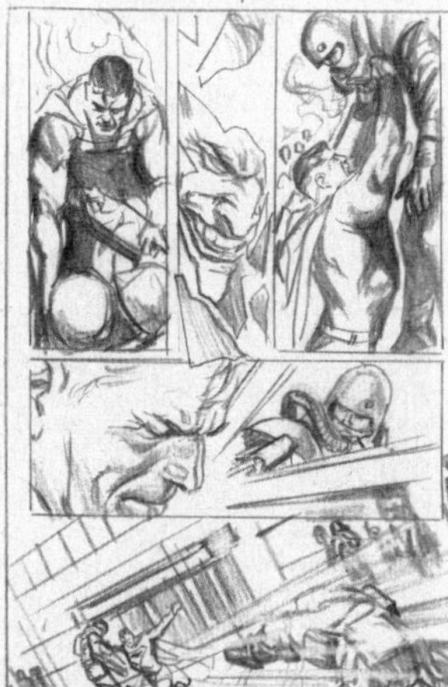

11

INTERROGATING WHAT HE BELIEVES TO BE THE LEADER, HE STILL FLASHES BACK TO JOKER. ONE MERCENARY FIRES AT HIM AGAIN, ONLY ANGERING HIM.

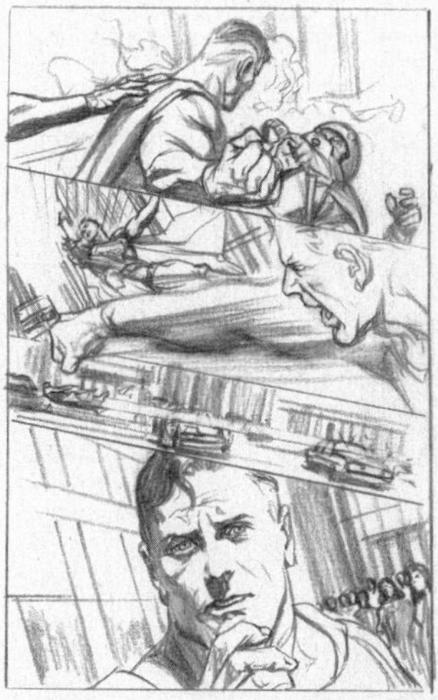

12

A HAND COMES FROM BEHIND AS HES CONTINUING HIS BLIND RAGE. HE TURNS AND PUNCHES WILDLY, SENDING SUPERMAN II(?) FLYING THROUGH THE STREET. HIS EYES FINALLY CLEAR AND HE QUICKLY REALIZES WHAT HE'S DONE.

Approaching the script was a long process where I put my visualization abilities first. Initially I wrote a detailed outline for Geoff and our editor, Mike, to read. Along with this I provided initial thumbnails which set the stage for my pacing the entire issue with detailed drawings. As you'll see from these examples, I put extensive notes below each page to help clarify where I was going in the storytelling.

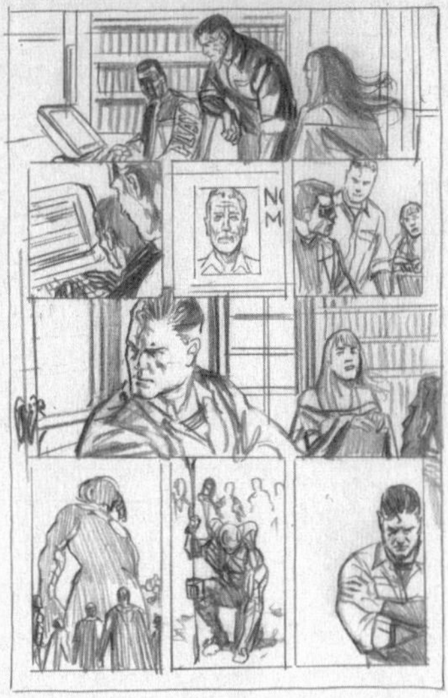

6

IN LIBRARY WITH MR. TERRIFIC LOOKING UP McCAY BASED ON DESCRIPTION, SUPERMAN LOOKING OFF THROUGH WALL AT DAILY PLANET. BOTTOM: RECALLING THE EVENTS OF GOG AND MAGOG'S COMING, AND FEELING RESPONSIBLE.

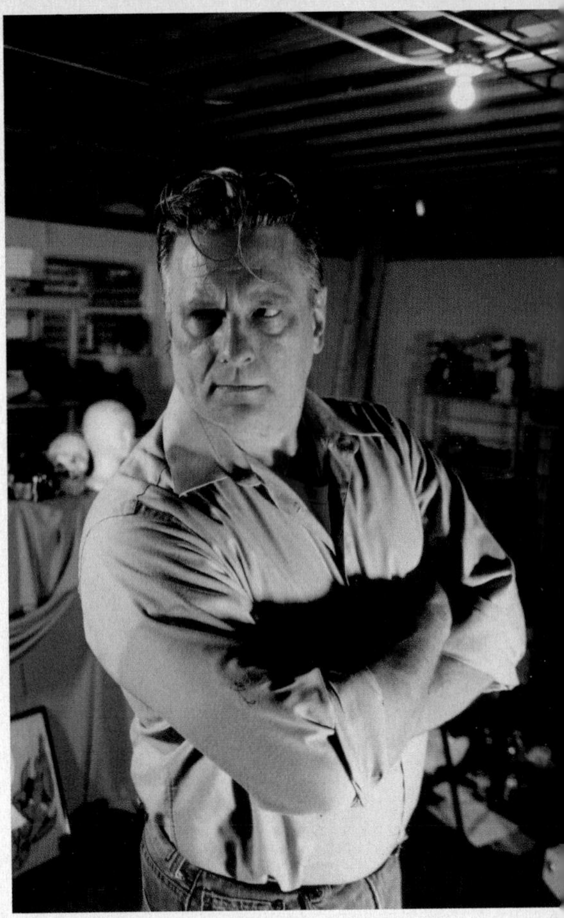

PAINTED PANELS FLASH BACK TO WHEN SUPERMAN MET HIS COUNTERPART, AND THE WORDS HE SAID.

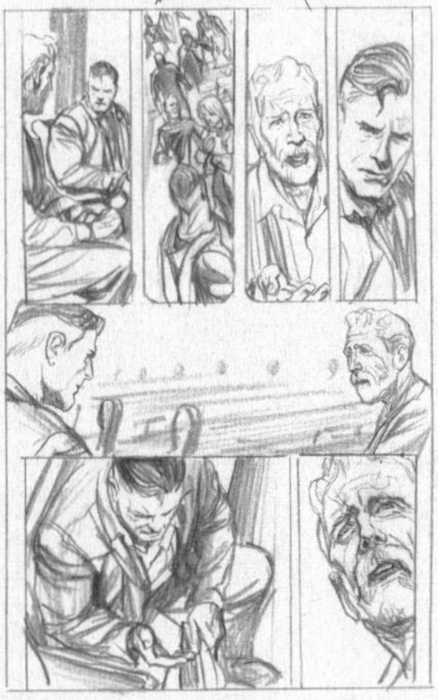

15

THEY TALK ABOUT REVELATION AND HOW IT RELATES TO SUPERMAN'S WORLD'S END AND McCAY ASKS, "ARE YOU SURE IT'S GONE?"

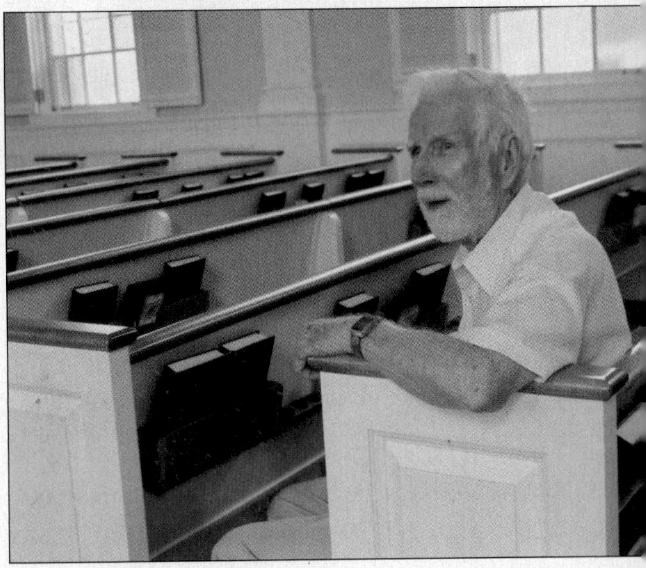

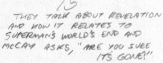

From these thumbnails, measuring about three inches by four-and-a-half inches, I began the reference process like I have for all my painted work and photographed friends as models for the characters. Key to my desire in this was a virtual reunion of my model for Superman, Frank Kasy, and my model for Norman McCay, Clark Ross (my dad).

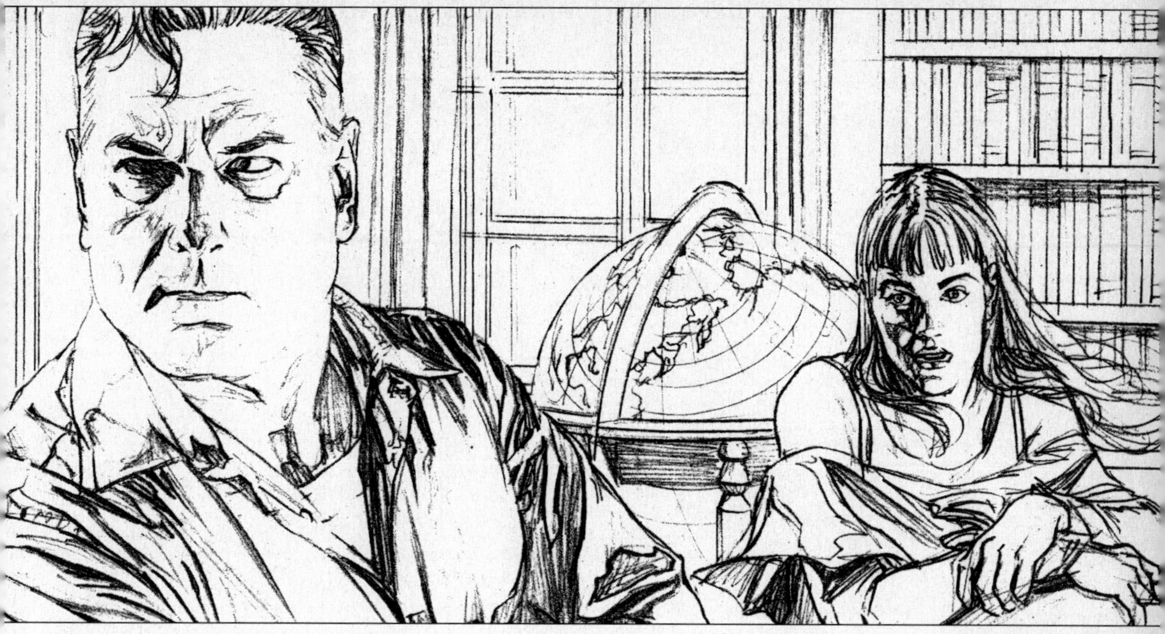

ng with my model for Cyclone and Lois Lane, Tobey Bartel, plus loads of reference of Chicago city eets and my dad's church, I had a plethora of images to study and learn from.

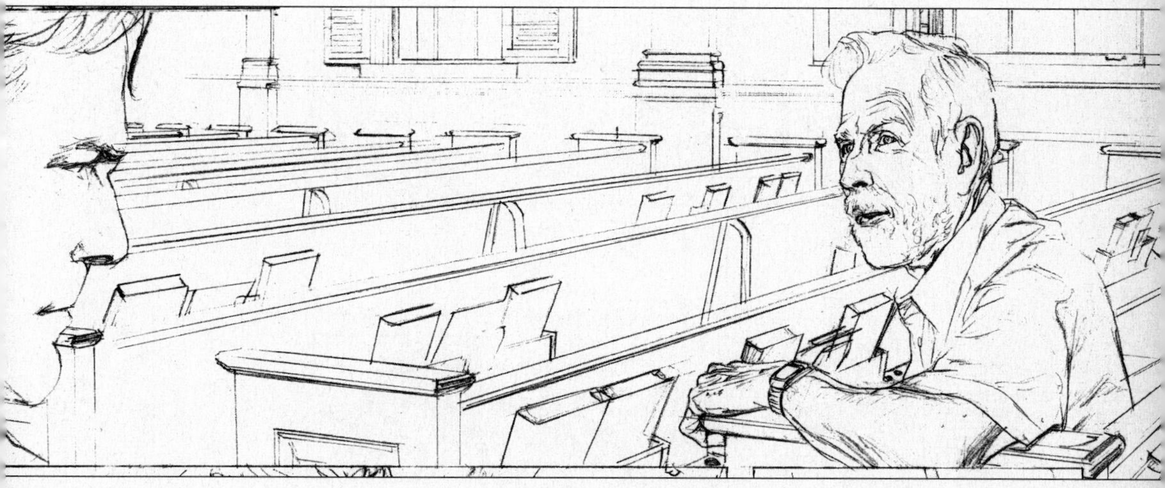

the start of drawing, I enlarged my detailed roughs to original art size and lightboxed the images. This s a new step for me, since for several years I've traced over my photocopied thumbnails by doing a phite carbon on the back and pressing through. That was all I knew until I finally tested my athmore Bristol (Series 500) 4-Ply paper over a light box and realized that I could see through it to re easily transfer my original drawing. Better late than never. And just to be clear, there is no cing over or projecting of photos onto my boards for me to follow. What you see is how my eye ws the reference and my hand interprets it as best it can or cares to.

Thumbnails presented at actual size.

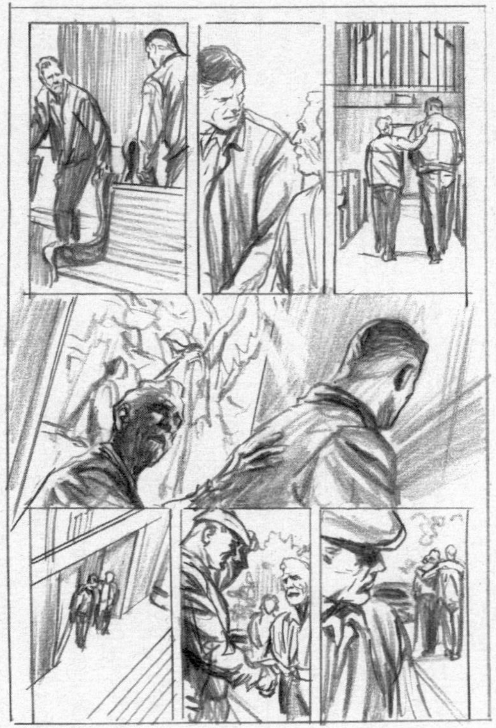

16

WALKING OUT, McCAY ADVISES THAT HE NEEDS TO OPEN HIS MIND TO THE POSSIBILITIES THAT LIE BEFORE HIM, AND WORK WITH THIS SECOND CHANCE. McCAY LEAVES WITH HIS WIFE WAITING.

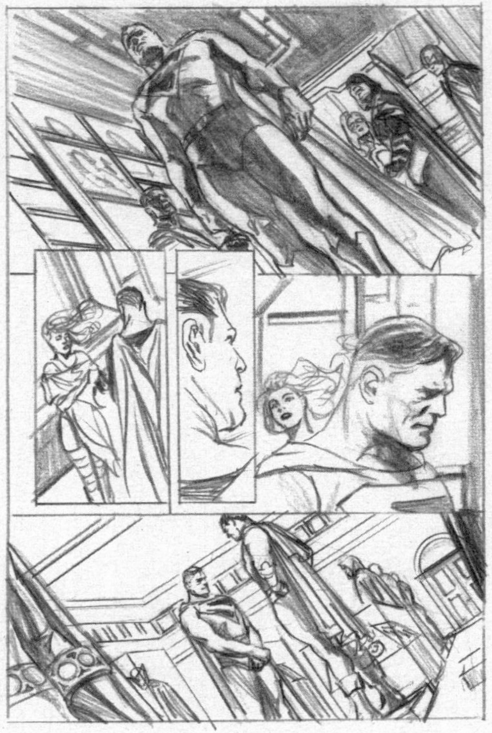

17

SUPERMAN WALKS SILENTLY AMONGST HIS JSA COMRADES. CYCLONE OFFERS HER SUPPORT WHEN HE HEARS A FAR AWAY PRESENCE APPROACH, AND EXCUSES HIMSELF TO PRIVATELY MEET HIS VISITOR IN THE TROPHY ROOM.

STANDING IN FRONT OF A STATUE OF CAPTAIN MARVEL.

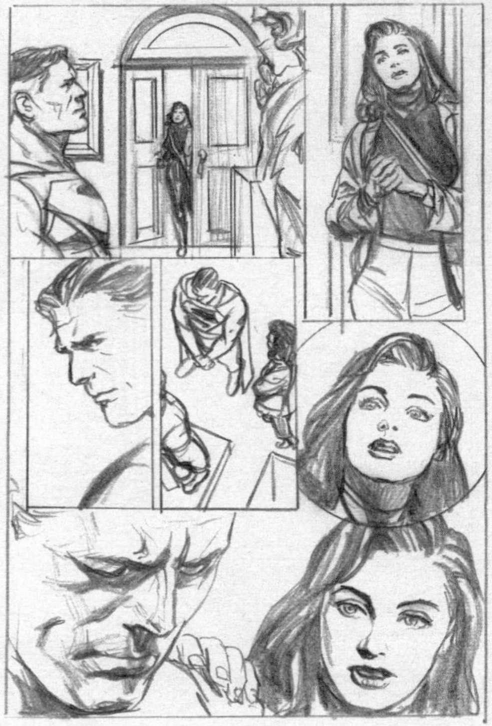

18

LOIS LANE OF THIS EARTH OPENS THE DOOR AND ASKS IF ITS OKAY TO TALK FREELY IN THERE. SHE SAYS "CAN'T YOU BEAR TO EVEN LOOK AT ME?" SHE PRESSES HIM TO RELEASE THE BURDEN OF HIS FULL STORY OF HOW HE LOST HIS LOIS.

BY GREEN SMOKE, THIS TIME IT WAS JOKER'S GAS.

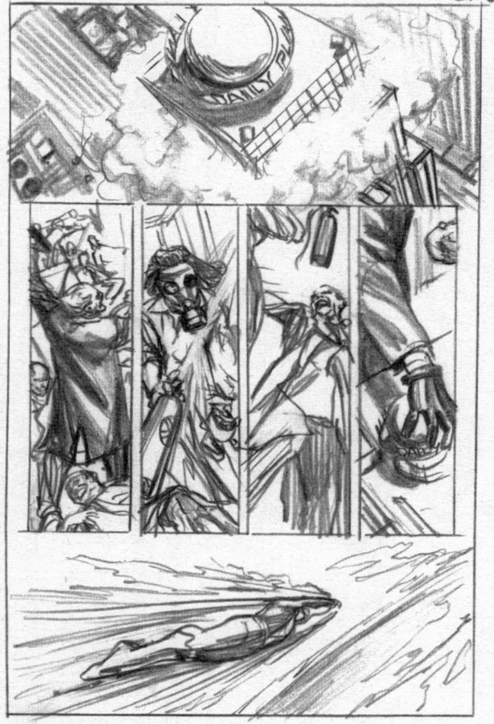

19

JOKER WALKS OVER THE DEAD GRIMACED PLANET EMPLOYEES, CELEBRATING JUST BEFORE LOIS (WITH GAS MASK ON) BEANS HIM WITH A FIRE EXTINGUISHER. JOKER STRIKES BACK, THEN GRABS THE PLANET PAPERWEIGHT AS SUPERMAN NARRATES HOW JOKER CRUSHED HER SKULL WITH IT.

HIMSELF UP INTENTIONALLY, LOOKING TO MAKE SOME SICK STATEMENT, POSSIBLY SETTING UP HIS OWN MURDER,

MOMENTS LATER.

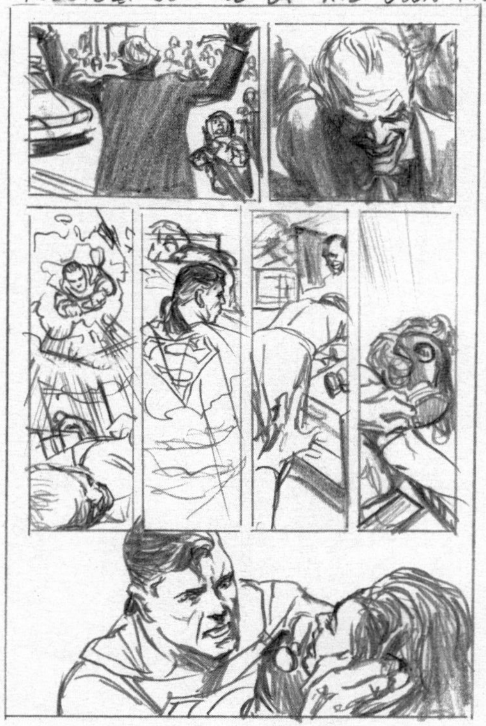

20

SUPERMAN BLASTS THROUGH THE PLANET'S CEILING, FINDING THE BODIES WITHIN. SUCKING ALL OF THE GAS OUT OF THE ROOM, HE MOVES TOWARD THE SLUMPED OVER FIGURE OF LOIS. TURNING HER OVER HE SEES THAT SHE'S WEARING A GAS MASK, ALIVE BUT BADLY, BADLY HURT.

IF HE CAN'T SAVE HER THIS ONE LAST TIME.

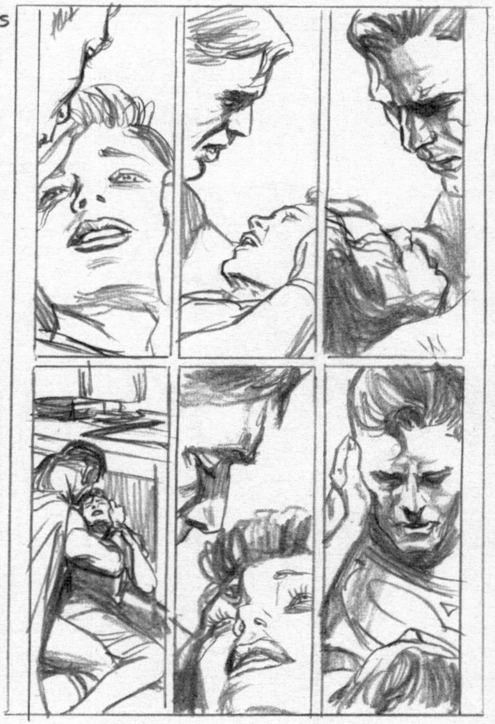

21

SHE PLEADS WITH HIM NOT TO BE ANGRY AS HE SEES THAT HER INJURY IS A FATAL BLOW. SHE DOESN'T WANT HIM TO LOSE THE PERSON SHE'S LOVED. SHE ALSO SAYS "I'M SORRY I COULDN'T GIVE YOU A..." AS HE CUTS HER OFF SAYING "NO, NO, NO, DON'T SAY THAT." (IT)

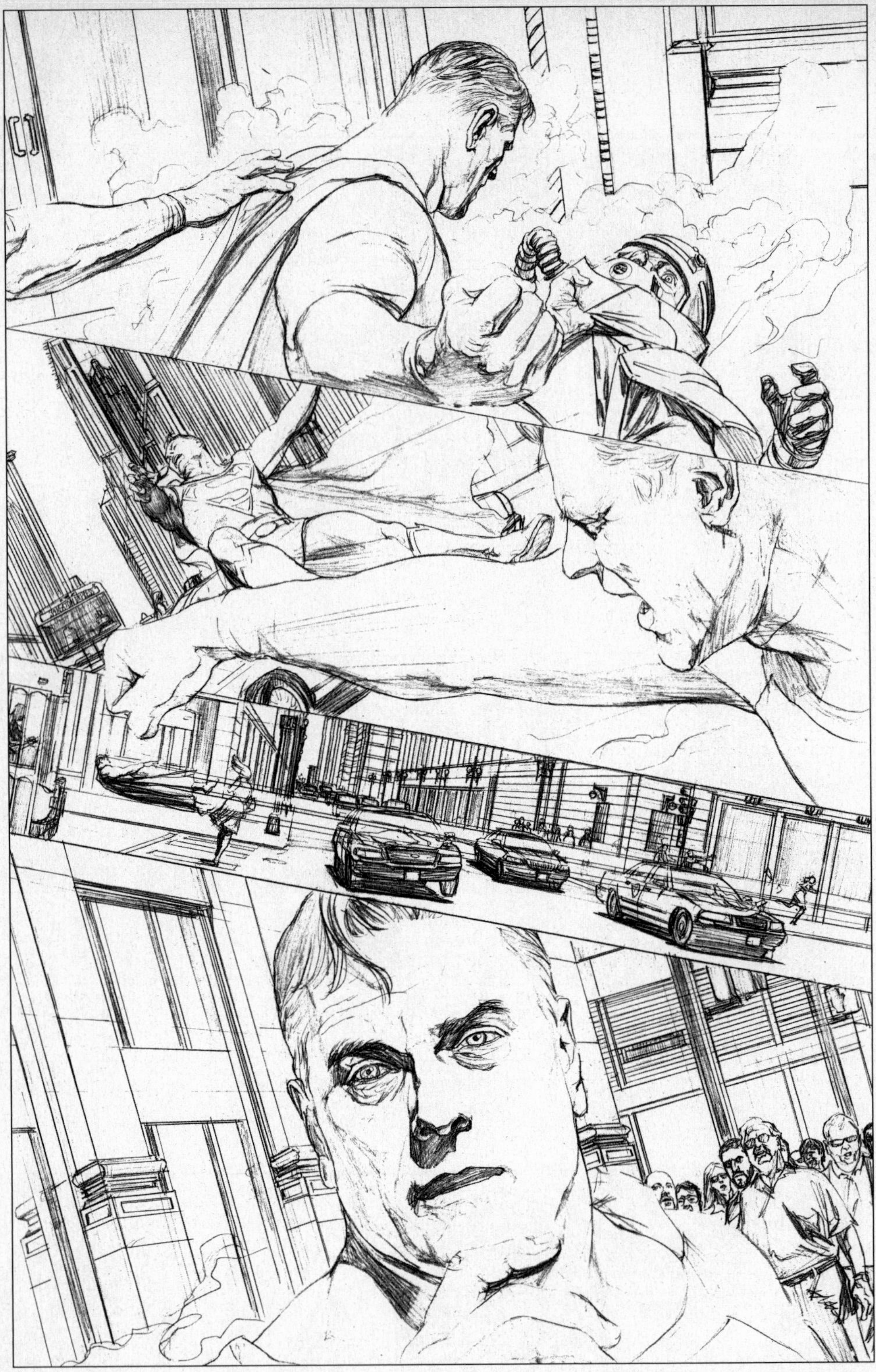

Going from pencils to inking was my first experiment in this book, trying an illustration approach I've avoided my whole career in comics. In the end, I still cheated. Because of current technologies of computer coloring, I still used a half-tone applied with a black Verithin Prismacolor pencil, once the darkest darks of the "inking" were done. As it was, I didn't use ink, either. I used a gouache jet black, which is as dark as ink, but it is a medium and texture I was comfortable with. When the work is scanned as a half-tone, as Alex Sinclair tutored me, you can hold the black lines as a full black but easily convert the half-tone gray as a shading guide in the coloring.

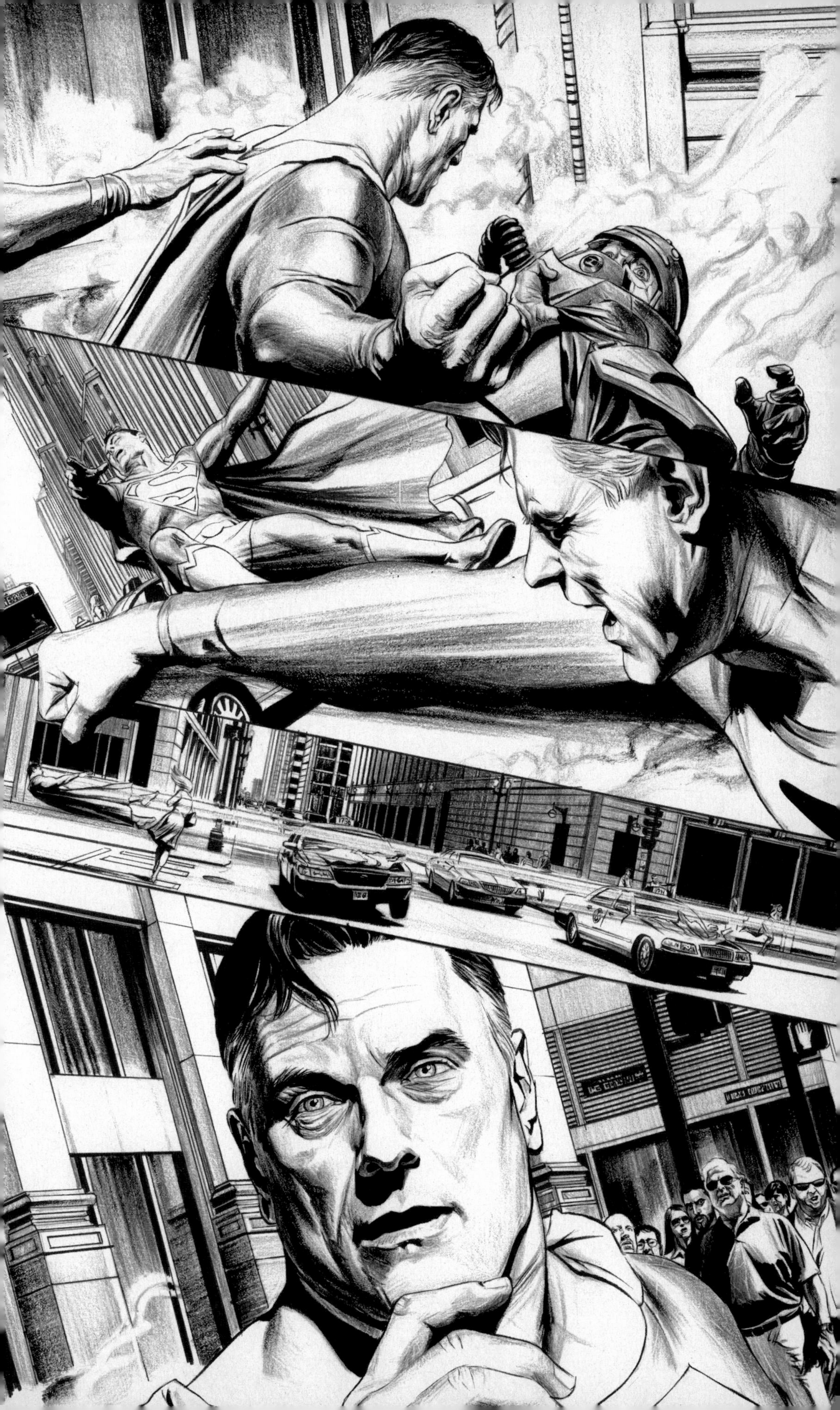

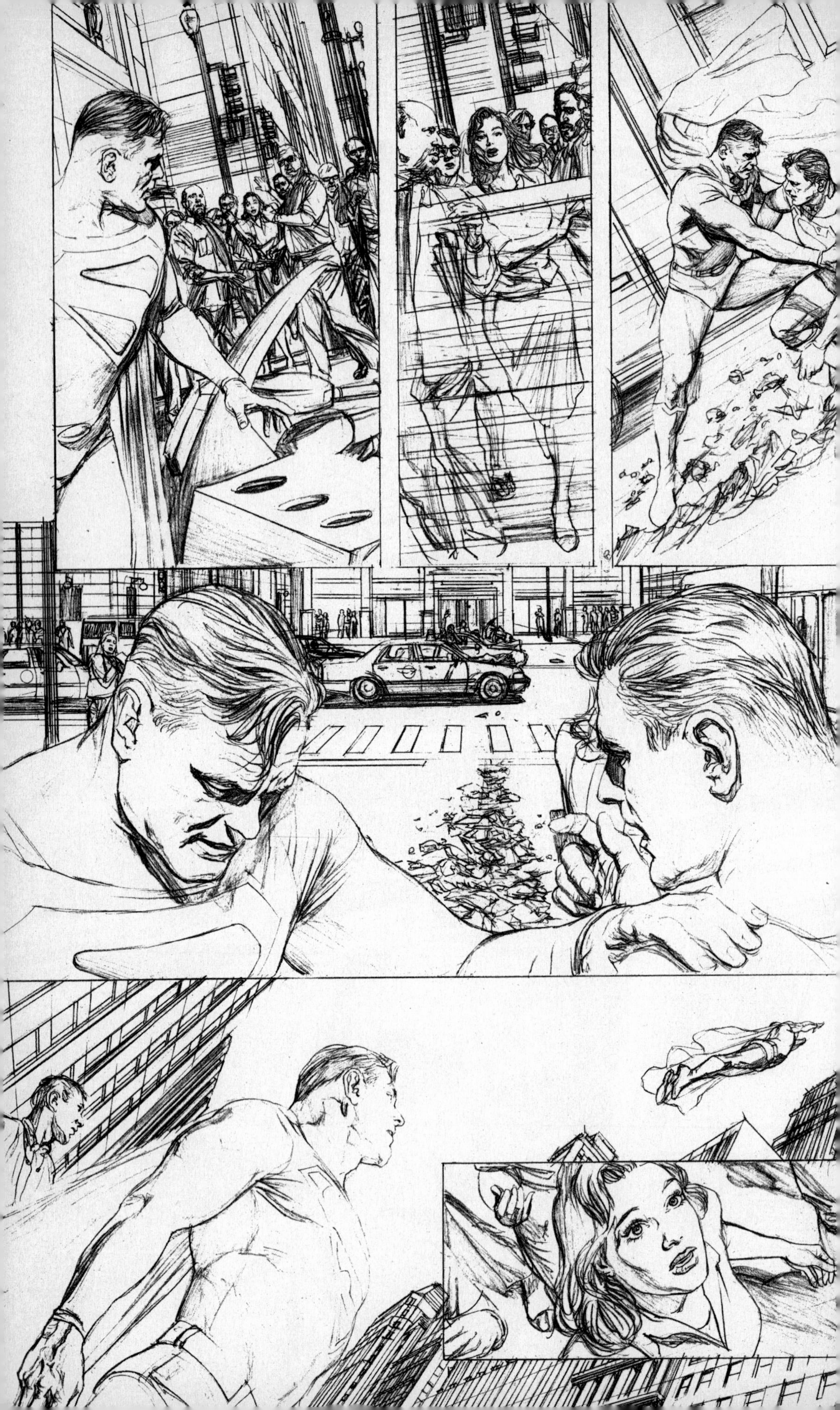

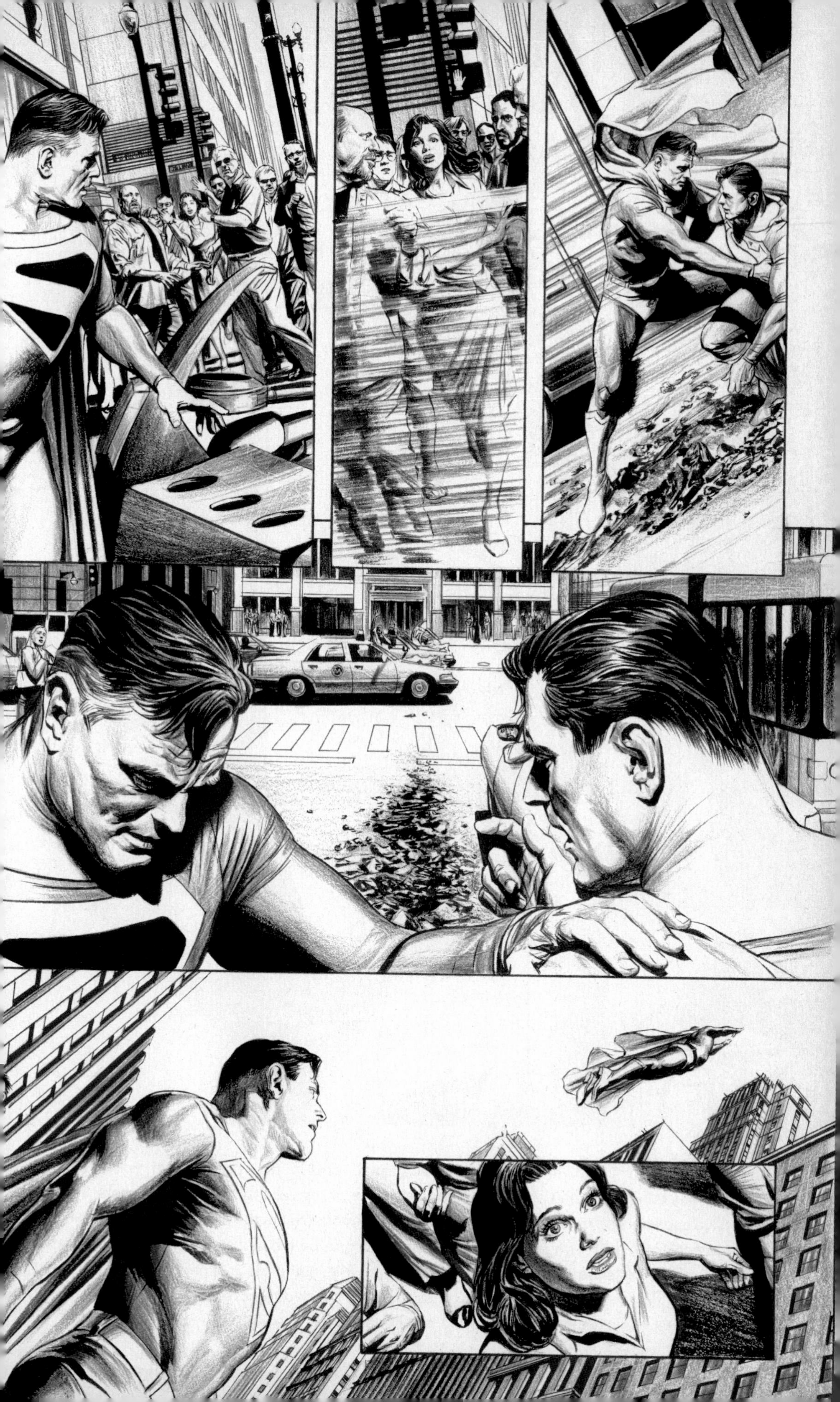

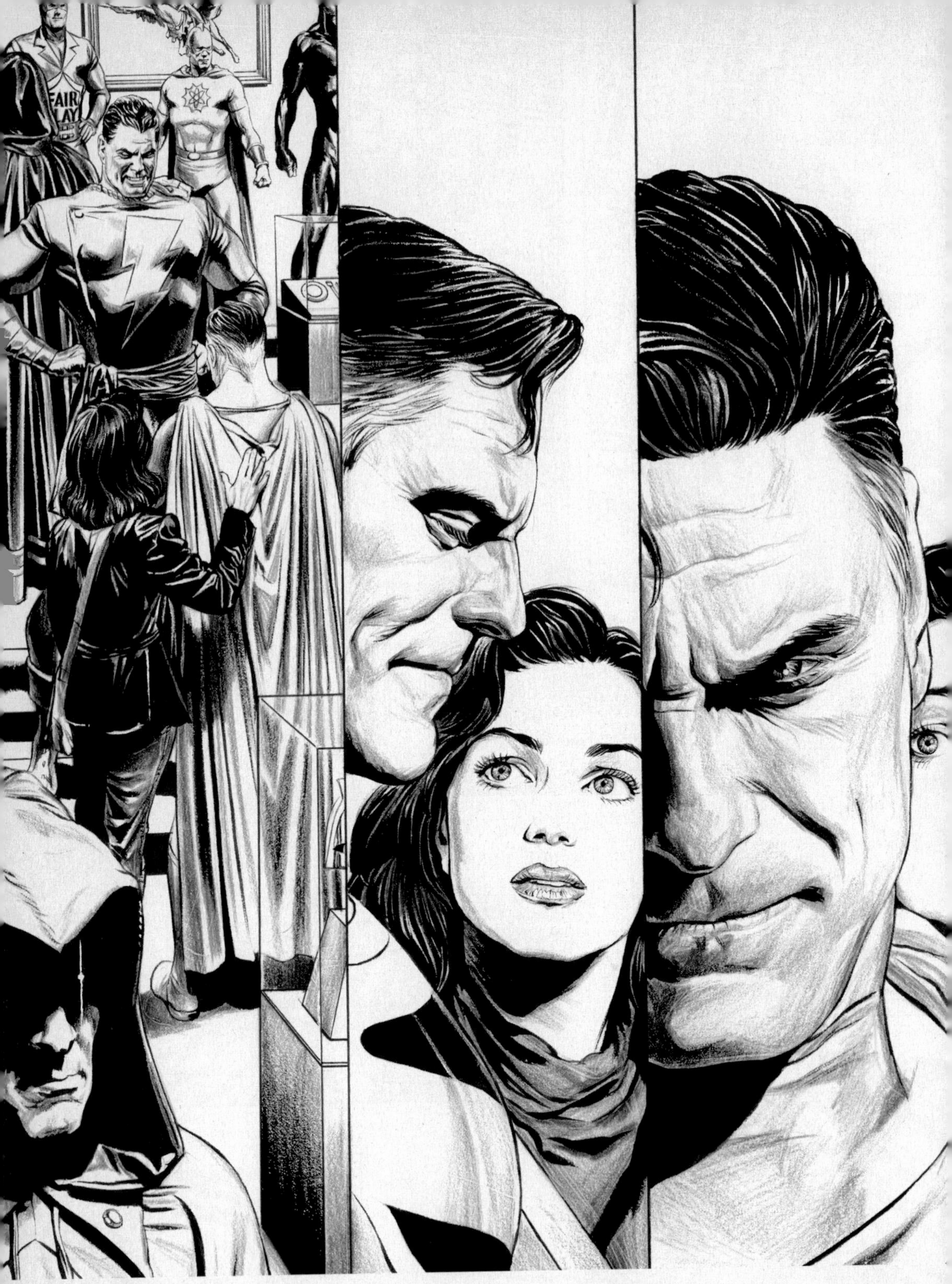
FAIR PLAY

When it was drawn, inked, and the additional painted panels and pages were finished, I deignec finally write this thing. From my abundant notes, reference of regular JSA scripts, and general inspiration, down to give captions and dialogue to my 23 pages. It was probably not the perfect order to do things, but m comics are constructed this way, allowing the final scripting to be the last stage. You find out then that if had a lot of excess dialogue there may be no room to put it in. Either way, experimenting with the art forr both writing and drawing the whole thing is an opportunity I'm glad to have had with the character I've c the most about. It has always been a pleasure and honor for me to spend time with Superman.

ADDITIONAL SKETCHES

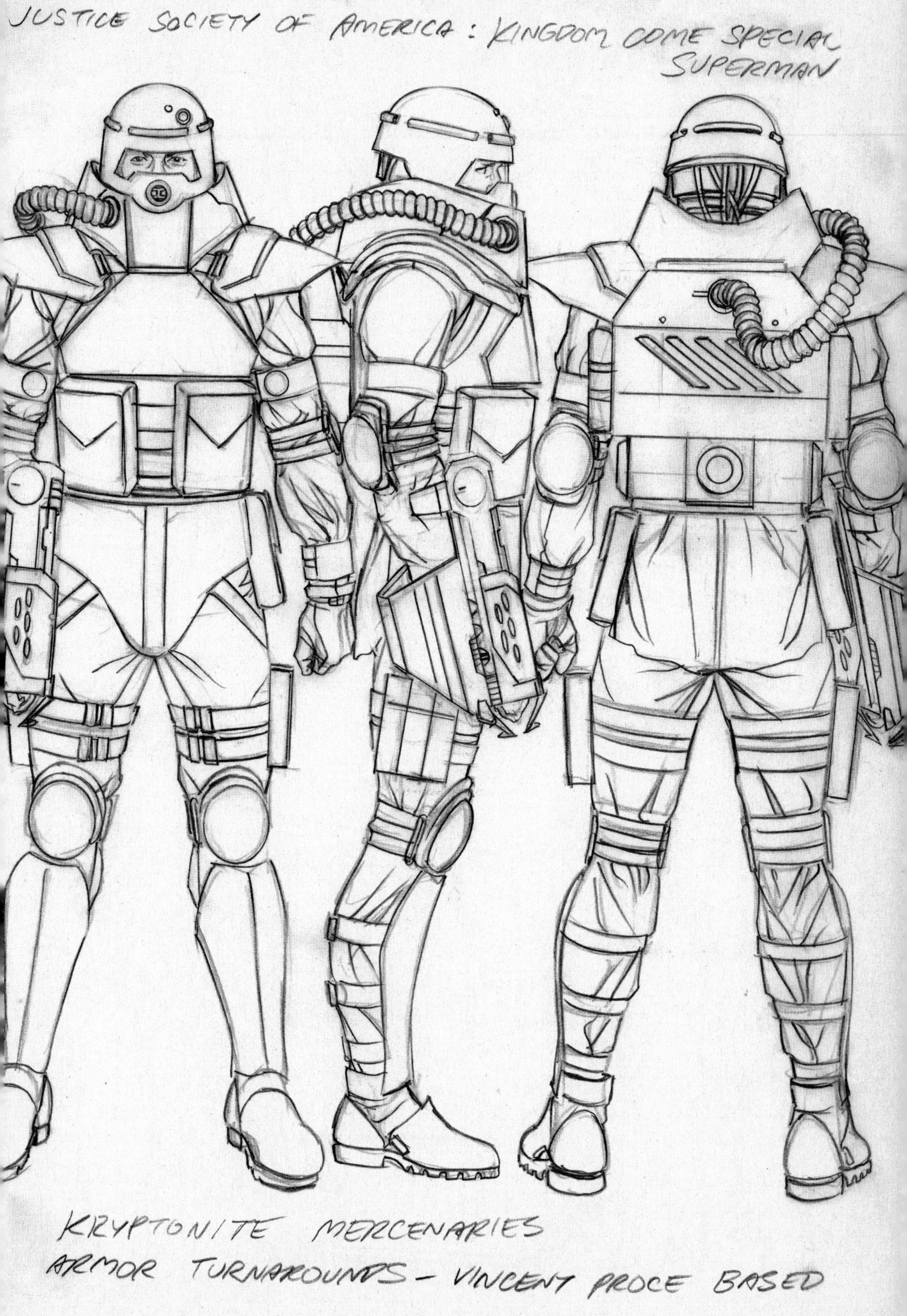
JUSTICE SOCIETY OF AMERICA: KINGDOM COME SPECIAL
SUPERMAN
KRYPTONITE MERCENARIES
ARMOR TURNAROUNDS - VINCENT PROCE BASED

KINGDOM COME SPECIAL : SUPERMAN

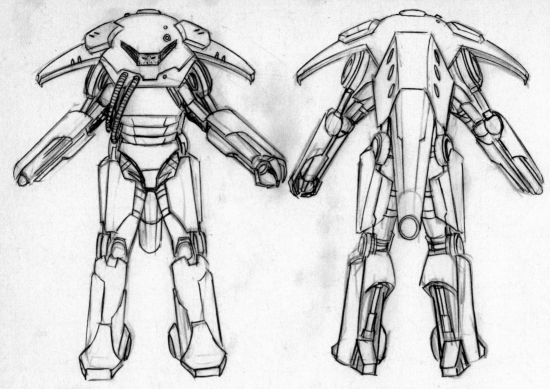

KRYPTONITE MERCENARY BATTLESUITS
ARMOR TURNAROUNDS - VINCENT PROCE BASED

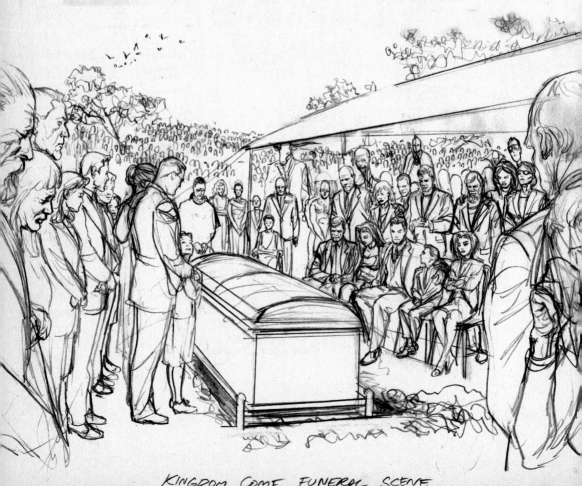

KINGDOM COME FUNERAL SCENE

BLACK BAR AT TOP

#18

JUSTICE SOCIETY OF AMERICA
KINGDOM COME SPECIAL
MAGOG

ANNUAL #1

REPLACE
BRAINWAVE JR.
W/ WILDCAT II

THIS PAGE AND NEXT:
Various cover sketches to the "Thy Kingdom Come" storyline.

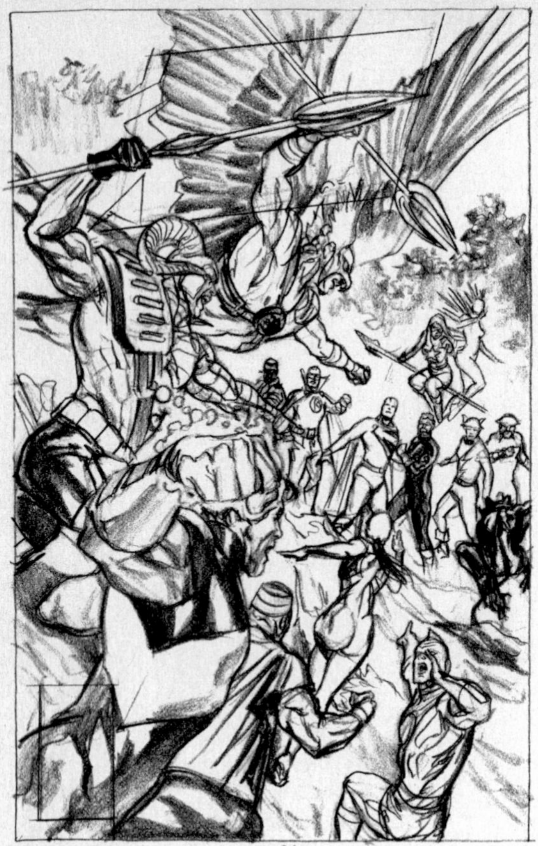

JSA #19

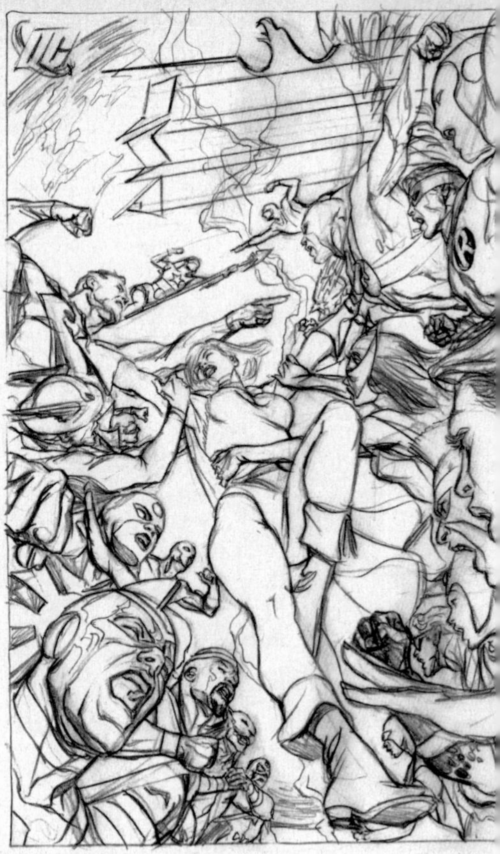

REPLACE 20
JUDOMASTER
CITIZEN STEEL
AMAZING MAN
WITH
LIBERTY BELL
HOURMAN
MR. TERRIFIC

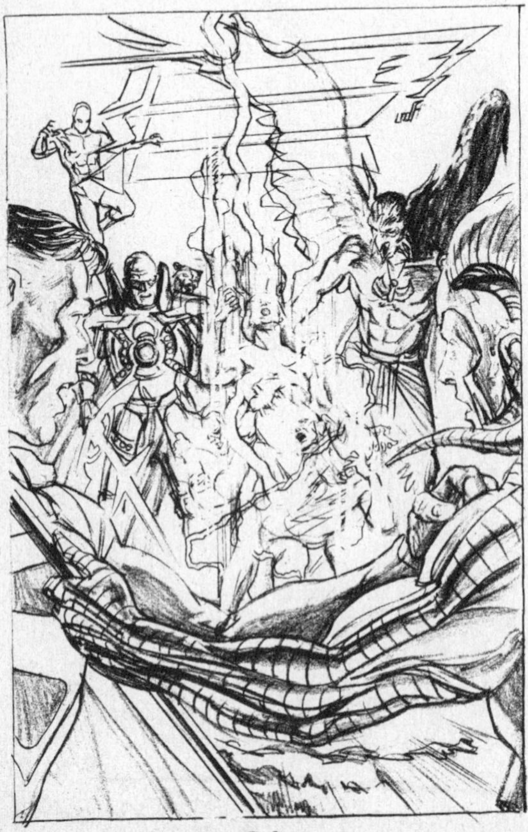

21

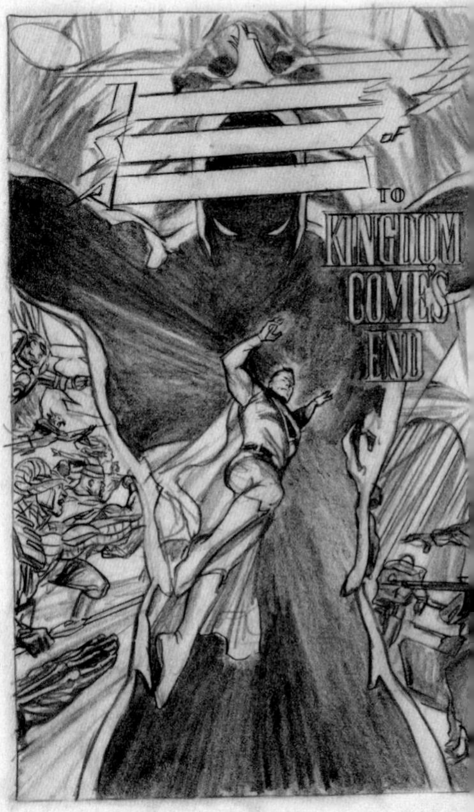
OF
TO
KINGDOM COME'S END

22

BLACK BAR AT TOP

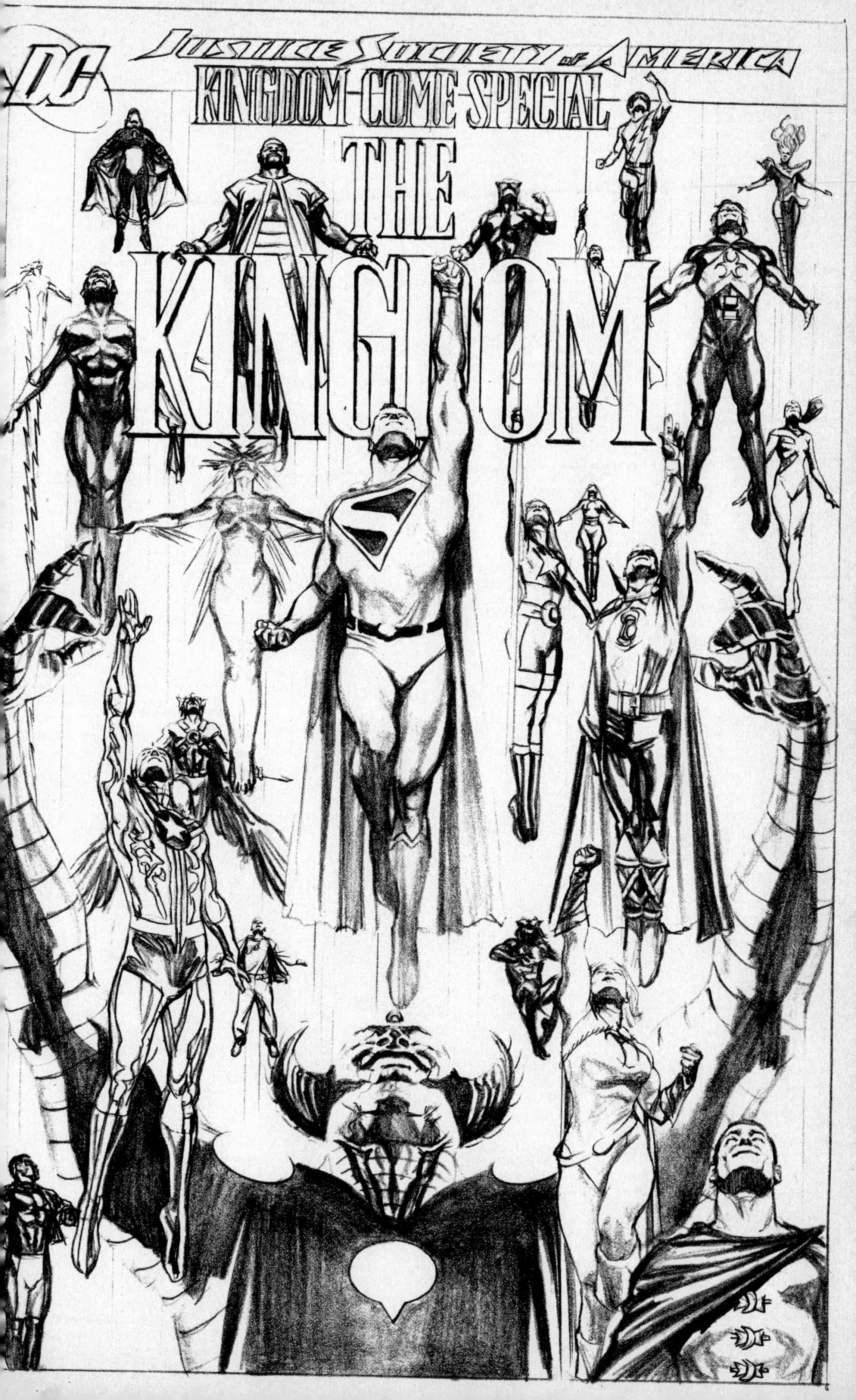
DC
JUSTICE SOCIETY of AMERICA
KINGDOM COME SPECIAL
THE KINGDOM

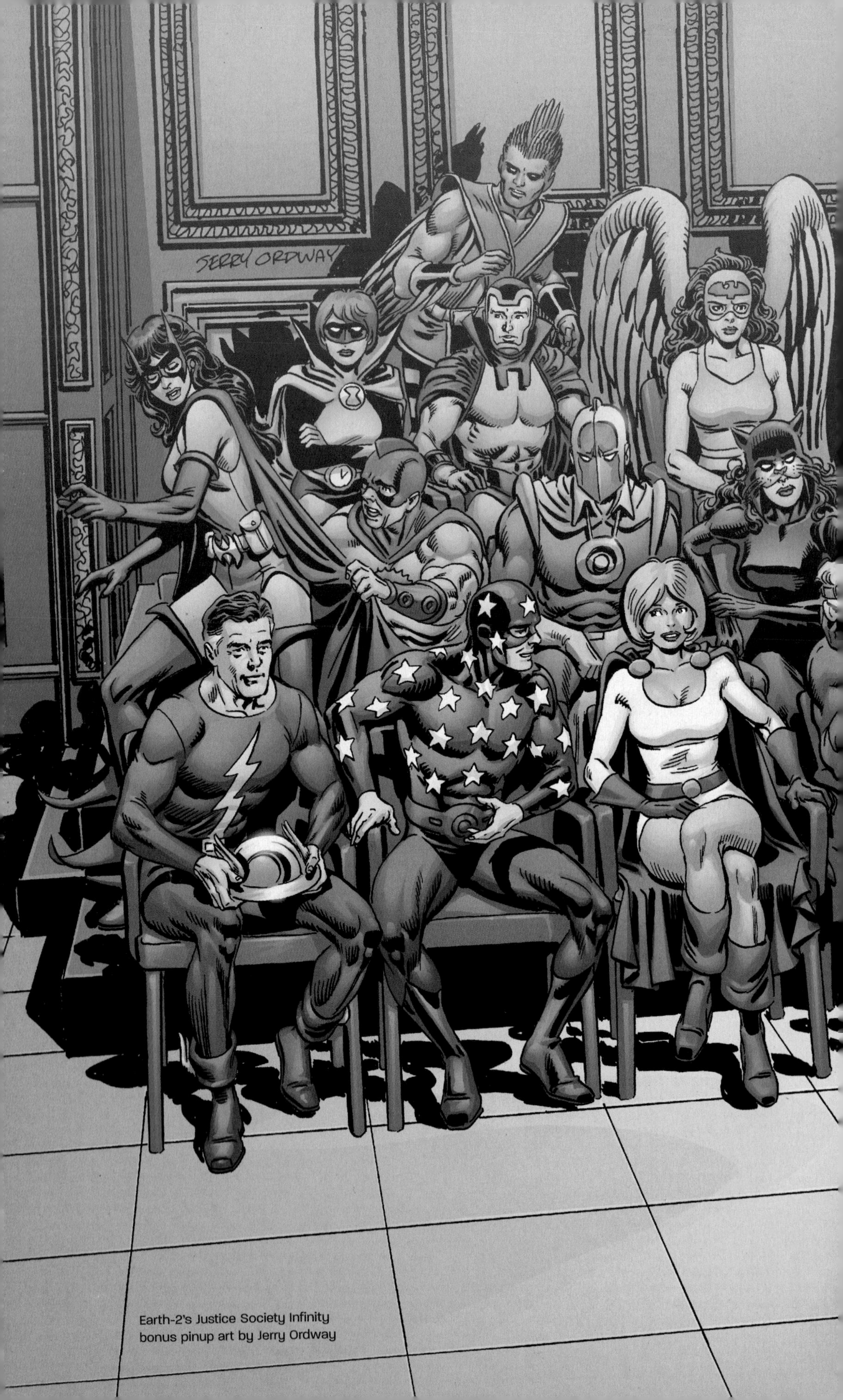
JERRY ORDWAY

Earth-2's Justice Society Infinity
bonus pinup art by Jerry Ordway

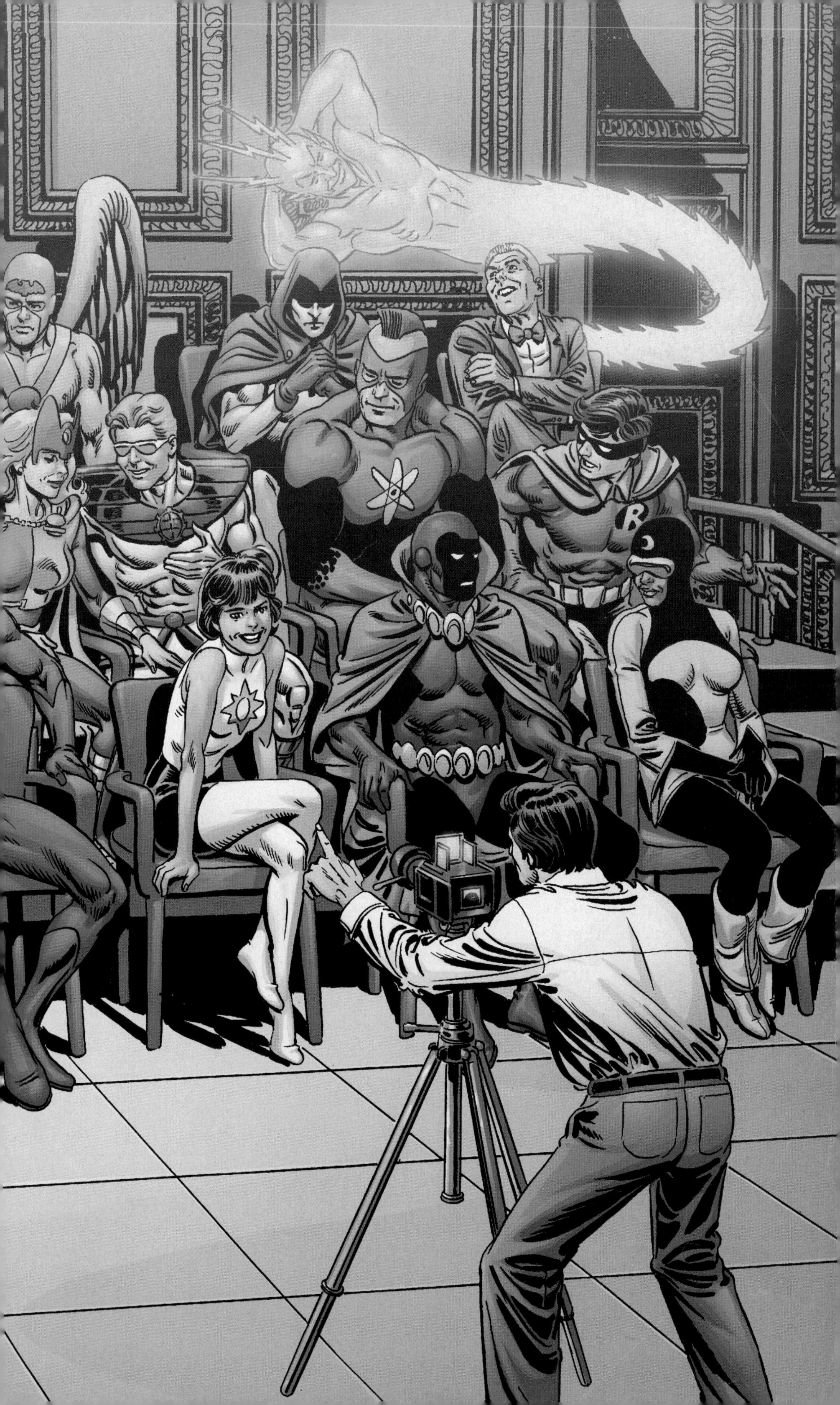